The Myth of the Noble Savage

The Myth of
the Noble Savage

TER ELLINGSON

University of California Press

BERKELEY   LOS ANGELES   LONDON

University of California Press

Berkeley and Los Angeles, California

University of California Press, Ltd.
London, England

© 2001 by Ter Ellingson

Library of Congress Cataloging-in-Publication Data
Ellingson, Terry Jay.
    The myth of the noble savage / Ter Ellingson.
        p .   cm.
    Includes bibliographical references and index.
    ISBN 0-520-22268-7 (alk. paper)—
    ISBN 0-520-22610-0 (paper : alk. paper)
    1. Anthropology—Philosophy.   2. Noble savage.   3. Noble savage
    in literature.   4. Racism in anthropology—History.   I. Title.
    GN33 .E44   2001
    301'.01—dc21   99-059341

Printed in the United States of America
9 8 7 6 5 4 3 2 1

10 9 8 7 6 5 4 3 2 1

The paper used in this publication meets the minimum requirements of
ANSI / NISO Z39.48-1992(R 1997) (*Permanence of Paper*).

To Linda

Advice from a World Wide Web search engine, after finding more than 1,000 references to the "Noble Savage":

Refine your search!

Contents

Illustrations

Preface

The title of this book will inevitably create some confusion, for there are a number of dimensions in which the Noble Savage intersects the field of the mythical. The fundamental myth is that there are, or ever were, any actual peoples who were "savage," either in the term's original sense of "wild" or in its later connotation of an almost subhuman level of fierceness and cruelty. The "Savage" and the "Oriental" were the two great ethnographic paradigms developed by European writers during the age of exploration and colonialism; and the symbolic opposition between "wild" and "domesticated" peoples, between "savages" and "civilization," was constructed as part of the discourse of European hegemony, projecting cultural inferiority as an ideological ground for political subordination. For most of the period from the sixteenth to the nineteenth century, the American Indians constituted the paradigmatic case for the "savage," and the term was most widely applied to them. If "savage" is not always flagged by quotes in the following citations and discussions of writings of this period, it should never be regarded as unproblematic; the idea that any people, including American Indians, are or were "savages" is a myth that should long ago have been dispelled.

However, the primary source of the ambiguity built into the title of this book is less obvious and more insidious. This is because the title refers to a living, contemporary myth that most of us accept as fact; and because the myth itself deceives us by claiming to critique and offer an exposé of another "myth," the existence of Savages who were really noble. The purported critique typically examines ethnographic or theoretical writings on "savage" peoples to problematize any potential claims to their "nobility." The supposed exposé asserts that the "myth" of savage nobility was created in the eighteenth century by Jean-Jacques Rousseau as part of a romantic glorification of the "savage" to serve as a paradigmatic counterexample for constructing attacks on European society, and that belief in the existence of actual Noble Savages has been widespread ever since.

Many accept this combination of critique and exposé as disproof of the "myth"; but the critique and the exposé were themselves a deliberate mythological construction, projected at a particular time in the history of anthropology for a specific political purpose. It is this construction, the false claim of widespread belief in the existence of the "Noble Savage," inspired by Rousseau, that constitutes the myth that is the subject of this book.

The real myth, in other words, is what we have been deceived into thinking is the reality behind the myth. Herein lies the difficulty of our task, for it involves calling into question some of our most deeply rooted beliefs and confronting an unexpectedly insidious influence that still continues to shape the construction of our disciplinary identity. In so doing, we must inevitably consider the possibility that something we have long taken pride in as evidence of our own intelligent, critical thinking was in fact no more than our gullible acquiescence in a scholarly hoax—a hoax that has been perpetrated on us for political reasons that many of us would dislike intensely, if we understood them.

The chronological framing of the following narrative seems to me to present a clear and consistent story, but it may seem rather like a mystery novel, with the reader having to follow obscure clues until the solution is revealed at the end. In fact, there is no mystery behind the myth of the Noble Savage, other than its continued success and longevity. Serious investigators have known since the 1920s that Rousseau did not create the myth, but its source has never been satisfactorily identified. This is the first great problem we face, and it suggests a first step toward a solution.

In a preliminary approach to the question, we will find that the failure to discover the source of the myth has resulted from a misguided substantivist orientation that has sought its origin in objective fact, accepting that there must actually have been a real belief in something called the "Noble Savage" reflected in the ethnographic and related literatures. In fact, since the claim of the reality of belief in the Noble Savage is part of the construction of the myth itself, any attempt to find its substantive basis in the world "out there" reinforces the myth by playing the game defined by its own rules and leads away from a solution to the problem of its source. For example, Bruce Trigger and Wilcomb Washburn (1996: 1/1:72), while alluding to "the noble savage as conceptualized by Jean-Jacques Rousseau," nevertheless suggest that "the so-called myth of the Noble Savage was not simply a product of the salons of Paris, as is often claimed." This is an important first step toward problematizing the substantive basis of the myth, but a clear critical understanding of it needs to be informed by an examination of its discursive foundations.

Thus, for example, it is hardly problematic that writers of the romantic period romanticized "savages," since this must necessarily be true merely by definition: that "romantic" writers romanticized the subjects of their writings is simply a circular statement. We would undoubtedly find it more problematically interesting if, instead, they had never found "savage" characters worthy of embodying romantic themes; for such a case would provide evidence of a racism so obtuse as to suggest that the evolution of Europeans beyond a bestial level of intelligence had been very recent indeed. But to take all such cases as prima facie evidence of belief in the "Noble Savage" not only ignores important questions of the meanings of various modes of romantic representation but also distracts from the more important issue of what is meant by the attribution of nobility and savagery. Terms used as essentializing labels become self-validating and draw attention away from themselves to the content to which they are affixed. But to understand the Noble Savage, what is needed is not a faith in its reality supported by self-validating repetitions of a formula but rather a suspension of faith that can support a serious investigation of its origin and meaning.

The solution, as we will see, is to treat the Noble Savage as a discursive construct and to begin with a rigorous examination of occurrences of the rhetoric of nobility as it was applied by ethnographic and other European writers to the peoples they labeled "savages." In focusing on the discursive rather than the substantive Noble Savage, which might be imagined to lurk behind any positive reference to "savages" anywhere in the literature, we will find that the term "Noble Savage" was invented in 1609, nearly a century and a half before Rousseau, by Marc Lescarbot, a French lawyer-ethnographer, as a concept in comparative law. We will see the concept of the Noble Savage virtually disappear for more than two hundred years, without reemerging in Rousseau or his contemporaries, until it is finally resurrected in 1859 by John Crawfurd, soon to become president of the Ethnological Society of London, as part of a racist coup within the society. It is Crawfurd's construction, framed as part of a program of ideological support for an attack on anthropological advocacy of human rights, that creates the myth as we know it, including the false attribution of authorship to Rousseau; and Crawfurd's version becomes the source for every citation of the myth by anthropologists from Lubbock, Tylor, and Boas through the scholars of the late twentieth century.

The chronological sequence of the following chapters also conceals the process followed in my own investigation of the myth. In fact, I began with a look at related historical problems in Rousseau's writings. Having absorbed the myth as part of my professional training, I was at first incidentally surprised and then increasingly disturbed by not finding evidence of either the discursive or the substantive Noble Savage in Rousseau's works. Finding this an interesting problem in its own right, I began to explore the secondary literature on the subject, beginning with Hoxie Neale Fairchild's *The Noble Savage* (1928), finding confirmation of my readings of Rousseau but no satisfactory investigation of the myth's real source.

Intrigued by how a myth that had been discredited for nearly seventy years had continued to dominate anthropological thinking and escaped serious critical examination for so long, I began to reexamine the ethnographic literature, where I had been convinced I had seen many references to the Noble Savage before. But all my critical reexaminations of ethnographic writings proved disappointing, until a systematic pursuit of possible earlier sources for Dryden's well-known 1672 reference to the Noble Savage revealed what was obviously an original invention of the concept by Lescarbot some sixty-three years earlier. However, since Lescarbot's Noble Savage was so different from that posited by the myth, further searching was necessary to find the reintroduction of the term and the construction of the myth itself.

Once again, since a temporal point of departure had been established by George W. Stocking, Jr.'s (1987: 153) identification of a reference to the myth in 1865 by John Lubbock, it was possible to establish a time frame for a search of the ethnographic and anthropological literature in the period between Rousseau and Lubbock. Examination of the sources most likely to have influenced Lubbock finally revealed a clearly original formulation of the myth as we know it in Crawfurd's 1859 paper. With the double invention of the concept and the myth established, it seemed necessary to conduct yet another survey of selected works of the ethnographic and derivative literatures from the intervening period, but from the new perspective of a concept once privileged by its embeddedness in the myth and the culture of anthropology now having become problematized by the new critical framing of the survey.

Thus the core of this narrative is contained in the beginning and ending sections, parts 1 and 4; and a concise view of my basic argument may be found in those sections, particularly chapters 2 and 17. The intervening parts are a frankly experimental project in rereading the ethnographic literature from the perspective provided by examining the construction of the Noble Savage in Lescarbot and Crawfurd. This project is necessarily incomplete, given the vast extent of the literature, but equally necessarily undertaken if one is to understand the broad outlines of the historical developments that led from Lescarbot's invention of the concept to its disappearance during the Enlightenment and its reemergence into the mainstream of anthropological discourse in Crawfurd's construction of the myth in the mid-nineteenth century.

Parts 2 and 3 must therefore be taken as tentative explorations of a much larger field, where further readings will certainly reveal many more examples of the rhetoric of nobility than those presented in this brief survey. It is, of course, quite likely that such examples will necessitate some revisions of the argument presented here—after all, it would be reckless to claim that the concept of the Noble Savage does not and could not exist in the writings between Lescarbot and Crawfurd. But it seems quite unlikely that additional examples of the rhetoric of nobility would displace either or both authors from their key roles in developing the concept and the myth into powerful currents in the stream of anthropological discourse, which is the primary focus of this book. Nevertheless, we cannot rule out such a possibility. Thus, to help in the evaluation of such additional examples, I have suggested some general principles for a critique of the rhetoric of nobility in the introduction to part 2, with discussions of particular critical issues raised in conjunction with the discussions of specific works throughout parts 2 and 3.

Obviously, then, this is a book with an empty center. As a study in the history of ideas, it leaves a frustrating sense of the nonexistence of any discernible "idea" of the Noble Savage after its first invention by Lescarbot. As a study in the history of discourse, it turns away from opportunities for technical analysis of discursive forms to explore fields of changing meaning in the energizing currents of cultural, historical, and political implications of the rhetoric of nobility. But these strategies seem the only feasible approach in this first attempt at a critical study. Its central subject does not exist, being only an illusory construction resulting from the conjunction of contingent causal and contributory circumstances. As a scholar whose fieldwork has long been situated in Buddhist cultures where assertions of nonexistence and illusion often serve as normative characterizations of the state of the world and knowledge of it, this is entirely familiar, natural, and intellectually intriguing to me. For some, it may be unfamiliar and disconcerting. I hope, though, that others will find the exploration of the process of deconstructing nonexistent entities and illusions as rewarding an experience as I have found in completing this study.

Some of the most familiar names from the history of anthropology are in the following pages, as are many unfamiliar writers who have long faded into obscurity but who have played key roles in the construction of the Noble Savage. Even in the cases of well-known writers, however, our investigation leads us to consider little-studied aspects of their work; so in the end, both cases involve the exposition of material that is new and unfamiliar. For this reason, I make considerable use of citations, often fairly extensive, from the various authors studied, to allow them their own "voice" as far as possible, to present their ideas in adequate depth to avoid superficial impressions, and to gain some appreciation of the cultural and intellectual forces that shaped their ideas and rhetoric. As this study is an ethnography of other times rather than other places, and of other anthropologists rather than other races, I think this is what we owe them; and I find the attention to their viewpoints repaid by what they give us in return.

But I am too much a product of my own temporocultural environment to sit respectfully and silently by as they speak, without engaging them in conversation or debate, asking questions, and even shouting back at some egregious diatribe about the physical or mental inferiority of some racial group; or applauding the open-mindedness of Rousseau, Prichard, or Boas; or vacillating between appreciation and loathing for a complex personality such as John Crawfurd, perhaps the most likably despicable racist I have ever encountered. Some may find this frustrating, and they deserve a revisitation of the subject by authors with a more neutral, balanced viewpoint; but, in the meantime, it seems to me, neutrality and balance could hardly have been adequate sources of inspiration for the writing of a book such as this one.

There is a vast secondary literature on the wide range of periods and topics that must necessarily be touched on by a study of this subject, given the long history of its creation and its perpetuation into the present. Although considerations of space and the necessary priority of primary sources preclude extensive consideration of the scholarly literature in the following discussion, readers will find an enriched understanding of the subjects covered here by exploring some of the most important scholarly studies available. For the Noble Savage concept and myth, and the question of Rousseau's authorship, the classic study is Fairchild's *The Noble Savage*. More recent treatments are provided by works such as Gaile McGregor's *The Noble Savage in the New World Garden* (1988) and Tzvetan Todorov's

On Human Diversity (1993). For *le bon sauvage* in French literature, Gilbert Chinard's *L'Amerique et le reve exotique dans la litterature française au XVIIe et XVIIIe siècle* (1913) is an influential work that offers interpretations very different from those presented here.

Rousseau, like Darwin, is the subject of a publishing industry in his own right, and at least a considerable share of a lifetime could be spent exploring the scholarly literature on him and his ideas. Maurice Cranston (1982, 1991) provides the best available multivolume biography, still unfinished, that incorporates a great deal of recent scholarship in a balanced, analytic way. Likewise, Cranston's translation of the *Discourse on Inequality* (Rousseau 1755b) may be the best available English rendition of the text that has been taken as emblematic of Noble Savage mythology. Some of the most important scholarly commentary on the issue, pro and con, is included in the works listed in the preceding paragraph. The issue of Rousseau's influence on the development of anthropology, it seems to me, still awaits adequate scholarly treatment; but Michele Duchet's *Anthropologie et histoire au siècle des lumières* (1971) helps to situate his anthropological ideas in the context of other leading thinkers of the time without, of course, linking him to the generation of the myth of the Noble Savage.

For the Renaissance ethnography that gave birth to the Noble Savage concept, the available resources are more diverse. Margaret T. Hodgen's *Early Anthropology in the Sixteenth and Seventeenth Centuries* (1964) discusses many of the important issues and problems in the ethnography of the period, including the interpretation of "savage" cultures in terms of the myth of the Golden Age, a subject covered from a more general historical perspective in Harry Levin's *The Myth of the Golden Age in the Renaissance* (1969). Renaissance ethnography has been given creative treatment by recent work in history, literary criticism, and cultural studies; two interesting and very different examples exploring themes covered in this study are Anthony Pagden's *The Fall of Natural Man* (1982) and Stephen Greenblatt's *Marvelous Possessions* (1991).

Even believers in the myth of the Noble Savage have long recognized the need to take note of the growing development, in the century after Rousseau, of increasingly negative representations of the "savage." Some have conceived this need in terms of a logically balanced opposition between the "noble" and the "ignoble Savage," an opposition given early popular currency by Mark Twain (cited in Barnett 1975: 71) and subjected to more comprehensive scholarly investigation in works such as Robert F. Berkhofer, Jr.'s *The White Man's Indian* (1978). Others, noting the real imbalance of positive and negative representations during this period, have focused their attention on the pervasively dominant imagery of the "ignoble savage." The definitive work of the "ignoble savage" scholarship, Roy Harvey Pearce's *The Savages of America* (1953; later retitled *Savagism and Civilization*, 1988), covers a wide range of ethnographic, philosophical, political, and popular writings over almost exactly the same historical time span as this study. Two more specialized works, Louise K. Barnett's *The Ignoble Savage* (1975) and Ronald Meek's *Social Science and the Ignoble Savage* (1976), explore the uses of negative representations of the "savage" in the fields of American literary fiction and Enlightenment European sociocultural evolutionary theory, respectively. A more broadly focused work, Olive P. Dickason's *The Myth of the Savage* (1984), is useful because of its combination of critical analysis with historical and ethnographic surveys of French Canada, an area of considerable importance to this study, and its inclusion of an overview of the often-contentious subject of Indians who had visited Europe and their reactions to what they saw. Gordon Sayre's *Les Sauvages Américains* (1997) is a wide-ranging exploration of the early ethnographic literature, with some provocative suggestions and interpretations that lend help in understanding the sometimes striking differences between representations of the "savage" in French and English literature. While most such recent studies explicitly or implicitly treat the savage as a constructed category, Andrew Sinclair's *The Savage* (1977) argues that "savages," in the etymological sense of "men of the forest," represent an ancient part of the human heritage that has been drawn into increasingly oppositional polarity with civilization—thus according the category a unique sort of deeper metaphysical valorization than it receives in other studies, including this one.

For the process leading up to the construction of the myth of the Noble Savage in the context of the rise of anthropological racism in nineteenth-century England, the single indispensable source is Stocking's *Victorian Anthropology* (1987). Some of Stocking's shorter works are also very helpful, particularly "What's in a Name?" (1971) and "From Chronology to Ethnology" (1973). The literature on race and racism is vast; but a recent historical survey of American racism, Audrey Smedley's *Race in North America* (1993), provides an anthropological perspective. For American racist anthropology, which had considerable influence on the ideas and rhetoric of British racists such as Burke and Hunt, William Ragan Stanton's *The Leopard's Spots* (1960) is a classic study despite its occasional tendency to idealize the scientific accomplishments of the American racists. George M. Fredrickson's *The Black Image in the White Mind* (1971) provides some critiques and counterinterpretations for some of Stanton's evaluations.

Stocking's *Race, Culture, and Evolution* (1968) furnishes wider-ranging and more sophisticated treatment of important issues relating to race and racism in the history of European and American anthropology. For the leading opponents in the struggles over racism in the Ethnological and Anthropological societies, Stocking's works contain the best available discussions of Prichard and James Hunt; and Amalie M. Kass and Edward H. Kass's *Perfecting the World* (1988) is a well-researched biographical study of Thomas Hodgkin. For Crawfurd, who would influence the thought and discourse of anthropology for a century and a half by his invention of the myth of the Noble Savage, there is no scholarly study available.

Finally, a technical note: I have generally preferred to cite first editions, contemporary translations, and facsimile reprints to reproduce the style as well as the content of works covering a wide historical range. Sometimes, however, either because of accessibility or enhanced clarity for contemporary readers, I have chosen to cite modern scholarly editions and translations or use my own translations. In all cases, though, I have chosen a form of citation that differs from ordinary anthropological conventions by privileging historical over commercial chronology. In simple terms, this means that I choose the date of first publication for the primary citation, rather than the date the particular copy on my bookshelf happened to have first been offered for sale. Thus, for example, if I cite two English translations of Rousseau's *Discourse on Inequality*, first published in 1755, they become Rousseau 1755a and 1755b. The actual publication dates of these particular editions, respectively 1761 and 1984, appear in a secondary position later in the citation. In primary position, they would visually suggest either the existence of two different Rousseaus writing identically titled works or a particularly long-lived individual; but their main problem is that Rousseau's critics, such as Chinard (1913), would appear to antedate the work they criticize (Rousseau 1984), a confusion more likely to occur in cases such as Smith (1755) and Rousseau (1761), where one might be less likely to guess that the "earlier" work is a critique of the "later" one.

Assuming that most of you share my interest in understanding the development of a discursive exchange on the Noble Savage, which entails understanding who said what and when, I have chosen to render the sequence of events as transparent as possible by giving primary emphasis to the times when particular ideas were voiced and were heard. In most cases, this means primary citation of the date of first publication; but there are some exceptions. Where important new elements are introduced in second or later editions, these are cited separately from the first edition. And in part 4, where month-to-month developments in the political takeover of the

Ethnological Society are of crucial importance, but the publication of papers was often delayed by two or more years, I cite key papers by the date that they were actually given before the society, rather than by the later date of their publication. Unpublished materials, of course, are cited by the date of their composition. If all this sounds complex and inconsistent, its goal—and, I hope, its result—is to provide a consistent interface that reveals as clearly as possible the complex sequence of events by which something as deviously powerful and debilitatingly consequential to anthropology as the myth of the Noble Savage was generated.

I owe particular thanks to Beverley Emery, Royal Anthropological Institute (RAI) Library Representative, and her colleagues at the Museum of Mankind, for facilitating my research in the RAI Archives in London. Research on topics related to this study has been supported by the Graduate School Research Fund and the Center for the Humanities at the University of Washington.

Introduction

More than two centuries after his death, Jean-Jacques Rousseau is still widely cited as the inventor of the "Noble Savage"—a mythic personification of natural goodness by a romantic glorification of savage life—projected in the very essay (Rousseau 1755a) in which he became the first to call for the development of an anthropological Science of Man. Criticism of the Noble Savage myth is an enduring tradition in anthropology, beginning with its emergence as a formalized discipline. George Stocking (1987: 153) has cited a reference as early as 1865 by John Lubbock, vice president of the Ethnological Society of London, the first anthropological organization in the English-speaking world; and other early citations include such leading figures as E. B. Tylor (1881: 408) and Franz Boas (1889: 68). The critique extends throughout the twentieth century, appearing in the work of scholars such as Marvin Harris.

> Although considerable difference existed as to the specific characterization of this primitive condition, ranging from Hobbes's "war of all against all" to Rousseau's "noble savage," the explanation of how some men had terminated the state of nature and arrived at their present customs and institutions was approached in a fairly uniform fashion. (Harris 1968: 38–39)

And it continues into the present. For example, a recent article begins with the assertion, "The noble savage, according to eighteenth-century French philosopher Jean-Jacques Rousseau, is an individual living in a 'pure state of nature'—gentle, wise, uncorrupted by the vices of civilization" (Aleiss 1991: 91). Michel-Rolph Trouillot (1991: 26), taking a more complex historical position, nevertheless states, "Rousseau . . . thus formalized the myth of the 'noble savage.'"

Clearly, in the 1990s the Noble Savage and Rousseau's purported role in its creation remains a leading critical concern both in anthropology and in the growing list of disciplines that take an interest in the ethnographic literature and the history of cross-cultural encounters between Europeans and non-Europeans. Where the Noble Savage is invoked, Rousseau's name is almost invariably found in close proximity, although sometimes with their linkage implied in ambiguous ways. Edna C. Sorber, for example, writes,

> They probably didn't plan it that way, but the perpetrators of the "noble savage" concept in 18th and 19th century America were doing the rhetorical criticism that more specialized rhetorical critics were ignoring. While the followers of the Rousseau point of view may have originally been the philosophers, as writings on the American Indian came to dominate such discussions other considerations took precedence. (1972: 227)

In a very few cases, Rousseau is identified not as the original author of the Noble Savage but rather as the most effective agent of its promotion. Bobbi S. Low (1996: 354), for example, writes, "Dryden (in *The Conquest of Granada*, 1672) seems to have been the first to use the term. Rousseau, of course, used the concept effectively to anathematize civilization"(cf. McGregor's discussion of Rousseau's role, below). But in most cases, attributions of authorship to Rousseau are straightforward and apparently unproblematic. Katherine A. Dettwyler (1991: 375) refers to "images of Rousseau's 'noble savage' transported to the past"; and Michael S. Alvard (1993: 355–56) charges that "Jean Jacques [*sic*] Rousseau's concept of the 'Noble Savage' has been extended and re-defined into the 'Ecological Noble Savage' by both conservationists and anthropologists." Even such a generally careful scholar as Stocking (1987: 17) remarks, "The ambiguous 'noble savage' of Rousseau's 'Discourse on Inequality' was not the only manifestation of primitivism or historical pessimism among the French philosophers of progress."

None of these authors apparently feels any need to support the claim of Rousseau's authorship with a citation; it is simply, unquestionably true, presumably one of those public-domain bits of information for which the citation is an implicit "Everyone knows . . ." After all, even the *Oxford English Dictionary* says:

> NOBLE (4 a) Having high moral qualities or ideals; of a great or lofty
> character. (Also used ironically.) NOBLE SAVAGE, primitive man, con-
> ceived of in the manner of Rousseau as morally superior to civilized
> man.

But like some other anthropological folklore, this particular invented tradition is not only wrong but long since known to be wrong; and its continuing vitality in the face of its demonstrated falsity confronts us with a particularly problematic current in the history of anthropology. A convenient
point of entry to this current is Fairchild's classic study, *The Noble Savage*.
Fairchild, an avowed enemy of the Noble Savage myth and an outspoken
critic of Rousseau's influence on romantic thought, investigated Rousseau's
writings (Fairchild 1928: 120–39) and was forced to conclude, as an earlier
examiner of Rousseau's "supposed romanticism" (Lovejoy 1923) had implied, that the linkage of Rousseau to the Noble Savage concept was un-
founded: "The fact is that the real Rousseau was much less sentimentally
enthusiastic about savages than many of his contemporaries, did not in any
sense invent the Noble Savage idea, and cannot be held wholly responsible
for the forms assumed by that idea in English Romanticism" (Fairchild
1928: 139).

Those few scholars who, since Fairchild, have bothered to look critically at the question have come to the same conclusion. Thus, although
anthropologists have generally tended to accept the legend of Rousseau's
connection with the Noble Savage more or less on faith, Stanley Diamond
(1974: 100–1) points out his critical perspective and his avoidance of the
term. Scholars of literary criticism and cultural studies who have examined
the issue in any depth have reached similar or stronger conclusions. For
example, Gaile McGregor, retracing Fairchild's investigation from a late-
twentieth-century perspective, says,

> Despite his undoubted influence, however, it is important to distin-
> guish Rousseau's own position on primitivism from popular assess-
> ments. As in Montaigne's case, the text itself contains elements which
> are obviously inhospitable to an unadulterated theory of noble sav-
> agery. While he does indeed, in Moore's words, lavish "uncommon
> praise on some aspects of savage life," Rousseau's overall estimate of
> that level of existence is far from enthusiastic. . . . Like Montaigne,
> then, Rousseau's aim was basically relativistic. (1988: 19–20)

And Tzvetan Todorov (1993: 277) similarly concludes, "Jean-Jacques Rousseau's thought is traditionally associated with primitivism and the cult of

the noble savage. In reality (and attentive commentators have been point-ing this out since the beginning of the twentieth century), Rousseau was actually a vigilant critic of these tendencies."

So it seems clear that we must conclude that Rousseau's invention of the Noble Savage myth is itself a myth. But this conclusion, unanimously supported by serious investigators and clear as it is, raises some obvious questions. If Rousseau did not create the concept of the Noble Savage, who did? How did it become associated in popular and professional belief with Rousseau, and with the origins of anthropology? And, perhaps less obvi-ously, why has belief in a discredited theory lingered on for seven decades after the publication of a clear disproof, particularly among anthropologists themselves? Is there something in the nature of anthropology itself, either in its intrinsic nature or in its historically contingent construction, that re-quires such a belief?

I will suggest in the following pages that there is; that not only is every-thing we have believed about the myth of the Noble Savage wrong, but it is so because our profession has been historically constructed in such a way as to require exactly this kind of obviously false belief. In outlining this suggestion, I will advance some apparently contradictory proposals: that belief in the Noble Savage never existed but that the Noble Savage was in-deed associated with both the conceptual and the institutional foundations of anthropology, and not only once but twice, in widely separated histori-cal periods, both before and after Rousseau's time; and finally, that there was indeed a single person who was the original source of both the Noble Savage concept and of the call for the foundation of a science of human di-versity but that this person was not Rousseau.

A ROSE AS REPRESENTED BY ANOTHER NAME MIGHT STINK

If Rousseau was not the inventor of the Noble Savage, who was? One who turns for help to Fairchild's 1928 study, a compendium of citations from romantic writings on the "savage," may be surprised to find *The Noble Savage* almost completely lacking in references to its nominal subject. That is, although Fairchild assembles hundreds of quotations from ethnogra-phers, philosophers, novelists, poets, and playwrights from the seventeenth to the nineteenth century, showing a rich variety of ways in which writers romanticized and idealized those whom Europeans of the period considered "savages," almost none of them explicitly refer to something called the "Noble Savage." Although the words, always duly capitalized, appear on nearly every page, and often several times per page, it turns out that in every instance, with four possible exceptions, they are Fairchild's words and not those of the authors cited. The myth of the Noble Savage suddenly seems very nebulous, and problematic in quite a different way than we might have expected.

But before concluding that the Noble Savage was a figment of the imagination or some kind of conceptual hoax, we should examine the apparent exceptions. Three of these date from after Rousseau's death. In Henry Mackenzie's novel *Man of the World* (1787), when a European captive who has lived several years with American Indians decides to return to civilization, his "imagination drew, on this side, fraud, hypocrisy and sordid baseness, while on that seemed to preside honesty, truth and savage nobleness of soul" (cited in Fairchild 1928: 92). While not an exact match, the wording is acceptably close, and the comparison of "savage nobleness" with civilized corruption seems to fit the myth as most have understood it. The comparison is, however, specifically identified as a construction of the imagination rather than as reality, and the context is not that of an idealization of the savage. For, as Fairchild (1928: 90–92) points out, Mackenzie places a noticeable emphasis on savage violence and cruelty, which seems incompatible with the Noble Savage myth. Furthermore, the passage leaves some doubt as to whether the construction "savage nobleness" implies equivalence or qualification: that is, might "savage" nobleness contrast with some other variety, such as "true nobleness"?

The other two cases are even more doubtful. In one, the wife of the poet Shelley describes the plot of one of his unfinished works written in 1822: "An Enchantress, living in one of the islands of the Indian Archipelago, saves the life of a Pirate, a man of savage but noble nature" (Fairchild 1928: 309). Here, despite the verbal similarity, the point is one of reference to qualities of an individual's nature rather than to man in a state of nature; and the "but" suggests an exceptional case that violates the normal opposition between "savage" and "noble" natures. The difference in implication of the application of the term "savage" to the pirate and to peoples living in a "state of nature" should be obvious enough to need no comment.

In the third case, Sir Walter Scott says in 1818 in *The Heart of Midlothian:* "One . . . stood upright before them, a lathy young savage. . . . Yet the eyes of the lad were keen and sparkling; his gesture free and noble, like that of all savages" (cited in Fairchild 1928: 317). Here again, despite the verbal resemblance, the nobility is of a different kind, a nobility of gesture; and the "savage" in question is actually a Scottish Highlander! Although Fairchild rightly points out, here and elsewhere, that attributions of savage wildness and natural goodness were often transposed from more exotic locales onto various groups of Europeans,[1] he also points out that Scott showed a rather obvious disinterest in the purported nobility of more ethnographically remote peoples.

Given the problematic nature of these three cases, we seem drawn more strongly toward an impression that there is little support in the literature for the idea that there was widespread belief, or even any belief at all, in the existence of something actually called "the Noble Savage." But is this really important? Why, after all, should we problematize the words "Noble Savage" rather than their conceptual content or objective field of reference? Isn't this mere empty formalism? After all, isn't there overwhelming evidence that "savages" were heavily laden by European writers with the baggage of romantic naturalism, which is the point of the critique, rather than the label attached to it?

But the fact is that both the label and the contents are problematic. In Fairchild's survey of "exotic" and "romantic naturalist" literature, for example, one finds the label "Noble Savage" affixed to literary representations ranging from the most absurd parroting of Parisian salon discourse by Huron warriors to African slaves lamenting their lost freedom. Are these really equivalent cases of "romantic naturalism," equally deserving of the critical scorn and derision implied by labeling them both "Noble Savage"?

In some of the cases Fairchild cites, "primitive" and "natural" ways of life seem so idealized and exalted that few readers could avoid wondering whether such paradises could ever exist on earth, or, if they did once, that anyone could ever exchange them for "civilization." And in some cases, "civilization" takes on such a quasi-hellish character that one wonders how it could ever have developed at all, or prevented its victims from mass desertion to happier states of existence. But in other cases, even the slightest criticism of European cruelty or corruption, or the least hint that non-European peoples might have any good qualities whatsoever, seems to qualify as "romantic naturalism," to be labeled as yet a further instance of belief in the "Noble Savage."

One can, of course, argue for the real merits of connecting such cases and maintain that any belief at all in things such as freedom or goodness is in reality nothing but romantic fantasy. But all such arguments, like the arguments against them, are necessarily problematic and require deliberate and careful construction. How much easier, instead, to have a ready-made polemic label such as "the Noble Savage" that assumes the validity of the connection even as it heaps scorn on any imaginable opposition, and saves the work of constructing an argument by assuming what it purports to critique? It seems that, given the problematic nature of its field of reference, we have no other choice but to also seriously consider the problematic nature of "the Noble Savage" as a discursive construct. Neither its content nor its verbal form should be accepted at face value, without further question.

But as soon as we begin to consider the Noble Savage concept as a discursive construct rather than as a substantive given element of objective or commonsense reality, we begin to further problematize it. The term is rather obviously a forced union of questionable assumptions. That men could ever be either savage, that is, wild, or noble, that is, exalted above all others either by an environmentally imposed morality or by their station of birth, is equally questionable; that the two could be causally related is absurd. The absurdity precludes serious belief in the concept, exactly the point of their juxtaposition. The Noble Savage clearly belongs to the rhetoric of polemic criticism rather than of ethnographic analysis, or even of serious credal affirmation.

As a discursive artifact, the term is further problematic in that it would appear to belong almost exclusively to Anglophone culture, to the English language and its writers in Britain and North America. The expression is simply not widely used in other languages: compare, for example, Todorov's (1993: 270) section called "The Noble Savage" in English translation, with "le Bon Sauvage," literally "the good savage," in the French original (Todorov 1989). A more striking comparison arises in juxtaposing the French, Spanish, German, and English abstracts of Georges Guille-Escuret's "Cannibales isolés et monarques sans histoire" (1992: 327, 345): the English "noble savage" contrasts noticeably with *bon sauvage, buen salvaje*, and *gute Wilde*, all sharing attributions of goodness and wildness but lacking the highly charged polarities of the English term. And one wonders why the editors found it necessary to mark only the English term by framing it in quotes. Could it be that communication with English readers on this subject requires a dramatically highlighted emotional intensity? If so, where did that intensity, or the need for it, come from?

One might protest that *le bon sauvage* and "the Noble Savage" simply mean the same thing, that they are dictionary equivalents, and that translation would never be possible if strict logical equivalence and formal congruity were always demanded (see Church 1950; Carnap 1955). In fact, the assertion of identity may be true of their extensive meaning, in the sense of reference to the "same" object; but intensively, they say something very different about it and so represent their objects very differently. The French *bon sauvage* and its cognates express a gentle irony; the English "Noble

Savage" drips with sarcasm, intensified by its obligatory framing in capitals and/or quotes. One usage embodies a critical stance that could, and sometimes does (see Atkinson 1924; Todorov 1989), include a dimension of critical appreciation; the other, a stance that is uncompromisingly hostile and polemic.

More specifically, nobility transcends mere goodness; it represents a more exalted state, and significantly, the exaltation implies an innate exaltation above other beings and their qualities. Nobility is a construction not only of a moral quality but also of a social class and social hierarchy. But is this not a contradictory association, given the supposed linkage of the term with eighteenth-century "romantic" advocates of egalitarian, democratic ideals? Perhaps the term represents a simple attempt to liberate by defeudalizing language, distinguishing "true" moral nobility from a class designation. Or perhaps the term's apparent link to orders of hierarchy and dominance is more than superficial. A look at its historical usage suggests this is in fact the case.

The single clear citation of the term "Noble Savage" in either Fairchild (1928) or McGregor (1988), which is also cited as the term's earliest occurrence by the *Oxford English Dictionary*, comes not from the romantic period or the eighteenth century but from John Dryden's seventeenth-century drama, *The Conquest of Granada by the Spaniards:*

> I am as free as Nature first made man,
> 'Ere the base Laws of Servitude began,
> When wild in woods the noble Savage ran.
> (Dryden 1672: 34)

Here, the freedom of the noble savage is not only associated with wildness and nature, and contrasted with a baseness that must be implicitly attributed to civilization, but the latter is associated with servitude linked to law. The combination is specific and complex enough to suggest an underlying argument or a conceptual foundation not clarified in the lines themselves. Dryden's words appear to be a poetic condensation of a preexisting construction that we must seek in earlier sources; a likely starting point would be the ethnographic sources on "savage" ways of life.

I

THE BIRTH OF THE
NOBLE SAVAGE

FIGURE 1. SAVAGE BEAUTY.
Renaissance assimilations of non-European peoples to classical
Greco-Roman ideals of innocence and beauty produced discursive and visual representations such as the myth of the Golden
Age and Theodor De Bry's sixteenth-century portrait of African
warriors as Greek nudes (De Bry, reprinted in Green 1745–47:
3:281, pl. 16).

1 Colonialism, Savages, and Terrorism

FIGURE 2. SAVAGE CRUELTY.
Assimilation with the negative classical imagery of the Anthropophages, reinterpreted as New World "cannibals," led to discursive and pictorial emphases on the cruelty of "savage" peoples, as in Jacques LeMoyne's sixteenth-century depiction of infant sacrifice in Florida (LeMoyne, redrawn and printed in Picart 1712–31).

European ideas of the "savage" grew out of an imaginative fusion of classical mythology with the new descriptions that were beginning to be conceived by scientifically minded writers as "observations" of foreign peoples by Renaissance travel-ethnographic writers. In the century and a half after Columbus, such "observations," often quite descriptively accurate and perceptive, gained power through their polarization within a field of potentialities defined by the negatively and positively highly charged classicist identifications, respectively, of native Americans with the "Anthropophages," or man-eaters—now relabeled "cannibals" by identification with the newly discovered Caribs of the West Indies—and with the inhabitants of the mythological "Golden Age" (fig. 1).

In terms of their emotional impacts, the contrasting constructions of the cannibals and the Golden Age reflect outcomes of two opposing representational strategies: alienation from and assimilation to the familiar world of European experiences and values. In terms of the process of their construction, however, both reflect a common process of assimilation of the unfamiliar to the familiar; for, as Leonardo da Vinci (1489–1518: 1:292–93) reminded artists of the period, monsters can only be constructed out of the animals we know. Thus both the cannibals and the Golden Age superimposed observations of unfamiliar peoples on idealized models drawn from Greco-Roman mythology, whether the idealization was given a negative or a positive valence. In turn, each became the locus for further assimilations of other negative or positive constructions. Where the actual practice of cannibalism was lacking, for example, human sacrifice, torture of prisoners, or any form of the "cruelty" inevitably found in human societies could fill its place in the axis of polarized representations, ensuring that all "savages" could be represented as at least some sort of virtual cannibals (fig. 2). Likewise, where the full litany of characteristics of the Golden Age (see below) was incomplete, almost any combination of its emblematic feature, nudity, with evocations of goodness and beauty could serve to construct the positive side of the polarization empowered by the underlying ideal of the Golden Age itself.

Although it would seem that the Golden Age, with its positive valence, should be the more relevant to our subject, in fact the more negative equation of "savages" with "cannibals" generated discourses of cultural relativism (e.g., Lery 1578; Montaigne 1588a) that would themselves be misperceived as representations of the "Noble Savage," or at least as closely related to them.[1] The Golden Age, in its turn, would generate many permutations that would reverberate through the centuries of changing discourses on the "savage." We must take note of both concepts here to recognize their vitalizing force in representations of the "savage," which, we must remind ourselves, given the horrific predominance of the imagery of cannibalism, were anything but generally positive, relativistic, romanticized, or "noble."

But, about a century after Columbus, new conceptual and discursive alternatives would appear, including the quite unexpected and unlikely concept of the Noble Savage. The ideas both of the Noble Savage and of an anthropological science of human diversity grew out of the writings of these Renaissance European traveler-ethnographers. Although work by many scholars will be needed to confirm the ultimate origin of either concept, both can be traced at least to the beginning of the seventeenth century, where they appear together in Lescarbot's (1609c) ethnography of the Indians of eastern Canada.

Lescarbot was a lawyer who, after having suffered setbacks in his Parisian legal practice, joined the Seigneur de Poutrincourt's colonial expedition to the Bay of Fundy in eastern Canada, where he spent a year in 1606–7 living among the "Souriquois" (Mi'kmaq, or "Micmac") Indians (Biggar 1907: x–xv). In response to Poutrincourt's invitation, Lescarbot said, "Not so much desirous to see the country . . . as to be able to give an eye judgment of the land, whereto my mind was before inclined; and to avoid a corrupted world I engaged my word unto him" (1609c: 61–62). In the new colonial setting, the urban professional, friend of noblemen, found a new and unexpected self-realization:

> I may say (and that truly) that I never made so much bodily work for the pleasure that I did take in dressing and tilling my gardens, to enclose and hedge them against the gluttony of the hogs, to make knots, to draw out alleys, to build arbours, to sow wheat, rye, barley, oats, beans, peas, garden-herbs, and to water them—so much desire had I to know the goodness of the ground by my own experience. So that summer's days were unto me too short, and very often did I work by moonlight. (1609c: 43)

This experience moved Lescarbot to philosophical reflections on problems in the "corrupted world" of his own society:

> But the Frenchmen and almost all nations at this day (I mean of those that be not born and brought up to the manuring of the ground) have this bad nature, that they think to derogate much from their dignity in addicting themselves to the tillage of the ground, which notwithstanding is almost the only vocation where innocency remaineth. And thereby cometh that everyone shunning this noble labour our first parents' and ancient kings' exercise, as also of the greatest captains of the world, seeking to make himself a gentleman at others' costs, or else willing only to learn the trade to deceive men or to claw himself in the sun, God taketh away his blessing from us, and beateth us at this day, and hath done a long time, with an iron rod, so that in all parts the people languisheth miserably, and we see the realm of France swarming with beggars and vagabonds of all kinds, besides an infinite number, groaning in their poor cottages, not daring, or ashamed, to show forth their poverty and misery. (1609c: 59–60)

By contrast, Lescarbot found a personal epiphany that led to self-fulfillment in the three culturally and personally significant dimensions of Christian theology, Renaissance classicism, and feudal-aristocratic patronage:

> Wherein I have cause to rejoice, because I was of the company and of the first tillers of that land. And herein I pleased myself the more, when I did set before mine eyes our ancient father Noah, a great king, great priest, and great prophet, whose occupation was to husband the ground, both in sowing of corn and planting the vine; and the ancient Roman Captain Seranus, who was found sowing of his field when that he was sent for to conduct the Roman army; and Quintus Cincinnatus, who all dusty did plough four acres of lands, bare-headed and open stomached, when the Senate's herald brought letters of the dictatorship unto him; in sort that this messenger was forced to pray him to cover himself before he declared his embassage unto him. Delighting myself in this exercise, God hath blessed my poor labour, and I have had in my garden as fair wheat as any can be in France, whereof the said Monsieur de Poutrincourt gave unto me a glean. (1609c: 138–39)

But Lescarbot found a fascination at least equally great in the discovery of the "savages" who inhabited his new world: "Having never seen any before, I did admire, at the first sight, their fair shape and form of visage" (1609c: 84).

The attraction the Indians exercised on Lescarbot was certainly enhanced by the complex circumstances under which he encountered them. Far from being a first encounter with a pristine culture, the French-Indian relationship at the time of Lescarbot's visit was the product of prolonged contact and increasingly sophisticated interactions. Although there was a hiatus in French colonial endeavors in Canada between Cartier's explorations in the 1530s and 1540s and Champlain's return there in the 1590s, the Indians had not remained isolated from European contacts. For a whole century, fishermen and traders of various nationalities, including French but most prominently Basque, had made yearly voyages to the Newfoundland banks and the Canadian coasts and drawn the Indians into increasingly profitable and complex trade networks and alliances. The more famous explorers whose names are known to history all mention these nameless fishermen and traders, and we may never know for sure who they were; but what they did is obvious by its results.

By the turn of the seventeenth century, when Lescarbot joined the pioneering colony in Acadia (Nova Scotia), the coastal Indians had developed trade networks with friendly peoples extending into the interior of the continent, and formed political alliances against potential and actual enemies and competitors, in pursuit of the increasingly profitable advantages of the fur trade with the Europeans. The competition had not yet developed into the international alliances with competing European powers, such as the famous French-Huron versus British-Iroquois alliances, that would grow up with Dutch and British expansion into New York and New England in the seventeenth century; but even the local competition among Indians for control of trade with transient Europeans and the initial French settlers was already intense. Some of the Indians began to appreciate the advantages of stabler, longer-term relationships with particular groups of Europeans and moved decisively to exploit the possibilities of the situation, making adjustments to their ways of life to accommodate their new strategies (for a useful overview, see Brasser 1978).

Thus, at the time of the settlement of Lescarbot's colony in Acadia, the Mi'kmaq Indians, under the leadership of their politically skillful chief and shaman Membertou, were engaged in aggressive pursuit of the advantages of a closer alliance with the French. It was under these circumstances that Lescarbot came into close and prolonged contact with the Indians, as they and the French colonists pursued every available means of strengthening an alliance that both sides found advantageous to their own interests. It is no wonder, then, that increasing familiarity, but also the beginnings of a new and wonderful kind of friendship between such very different peoples, began to grow. Lescarbot describes the festive dinners of the colonists:

> In such actions we had always twenty or thirty savages, men, women, girls, and boys, who beheld us in doing our offices. Bread was given to them gratis, as we do here to the poor. But as for the Sagamos [chief] Membertou and any Sagamos (when any came to us), they sat at table eating and drinking as we did; and we took pleasure in seeing them, as contrariwise their absence was irksome unto us. (1609c: 118–19)

Yet, while Lescarbot's liking for Membertou and the Indians seems genuine enough, he recognized the complexity of the relationship and of their motives.

> As it came to pass three or four times that all went away to the places where they knew that game and venison was, and brought one of our men with them, who lived some six weeks as they did without salt, without bread and without wine, lying on the ground upon skins, and that in snowy weather. Moreover, they had greater care of him (as also of others that have often gone with them) than of themselves, saying that, if they should chance to die, it would be laid to their charges to have killed them. And hereby it may be known that we were not (as it

were) pent up in an island as Monsieur de Villegagnon was in Brazil.[2]
For this people love Frenchmen, and would all, at a need, arm themselves for to maintain them. (1609c: 119)

There can be little doubt that the Indians Lescarbot knew valued their
relationship with the French settlers; and he gives several colorful instances of their positive actions, including their farewell to the departing
colonists.

> But it was piteous to see at his departing those poor people weep, who
> had been always kept in hope that some of ours should always tarry
> with them. In the end, promise was made unto them that the year fol-
> lowing households and families should be sent thither, wholly to in-
> habit their land and teach them trades for to make them live as we do,
> which promise did somewhat comfort them. (Lescarbot 1609c: 139)

Is this merely the wishful thinking of ethnocentric Europeans, complacent
in their own sense of cultural superiority? We must remember that the
Mi'kmaq were pursuing an aggressive strategy of alliance with the French,
apparently based on the principle that the stronger and more durable the
connection was, the more they stood to gain. In arousing French hopes of
their own amalgamation with colonial society, it seems that their strategy
was quite successful in evoking a perception in their trading partners of the
strength and permanency of the bonds between them.

> The meanwhile the savages from about all their confines came to see
> the manners of the Frenchmen, and lodged themselves willingly near
> them: also, in certain variances happened amongst themselves, they did
> make Monsieur de Monts judge of their debates, which is a beginning
> of voluntary subjection, from whence a hope may be conceived that
> these people will soon conform themselves to our manner of living.
> (Lescarbot 1609c: 24)

It hardly needs to be said that Lescarbot's perception of "a beginning
of voluntary subjection" reflects a French rather than an Indian viewpoint.
Rather than Lescarbot's legalist vision of a French-style judge with absolute power over the subjects of the monarch he represents, the Indians
probably placed de Monts more in the role of a tribal mediator in a dispute
between equals, or perhaps even of a neutral referee such as other Northeastern tribes used for ball games and other sporting contests (Morgan
1851: 295 ff.). And in reflecting on the success of the Mi'kmaq strategy
of courtship of the French alliance, we might also consider the propagandistic focus of Lescarbot's writing, designed to encourage French settlers

and allay their anxieties over the alien nature of the new world and its inhabitants by arousing expectations of their domesticability. Toward this
end, he stresses the richness and comfort of the new land, the enjoyment
of which was substantially enabled by the assistance of the Indians; and in
so doing, he reveals something of the economic strategies and practices that
facilitated the cooperation of French and Indians:

> For our allowance, we had peas, beans, rice, prunes, raisins, dry cod,
> and salt flesh, besides oil and butter. But whensoever the savages
> dwelling near us had taken any quantity of sturgeons, salmons, or
> small fishes—item, any beavers, elans, carabous, (or fallow-deer), or
> other beasts . . . they brought unto us half of it; and that which re-
> mained they exposed it sometimes to sale publicly, and they that would
> have any thereof did truck bread for it. (1609c: 119)

Lescarbot's recognition of complexity and realism in the relationship
continues in his analysis of the Indians' generosity.

> For the savages have that noble quality, that they give liberally, casting
> at the feet of him whom they will honour the present that they give
> him. But it is with hope to receive some reciprocal kindness, which is a
> kind of contract, which we call, without name: "I give thee, to the end
> thou shouldest give me." And that is done throughout all the world.
> (1609c: 100–1)

In this proto-Maussian characterization of the obligation inherent in
the gift, the awareness of reciprocity, and its widespread occurrence in human life, we catch something of the way of thinking that led Lescarbot to
become one of the first advocates of an anthropological science (see chap. 2).
Indeed, his impressions of the Indians are pervaded by comparativist and
relativist perspectives.

> So we see that one selfsame fashion of living is received in one place
> and rejected in another. Which is familiarly evident unto us in many
> other things in our regions of these parts [Europe and France], where
> we see manners and fashions of living all contrary, yea, sometimes un-
> der one and the same prince. (1609c: 191)

And this comparative-relativist viewpoint leads Lescarbot again and
again to draw unfavorable comparisons of European to Indian conduct and
to criticize what he sees as corruptions and injustices in his own society.
This is hardly surprising in a writer of the time, given the strong development of such themes by Renaissance ethnographers and humanist

commentators on the "savage" such as Jean de Lery (1578) and Michel de Montaigne (1588a). Lescarbot is in many ways a typical Renaissance humanist writer: for instance, in his repeated questioning and occasional outright rejection of the claims of written authority (e.g., Lescarbot 1609c: 21, 49, 51), even as he constantly cites classical authorities as a source of comparative data and interpretive concepts. The dynamic tension between the use of classical authority for ethnographic comparisons, on the one hand, and observation as a challenge to authority, on the other, provides an energizing polarity in many Renaissance ethnographies; and so it does also in Lescarbot. His interest in classical Greek and Roman antiquity is expanded in his ethnographic description (1609c: 145 ff.) into a chain of comparisons of the ways of the "savages" with the classical civilizations of Europe—not, indeed, as a means of alienation through detemporalization (Fabian 1983) but rather as a means of bringing their experiences closer to those of Europeans, a kind of time-shifting manipulation to bridge the gaps of geographic distance and cultural contrasts.

Nevertheless, Lescarbot's overall view of the Indians remains that of a committed advocate of colonial domination and, as such, is diametrically opposed to any project of idealization. Indeed, as a colonist confronting not only Indian alliances and friendship but also hostile peoples whose opposition sometimes violated European norms of the sanctity of property, and sometimes embraced the use of lethal force, Lescarbot presents one of the most remarkable rhetorical stances in the French colonial literature in his oscillation between strongly positive and negative rhetoric, the latter extending so far as the evocation of an incipient theory of terrorism.

> We would have made them to eat of the grape, but, having taken it into their mouths, they spitted it out, so ignorant is this people of the best thing that God hath given to man next to bread. Yet, notwithstanding, they have no want of wit, and might be brought to do some good things if they were civilized and had the use of handy crafts. But they are subtle, thievish, and traitorous, and, though they be naked, yet one cannot take heed of their fingers, for if one turn never so little his eyes aside, and that they spy the opportunity to steal any knife, hatchet, or anything else, they will not miss nor fail of it; and will put the theft between their buttocks, or will hide it within the sand with their foot so cunningly that one shall not perceive it.
>
> Indeed, I do not wonder if a people poor and naked be thievish; but when the heart is malicious, it is inexcusable. This people is such that they must be handled with terror, for if though love and gentleness one give them too free access, they will practise some surprise. (1609c: 103)

The ideological justification and practical application of this policy of "terror" (*terreur*) is elaborated in Lescarbot's narrative of an encounter with another group.

> After certain days, the said Monsieur de Poutrincourt, seeing there great assembly of savages, came ashore, and, to give them some terror, made to march before him one of his men flourishing with two naked swords. Whereat they much wondered, but yet much more when they saw that our muskets did pierce thick pieces of wood, where their arrows could not so much as scratch. And therefore they never assailed our men as long as they kept watch. . . .
>
> They were five [Frenchmen], armed with muskets and swords, which were warned to stand still upon their guard, and yet (being negligent) made not any watch, so much were they addicted to their own wills. The report was that they had before shot off two muskets upon the savages, because that some one of them had stolen a hatchet. Finally, those savages, either provoked by that or by their bad nature, came at the break of day without any noise (which was very easy to them, having neither horses, waggons, nor wooden shoes), even to the place where they were asleep; and, seeing a fit opportunity to play a bad part, they set upon them with shots of arrows and clubs, and killed two of them. The rest being hurt began to cry out, running towards the sea-shore. . . .
>
> But the savages ran away as fast as ever they could, though they were above three hundred besides them that were hidden in the grass (according to their custom) which appeared not. Wherein is to be noted how God fixeth I know not what terror in the face of the faithful against infidels and miscreants, according to His sacred Word, when he saith to his chosen people [Deut. xi.25]: *"None shall be able to stand before you. The Lord your God shall put a terror and fear of you over all the earth, upon which you shall march."*
>
> . . . The said Monsieur de Poutrincourt, seeing he could get nothing by pursuing of them, caused pits to be made to bury them that were dead, which I have said to be two; but there was one that died at the water's side, thinking to save himself, and a fourth man which was so sorely wounded with arrow-shots that he died being brought to Port Royal; the fifth man had an arrow sticking in his breast, yet did scape death for that time; but it had been better he had died there, for one hath lately told us that he was hanged in the habitation that Monsieur de Monts maintaineth at Quebec in the great river of Canada, having been the author of a conspiracy made against his Captain Monsieur Champlain, which is now there. . . .
>
> Nevertheless, the last duty towards the dead was not neglected, which were buried at the foot of the Cross that had been there planted,

as is before said. But the insolency of this barbarous people was great, after the murders by them committed; for that as our men did sing over our dead men the funeral service and prayers accustomed in the Church, these rascals, I say, did dance and howled a-far off, rejoicing for their traitorous treachery, and therefore, though they were a great number, they adventured not themselves to come and assail our people, who, having at their leisure done what we have said before, because the sea waxed very low, retired themselves unto the barque, wherein remained Monsieur Champdoré for the guard therof. But being low water and having no means to come a-land, this wicked generation came again to the place where they had committed the murder, pulled up the Cross, digged out and unburied one of the dead corpses, took away his shirt, and put it on them, showing their spoils that they had carried away; and, besides all this, turning their backs towards the barque, did cast sand with their two hands betwixt their buttocks in derision, howling like wolves: which did marvellously vex our people, which spared no cast pieces shots at them; but the distance was very great, and they had already that subtlety as to cast themselves on the ground when they saw the fire put at it, in such sort that no one knew not whether they had been hurt or no, so that our men were forced to drink that bitter potion, attending for the tide, which, being come and sufficient to carry them a-land, as soon as they saw our men enter into the shallop, they ran away as swift as greyhounds, trusting themselves on their agility. . . . [S]o they set up the Cross again with reverence, and the body which they had digged up was buried again, and they named this Port Port Fortuné. (1609c: 107–12)

Thus far Marc Lescarbot, lawyer, traveler, and farmer; friend to Membertou, critic of civilized injustices, vivid chronicler of anticolonial resistance, and exponent of terrorism. He is certainly one of the most complex and interesting ethnographic writers of the French colonial enterprise. Even the abbreviated excerpt above might almost be the basis for a book in itself, so rich is it in the tropes and images of colonialism and resistance. The unexpected reframing by the Indians, for example, of the French psalm singing into one side of an Indian war-song duel between opposing tribes is as striking a case of "ethnographic" transformation as any European construction of Indians as the inhabitants of a "golden age"; and it must have been as shocking, in its own way, as the Indians' "mooning" their French adversaries. But Lescarbot's work would become even more complex and interesting when it passed beyond travel narrative to systematic ethnography, and to serious analysis of the nature of "savage" society.[3]

2 Lescarbot's Noble Savage and Anthropological Science

FIGURE 3.
NOBLE HUNTER.
Because all Mi'kmaq
men practiced hunting,
enjoying a right that
was restricted by law
to the nobility in
Europe, Lescarbot
drew the comparative
conclusion that "the
Savages are truely
Noble." Eighteenth-
century portrait of a
Mi'kmaq hunter by
J. G. Saint-Sauveur and
J. Laroque, courtesy
of National Archives
of Canada, negative
no. C21112.

Lescarbot's *Histoire de la Novvelle France*, a compendium of French New World voyages, including his own, together with his ethnographic treatise on the Indians, was published in Paris in 1609 after his return to France. An excerpted English translation of Lescarbot's own voyage and ethnography, *Nova Francia*, was published in London the same year. With its appearance, the Noble Savage also made his entrance into English literature.

> Now leaving there those *Anthropophages* Brazilians, let us return to our New France, where the Men there are more humane, and live but with that which God hath given to Man, not devouring their like. Also we must say of them that *they are truely noble* [emphasis added], not having any action but is generous, whether we consider their hunting,

or their employment in the wars, or that one search out their domesti-
cal actions, wherein the women do exercise themselves, in that which
is proper unto them, and the men in that which belongeth to arms,
and other things befitting them, such as we have said, or will speak
of in due place. But here one must consider that the most part of the
world have lived so from the beginning, and by degrees men have
been civilized, when that they have assembled themselves, and have
formed commonwealths for to live under certain laws, rule, and policy.
(Lescarbot 1609c: 276; emendations from 1609a: 257)

Here we seem to have the solution of our problem. The nobility of the
Indians is associated with moral qualities such as generosity and proper and
fitting behavior; and their primordial lifestyle is set off against later civilizations where men "have assembled themselves and have formed commonwealths for to live under certain laws, rule, and policy." Clearly, this
must be the source of Dryden's poetic image. To complete the impression
that we have discovered the source of the full-blown Myth of the Noble
Savage, we have Lescarbot's Contents heading for this part of the chapter:
"The Savages are truely Noble" (Lescarbot 1609a: n.p.)! Moreover, we
must reassess our hypothesis that the Noble Savage is a product of English
rather than French literature, for the French text contains the same words:
"Sauvages sont vrayement nobles" (Lescarbot 1609b: n.p.). And yet, surprisingly, a closer look at Lescarbot reveals that his Noble Savage is entirely
different from the one known to later myth.

If there is a key to understanding Lescarbot's ideas, it is to constantly
remind ourselves that he is a lawyer and that his profession shapes his
perception and representation of his ethnographic experiences. Thus, for
example, when dealing with other ethnographers' writings on America,
and the ubiquitous Renaissance plagiarism that all too often resulted in
the repetition of previous scholars' mistakes, he presents a legalist's viewpoint on the evaluation of evidence and the need for citation of sources:
"One must needs believe, but not everything; and one must first consider
whether the story is in itself probable or not. In any case, to cite one's authority is to go free from reproach" (1609d: 2:176).

"The Savages are truly Noble" is the concluding section of a chapter of
Lescarbot's ethnography devoted to a subject—hunting—that we might
perhaps not have expected as the context for the introduction of such a historically significant concept. Hunting was a primary means of subsistence
in some American Indian societies and an important dietary supplement in
agriculturally based societies, both for Indians and for European colonists.
European writers tended to view it from a pragmatic standpoint, exagger-

ating its importance for some Indian groups, ignoring its widespread religious connotations (Lescarbot noted in passing the consultation of shamans
in hunt planning), and generally treating it in utilitarian, technical terms.
It seems an unlikely site for the construction of a concept such as the Noble
Savage. Yet, if we recall that Lescarbot was a lawyer and reflect on the legal
status of hunting in late Renaissance Europe, we can see why exactly this
subject should have led him to reflect on matters of nobility (fig. 3).

> God, before sin, gave for food unto man every herb . . . without mak-
> ing mention of the spilling of the blood of beasts. . . . But, after the
> flood, God, renewing his covenant with man: *"The fear and dread of
> you . . . shall be upon every beast of the earth, and upon every fowl of
> the heaven . . . all that moveth having life shall be unto you for meat"*
> [Gen. 9:2, 3]. Upon this privilege is formed the right of hunting, the
> noblest right of all rights that be in the use of man, seeing that God is
> the author of it. And therefore no marvel if Kings and their nobility
> have reserved it unto them, by a well-concluding reason that, if they
> command unto men, with far better reason may they command unto
> beasts; and, if they have the administration of justice to judge male-
> factors, to overcome rebels, and to bring to human society wild and
> savage men, with far better reason shall they have it for to do the same
> towards the creatures of the air, of the forests and of the fields. . . . And
> seeing that Kings have been in the beginning chosen by the people for
> to keep and defend them from their enemies whilst that they are at
> their necessary works, and to make war as much as need is for the repa-
> ration of injury and recovery of that which hath been wrongfully
> usurped or taken away, it is very reasonable and decent that as well
> them as the nobility that do assist and serve them in those things have
> the exercise of hunting, which is an image of war, to the end to rouse
> up the mind and to be always nimble, ready to take horse, for to go to
> encounter with the enemy, to lie in ambush, to assail him, to chase
> him, to trample him under feet. . . .
>
> Hunting, then, having been granted unto man by a heavenly privi-
> lege, the savages throughout all the West Indies do exercise themselves
> therein without distinction of persons, not having that fair order estab-
> lished in these parts whereby some are born for the government of the
> people and the defence of the country, others for the exercising of arts
> and the tillage of the ground, in such sort that by this fair economy
> everyone liveth in safety. (Lescarbot 1609c: 267–68)

It takes some reflection for the point of this discussion to sink in: that
by their free practice of hunting, which is also an "image of war" and defense of the innocent, the "savages" of America occupy a status that corre-
sponds, from a legal standpoint, to the nobility of Europe. By exercising

"without distinction of persons" a "heavenly privilege" reserved in Europe for the nobility, they have in effect constituted for themselves as a people, rather than restricting to a privileged class, the status defined in Europe as "noble." In a technical legal sense, then, the conclusion is not only appropriate, but legally inescapable, that "the Savages are truly Noble."

Hunting was, after all, one of the *marques de noblesse*, the emblematic privileges that distinguished nobles from commoners. As Ellery Schalk explains,

> The hunt, seen as a right of nobles only, was originally justified because it served two purposes: the nobles killed wild animals and thus theoretically protected the people, and it kept them in good condition and training for fighting. From the sixteenth century on it was associated very closely and almost unconsciously with the nobility. . . . It was legalized by the king in various ordinances, and even some of the *cahiers* of the Third Estate . . . accepted and indeed argued that the hunt be limited to just the nobility. (1986: 149–50)

And Lescarbot reinforces the inevitability of the conclusion that hunting was proof of noble status with further legal comparisons; for example, in his chapter on falconry.

> If hunting, then, be a noble exercise . . . hawking is far more noble, because it aimeth at an higher subject, which doth participate of heaven, seeing that the inhabitants of the air are called in the sacred Scripture *volucres coeli*, the fowls of [heaven]. Moreover, the exercise thereof doth belong but to kings and to the nobles, above which their brightness shineth as the sun's brightness doth above the stars. And our savages being of a noble heart, which maketh no account but of hunting and martial affairs, may very certainly have right of usage over the birds that their land doth afford them. (1609c: 277)

Again, the technical nobility of the "savages" is legally indisputable. If possession is nine points of the law, and the Indians possess "right of usage" of falconry, and that right "belongs but to kings and to the nobles," then the conclusion of their legal nobility is inevitable.

The Noble Savage is obviously, "beyond the shadow of a doubt," a legal concept, a technical analysis of the legal status of "savage" peoples from the standpoint of comparative law. For those of us conditioned by a lifetime of folklore and more than a century of professional polemic masquerading as history, the blatant contradiction between this historical evidence and the myth of Rousseauian "romantic naturalism" must give rise to feelings of shock and denial; and yet it can help us to appreciate the reasons for the absence of the concept in the writings of Rousseau and his contemporaries. By the mid-eighteenth century, intellectuals were no longer so willing to accept that the nobility's "brightness shineth as the sun's brightness doth above the stars," or that "it is very reasonable and decent" for "heavenly" privileges to be restricted to them and denied to ordinary men. In contemporary terms, a model once privileged had become problematized, and nowhere more so than in the thought of Rousseau.

But if Lescarbot's construction of the Noble Savage was, first of all, advanced as a technical analytic concept in comparative law, it was more than that. In fact, it offered at least a partial solution to the greatest ethnological problem of the age of discovery, the problem of comparative negation, often expressed through the metaphor of savage nakedness. The nakedness of "savage" peoples, dwelt on by virtually every ethnographic account, had assumed an emblematic status for framing the problem of every kind of perceived negativity, from a European comparative standpoint, of features lacking in their cultures. They were said to have "no laws," "no property," "no religion," no analogue of almost any feature that Europeans assumed to be an indispensable characteristic not only of civilization but even of human society. For many European writers from the time of Columbus onward, a solution suggested itself in the Greco-Roman myth of the Golden Age of mankind, from which men had degenerated in their rise to civilization.

> For it is certeyne, that amonge them, the lande is as common as the sonne and water: And that Myne and Thyne (the seedes of all myscheefe) haue no place with them. They are contente with soo lyttle, that in soo large a countrey, they haue rather superfluitie then scarsenes. Soo that (as wee haue sayde before) *they seeme to lyue in the goulden worlde*, without toyle, lyuinge in open gardens, not intrenched with dykes, dyuyded with hedges, or defended with waules. They deale trewely one with another, without lawes, without bookes, and without Iudges. They take hym for an euyll and myscheuous man, which taketh pleasure in doinge hurte to other. And albeit that they delyte not in superfluities, yet make they prouision for th[e] increase of suche rootes, wherof they make theyr breade, . . . contented with suche simple dyet, wherby health is preserued, and dyseases auoyded. (Martyr 1511–21: 78; emphasis added)

The myth of the Golden Age, constructed on the rhetorical foundations of a litany of comparative negations and invocation of the corrupting power of "mine and thine" (*meum et tuum*), posited both a continuity and a seemingly insurmountable disjunction between European and "savage" cultures. By projecting the Indians as a mirror image of the European past, it excluded them from a cultural present in which laws, books, and judges, and above all the property distinctions of "mine and thine," were the indispensable foundation blocks of civil society. It was not so much that the Indians themselves lived in the past as that they lived in a kind of temporal parallel universe, where the Golden Age extended into adjoining spacetime by the confluence of ecological abundance and a "Zen strategy" (Sahlins 1972: 1–2) of satisfaction with available resources. But their very ability to coexist thus presented problems to European thinkers; not the least of which was the validity of European assumptions of cultural superiority, on the one hand, and the viability of cultures that seemed to be built out of nothing, on the other, at least insofar as their representations were constructed, and their essential natures projected, in terms of the enumeration of comparative negations.

With regard to these problems, Lescarbot offered a new perspective and a new solution:

> Furthermore, all savages generally do live everywhere in common—the most perfect and most worthy life of man, seeing that he is a sociable creature, the life of the ancient golden age. . . . If it happens, then, that our savages have venison or other food, all the company have part of it. They have this mutual charity, which hath been taken away from us since that *mine* and *thine* have come into the world. They have also hospitality, a virtue peculiar to the ancient Gauls . . . , who did constrain travellers and strangers to come into their houses and there to take their refreshing: a virtue which seemeth to have conserved herself only with the nobility and gentry, for among the other sort we see her very weak and at the point of death. . . . So do our savages, which, stirred up with a human nature, receive all strangers (except their enemies), whom they accept in their commonality of life. (1609c: 227–28)

Here Lescarbot draws on an old argument raised by opponents of the Renaissance humanists' project to defeudalize the concept of nobility and redefine it in terms of moral goodness alone: "the chief and highest part of noblesse must rest in liberality" (Skinner 1987: 138). The virtues of the Golden Age, it turns out, have been partially preserved, not only by the "savages" but also by their legal equivalents, the nobility. The absence of property, or the negation of its absolute significance in the practice of unlimited hospitality, shows us that problems of comparative negation pose no insurmountable barrier to the construction of a just and workable human society; indeed, the example of the savages provides a direct link between the perfection of myth and the most exalted state of contemporary society. The nobility of the savages negates the comparative negation by showing how the apparent absence of a trait such as property, formalized law, or class divisions may actually represent a continuity rather than a contradiction, a juncture of past and present, a linkage of golden myth with present power and privilege. And it can also point to the future; for Lescarbot's vision includes a project for the construction of a newer and better golden age than that of Greek myth, and a newer and better nobility as well:

> This is the contentment which is prepared for them that shall inhabit New France, though fools do despise this kind of life, and the tilling of the ground, the most harmless of all bodily exercises, and which I will term the most noble, as that which sustaineth the life of all men. They disdain (I say) the tillage of the ground, and notwithstanding all the vexations wherewith one tormenteth himself, the suits in law that one follows, the wars that are made, are but for to have lands. Poor mother! what hast thou done that thou art so despised? The other elements are very often contrary unto us: the fire consumeth us, the air doth infect us with plague, the water swalloweth us up, only the earth is that which, coming into the world and dying, receiveth us kindly—it is she alone that nourisheth us, which warmeth us, which lodgeth us, which clotheth us, which contrarieth us in nothing; and she is set at naught, and them that do manure her are laughed at, they are placed next to the idle and blood-suckers of the people. All this is done here among us; but in New France the golden age must be brought in again. (1609c: 300)

To understand Lescarbot's vision of the Golden Age, the Noble Savage, and the future, we must consider his vision of a future anthropological science:

> BOOK 2 [French ed. Book 6]: THE PREFACE. Almighty God, in the creation of this world hath so much delighted himself in diversity that, whether it be in heaven or in the earth, either under the same or in the profound depth of waters, the effects of his might and glory do shine in every place. But the wonder that far exceedeth all others is that in one and the selfsame kind of creature, I mean in Man, are found more variety than in other things created. For if one enters into the consideration of his face, two shall not be found who in every respect do resemble one another: if he be considered in the voice, the same variety shall be found: if in the speech, all nations have their proper and peculiar language, whereby one is distinguished from the other. But in manners and fashion of life there is a marvelous difference, which (without troubling ourselves in crossing the seas to have the experience thereof) we see visibly in our very neighbourhood. Now forasmuch as it is a small matter to know that people differ from us in customs and man-

ners, unless we know the particularities thereof, a small thing is it like
wise to know but that which is near to us; but the fair science is to
know the manner of all nations of the world, for which reason Ulysses
hath been esteemed, because he had seen much and known much. It
hath seemed necessary unto me to exercise myself in this second Book
upon this subject, in that which toucheth the nations spoken of by us,
seeing that I have tied myself unto it, and that it is one of the best parts
of an history, which without it would be defective, having but slightly
and casually handled hereabove those things that I have reserved to
speak of here. Which also I do, to the end, if it please God to take pity
of those poor people and to work by his holy spirit that they be brought
into his fold, their children may know hereafter what their fathers
were, and bless them that have employed themselves in their conversion, and reformation of their incivility. Let us therefore begin with
man from his birth, and having in gross marked out what the course of
his life is, we will conduct him to the grave, there to leave him to rest,
and also to repose ourselves. (1609c: 145–46)

Lescarbot's vision of "the fair science" of human diversity is as remarkable
as his conception of it in terms of a salvage ethnography of cultures
doomed to disappear. In the light of this grim vision of the future of "savagery," we should examine more closely his conception of the relative merits of savagery and civilization, the relationship of whatever he found to
praise in savage society to his conception of European civilization, and his
vision of their respective futures.

CHAPTER XX: OF THE VIRTUES AND VICES OF THE SAVAGES Virtue, like unto
wisdom, disdaineth not to be lodged under a mean roof. The Northerly
nations [of Europe] are the last that have been brought to civility; and,
notwithstanding, before that civility, they have done great actions. Our
savages, although they be naked, are not void of those virtues that are
found in men of civility. . . . For first concerning fortitude and courage,
they have thereof as much as any nation of the savages. . . . One point
maketh this virtue of force and courage imperfect in them, that is they
are too revengeful, and in that they put their sovereign contentment,
which inclineth to brutishness. But they are not alone, for all those
nations how far soever they may stretch themselves from one pole to
the other, are infected with this vice. The Christian religion only may
bring them to reason, as in some sort she doth with us (I say in some
sort) because that we have men very imperfect as well as the savages.
   Temperance is another virtue, consisting in the mediocrity in things
that concern the pleasures of the body. . . . Our savages have not all the
qualities requisite for the perfection of this virtue. For as for meats, we
must acknowledge their intemperance, when they have wherewith and
they do eat perpetually, yea, so far as to rise in the night to banquet.

> But seeing that in these our parts many are as vicious as they, I will not
> be too rigorous a censurer of them. As for the other actions, there is no
> more to be reproved in them than in us—yea, I will say less, in that
> which concerneth the venereal action, whereto they are little addicted.
> (1609c: 260–62)

Although there is praise for the "savages" here, there is certainly no
idealization. Rather, every assertion of their virtues is balanced by an
enumeration of their vices, which is in turn counterbalanced by a reminder
of the equal vices of Europeans. From one perspective, there is nothing remarkable in this. The dialectic of vice and virtue had been part of the modern European ethnographic tradition at least since the thirteenth-century
ethnographies of the Mongols (Plano Carpini 1248; Rubruck 1255); and
Renaissance ethnographic discourse on the New World "savage" was continually charged with the oscillating positive/negative symbolic polarities
of the Golden Age and the cannibal (e.g., Martyr 1511–21; Lery 1578).
Lescarbot's project, however, is more original and interesting than simple
reproduction of preexisting models. The dialectic of vice and virtue continues in Lescarbot's assessment of savage law and justice.

> As for justice, they have not any law, neither divine nor human, but
> that which Nature teacheth them—that one must not offend another.
> So have they quarrels very seldom. And if any such thing do chance to
> happen, the Sagamos quieteth all, and doth justice to him that is of-
> fended, giving some bastinados to the wrongdoer, or condemning him
> to make some presents to the other, for to pacify him, which is some
> form of dominion. If it be one of their prisoners that hath offended, he
> is in danger to go to the pot. For, after he is killed, nobody will revenge
> his death. The same consideration is in these parts of the world [France
> and other European countries]. There is no account made of a man's life
> that hath no support. (1609c: 264)

The Renaissance negativist assessment "they have not any law . . .
but that which Nature teacheth them" proceeds to a brief but sympathetic ethnographic description of their actual practices, a balancing critical description of their injustice to prisoners, followed once again by a
counterbalancing reminder of the injustices facing the powerless in Europe.
Throughout Lescarbot constructs his case in the form of opposition of evidence to counterevidence, argument to counterargument, as if in a court-
room trial. Seeming at first glance to act as an impartial judge, but on closer
examination revealing himself in the dual, alternating roles of advocates
for both the plaintiffs and the defendants in the case, he states and chal-

lenges the claims of both savages and civilization. At times the balance
shifts in favor of the savages.

> That which also procureth the health of our savages is the concord
> which they have among them, and the small care they take for the
> commodities of this life, for the which we torment and vex ourselves.
> They have not that ambition which in these parts gnaweth and fretteth
> the minds and spirits, and filleth them with cares, making blinded men
> to go to the grave in the very flower of their age, and sometimes to
> serve for a shameful spectacle to a public death. . . . Also corruption is
> not among them, which is the fostering mother of physicians and of
> magistrates, and of the multiplicity of officers, and of public extortion-
> ers, which are created and instituted for to give order unto it and to cut
> off the abuses. They have no suits in law (the plague of our lives), to
> the prosecuting whereof we must consume both our years and our
> means, and very often one cannot obtain justice, be it either by the
> ignorance of the judge, to whom the case is disguised, or by his own
> malice, or by the wickedness of an attorney that will sell his client.
> And from such afflictions do proceed the tears, fretfulnesses, and deso-
> lations, which bring us to the grave before our time. (Lescarbot 1609c:
> 242–43)

Here Lescarbot faces what to him is the real evidence of their comparatively better health and longer lives and finds a plausible explanation of the
disparity in the stresses and corruptions of his own society. In such cases,
Lescarbot speaks not from the standpoint of a neutral observer, and certainly not from the idealized stance of the true believer in Western law,
such as we still find examples of in legal anthropology, who steadfastly
affirms the rationality and impartiality of Euro-American legal codes and
institutions as a standard against which all others are to be measured and
found wanting. Rather, Lescarbot accepts the adversarial pragmatics he sees
as the basis of both "savage" and "civilized" law, in which judgment proceeds from the problematics of conflicts that must be investigated from a
stance of initial neutrality, but which must finally be resolved by moving
beyond the stalemate of neutrality to the fair and rational determination of
winners and losers. In accepting the practical necessity for such a judgment, however, he argues as an advocate of both the plaintiffs and the
defendants; and in favor of the latter's case, he voices his personal and professional experiences of injustice in a system to which, in the end, he still
remains committed but has learned too much about to be able to idealize.

What, then, is the issue of the case Lescarbot builds with his dialectic of
vice and virtue, of balance and counterbalance? Who is the judge, and what

is the verdict? We see at the beginning of Lescarbot's first volume that his case is addressed "To France" (Lescarbot 1609d: 12–18); and the French people, from the king and nobility down to the farmers and merchants, must necessarily be his judges. Ultimately, the case being argued is that for his project of building a new golden age in the colonies of Canada, which requires colonists able to reject both the claims of superiority of French society to the extent required to wish to escape it and the claims of the "savages" to a moral right of possession of their own lands.

> And as the overconscientious make difficulties everywhere, I have at times seen some who doubted if one could justly occupy the lands of New France, and deprive thereof the inhabitants; to whom my reply has been in few words, that these people are like the man of whom it is spoken in the Gospel, who had wrapped up in a napkin the talent which had been given unto him, instead of turning it to account, and therefore it was taken away from him. And therefore, as God the Creator has given the earth to man to possess it, it is very certain that the first title of possession should appertain to the children who obey their father and recognise him, and who are, as it were, the eldest children in the house of God, as are the Christians, to whom pertaineth the division of the earth rather than to the disobedient children, who have been driven from the house, as unworthy of the heritage and of that which dependeth thereon.[1] (Lescarbot 1609d: 1:16–17)

But if the verdict is to go so uncompromisingly against the Indians, what then was the point of building such a strong case in their favor, with so many citations of their virtues and counterbalancing evidence of European vices? Simply that, as Lescarbot foresaw, the colonialist project might lead to far more draconian consequences than simple dispossession, or even destruction of culture, and he wished to offer a special plea for clemency on their behalf.

> But I would not have these tribes exterminated, as the Spaniard has those of the West Indies, taking as pretext the commandments formerly given to Joshua, Gideon, Saul, and other warriors for God's people. For we are under the law of grace, the law of gentleness, piety, and pity, wherein our Saviour hath said: " . . . I am meek and lowly in heart," and likewise, " . . . I will give you rest"; and not, "I will root you out." Moreover, these poor Indian tribes were defenceless in the presence of those who have ruined them, and did not resist as did those peoples of whom the Holy Scripture makes mention. And further, if it was intended that the conquered be destroyed, in vain would the same

Saviour have said to his Apostles: "Go ye into all the world, and preach the Gospel to every creature."

The earth pertaining, then, by divine right to the children of God, there is here no question of applying the law and policy of Nations, by which it would not be permissible to claim the territory of another. This being so, we must possess it and preserve its natural inhabitants, and plant therein with determination the name of Jesus Christ and of France, since today many of your children have the unshakable resolution to dwell there with their families. The inducements are great enough to attract men of valour and of worth, who are spurred on by a goodly and honourable ambition to be the first in the race for immortality by this action, which is one of the greatest men can set before themselves. . . . [S]o, dearest Mother, those of your children who would fain leave this salt sea to go to drink of the fresh waters of Port Royal in New France, will soon find there, by God's aid, a retreat so agreeable, that they will greatly desire to go thither to people the province and to fill it with offspring. (1609d: 1:17–18)

Thus we can resolve one of our apparent paradoxes: the concept of the Noble Savage did indeed exist, and in fact was brought into existence together with the call for the foundation of an anthropological science. But Lescarbot's Noble Savage concept is not in any way the same as that which later came to be criticized as part of the Noble Savage myth. Rather than an idealized equation of morality with nature, it was a technical concept based on legal theory, attempting to account for the problem of societies that could exist in the absence of anything Europeans might recognize as legal codes and institutions, by projecting a model drawn from European "nobility" that could satisfactorily account for the absence of a wide range of European-style political and legal constructs. And rather than being associated with an idealization of "savage" peoples or promotion of them to the status of exemplars for revealing European corruption, it was instead offered in the context of a colonialist project that would promote European dominance, guided by a salvage ethnology that would show later generations how their forefathers had lived, once the inevitable destruction of their culture had been achieved. If, in such a context, Lescarbot's plea to spare the Indians from outright genocide were taken as idealistic, it is a singularly impoverished form of idealism, as marginalized a survival as the destiny he foresaw for the people he called "noble."

On the other hand, we might be tempted to see in Lescarbot's argument another kind of idealism—a concealed egalitarian agenda subversive to established authority and privilege—insofar as his concept of a new golden age in the Canadian colonies was linked to the rise of a new nobility, better than the old European nobility but drawn from a range of potential recruits not restricted to the hereditary noble class. In fact, however, the elevation of commoners to noble rank was so widespread in Lescarbot's time that, far from being subversive, it might be seen as a mainstay of the system of nobility itself. In the pursuit of elevation to ennoblement, one effective strategy was to adopt an "honorable profession" associated with persons of noble rank and status; interestingly, one of these was Lescarbot's own legal profession (Bitton 1969: 97). Another strategy open to successful members of any profitable occupation was to be recognized as noble by acquiring the marks and possessions of nobility: weapons, silk clothing, country estates, and other things and practices generally recognized as emblematic of noble rank (Bitton 1969: 92–117). Thus, if Lescarbot's argument implied that the French Canadian colonists would be elevated to noble status by their necessary assumption of noble perquisites such as the possession of land and the practice of hunting and warfare, the result would be a strengthening of the feudal system through its geographic-demographic expansion, rather than its subversion by egalitarian ideals. It may even be that Lescarbot saw this new, expanded nobility as open to the converted and Christianized descendants of the Indians; but, of course, this would require the destruction, rather than admiration and emulation, of their previous state of "noble savagery."

And yet Lescarbot's project in the long run probably contributed more to the humanistic tradition of relativist, balanced sympathetic critique than to the colonial enterprise that it promoted. His plea for clemency together with the evidence he cited in support of it, in the end, outweighed his pro-colonialist citation of savage vices. Thus, for Atkinson (1924: 67–69), Lescarbot represents simply another uncritical, unproblematic exponent of *le bon sauvage;* and Chinard (1913: 100–15), although he takes a more complex view that recognizes Lescarbot's colonialist project, also sees him as an important contributor to the construction of the image of *le bon sauvage*. In later centuries, with colonialism so long and thoroughly established as to have faded into the European intellectual background and policies of terrorism, if not entirely ethically unproblematic, at least widespread enough for literary allusions to them not to attract special notice, Lescarbot would be primarily remembered as an advocate of the goodness of the "savages" and his work as evidence in their favor.

But at the time his work was published, Lescarbot's construction of a case for a nobility associated not only with moral goodness and freedom from legal restrictions but also with inherited privilege, magnificence, and wealth sufficient to support unlimited generosity put him in direct opposition to the mainstream of humanist thought, which overwhelmingly supported a deconstruction of all such linkages in favor of the *vera nobilitas,* the "true nobility" based on moral goodness alone (Skinner 1987: 135–47, 152–57). Hence the concept of the Noble Savage itself, so strikingly original a part of Lescarbot's legal and anthropological analysis,[2] became a dismal failure rather than a widely emulated paradigm. Too much a part of the vanishing feudalism of the age that inspired it, it simply failed to catch the imagination or the interest of humanist writers, or of their Enlightenment successors who were inspired by new realities and new paradigms.

In the eighteenth century, ideals of divine right and aristocratic paternalism would be replaced by ideals of natural rights and *fraternité,* and the aristocratic paradigm of nobility would give way to new, more bourgeois-centered reinterpretations of the "social contract" that emphasized the equality of the consenting parties. Thus when Atkinson (1924: 68–69) notes Lescarbot's use of the Noble Savage concept, it is more or less a passing observation in the context of noting his early "opposition of primitive man, who is good and noble, and the development of governments." No special attention is given to Lescarbot's unique use of the term "noble": the issue is *le bon sauvage,* since the "Noble Savage" never became a significant element in the French intellectual tradition. At most, it had a marginalized and sporadic survival in English poetic fiction, where it caught the attention of Dryden, who gave it passing mention that may have, perhaps but by no means certainly, briefly caught the emulative attention of a few later writers. But for all practical purposes, after Dryden's brief evocation of the term, the Noble Savage disappeared from view for the next two hundred years.

3   Poetic Nobility
Dryden, Heroism, and Savages

FIGURE 4. FEUDAL-HEROIC
NOBILITY "Athabaliba, the last
King of the Peruvians," shown
in the iconographic style of
a European monarch with
"savage" heraldic insignia, in
an imaginative projection of
the Inca Atahuallpa from John
Ogilby's *America* (1671).

Tracing the fate of the Noble Savage after Lescarbot leads in complex and
ambiguous directions. Since I have already mentioned Dryden's reference
to the Noble Savage, apparently derived from Lescarbot's work, I might begin by examining it more closely. It appears in the first act and scene of
Dryden's play, *The Conquest of Granada by the Spaniards*, when Almanzor, the hero, defies the king's command by coming to the aid of unarmed
victims and kills their attacker in self-defense. The king threatens him with
death for his disobedience, and Almanzor responds:

> No man has more contempt than I, of breath;
> But whence hast thou the right to give me death?
> Obey'd as Soveraign by thy Subjects be;

But know, that I alone am King of me.
I am as free as Nature first made man,
'Ere the base Laws of Servitude began,
When wild in woods the noble Savage ran.
(Dryden 1672: 34)

This is the play's first and last mention of savages, for its true focus is on individual heroism in a civilized society. The king replies contemptuously,

Since, then, no pow'r above your own you know,
Mankind shou'd use you like a common foe.
You shou'd be hunted like a Beast of Prey . . .

(34)

So much for the freedom of savages. But in the contest of wills that follows, Almanzor, by force of character, wins over the king and awes the warring factions into submission. Here is the source of true nobility; and later in the scene, the king muses, "'Tis true, from force the noblest title springs" (37). And the king's brother passes judgment on Almanzor in these words:

How much of vertue lies in one great Soul
Whose single force can multitudes controll!

(36)

It might be thought that the play's setting among the Moors together with its Moorish hero reflect a tendency to ennoble or at least exalt non-Europeans (or non-Christians) as examples for emulation. Indeed, there are good Muslims in the play; and the late seventeenth century was a time of exotic stage heroes, from the magnanimous Turks of Molière's *Bourgeois Gentilhomme* (1670) and Daniel Speer's *Türkischer Eulen-Spiegel* (1688) to the Hindustani Muslims of Dryden's own *Aureng-Zebe* (1675) and the Aztecs and Incas of his *Indian Queen* (1664) and *Indian Emperour* (1665). However, the worst examples of villainy in *Conquest of Granada* are provided by Moorish characters; while Almanzor, the paradigm of noble virtue and heroism, is revealed in the end to be the long-lost son of a Spanish Christian royal princess! The play, as it turns out, is about nobility in its familiar Euro-Christian form, and there is no further need for talk about Noble Savages.

No more is there any mention of Noble Savages in Dryden's two plays about American Indians, *The Indian Queen* and *The Indian Emperour*. But nevertheless, in the latter play, we find that Dryden does indeed take an interest in contemporary discourse and ideas of the "savage" and in fact has developed an interesting position of his own, combining a Lescarbot-like acceptance and defense of feudalistic-chivalrous conceptions of hereditary class nobility with myths of the Golden Age, and with Renaissance humanist notions of relativism and the critique of European corruption and oppression. We find this combination of ideas articulated, amazingly enough, by none other than Hernán Cortés as he leads his conquistador army to conquer the Aztecs of Mexico:

> *Cortez:* On what new happy Climate are we thrown,
> So long kept secret, and so lately known;
> As if our old world modestly withdrew,
> And here, in private, had brought forth a new!
>
> *Vasquez:* Corn, Wine, and Oyl are wanting to this ground,
> In which our Countries fruitfully abound:
> As if this Infant world, yet un-array'd,
> Naked and bare, in Natures Lap were laid.
> No useful Arts have yet found footing here;
> But all untaught and salvage does appear.
>
> *Cortez:* Wild [i.e., "salvage"] and untaught are Terms
>   which we alone
> Invent, for fashions differing from our own:
> For all their Customs are by Nature wrought,
> But we, by Art, unteach what Nature taught.
>
> (Dryden 1665: 30)

Cortés, the cultural relativist! But it turns out that Dryden has been reading, and apparently thinking quite seriously, about the writings of Montaigne, particularly Montaigne's manifesto of cultural relativism, "Of the Caniballes."

> I finde (as farre as I have beene informed) there is nothing in that nation, that is either barbarous or savage, unlesse men call that barbarisme which is not common to them. As indeed, we have no other ayme of truth and reason, than the example and *Idea* of the opinions and customes of the countrie we live in. There is ever perfect religion, perfect policie, perfect and compleat use of all things. They are even savage, as we call those fruits wilde, which nature of her selfe, and of her ordinarie progresse hath produced: whereas indeed, they are those which our selves have altered by our artificiall devices, and diverted from their common order, we should rather terme savage. In those are the true and most profitable vertues, and naturall properties most lively and vigorous, which in these we have bastardized, applying them to the pleasure of our corrupted taste. . . .

> Those nations seeme therefore so barbarous unto me, because they
> have received very little fashion from humane wit, and are yet neere
> their originall naturalitie. The lawes of nature doe yet command them,
> which are but little bastardized by ours. (Montaigne 1588a: 37–39)

Nor is "Of the Caniballes" Dryden's only source of ethnographic information and ideas. He has drawn on Montaigne's essay "Of Coaches" for his
construction of a scene of debate and critique of Christian hypocrisy by
Montezuma while under torture by Pizarro and a Catholic priest (Loftis
1966: 311 ff.). Moreover, Dryden appears to have consulted Spanish ethnographic sources, including Bartolomé de Las Casas (1542/1552), with his
passionate defense of the rights of the Indians against European cruelty
and oppression, as well as Samuel Purchas's 1625 ethnographic collection
(Loftis 1966: 309–14), through which he may first have become acquainted
with the work of Lescarbot.

With such sources it is no wonder that Dryden was able to build dialogues evoking the simplicity and innocence of Indians against the cruelty
and avarice of Europeans and to express their arguments with striking poetic skill. Yet, in the end, the Spanish conquest is a foreordained outcome;
and Dryden here, as in all his dramas, is not concerned with the clash of
ethnic groups or cultures except to the extent that they provide plot, motivation, and coloring for the clash of noble-minded heroes. If some of these
be Indians, they are not Noble by virtue of their "savage" state, but Nobles,
pure and simple (fig. 4). So, in *The Indian Queen*, Montezuma, a chivalrous
but unknown hero like Almanzor in *Conquest of Granada*, turns out to be
a member of the hereditary nobility, the long-lost son of the murdered
king and exiled queen of Mexico (Dryden and Howard 1664: 227 ff.).

Nobility, in the end, comes from hereditary descent; and things such as
freedom and bravery follow from it, rather than the other way around.
Dryden is a royalist defending royalty in the restoration of monarchy after the failure of Cromwell's Commonwealth in England, and he defends
it eloquently. All in all, there is little to indicate that Dryden's views on nobility, savages, or their relationship are any less embedded in notions of
hereditary dominance or European superiority than those of Lescarbot,
from whom Dryden borrowed the idea of the Noble Savage. Indeed, in *The
Indian Queen* Dryden gives us one of the most remarkable apologies of the
period for colonialism, as an Aztec boy and girl watch the arrival of the in-
vading Incas (!), coming to conquer them:

> *Boy:* Wake, wake, Quevira, our soft Rest must cease,
> And fly together with our Country's Peace . . .

Quevira: Why should men quarrel here, where all possess
As much as they can hope for by success?
None can have most, where Nature is so kind
As to exceed Man's Use, though not his Mind.

> (Dryden and Howard 1664: 184)

As in the dialogue between Cortés and his lieutenant, Dryden invokes the rhetoric of the Golden Age, by now an established convention of the travel-ethnographic literature, and so virtually guaranteed to meet the expectations and arouse the interest of his audience. The dialogue continues:

Boy: By ancient Prophecies we have been told
Our World shall be subdu'd by one more old;
And see, that World already's hither come.
Quevira: If these be they, we welcom then our Doom.
Their Looks are such that Mercy flows from thence,
More gentle than our Native Innocence.
Boy: Why should we then fear these are Enemies,
That rather seem to us like Deities?
Quevira: By their protection let us beg to live:
They come not here to Conquer, but Forgive.

> (184)

As we say in the early twenty-first century, well, pardon me for living! But here, in what was after all an age when the highest poetic expression of European religious sentiment would often take the form of abject declarations of one's own sinfulness and guilt, the idea of the victim seeking the forgiveness of the aggressor seems to be taken quite seriously. At least we do not have to ask who these wonderfully gentle and forgiving conquerors really are; their Inca masks are all too transparent, and the mythic justification of conquest of a new world "by one more old" all too obvious.

But it would be as problematic to lay too much emphasis on Dryden as an apologist for colonialism as it would to emphasize too strongly his occasional choice of Muslims or Indians as heroes and heroines. Dryden's theme is heroism itself, not the ethnicity of the hero. His dramas, and above all their tragic conflicts, are generated out of the uncompromising oppositions of characters perfectly faithful to their principles. This perfect faith is "noble"; as such, it is the universal characteristic of hereditary nobles of all nations, and its nobility consists in the chivalry in love and war of the divinely established aristocracy. If the tragic clash of chivalrous convictions sometimes gives rise to noble-minded Europeans meeting their nemesis in noble "savages," then, we might ask, what better way to dramatize the tragedy than by showing men compelled to it by innately and universally noble urges to defend the most incompatible lifestyles and domains? Nothing could make for a more vivid story, and the right side always wins.

> You see what Shifts we are inforc'd to try
> To help out Wit with some Variety;
> Shows may be found that never yet were seen,
> 'Tis hard to finde such Wit as ne're has been:
> You have seen all that this old World cou'd do,
> We therefore try the fortune of the new,
> And hope it is below your aim to hit
> At untaught Nature with your practic'd Wit:
> Our naked *Indians* then, when Wits appear,
> Wou'd as soon chuse to have the *Spaniards* here . . .
>   (Dryden and Howard 1664: 231; emphasis in original)

Although it is certainly possible for a writer to have a "message," Dryden's first priority is elsewhere. "For I confess," he says, "my chief endeavours are to delight the Age in which I live" (Dryden 1668: 7). If Dryden is an interesting thinker who complexly interweaves ideas from both the feudalist and the Renaissance humanist traditions, he is nevertheless an entertainer whose first concern must always be to present a good story. Such a story will be constructed with as much colorful elaboration as necessary to gain his audience's attention and patronage, adding in only such "messages" as will not bore or alienate them, and which themselves may constitute part of the exotic color of the play. Professional writers of prose or poetic or dramatic fiction who depend on sales for their fame and/or survival necessarily share this order of priorities, however large or exclusive their projected target audience. Dryden's target audience is a special one, with special interests.

> The favour which Heroick Plays have lately found upon our Theaters has been wholly deriv'd to them, from the countenance and approbation they have receiv'd at Court, the most eminent persons for Wit and Honour in the Royal Circle having so far own'd them, that they have judg'd no way so fit as Verse to entertain a Noble Audience, or to express a noble passion. (Dryden 1665: 23)

Thus, to please his "Noble Audience," themes of nobility and exaltation play a strategic role. In addressing himself to real members of the English noble classes, Dryden shows no restraint in the dramatic intensity by which he exalts their virtues.

> To receive the blessings and prayers of mankind, you need only to be seen together; we are ready to conclude that you are a pair of Angels sent below to make Virtue amiable in your persons. . . . For Goodness and Humanity, which shine in you, are Virtues which concern Mankind, and by a certain kind of interest all people agree in their commendation, because the profit of them may extend to many. 'Tis so much your inclination to do good that you stay not to be ask'd; which is an approach so nigh the Deity, that Humane Nature is not capable of a nearer. (Dryden 1665: 24)

And if personal acquaintances can be so idealized to please the "Noble Audience," then how realistic a treatment should we expect of the remote and "savage" characters, or of the author's "true" opinion of them, when they are inserted into a work for the same reason?

> [Montezuma's] story is, perhaps the greatest, which was ever represented in a Poem of this nature; (the action of it including the Discovery and Conquest of a New World.) In it I have neither wholly follow'd the truth of the History, nor altogether left it: but have taken all the liberty of a Poet, to adde, alter, or diminish, as I thought might best conduce to the beautifying of my work; it being not the business of a Poet to represent Historical truth, but probability. (Dryden 1665: 25)

Whether ethnographic writings should also be considered works of "fiction" shaped by similar kinds of priorities is arguable; at least, the fiction writer has generally been implicated in a different kind of professionalism than the ethnographer at any given period, entailing necessary differences in their respective priorities and representational techniques and values. But since the ethnographers are the primary source of material for both "exotic" fiction and comparativist philosophical writers, it is to them that we should turn next.

II

AMBIGUOUS NOBILITY

*Ethnographic Discourse on
"Savages" from Lescarbot
to Rousseau*

4   The Noble Savage Myth and Travel-Ethnographic Literature

FIGURE 5. SAVAGE RELIGION.
Assimilation of New World practices to European models could include negative overtones in even relatively neutral or positive representations, as in Jacques Le Moyne's sixteenth-century portrayal of a sacrifice of deer to the sun by Indians in Florida, a powerful and beautiful image that still shows similarities to biblical illustrations of the idolatrous worship of the Golden Calf by the Children of Israel (LeMoyne, redrawn and printed in Picart 1712–31).

In the interval between Lescarbot's invention of the Noble Savage concept at the beginning of the seventeenth century and its reemergence as a full-blown myth in the 1850s, the Noble Savage appears to have receded into a state of virtual nonexistence. Although no one could say with certainty how many instances of discursive linkage of the terms "noble" and "savage" occur in the thousands of travel-ethnographies produced during this period, anyone who takes the trouble to carefully read more than a few of them can verify that such linkages do not occur in the vast majority of works. Most writers, even in the eighteenth century, when popular myth has it that belief in the Noble Savage was almost universal, simply do not juxtapose the two terms. In the few cases where they do occur together, a closer look reveals that juxtapositions of nobility and the "savage" reveal only the most ambiguous and vestigial links with either Lescarbot's Noble Savage concept or the later myth. To understand this, we need to consider some of the characteristic features of the myth itself.

First, the Noble Savage myth posits an ontologically essential rather than a trait-ascriptive nobility. That is, according to the myth, there were many who believed that "savages" *were* noble by nature, rather than displaying isolated traits, such as ways of moving or speaking, or other elements to which qualities of nobility could be ascribed. Thus, for example, when Joseph-François Lafitau says in 1724 that "the Huron language is noble, majestic and more regular than the Iroquois dialects" (2:263), the ascription of nobility as an aesthetic quality of their language is far from being an ontological claim about the Hurons themselves. Many ascriptions of "nobility" during this period follow this same trait-ascriptive pattern. We have already seen several examples of this kind in the writings cited by Fairchild, and we will encounter a greater variety of them as we pursue our investigation.

Second, the nobility of the Noble Savage myth is an absolute rather than a relative quality. To say "Some Indians are more honest than others" is a very different kind of statement than "Indians are honest" (or "noble"!). For example, when William Howitt says in 1838 that "Philip was one of the noblest specimens of the North American Indian" (352), the comparison presupposes that other Indians were less noble than this outstanding "specimen"—a term that itself ought to connote an exemplar typical of its species and hence a typical example of the skewed application of scientific rhetoric to ethnography. The relative quality of this comparison highlights its divergence from the mythical nobility of "the savage," whose absolute nobility ought to be characteristic of a "nation" or "race" (depending on the period of writing) rather than an individual, as it is the result of a natural way of life shared by all members of the group.

Furthermore, the nobility of the mythical Noble Savages consists of their shared moral superiority to Europeans, not a status superiority to each other. When a writer singles out a chief or leader as an exemplar of nobility, as Howitt does in the above quote, again the implication is that some other "savages" are less noble by comparison—or, perhaps, not very noble at all. But according to the myth, the nobility of the "savages" should not be a nobility of distinction of status of one over another but rather a nobility of inclusion of all in the state of moral superiority engendered by their natural way of life.

Finally, we should also remember that the myth vaguely associates belief in the Noble Savage with the egalitarian ideals of the Enlightenment, an association implicit in its linkage with Rousseau, and whose significance will only become clear as we look into the history of the myth itself. With these features in mind, then, let us consider some of the discourse on "savages" and "nobility" in the centuries after Lescarbot.

THE UNPHILOSOPHICAL TRAVELERS AND THE SAVAGE

In surveying the ethnographic literature, a useful point of departure might be to note that in the great collections of travel narratives, with their hundreds of authors and thousands of pages, from Richard Hakluyt (1589) and Samuel Purchas (1625) in Lescarbot's lifetime to John Green (1745–47) in Rousseau's, we find little discourse on nobility. In the relatively few instances where it does occur, the only non-Europeans we are likely to find described as "noble" are the hereditary aristocrats of royal courts. The same pattern generally holds true of individual travel-ethnographies. We may find representations of nobility in descriptions of stratified societies and, especially, the royal courts and palaces of places such as the Ottoman Empire (Nicolay 1567–68; Montagu 1716–18), India (della Valle 1665), Persia (Chardin 1686), or China (Du Halde 1735; Barrow 1804), but they obviously have little to do with the "wild" condition of humans in a "state of nature." In omitting further consideration of discussions of the nobility of distinction of the hereditary elites of centralized and urbanized states and empires, we take a necessary and logical step; but we should recognize that it immediately eliminates from consideration the largest share of European discourse on "nobility" among non-European peoples.

Of the traveler-ethnographers of the Age of Exploration, the majority could be characterized as "unphilosophical travelers" who, unlike Lescarbot, describe without reflecting much on the significance of what they see, particularly on the meanings of similarities and differences in the ways of life of human communities. They seem to wander almost at random between positive and negative interpretations of what they observe; but even in relatively neutral or positive moments, negative overtones make their appearance, giving a generally negative cast to the whole (fig. 5). Since the American Indians provided the paradigm case for views of the "savage," let us consider a few examples of accounts of them. Jacques Cartier, one of the first European voyagers to the region later treated by Lescarbot, describes some of his encounters with Canadian Indians:

> They were more than three hundred men, women, and children: some of the women which came not over, we might see them stande up to the knees in water, singing and dauncing, the other that had passed the river where we were, came very friendlye to us, rubbing oure armes with their owne handes, then woulde they lifte them uppe towarde heaven, shewing manye signes of gladnesse: and in such wise were we assured one of another, that we very familiarly beganne to trafficke of whatsoever they had, till they had nothing but their naked bodies, for they gave us al what soever they had, and that was but of small value. We perceived that this people might verie easily be converted to our religion. . . . We gave them knives, combs, beades of glas, & other trifles of smal value, for which they made many signes of gladnesse, lifting their handes up to Heaven, dauncing and singing in their boates. These men may very wel & truely be called *Wilde* [*sauvage*], bicause there is no poorer people in the world. . . . [W]e with our boates wente to the bancke of the river, and freelye went on shore among them, whereat they made many signes of gladnesse, and al their men in two or three companies began to sing and daunce, seeming to be very glad of our comming. They had caused al the yong women to flee into the wood, two or three excepted, that staed with them, to each of which we gave a combe, and a little bell made of Tinne, for which they were very glad, thanking our Captaine, rubbing his armes and breastes with theyr handes. . . . These women were about twentie, who altogither in a knot fell upon our Captain, touching and rubbing him with their hands, according to their manner of cherishing and making muche of one, who gave to eache of them a little Tinne bell: then sodainely they began to daunce, and sing many songs. (1580: 18–20)

Although there is nothing in Cartier's account to suggest "nobility," there is also no overt hostility. Rather, we seem to get a curious foretaste of the fantasies of an intertwined erotic and commercial gratification that would assume its full-blown form in the later colonial dreams of the South Seas tropical paradise. But Cartier does not reflect, he only describes; and for him, the meaning of what it is to be "wel & truely called *Wilde*"—that is, "Savage"—is to be truly poor.

Samuel de Champlain, the leading French New World explorer of the seventeenth century, made extensive voyages to Canada, one of them in the same expedition that brought Lescarbot there. A few years earlier, in 1603, Champlain had published a book titled *Des sauvages* (Of the Savages), a work that, like Cartier's, must be classed with the ethnographic contributions of the typical unphilosophical traveler. Quantitatively, its ethnography is scanty by comparison with Lescarbot: where Lescarbot devotes a chapter to a subject, Champlain is typically content with a paragraph. Champlain's specifically ethnographic sections total about two or three chapters out of thirteen. The remainder of the ethnographic information in the book occurs incidentally in narratives of exploration and adventure, with the typical geographic-military-commercial priorities that we find in most such narratives. Indeed, we find a strong resemblance to Cartier's narrative in Champlain's repeated descriptions of how, in his encounters with the Indians, they would perform dances in which the women "stripped themselves stark naked" (Champlain 1603: 107–8, 180). Even in the chapters devoted to a specific focus on ethnographic subjects, Champlain reveals himself as a conventional, unreflective observer:

> I asked him what ceremony they used in praying to their God. He told me, that they did not make much use of ceremonies, but that every one prayed in his heart as he thought good. This is why I believe they have no law among them, nor know what it is to worship and pray to God, and that most of them live like brute beasts; and I think they would speedily be brought to be good Christians, if their country were colonised, which most of them would like. (1603: 117)

The representation of the Indians' favorable attitude toward colonization may be more than simple wishful thinking; for, far from encountering a scene of pristine "wild" peoples and cultures in their primordial state, the French travelers of even this early period moved in a complex network of alliances and hostilities, in which strengthened relationships could be highly profitable to both parties, if not crucial to survival. But in any case, the negative comparisons and bestial similes of Champlain's narrative bear no affinity to concepts of the nobility of the savage. Indeed, Champlain provided those who wished to draw favorable comparisons from "savage" life with a discursive alternative untinged by nobility and idealism:

> We had recognized him all the time we were there as a *bon sauvage,* even though he had the reputation of the greediest and most treacherous of all his nation. (1613a: 107)

Here, the goodness of the savage assumes nothing about the goodness of savages in general, or even about the general goodness of the particular individual under consideration. It is a purely contingent, instrumental value, reflecting only the strategic usefulness to the observer of the object of observation, who otherwise is viewed in overwhelmingly negative terms. But, ironically, this ambivalent prototype of the *bon sauvage* was none other than Membertou, chief of the Mi'kmaq, so recently eulogized by Lescarbot as the shining exemplar of the savages who were "truely noble."

We see in this vignette of faint praise from Champlain's narrative one of the characteristics of the ethnographic literature that has fostered the illusion of the widespread existence of the Noble Savage concept: namely, that it is possible for isolated bits of positive rhetoric to exist within a context of overall negativity. For example, Gabriel Sagard, the seventeenth-century missionary-ethnographer of the Hurons, actually connects them with nobility in one passage:

> Among all these Nations there is none that does not differ in some thing, whether in its manner of living and subsisting, or in clothing and adornment, each Nation considering itself the wisest and best advised of them all, for the way of a fool is always right in his own eyes, says the wise man. And to give my opinion about some of them, and to say which are the most happy or miserable, I consider the Hurons and other Sedentary peoples as the Nobility, the Algonquin Nations as the Bourgeois, and the other Savages nearer us, such as the Montagnais and Canadians, as the villagers and poor people of the country. (1632a: 342)

This, though, is clearly a case of class or status nobility rather than moral nobility; and, moreover, a case of "some savages are more noble than others" rather than an ontological attribution of nobility to all "savages." In fact, the Hurons and others can be likened to the European nobility only because they practice a sedentary life, that is, because they are more "civilized," and less "savage," than the nomadic hunter-gatherer tribes. The latter, precisely because they are closest to a "state of nature," are thus necessarily the least "noble." And the contextualization of the comparison in the "a fool is always right in his own eyes" model of cultural differences does not do much to convince us that we have found a believer in the Noble Savage as a paradigm of natural wisdom.

Sagard (1632b: 139–42), indeed, continues the long-established ethnographic tradition of the dialectic of virtues and vices; and he not only finds things to praise in Huron character, he even cites some of their criticism of Europeans:

> They reciprocate hospitality and give such assistance to one another that the necessities of all are provided for without there being any indigent beggar in their towns and villages; and they considered it a very bad thing when they heard it said that there were in France a great many of these needy beggars, and thought that this was for lack of charity in us, and blamed us for it severely. (1632b: 88–89)

But in the end, Sagard's narrative includes far more strongly negative than positive evaluations of the Hurons. He finds their ceremonies "ridiculous" (1632a: 331), "absurd" (1632b: 185), and "damnable and wicked" (1632b: 120). As for comparisons with Europeans,

> This [chief] had no small opinion of himself, when he desired to be spoken of as brother and cousin of the King and on an equality with him, like the two forefingers on the hands which he showed us touching one another, making a ridiculous and absurd comparison thereby. (1632b: 149)

Sagard's overall evaluation of "savage" life, and his perspective on ethnography, is given in his introduction:

> It will not be in imitation of Apollonius, to cultivate my mind and become wiser, that I shall visit these wide provinces. There savagery and brutishness have taken such hold that the rest of this narrative will arouse in your souls pity for the wretchedness and blindness of these poor tribes. . . . You shall see as in a perspective picture, richly engraved, the wretchedness of human nature, tainted at the source, deprived of the training of the faith, destitute of morality, and a victim of the most deadly barbarism to which in its hideousness the absence of any heavenly illumination could give birth. (1632b: 17–18)

Two decades earlier, one of the first Jesuit missionaries in Canada, Father Pierre Biard, had likewise assessed the "savages" in strongly negative terms:

> The nation is savage, wandering and full of bad habits; the people few and isolated. They are, I say, savage, haunting the woods, ignorant, lawless and rude: . . . as a people they have bad habits, are extremely lazy, gluttonous, profane, treacherous, cruel in their revenge, and given to all kinds of lewdness. . . . With all these vices, they are exceedingly vainglorious: they think they are better, more valiant and more ingenious than the French; and, what is difficult to believe, richer than we are. . . . They consider themselves better than the French: "For," they say, "you are always fighting and quarreling among yourselves; we live peaceably. You are envious and are all the time slandering each other; you are thieves and deceivers; you are covetous, and are neither generous nor kind; as for us, if we have a morsel of bread we share it with our neighbor." They are saying these and like things continually. (1611: 173–74)

The prejudicial character of this early Jesuit reaction may be better appreciated by reflecting that the people Biard describes are the Mi'kmaq, the same people who were called "truly noble" by Lescarbot just two years earlier. But if Jesuit and Recollect missionaries shared a tendency toward equally negative views of the Indians early in the seventeenth century, over the next century and a half their views would diverge into a nearly diametric opposition. Lahontan, the promoter of semifictionalized "savage" critiques of French culture, noted the difference at the end of the century:

> The Recollets brand the Savages for stupid, gross and rustick Persons, uncapable of Thought or Reflection: But the Jesuits give them other sort of Language, for they intitle them to good Sense, to a tenacious Memory, and to a quick Apprehension season'd with a solid Judgment. The former allege that 'tis to no purpose to preach the Gospel to a sort of People that have less Knowledge than the Brutes. On the other hand the latter (I mean the Jesuits) give it out, that these Savages take Pleasure in hearing the Word of God, and readily apprehend the meaning of the Scriptures. In the mean time, 'tis no difficult matter to point to the Reasons that influence the one and the other to such Allegations. (1703a: 2:423)

James Axtell's *The Invasion Within* (1985: chaps. 2–6, esp. chap. 4) provides a clear overview of divergences between Recollect and Jesuit strategies and practices, while George R. Healy's "The French Jesuits and the Idea of the Noble Savage" (1958), despite its partial acceptance of the Noble Savage myth, provides a deeper look at the ideological framing of their contrasting representations of Indian cultures. As Healy (1958: 145) cautions us, "The Jesuit literature did not, in sum, represent the Indian in as noble a posture as is sometimes imagined. Any quantitative analysis . . . must conclude that most of them considered pagan Indian life a thoroughly miserable existence." Yet the contrast between later Jesuit and Recollect views is indeed striking. The reasons behind the divergent views of the two orders include the increasingly greater success of the Jesuits in gaining converts as the Recollect missions were declining after an early head start, together with the consequences this entailed for the relative ability of the two orders to attract financial and political support for their missions.

But there were in fact philosophical differences between the two orders that lent ideological energy to their movement away from common ground into increasingly polarized opposition: for the Jesuits, an inclination toward classical humanist traditions and theological movements that encouraged a positive outlook on the state of nature and natural goodness; and for the Recollects, increasing involvement with the Jansenist movement in Catholic thought, with its uncompromising condemnation of the sinfulness of natural man (Healy 1958). On the Jesuit side, this led to increasingly positive constructions of at least some aspects of Indian character and culture and to a practical policy of encouraging the formation of isolated Indian Christian communities in order to reduce contact with some of the more harmful elements of French culture, such as the alcohol used as a come-on by the fur traders. From the Recollect perspective, "Frenchifying" (*franciser*) the Indians was necessary before they could be Christianized, since their own culture was irredeemably permeated with the sinfulness of man's natural state (Healy 1958).

Thus, if the diverging positions of the Jesuits and Recollects were, in a sense, equally "philosophical" in terms of adherence to explicit ideological principles, they led to markedly contrasting results from the standpoint of the "love of knowledge" that constitutes the root meaning of "philosophy." For the Jesuits' stance impelled them toward a relatively greater respect for Indian cultures and the acquisition of broader and deeper ethnographic knowledge about them; while the Recollects' hard-line ideology ended up reinforcing old prejudices, discouraging the kind of ethnographic inquiries that might lead to deeper knowledge of, and perhaps sympathy for, the subjects, and promoting an intensification of negative energy in their characterization.

If we compare the two most famous Recollect accounts of Indians from the seventeenth century, Sagard's narrative from the 1630s and Father Louis Hennepin's accounts of Indian life from later in the century (Hennepin 1683: 273–339; 1698: 2:448–588), we find the later author's antiphilosophical, Jansenist-inspired constructions reflecting even more negativistic prejudices than those entertained by his predecessor. Hennepin's only uses of the rhetoric of nobility are applied to gifts of food, whether given by Indians or Europeans:

> They gave us also a Noble Treat according to their own way, which I lik'd very well. (1698: 1:196)

> We regal'd the three Savages for their good News very nobly, having plenty of Provisions at that time. (1698: 1:300)

If this very limited use of the rhetoric of nobility has any meaning beyond the aesthetic, it can only be in terms of the old feudalistic ideal, "the chief and highest part of noblesse must rest in liberality" (see chap. 2 above), already rejected by humanist writers of the period. As for substantive nobility, Hennepin offers little in the way of praise of "savage" life. It is true that in one case, delighted by a map of a canoe route that an Indian drew for him, he speaks with high enthusiasm:

> After this, with a Pencil, he mark'd down on a Sheet of Paper, which I had left, the Course that we were to keep for four hundred Leagues together. In short, this natural Geographer describ'd our Way so exactly, that this Chart serv'd us as well as my Compass cou'd have done. For by observing it punctually, we arriv'd at the Place which we design'd, without losing our way in the least. (1698: 1:298–99)

But this is an isolated description of an outstanding individual, a chief of whom Hennepin had high hopes for cooperation in establishing a trading monopoly. Even in cases of other exceptional individuals, in whom Hennepin saw good qualities that distinguished them from their less praiseworthy compatriots, the good he sees usually consists in their adoption of European customs; and, even so, his praise is never given without reservation:

> There are few that salute after the mode of *Europe*. . . . Another Captain of the *Hojogoins* [Cayugas] seeing his little Daughter which he had given to the Count *de Fontenac* to be instructed, said very civilly to him, *Onnontio,* . . . thou art the Master of this Girl; order the business so that she may learn to write and read well; and when she grows great, either send her home, or take her for a Wife. Which shows you, that the *Iroquois* look upon themselves as much as the greatest Persons in the World.
>
> I knew another *Iroques* who was called *Atreovati* [Fr. Grande Guele, or "Grangula"; cf. Lahontan's description of the same individual, chap. 5], which signifies *great Throat:* this Man eat [*sic*] as the Europeans do; he washed his Hands in a Bason with the Governour; he sat last down at the Table, and opened his Napkin handsomly, and eat with his Fork; and did all things after our mode: But often he did it out of Craft or Imitation, to get some Present from the Governour. (1698: 2:550–51)

Indeed, Hennepin repeatedly succumbs to grudging admiration of the Indians' skillful pursuit of their own self-interest. He remarks, "These Barbarians want no Wit; on the contrary, their Natural Parts are extraordinary" (1698 1:298); and further explains: "We are not to imagine that these People are Brutes, and irrational; no, they understand their own Interest thorowly, and order their Affairs very discreetly" (2:515). For example,

> 'Tis to be observ'd here, that the Savages, though some are more cunning than others, are generally all addicted to their own Interests; and therefore though the *Iroquese* seem'd to be pleas'd with our Proposals,

they were not really so; for the *English* and *Dutch* affording them the *European* Commodities at cheaper Rates than the *French* of *Canada*, they had a greater Inclination for them than for us. (Hennepin 1698: 1:86)

When Hennepin focuses on the differences between different "savage" peoples, as when he discusses outstanding individuals, his language sometimes takes on a tone of high praise, extending even to favorable contrasts of "savage" behavior with that of Europeans:

One of them . . . came to the Shoar with the Women and Children to receive us, which they did even with more Civility than they had express'd the first time. Our Men suspected that this was only to get our Commodities, which they admir'd; but they are certainly a good sort of People; and instead of deserving the Name of a Barbarous Nation, as the Europeans call all the Natives of *America,* I think they have more Humanity than many Natives of *Europe,* who pretend to be very civil and affable to Strangers. (1698: 1:206)

However, this passage is from a part plagiarized, part fantasized account of an imaginary journey. Hennepin, like the Baron de Lahontan who would soon follow his route from Canada through the Great Lakes to the Mississippi, had expanded his physical journey into a metaphysical excursion to more remote peoples and places than he was actually able to visit (Thwaites 1905: 1:xxxiii–xxxix, 155); and the people singled out for such high praise here were ones that the explorer himself knew only through secondhand reports. As in Lahontan's case, Hennepin's most positive language is received for the peoples he met on his imaginary journey: "The Manners and Temper of that Nation [Taensa] is very different from that of the *Iroquese, Hurons,* and *Illinois.* These are Civil, Easie, Tractable, and capable of Instructions; whereas the others are meer Brutes, as fierce and cruel as any wild Beasts" (1698: 1:195).

Here, the nations Hennepin actually knew are reduced to the level of "meer Brutes." Elsewhere, he treats them in terms of a version of the dialectic of vices and virtues that seems curiously heightened in both positive and negative intensity.

The *Iroquese* are an Insolent and Barbarous Nation, that has shed the Blood of more than Two millions of Souls in that vast-extended Country. They would never cease from disturbing the Repose of the *Europeans,* were it not for fear of their Fire-Arms. . . .
These Savages are for the most part tall, and very well shap'd, cover'd with a sort of Robe made of Beavers and Wolves-Skins, or of black

Squirrels, holding a Pipe or *Calumet* in their Hands. The Senators of *Venice* do not appear with a graver Countenance, and perhaps don't speak with more Majesty and Solidity, than those ancient *Iroquese*. (1698: 1:44, 82)

Unlike the Iroquois, in whose country Hennepin had lived for four years, the Illinois, among whom the exploring expedition stopped for two months, were for him partly known and partly imagined. Thus sometimes they receive the kind of high praise he accorded to others described in his fantasy travels.

The Union that reigns amongst that Barbarous People, ought to cover with Shame the Christians; amongst whom we can see no Trace of that brotherly Love, which united the Primitive Professors of Christianity. (1698: 1:153)

At other times, however, the dialectic of vices and virtues appears to be slanted strongly in a more negative direction.

They are tall, strong, and manage their Bows and Arrows with great dexterity; for they did not know the use of Fire-Arms before we came into their Country. They are Lazy, Vagabonds, Timorous, Pettish, Thieves, and so fond of their Liberty, that they have no great Respect for their Chiefs. (1698: 1:167)

And in the end, Hennepin leaves no doubt as to his final assessment of the general character of the Illinois, and of the other "savage" peoples he encounters.

The *Illinois*, as most of the Savages of America, being brutish, wild, and stupid, and their Manners being so opposite to the Morals of the Gospel, their Conversion is to be despair'd of, till Time and Commerce with the *Europeans* has remov'd their natural Fierceness and Ignorance, and thereby made 'em more apt to be sensible of the Charms of Christianity. (1698: 1:168–69)

George Healy juxtaposes this passage of Hennepin to a remark by the Jesuit Claude Dablon made in the early 1670s.

His [the chief of the Illinois] countenance, moreover, is as gentle and winning as is possible to see; and, although he is regarded as a great warrior, he has a mildness of expression that delights all beholders. The inner nature does not belie the external appearance, for he is of a tender and affectionate disposition. . . . And what we say of the chief may be said of all the rest of this nation, in whom we have noted the same disposition, together with a docility which has no savor of the barbarian. (Dablon 1670–71, cited in Healy 1958: 146)

If we find that Hennepin's version of the dialectic of vices and virtues leads to strongly negative constructions, the same is true of his version of the litany of comparative negations.

> The Apostolick Man [missionary] ought much more to acknowledg this dependance upon the Sovereign Lord, in respect of those barbarous Nations who have not any regard of any Religion true or false, who live without Rule, without Order, without Law, without God, without Worship, where Reason is buried in Matter, and incapable of reasoning the most common things of Religion and Faith. Such are the people of *Canada*. (Hennepin 1698: 2:616)

Or, perhaps more to the point:

> They live without any subordination, without Laws or any form of Government or Policy. They are stupid in matters of Religion, subtle and crafty in their Worldly concerns; but excessively superstitious. (Hennepin 1698: 2:456)

Here the litany of comparative negations does not resolve into a golden age but only into a virtually impenetrable darkness of brute stupidity. Thinking of the obstacle they pose to his missionary endeavors, Hennepin's cold contempt for them reduces him to a frozen state of helplessness:

> These miserable dark Creatures listen to all we say concerning our Mysteries, just as if 'twere a Song; they are naturally very vitious, and addicted to some Superstitions that signifie nothing; their Customs are savage, brutal and barbarous; they will suffer themselves to be baptized ten times a Day for a Glass of Brandy, or a Pipe of Tobacco, and offer their Children to be baptiz'd, but all without any Religious Motive.
>
> When we dispute with them, and put them to a nonplus, they hold their tongues; their Minds are stupid, their Faculties are besotted. If we propose our Mysteries to them, they heed them as indifferently as their own nonsensical Whimsies. I have met with some of them, who seem to acknowledg that there is one first Principle that made all things; but this makes but a slight Impression upon their Mind, which returns again to its ordinary Deadness, and former Insensibility. (1698: 2:460, 466)

Indeed, it seems at times that Hennepin is driven into a frenzy, reduced to mindless ranting and raving. His chapter "Of the barbarous and uncivil Manners of the Savages" (2:547 ff.) consists mainly of vituperations and attributions of bestiality, rivaling the worst diatribes of the racist writers of the nineteenth century.

> They eat sometimes snuffling and blowing like Beasts. As soon as they enter into a Cabin, they fall a smoking. If they find a pot covered, they make no difficulty to take off the Lid to see what's in it. They eat in the Platter where their Dogs have eaten, without wiping it. When they eat fat Meat, they rub their Hands upon their Face and Hair to clean them: They are perpetually belching.
> Those that have trucked Shirts with the Europeans, never wash them; they commonly let them rot on their backs: They seldom cut their Nails: They seldom wash the Meat they dress. Their Cabins in the North are commonly filthy. I was surprized one day to see an old Woman bite the Hair of a Child, and eat the Lice. The Women are not ashamed to make water before all the World: abut they had rather go a League in the Woods than any body should see them go to stool. When the Children have pissed their Coverlets, they cast away their piss with their hands. One may often see them eat lying along like Dogs. In a word, they act every thing brutally. (Hennepin 1698: 2:548–49)

But perhaps surprisingly in a narrative so freely sprinkled with rhetoric of "brutishness" and "stupidity," Hennepin repeatedly praises the "Civilities" of the Indians: "The Chief Captains of that people receiv'd us with great Civilities after their own way" (1698: 1:115); "For all that there are many things found among them honest and civil" (1698: 2:549); or:

> The chief of that Nation had been formerly in *Canada,* and had an extraordinary Respect for Count *Frontenac,* who was Governour thereof; and upon that account receiv'd us with all the civility imaginable, and caus'd his Men to dance the *Calumet,* or Pipe, before us. This is a piece of Civility we shall describe anon. (1698: 1:119)

Hennepin's emphasis on Indian "Civility" sometimes seems to suggest a tolerant, relativistic acceptance of cultural differences, assimilating "savage" customs and values with those of civilization. However, there are other times when the word is used in contexts alien enough to have shocked or disgusted a contemporary reader.

> These Savages have more Humanity than all the others of the Northern *America.* . . . They rubb'd our Legs and Feet near the Fire, with Oil of Bears and Wild Bulls Fat, which, after much Travel, is an incomparable Refreshment; and presented us some Flesh to eat, putting the three first Morsels into our Mouth with great Ceremonies. This is a great piece of Civility amongst them. (1698: 1:157)

This seems rather close to the many ironic, patronizing references to the "beauty, such as it is," of non-European women that we find littering the ethnographic literature. Clearly, the civilities of "savages" are not those of civilization, and may ultimately even be worse than the "barbarous and uncivil Manners" to which Hennepin (1698: 2:547) devotes a chapter. Indeed, he finds one of their civilities highly problematic:

> That People, tho' so barbarous and rude in their Manners, have however a Piece of Civility peculiar to themselves; for a Man would be accounted very impertinent, if he contradicted any thing that is said in their Council, and if he does not approve even the greatest Absurdities therein propos'd; and therefore they always answer, *Niaoua*; that is to say, *thou art in the right, Brother; that is well.*
>
> Notwithstanding that seeming Approbation, they believe what they please and no more; and therefore 'tis impossible to know when they are really persuaded of those things you have mention'd unto them, which I take to be one of the greatest Obstructions to their Conversion; for their Civility hindring them from making any Objection, or contradicting what is said unto them, they seem to approve of it, though perhaps they laugh at it in private, or else never bestow a Moment to reflect upon it, such being their Indifference for a future Life. From these Observations, I conclude that the Conversion of that People is to be despair'd of, 'till they are subdu'd by the *Europeans*, and that their children have another sort of Education, unless God be pleas'd to work a Miracle in their Favour. (1698: 2:86–87)

For Hennepin, this "civility" of mutual self-respect, of believing everyone entitled to the integrity of his own opinion, proved the most frustrating and maddening feature of "savage" life. Again and again, he would cite instances of Indian opposition to European claims of the right to unquestioning acceptance and obedience based on scriptural authority; and the dialogues he recorded often prefigure, in logical construction and rhetorical style, the "imaginary" dialogues that the religious skeptic Lahontan would publish a decade later.

> When I told them it was a Foolery to believe so many Dreams and Fancies; they ask'd me how old I was? You are not above thirty five or forty years old, and do you pretend to know more than our Antient Men? Go, go, you know not what you say; you may know what passes in your own Country, because your Ancestors have told you, but you cannot tell what has passed in ours, before the *Spirits*, that's to say the Europeans, came hither.

I reply'd to these Barbarians, that we knew all by the Scripture, which the great Master of Life has given us by his Son; that this Son died to deliver Men from a place where burns an eternal Fire, which would have been their lot, if he had not come into the World to save us from Sin and from Death; that all Mankind were Sinners in *Adam*, the first Man of the World. These Savages, who have a large share of common Sense, often ask'd me, Did you *Spirits* know of our being here before you came hither? I answered them, No: You do not learn therefore all things by Scripture; it tells you not all things, reply'd they. (Hennepin 1698: 2:535–36)

When one speaks to them of the Creation of the World, and of the Mysteries of the Christian Religion; they say we have Reason: and they applaud in general all that we say on the grand Affair of our Salvation. They would think themselves guilty of a great Incivility, if they should shew the least suspicion of Incredulity, in respect of what is proposed. But after having approved all the Discourses upon these Matters; they pretend likewise on their side, that we ought to pay all possible Deference to the Relations and Reasonings that they make on their part. And when we make answer, That what they tell us is false; they reply, that they have acquiesced to all that we said, and that it's want of Judgment to interrupt a Man that speaks, and to tell him that he advances a false Proposition. All that you have taught touching those of your Country, is as you say: But it's not the same as to us, who are of another Nation, and inhabit the Lands which are on this side the great Lake. (Hennepin 1698: 2:541)

But if Lahontan would find in such verbal resistance a basis for admiring the Indians and criticizing Europeans, Hennepin saw in them a unique reason for condemning the Indians:

Another hindrance lies in a Custom of theirs, not to contradict any Man; they think every one ought to be left to his own Opinion, without being thwarted: they believe, or make as if they believed all you say to them; but 'tis their Insensibility, and Indifference for every thing, especially Matters of Religion, which they never trouble themselves about.

America is no place to go to out of a desire to suffer Martyrdom, taking the Word in a Theological Sense: The Savages never put any Christian to death upon the score of his Religion; they leave every body at liberty in Belief: They like the outward Ceremonies of our Church, but no more. These Barbarians never make War, but for the Interest of their Nation; they don't kill people, but in particular Quarrels, or when they are brutish, or drunk, or in revenge, or infatuated

with a Dream, or some extravagant Vision: they are incapable of taking
away any Person's Life out of hatred to his Religion. (1698: 2:468–69)

What a reason to condemn a people as "savages" and "barbarians": because
they will not kill you for your religious beliefs! But Hennepin is genuinely
true to his temporocultural milieu; and he would certainly not be the last
to find the ultimate damnation of the "savages" in their "liberty." However, he is moved to flirt with theological heresy:

> They have Skill enough to make a little Cloke or sort of Robe with
> dress'd Skins of Bears, Bevers, Otters, black Squirrels, Wolves, Lions,
> and other Animals. . . . But the Savages of our last discovery betwixt
> the frozen Sea and new *Mexico*, appear always naked upon all occa-
> sions; from whence I took occasion to tell Father *Gabriel* one day,
> whilst we were among the *Illinois,* that probably these Savages did not
> sin in *Adam;* because he cover'd himself with Leaves, and then had a
> Habit of Skins given him after he had sinned: These Savages have re-
> ally no manner of Shame to see themselves naked; nay they seem to
> glorify in it. When they talk with one another, they often make use of
> those Terms, *Tchetanga,* which are obscene, and would make me write
> 'em down, when I was about composting a Dictionary, and they nam'd
> the Parts of the Body to me. [But] Whatever I might say to Father *Ga-
> briel de la Ribourd,* I am nevertheless perswaded by the Scripture, that
> all Mankind are descended from *Adam;* and therefore the Savages as
> well as others, are Sinners, and corrupted by their Birth, and that they
> will perish in their Sins if they don't receive the Gospel; for there is no
> other name by which Men can be saved but the Name of Christ. I know
> very well that Habits don't save any body; but in short, if these poor
> People would observe the Precepts of the Law of Nature, God would
> work a Miracle in their favour, rather than suffer 'em to perish in their
> Ignorance; and therefore he would lead 'em into the knowledg of the
> Truth, by means worthy of his Wisdom. But these unhappy Barbarians
> violate the Precepts of the Law of Nature, and live in Stupidity, and in
> the disorders of a dreadful Corruption, which makes them fit Subjects
> of God's Wrath. (1698: 2:494–95)

It seems strange in retrospect that if Europeans could have imagined
the existence of a Law of Nature, they could also imagine it possible for
creatures of nature to "violate" it. But at the time, scientific concepts of
universal and inviolable natural "laws" were only tentatively beginning to
become differentiated from their paradigmatic inspiration in the older concepts of Royal and Divine Laws; and notions of violation and just retribution could as well be applied to the one as to the others. For Hennepin, the

sense of the Indians' guilt seems to have been strong enough that it made little difference under which code of "Law" they were to be accused, convicted, and punished. The severity of his attitude set him at odds with La Salle, the commander of the exploring expedition.

> M. *de la Salle* had often entertain'd me with the unheard of Cruelties exercised by the *Spaniards* in New *Mexico*, and *Peru*, against the Inhabitants of those vast Empires, whom they destroyed as much as ever they could, preserving only their Children to make new People. He exclaimed against that Cruelty of the *Spaniards*, as unworthy of Men of Honour, and contrary to the Doctrine of the Christian Religion. I blamed them my self; but yet I offered now and then some Reasons to excuse them, as the Necessities they found themselves under of exterminating those Nations, or perishing themselves, and forsaking their Conquest; for whenever they thought themselves safe, they were suddenly invaded by great Armies, and therefore in a perpetual Danger. (Hennepin 1698: 2:398–99)

To do him justice, Hennepin expressed a preference for methods other than genocide, even if he was willing to excuse it as an occasional "necessity":

> From these observations we may conclude, that Meekness and Charity so much recommended in the Gospel, are two Vertues absolutely necessary for the establishment of Colonies in those new Countries; for otherwise the new Inhabitants must destroy the Ancient, or be destroyed by them, either of which is a cruel Necessity unworthy of a Christian. (1698: 2:399)

Still, the Christian missionary ultimately did not regard the deaths of "savages" as worthy of regret; and for this attitude, too, he found a theological justification.

> I found the Infant-Child of one call'd *Mamenisi*, very sick. Having a little examin'd the Symptoms of its Distemper, I found the Child past hopes of Recovery . . . I thought my self oblig'd in Conscience to baptize it. . . . I am sure I saw it laughing the next Day in its Mother's Arms, who believ'd I had cur'd her Child. However it dy'd some time after, which affected me more with Joy than Grief.
>
> Had this Child recover'd, 'twas much to be fear'd 'twou'd have trod in the Steps of its Fore-fathers, and been overgrown with their infamous Superstitions, for want of a Preacher to instruct it. For indeed, if those of its Nation dwelling in Darkness and Ignorance, *continue to sin without Law, they shall also perish without Law*, as we are told by the Apostle. Upon these Considerations I was glad it had pleas'd God to take this little Christian out of the World, lest it might have fall'n into

Temptations, had it recover'd, which might have engag'd it in Errour and Superstition. I have often attributed my Preservation amidst the greatest Dangers which I have since run, to the Care I took for its Baptism. (1698: 1:263–65)

The above random selection of early travel-ethnographic writings present us with a continuum of negativity, extending from Cartier's relatively indifferent treatment of the Indians as potential objects of commercial exploitation and erotic gratification to Hennepin's deeply negative assessment of the value of their lives. It would be no great challenge to multiply into the hundreds such negativistic portrayals of "savagery" from the writings of the unphilosophical travelers, complacent in their Eurocentric prejudices. Their views have to be taken into account if only for the sake of balance, to counteract the tendency built up over a century and a half of unquestioning acceptance of the myth of the Noble Savage, to assume that belief in the nobility of "savages" was ever predominant in the ethnographic literature. But once the overall balance has been taken into account, it would be overkill to dwell on the negativity that pervades European views of the "savage." Let us continue, instead, with the more complex and interesting task of exploring the works of writers who have been perceived as advocates of positive interpretations of "savage" life, with emphasis on writers on the North American Indian, who continues to represent the paradigm case of the "savage" as we move ahead into the eighteenth century and the period known as the Enlightenment.

5 Savages and the Philosophical Travelers

FIGURE 6. THE SAVAGE CONFRONTS CIVILIZATION. Lahontan's philosophically constructed savage, with his Greco-Roman head and fig leaf superimposed on a naked dark body, treads book of "laws," crown, and scepter underfoot (Lahontan 1703a: 2:frontispiece).

There is no clear and unambiguous dividing line between the ethnographic writings of the Renaissance and those of the Enlightenment. Our historical periods represent not so much discretely bounded blocks of time as temporal convergence zones, which seem to attract both concentrations of similar kinds of events and the concentration of our own attention, drawn by a mixed configuration of historical and contemporary attractors. At most, we can recognize that an author such as Lescarbot embodies such "typical" Renaissance tendencies as the dynamic tension between a strong interest in classical humanist writers and ideas and a critical stance toward traditional authority, whereas the authors we are about to consider embody trends that seem equally characteristic of Enlightenment concerns. We must nevertheless recognize that continuities extending across historical periods can be at least as interesting as the contrasts between them. This is the case with the next two authors to be considered.

Among the eighteenth-century writers on the American Indians, those who have attracted the most attention are Lahontan and Lafitau. Lafitau is perhaps almost stereotypically an Enlightenment scholar in the Foucauldian sense of his tendency toward the "mathesis" (Foucault 1970: 71 ff.) constructed by the tabularization of ethnographic knowledge into a systematic and comprehensive form; but in so doing, his primary focus is an extension of the comparison of American Indians with classical antiquity promoted so vigorously by Lescarbot. Lahontan, by contrast, continues and expands on the skeptical and critical tendencies that we see so strikingly present in Lescarbot; but he does so in a way that aims less at a typically Renaissance project of reformation and restoration of an ethically purified nobility and authority than at a revolutionary rejection of it, a stance more typical of some of the philosophes of the Enlightenment and the French Revolution.

NOBLE FANTASIES: LAHONTAN'S ETHNOGRAPHY AND DIALOGUES

Louis Armand de Lom d'Arce, baron de Lahontan (1666–1715?) is one of the two key figures selected by Todorov to exemplify the construction of *le bon sauvage* (or, of course, "The Noble Savage" in the English edition; Todorov 1993: 270–76). Gilbert Chinard points out his unique significance:

> The contribution of Lahontan is of the greatest importance. Since the beginning of the great geographic discoveries, that is, since the beginning of the XVIth century, hundreds of voyagers had noted in passing the goodness of primitive peoples, without for all of that pronouncing a radical condemnation upon our society. . . . At the very least, he had definitively fixed the character of the "*bon sauvage*," of the "natural man" whose figure would dominate all the literature of the century to come. (1931: 71–72)

Other writers had, in fact, launched more direct and strongly worded attacks on the evils and abuses of European society—the outstanding example being Las Casas's (1542/1552) denunciation of Spanish atrocities against the Indians—but, by contrast with such reformist projects, Lahontan's fundamental condemnation of features inherent in European laws and institutions themselves can certainly be seen as more "radical." In any case, Lahontan is one of the most colorful travel-ethnography writers of the colonial era. A minor nobleman who lost his estate through legal machinations aided by political corruption, he resembles Lescarbot in presenting himself as a critic of his own society with personal experience of its capacity for injustice. But, unlike Lescarbot, he had quickly lost hope of reintegration into the system as his personal situation went from bad to worse, and his black-humored cynicism gives his writing a far sharper bite than Lescarbot's. His continual jibes at the hypocrisies of European and colonial society make for highly entertaining reading.

> As for my own part, I have lost my whole Estate by being cast in three or four Law-Suits at *Paris;* but I would be loth to believe that the Judges are in fault, notwithstanding that my Adversaries found both Mony and Friends to back bad Causes. 'Twas the Law that gave it against me, and I take the Law to be just and reasonable, imputing my surprize upon the matter, to my unacquaintedness with that Study. (Lahontan 1703a: 2:560)

In denouncing the corruption of his own society, Lahontan seizes on the character of the Indians as a rhetorical counterfoil that he wields with all the uncompromising enthusiasm appropriate to his nothing-to-lose position:

> This I only mention by the bye, in this my Preface to the Reader, whom I pray the Heavens to Crown with Prosperity, in preserving him from having any business to adjust with most of the Ministers of State, and Priests; for let them be never so faulty, they'll still be said to be in the right, till such time as Anarchy be introduc'd amongst us, as well as the *Americans,* among whom the sorryest fellow thinks himself a better Man, than a Chancellor of *France.* These People are happy in being screen'd from the tricks and shifts of Ministers, who are always Masters where-ever they come. I envy the state of a poor Savage, who tramples upon Laws, and pays Homage to no Scepter. I wish I could spend the rest of my Life in his Hutt, and so be no longer expos'd to the chagrin of bending the knee to a set of Men, that sacrifice the publick good to their private interest, and are born to plague honest Men. (1703a: 1:11)

Lahontan, of course, did not spend the rest of his life in their huts; and on his return to Europe, he gave vent to remarks that at least seem to problematize his apparent belief in the superiority of Indian over European culture.

> I am glad my Memoirs of *Canada* please you, and that my Savage Style did not turn your Affection: Tho' after all, *you* have no reason to criticise upon my Jargon, for both you and I are of a Country, where no

body can speak *French* but when they are not able to open their
Mouths: Besides, 'twas not possible for me who went so young to
America, to find out in that Country, the Mystery of Writing Politely.
That's a Science that is not to be learn'd among the Savages, whose
Clownish Society is enough to fasten a brutish twang upon the Politest
Man in the World. (Lahontan 1703a: 2:620)

Although "clownish" might seem an exaggerated and distorted English
gloss for Lahontan's French *rustique* (1703b: 107–8), in fact it was an accurate translation. "Clown" in sixteenth- through eighteenth-century English denoted, like "boor" (see below), a peasant or rustic country person;
and its adjectival form denoted someone who was "rude, boorish; unculti-
vated, ignorant, stupid; awkward, clumsy; rough, coarse" (*OED*). Derived
from West Germanic roots denoting a "clod, clot, or lump" (*OED*), it was
nearly synonymous with the term "blockish" favored by other writers on
comparative ethnography (e.g., Heylyn 1629: 333), the most common
context for either term being a complementary conjunction with " . . . and
stupid."

As one of the more colorful weapons in the arsenal of English ethnographic invective, "clownish" managed to last though the whole century,
from the English edition of Lahontan's book in 1703 to the description of
China by William Winterbotham in 1795. Winterbotham, for example,
characterizes the Tibetan lamas (*bla ma*) as "a set of clownish, ignorant,
and licentious priests" (1795: 134), and some Tibetan groups as "the most
clownish and wretched," while others "are of a noble and independent
spirit" (1795: 145). If anything, the ease with which one author juxtaposes
"clownishness" and trait-ascriptive nobility, without any apparent sense
of contradiction, might serve to remind us that the other's "true" opinion
of the people he wrote of need not have been fully committed to either a
single-mindedly positive or negative extreme: for, while global, exclusive,
and unambiguous affirmations of positivity or negativity may be found in
propagandistic constructs like the myth of the Noble Savage, they are relatively rarely encountered in real-world ethnographic narratives. In any
case, Lahontan does not use the word *noble,* except in two special contexts.

Perhaps to enhance the sales potential of his book in the context of his
declining fortunes, Lahontan interspersed passages of sharply observed
ethnographic description with flights of ethnographic science-fiction fantasy. These took two forms. The first was to add to his description of his
military journey to the western Great Lakes region, a fantasy journey to
the imaginary "Long River" or "River Long," supposed to flow into the

Mississippi from the West (Lahontan 1703a: 1:179–97). The river, not found in the specified location by any later explorers, has generated controversy over the years as to whether it was simply fantasized by Lahontan or perhaps represented a possible case of mislocation or misidentification of one or another real Mississippi tributary. Not so the Indians Lahontan describes as inhabiting its banks; for these peoples—peoples such as the supremely polite "Gnacsitares," with their great houses, game parks, and sexual hospitality; the bushy-bearded "Mozeemleck," with their "six noble Cities" and despotic government; and the bearded, metalworking "Tahuglauk," with their domesticated buffalo, knee-length garments and knee boots, and secluded women—could not be mistaken for any of the Indians that later explorers would find west of the Mississippi.

Whether Lahontan, in this episode, is taking on faith (and perhaps embellishing) the uncertainly translated tales and legends told by people he met about the little-known peoples farther beyond the frontier—a likely source for many of the exotic prodigies and monsters that haunt the travel-ethnographic literature—or whether he has simply unleashed his own imagination, filled with Eurasian ethnographic and legendary images, the discursive balance has obviously shifted almost entirely from observation to imagination. And it is here, in this imaginative construction, that we find Lahontan employing the discourse of nobility:

> I pray'd him to send six Warriours to accompany me to the long River, which I design'd to trace up to its Source. . . . At the same time he caution'd me not to venture too far up that Noble River. . . . I stay'd two days with this General, during which time he regal'd me nobly. . . . The four Slaves of that Country inform'd me, . . .[t]hat the lower part of that River is adorn'd with six noble Cities. . . . Had I been of the same mind with the *Outagamis,* we had done noble Exploits in this Place. (1703a: 1:176, 194, 202)

It seems entirely appropriate that the imaginary realm of the Long River, filled with imaginary peoples, should also be the only part of Lahontan's narrative to be filled with the rhetoric of nobility.

The second fictionalized part of Lahontan's narrative was an imaginary dialogue with a real Indian, the Huron (Wyandot) chief Kondiaronk, known to the French as "The Rat," whom Lahontan (1703a: 2:517–618) transforms into a "naked philosopher" called Adario. The "naked philosophers" (Lahontan 1703a: 1:7) of Lahontan's narrative of course recall the Gymnosophists, the "naked philosophers" of classical European ethnography, who were in fact based on the Brahmins of India; and this echo of classicism in Lahontan's text may indicate something of his possible sources of inspiration (fig. 6). In fact, Thwaites (1905: xliv) identifies the "Adario" dialogues as based on the Dialogues of Lucian; they could also be seen in more recent European terms as a kind of latter-day Anselmic dialogues, in which Lahontan himself plays the "Boso" role of the ineffectual straight man. As such, he shows little capability of withstanding the rapier thrusts of the witty and eloquent Adario, who not only stands on the firm ground of natural wisdom and honesty but also holds the advantage of having traveled to France to learn the weaknesses and disadvantages of his "civilized" opponents:

> ADARIO. When you speak of *Man,* you ought to say *French-Man.* . . . Your *French* Men have reason to say, *That 'tis impossible to keep that Law:* so long as the distinction of *Meum* and *Tuum*[1] is kept up among you: You need no other proof for this than the Example of all the Savages of *Canada,* who notwithstanding their Poverty are Richer than you, among whom all sorts of Crimes are committed upon the score of that *Meum* and *Tuum.*
>
> LAHONTAN. I own, my dear Brother, that thou'rt in the right of it; and I can't but admire the Innocence of all the Savage Nations. . . .
>
> (Lahontan 1703a: 2:539–40)

No one could blame Lahontan here for giving in to an adversary not only armed with innocence and ethnographic experience of his own but also fully in control of the rhetorical weapon of "mine and thine," the fundamental critical-discursive trope of the Golden Age tradition. Occasionally, however, Lahontan is able to rise to a more spirited resistance.

> LAHONTAN. Indeed, my Friend, thy way of Reasoning is as Savage as thy self. I did not think that a Man of Sense, who hath been in *France* and *New England,* would speak after that Fashion. What benefit hast thou reap'd by having seen our Cities, Forts and Palaces? When thou talk's of severe Laws, of Slavery, and a Thousand other idle Whims, questionless thou preachest contrary to thy own Sentiments. Thou takest pleasure in discanting upon the Felicity of the *Hurons,* a set of Men who mind nothing but Eating, Drinking, Sleeping, Hunting, and Fishing; who have not the enjoyment of any one Conveniency of Life, who travel four Hundred Leagues on Foot to knock four *Iroquese* on the Head, in a Word, who have no

more than the shape of Men: Whereas we have our Conveniences, our unbending Diversions, and a Thousand other Pleasures, which render the Minutes of our Life supportable.

(1703a: 2:555)

But Lahontan is repeatedly, and ultimately, forced to retreat before Adario's uncorrupted honesty, clear-minded wisdom, and devastating wit.

ADARIO.   Nay, you are miserable enough already, and indeed I can't see how you can be more such. What sort of Men must the *Europeans* be? What Species of Creatures do they retain to? The *Europeans*, who must be forc'd to do Good, and have no other Prompter for the avoiding of Evil than the fear of Punishment. If I ask'd thee, what a Man is, thou wouldst answer me, *He's a Frenchman*, and yet I'll prove that your *Man* is rather a *Beaver*. For *Man* is not intitled to that Character upon the score of his walking upright upon two Legs, or of Reading and Writing, and shewing a Thousand other Instances of his Industry. I call that Creature a *Man*, that hath a natural inclination to do Good, and never entertains the thoughts of doing Evil. . . . In earnest, my dear Brother, I'm sorry for thee from the bottom of my Soul. Take my advice, and turn *Huron*; for I see plainly a vast difference between thy Condition and mine. I am Master of my own Body, I have the absolute disposal of my self, I do what I please, I am the first and the last of my Nation, I fear no Man, and I depend only upon the Great Spirit: Whereas thy Body, as well as thy Soul, are doom'd to a dependance upon thy great Captain [King]; thy Vice-Roy disposes of thee; thou hast not the liberty of doing what thou hast a mind to; thou'rt affraid of Robbers, false Witnesses, Assassins, &c. and thou dependest upon an infinity of Persons whose Places have rais'd 'em above thee. Is it true, or not? Are these things either improbable or invisible? Ah! my dear Brother, thou seest plainly that I am in the right of it; and yet thou choosest rather to be a *French* slave than a free *Huron*.

(1703a: 2:553–54)

In fact, this was the single most crucial insight facing many of the European travelers and colonists: that their identity, their ethnicity, their freedom were actually subject to their own choice; and enough of them chose the freedom that they saw available to them by defecting to the Indian side that colonial governments were sometimes moved to institute draconian punishments for Europeans who "went native." Nevertheless, such defectors were common and widely known. Charlevoix, the Jesuit historian, describes an encounter with two of them:

> They had in a short time so completely adopted Indian habits, that they would never have been taken for Europeans. Not only were they naked, but they had their whole body painted and tattooed. They were married, and had several wives. . . . [A]s long as their powder lasted, they had won admiration by the effect of their muskets; but as soon as their ammunition failed, they were obliged to handle the bows and arrows. The loose life which they led had great attractions for them, and they had scarcely a sentiment of religion left. (1744b: 4:101)

In this discourse of identity and freedom, the most powerful part of his narrative, Lahontan may be fictionalizing the historical truth of individual identities and the particular instances of their words and interactions, but the result is a clear and direct representation of one of the profoundest and most unsettling experiential truths confronted by both colonists and Indians. If Lahontan recognizes and even foregrounds the problematic nature of identity as something that can be constructed by choice, in the end he evades the necessity of choice by denying it through an argument that represents the Indians as not fully human—or, at least, not of the same species as Europeans. This argument is elaborated in a dialogue with an unnamed Portuguese physician, whom Lahontan says he met at an inn in Nantes in 1693. In this dialogue, as in his dialogue with Adario, Lahontan acts the part of the defender of the orthodox Christian doctrine of the unity of mankind, against his opponent's powerful argument "that the People of the Continent of *America, Asia,* and *Africa,* were descended from three different Fathers" (Lahontan 1703a: 1:282). After raising many of the same questions of physical and cultural differences, and the problematics of migration, heredity, and climatological explanations of human differences that would be raised by the polygenist anthropologists of the nineteenth century, the doctor goes on to challenge orthodox doctrines of the damnation of non-Christians, asking, "Who can tell but God has a mind to be honour'd by infinite ways of paying him Homage and Respect, as by Sacrifices, Dances, Songs, and the other Ceremonies of the *Americans?*" (Lahontan 1703a: 1:286). To all these points, Lahontan offers protests but

no credible counterargument; and he will face another polygenist challenge, equally unanswerable, in the course of his debates with Adario:

> ADARIO.   . . . Our Temperaments and Complexions are as widely dif-
> ferent from yours as Night from Day: And that remarkable
> difference that I observe between the *Europeans* and the
> People of *Canada*, upon all things in general, is to me an
> Argument that we are not descended of your pretended
> *Adam*.
>
> (1703a: 2:594)

Undoubtedly, Lahontan's transformation of "The Rat" into the philosophical Adario is one of the more remarkable creations of ethnographic
science fiction. Too bad "The Rat," as the historical person Kondiaronk, had
as far as we know never actually visited France; and how fortunate, to the
extent that we can admire original creations of the imagination, that Lahontan was able and willing to lend him the vehicle of his own imagination
and experience to make the trip. His character here is a fantasy mind-meld,
in which the physical reality of every statement is a mythic utterance spoken through the mouth of the medium, Lahontan himself. And yet, taken
as such a composite construct, Adario may not be quite so problematic as
has often been supposed.

In constructing Adario, Lahontan made use of several elements, one
being the historical Kondiaronk himself. Superimposed on the historical
character were Lahontan's individual acquaintances with Indians who had,
in fact, visited France—including Iroquois Catholic converts treacherously
kidnapped, tortured, and sent to France as galley slaves, and who were quite
understandably vehement in their criticism of French mendacity and hypocrisy (Lahontan 1703a: 1:121–24, 233). Similar kinds of native criticisms were, after all, scattered throughout the writings of virtually every
traveler, missionary, and colonial administrator of the exploratory and
colonial eras, however unsympathetic to indigenous peoples they might
have been (e.g., Sagard and Biard, chap. 4). Besides constituting part of a
widespread resistance to oppression and atrocity from the victims' standpoint, such critiques were, from the Europeans' side, among the more colorful "curiosities" of exotic travel that could not but produce a striking
impression on the travel writers themselves, as well as on their intended
audiences.

Another important element contributing to the construction of Adario
was Lahontan's more general acquaintance with the power of Indian rhetoric and eloquence. He had, in fact, been so impressed early in his travels

with the oratorical power of an Iroquois chief known to him as "the Grangula" that he attempted to give an extensive translation, as literal as possible, in one of the letters he would later compile to form the basis of his travel narrative (Lahontan 1703a: 1:80–84). This experiment in opening ethnographic narrative to "the voice of the Other" was a dismal failure, as Lahontan explains his audience's reaction:

> Farther; I would not have the Reader to take it amiss, that the thoughts of the Savages are set forth in an *European* Dress. The occasion of that choice proceeded from the Relation I Corresponded with; for that honest Gentleman ridiculed the Metaphorical Harangue of the *Grangula;* and intreated me not to make a literal Translation of a Language that was so stuff'd with Fictions and Savage Hyperboles. 'Tis for this reason that all the Discourses and Arguments of those Nations, are here accommodated to the *European* Style and way of Speaking; for having comply'd with my Friend's Request, I contented my self in keeping only a Copy of the Letters I writ to him, during my Pilgrimage in the Country of these naked Philosophers. (1703a: 1:7)

Toward the end of the century, Diderot (1772a: 129) would offer a similarly disingenuous explanation for the patently European discourse of his own fictionalized dialogue with the non-European "Other." But Lahontan, unlike Diderot, had "been there and known them"; and his representations of Indian discourse, even when "set forth in an *European* dress," retained enough resemblance to the original that, a century and a half later, Lewis Henry Morgan (1851: 175–76, 200) was able to recognize parallels with Iroquois discourses provided him by Ely Parker, his Seneca collaborator and translator, and use Lahontan's representations of Indian rhetoric for historical and comparative amplification of his own ethnographic work (cf. Lahontan 1703a: 2:472, 449). Clearly, the European style of Lahontan's dialogues was in itself no automatic disqualifier either of their Indian content or of their possible inspiration in Indian discourse. The most that can be said with any certainty is that it rendered them more intuitively accessible to Europeans—a goal that, if any of their content was in fact inspired by Kondiaronk, he would have presumably shared with Lahontan.

As for Kondiaronk himself, Lahontan could not have chosen a better model for Adario. Lahontan's ideological enemy and critic, the Jesuit historian Charlevoix, describes Kondiaronk as "a man of ability, extremely brave, and the Indian of the highest merit that the French ever knew in Canada" (Charlevoix 1744b: 4:12). At his death, "it was the general opinion that no Indian had ever possessed greater merit, a finer mind, more valor, prudence or discernment in understanding those with whom he had to deal"; and he was given a full French military funeral and buried in the cathedral of Montreal (Charlevoix 1744b: 5:146–48). Moreover, besides his outstanding intelligence and character, there was also general agreement on his excellence as an orator.

> In fact he never opened his lips in council without receiving such applause even from those who disliked him. He was not less brilliant in conversation in private, and they often took pleasure in provoking him to hear his repartees, always animated, full of wit and generally unanswerable. In this he was the only man in Canada who was a match for the Count de Frontenac [governor of Canada], who often invited him to his table to give his officers this pleasure. (Charlevoix 1744b: 5:146)

But recalling that it is Lahontan's adversary speaking here, we might well be surprised to find a picture of the historical Kondiaronk that so perfectly characterizes the "fictional" Adario, as an "unanswerable" match in witty repartee for one of the most cultivated representatives of the French nobility. We might also be surprised to reflect that, as described here in Charlevoix's narrative, Kondiaronk seems to continue a role filled by Membertou as a frequent guest and pleasurable companion at the dinner table of the colonial governor in Lescarbot's time, a century earlier.

Perhaps Indians who knew how to engage in discourse and repartee with Frenchmen were not all that fantastic, after all; and if some had not journeyed to France, at least they had regularly observed Frenchmen in French cultural settings and had more than a slight opportunity to learn their ways and ideas. But what was actually said in these nightly dinner colloquies, full of witty and animated disputations? We have only Lahontan's "curious dialogues" in their "French dress" as a problematic example, for which he nevertheless claimed the collaboration of Frontenac himself, who according to Lahontan was delighted with a rough draft and helped to edit them into a more coherently organized and publishable form. Even Chinard (1913: 170; 1931: 29, 47 ff.), Lahontan's harshest modern critic, admits that the claim of Frontenac's collaboration cannot be rejected. If the claim of Frontenac's participation is true, the fictionalized dialogues were underwritten by a much less marginalized figure than Lahontan, in fact a pillar of French society, who was in the best position of anyone then living to support their authenticity as a representation of Kondiaronk's personality and discourse.

Charlevoix (1744b: 5:146) insists that Kondiaronk, in his last few years, determined "to embrace Christianity, or at least to live in conformity to the maxims of the gospel." Yet Charlevoix also provides the most detailed account of his opposition to French colonial policies in describing a Machiavellian set of political machinations in which he used a French truce to ambush Iroquois ambassadors, killed some and sent others home filled with lies to provoke anti-French warfare, and managed to persuade all parties to blame the entire treacherous operation on the French colonists (Charlevoix 1744b: 4:12 ff.). Given the agreement of both Lahontan and Charlevoix concerning both "The Rat's" rhetorical power and elegance and his "treachery" in this sophisticated political resistance to the French enterprise, who can doubt that he was a critic of European colonial practices and ideology? Ultimately, Lahontan's fictionalized representation of Kondiaronk as Adario may be less problematic than his own self-image as either Adario's opponent or a believer in the superiority of the Hurons' way of life; and perhaps Pagden (1993: 120 ff.) is right, in his discussion of their dialogues, in framing "Lahontan" rather than Adario in quotes as a marker of representational ambiguity.

As part of their discussions, Adario and Lahontan debate the restriction of hunting to the nobility, the very point of European law that stimulated Lescarbot to invent the Noble Savage.

> ADARIO. I protest I don't understand one word of what thou hast said; for I know the contrary of what thou sayest to be true, and those who inform'd me so of the Judges are Men of undisputed Honour and Sense. But if no body had given me any such Information, I am not so dull Pated as not to see with my own Eyes, the Injustice of your Laws and your Judges. I'll tell thee one thing my dear Brother; I was a going one day from *Paris* to *Versailles*, and about half way, I met a Boor [peasant] that was going to be Whipt for having taken Partridges and Hares with Traps. . . . These poor Men were punish'd by your unjust Laws, for endeavouring to get Sustenance to their Families. . . . If things go at this rate, where are your just and reasonable Laws; where are those Judges that have a Soul to be Sav'd as well as you and I? After this, you'll be ready to Brand the *Hurons* for Beasts. In earnest, we should have a fine time of it if we offer'd to punish one of our Brethren for killing a Hare or a Partridge. . . .
>
> LAHONTAN. Very fine, my dear Friend; thou goest too fast; believe me, thy Knowledge is so confin'd, as I said before, that thy Mind can't reach beyond the appearances of things. Wouldst thou but give Ear to Reason, thou wouldst

presently be sensible that we act upon good Principles,
for the support of the Society. You must know, the Laws
Condemn all without exception, that are guilty of the
Actions you've mention'd. In the first place, they pro-
hibit the Peasants to kill Hares or Partridges, especially
in the Neighbourhood of *Paris;* by reason that an un-
controul'd liberty of Hunting, would quickly exhaust
the whole Stock of those Animals. The Boors Farm the
Grounds of their Landlords, who reserve to themselves
the Priviledge of Hunting, as being Masters. Now, if
they happen to kill Hares or Partridges, they not only
rob their Masters of their Right, but fall under the Pro-
hibition enacted by the Law.
(Lahontan 1703a: 2:560–62)

Here, again, is the confrontation of civilized corruption and self-serving
rationalization with "savage" critique. But, unlike Lescarbot on this issue,
Lahontan does not draw the conclusion of "savage" nobility, and the discursive Noble Savage remains absent from his work.

Aside from the fantasy description of the Long River, Lahontan's sole
mention of nobility is, indeed, a haunting evocation of Lescarbot, although
it does not apply to "savages":

In earnest, Sir, the Boors of those Manors live with more ease and con-
veniency, than an infinity of the Gentlemen in *France.* I am out indeed
in calling them Boors, for that name is as little known here as in *Spain;*
whether it be that they pay no Taxes, and injoy the liberty of Hunting
and Fishing; or that the Easiness of their Life, puts 'em upon a level
with the Nobility. (1703a: 1:34–35)

It would seem that Lescarbot's dream of a new golden age and a new kind
of nobility had become realized in less than a century, and was perceived as
such by Lahontan for the very reasons that Lescarbot had argued the nobility of the "savages." But now, in fact, it was the colonial peasants of New
France, rather than the Indians, who were "put upon a level with the Nobility," exactly as Lescarbot had foreseen.

VESTIGIAL NOBILITY: LAFITAU'S COMPARATIVE ETHNOLOGY

Among the more philosophically interesting eighteenth-century writers
on American Indians is the Jesuit scholar Joseph-François Lafitau (1681–
1746), identified by some (e.g., Pagden 1982: 199 ff.) as a key figure in the
development of comparative ethnological method, while others (e.g., Fen-

ton and Moore 1974: 1:xxx) point out his anticipation of Morgan's nine-teenth-century research in the recognition of classificatory kinship among the Iroquois. Lafitau's work, *Customs of the American Indians Compared with the Customs of Primitive Times* (1724), is an ethnography of time-shifting, in which the Indians are compared with the Europeans of classical antiquity in a way that seems less a detemporalizing removal from the contemporaneity of shared humanity (cf. Fabian 1983) than a distance-nearing affirmation of common kinship. In fact, Lafitau's comparison of American Indians with earlier Europeans was an elaborated and system-atized extension of a project initiated by Lescarbot; and a reader of Lafitau cannot help but be impressed by echoes of Lescarbot's equation of Indian practices with those of European feudalistic chivalry.

> *Initiations of the Ancient Chivalry of Europe:* All that I have related about the initiations of warriors among the barbarous and more civilized nations of America must make anyone who has any idea of the ancient chivalry of our European peoples realize that the tests which had to be undergone by aspirants to the honourable estate of knighthood were almost like those which I have just described in detail [as given] by peoples, at a time when, still barbarous, they were plunged in the darkness of idolatry. (Lafitau 1724: 1:210)

On closer investigation, we see that the resemblance to Lescarbot is more than coincidental. Consider another passage from Lafitau.

> *Chapter 3: Warfare:* The men, who are so idle in their villages, make their indolence a mark of honour, giving it to be understood that they are properly born only for great things, especially for warfare. This ex-ercise, which exposes their courage to the rudest tests, furnishes them frequent occasions to put in its brightest light all the nobility of their sentiments and the unshakeable firmness of a truly heroic greatness of mind. They like hunting and fishing which, after warfare, take their attention, only because they are the image of warfare. Perhaps they would leave these occupations as well as that of subsistence and all oth-ers to women if they did not consider hunting and fishing exercises which get them into shape to be a terror to enemies even more formi-dable than wild beasts.
>   . . . If my conjectures as to the origin of the Americans are well founded, we may say that their courage serves to lend even more force to this [theory]. They all have haughty hearts. They have an air of pride and nobility. They make their claim to glory their courage, and their reputation is established only by the frequent proofs that they have given of an intrepid firmness. (1724: 2:98)

This passage is clearly based on Lescarbot, as we see by the characterization of hunting and fishing as "the image of warfare," a direct quotation from Lescarbot's discussion of the subject. Even so, we see that Lafitau does not follow Lescarbot to the conclusion that "the Savages are truly noble" but rather limits himself to remarking on "all the nobility of their sentiments" and "an air of pride and nobility." This is a case of the narrower, trait-ascriptive and aesthetic nobility rather than the all-pervading ontological nobility that essentially defines the mythical Noble Savage; and we see that Lafitau's carryover from Lescarbot of a discursive linkage between "savages" and nobility is a kind of vestigial nobility, not as strong as the "true" feudalistic nobility of Lescarbot's argument or of the Noble Savage of the myth that would emerge in the next century.

Lafitau certainly does not idealize or essentialize his subjects by presenting them as personifications of unadulterated goodness. If we are inclined to view his classical-comparativist method as, in one sense, a continuation of the Golden Age rhetoric and imagery projected on the Indians by Renaissance writers, then we should be prepared to recognize other aspects of his work as a continuation of the counterbalancing negative imagery of the cannibal, the darker underside of European constructions of the "savage." As with Lescarbot and the others who had preceded him in Canada, Lafitau found a suitably horrific substitute for the locally absent cannibalism in the widespread practice of systematic torture of prisoners of war, a practice that he describes in gory detail, with this conclusion:

> Thus ends this bloody tragedy. I do not know at what one should marvel more, the brutal ferocity of these inhuman beings who treat so cruelly poor captives brought from such a distance that they could not be guilty of any offence towards their murderers, or the constancy of these same captives who, in the midst of the most frightful torture, retain an unimaginable greatness of soul and heroism.
>
> This heroism is real and the result of a great and noble courage. What we have admired in the martyrs of the primitive church which was, in them, the result of grace and a miracle, is natural to these people and the result of the strength of their morale. . . . I do not know whether one should call barbarian such manly courage, but I do know that we find more examples of this intrepid courage among those whom we treat as barbarians, than among the civilized nations to whom the arts and all that serves to polish and humanize them, give an abundance and gentleness of life which serves only to render them cowardly and soft. (1724: 2:157–58)

Is this a case of "some are more noble than others"? We have to bear in mind that the victims, with their "unimaginable greatness of soul and heroism" and their "great and noble courage," are the same persons, at different times in their lives and under the changing fortunes of war, as the "inhuman beings" who give vent to their "brutal ferocity" in torturing them. The heroism on one side and the cruelty on the other are the alternating polarities energizing and driving the warfare complex; and the victims sing proudly of their own lack of mercy in torturing the kinsmen of their torturers. What, then, is Lafitau's "real" opinion of the Indians—noble heroes or inhuman brutes? To choose one alternative as an exclusive or predominant characterization would be for us, as for him, an oversimplification of what he represents as ambivalent complexity. Rather than suppress one or another of the two polarities, he adopts them and turns them in another direction: comparison of Indian and European qualities.

Here, indeed, we find the Indian as exemplar for European self-critique, but in a strangely disturbing way. Is the missionary, the man of religion and peace, reproaching Europeans for their lack of a heroism that he himself recognizes and represents as constructed by complementary interaction with killing, torture, and "inhuman" cruelty? Both his descriptions of Indian warfare and his comparative citations of cases from European classical antiquity suggest a considerable degree of admiration for warlike peoples and militaristic virtues. Expressions of appreciation for military-style courage and discipline might be expected to arise from time to time among some members of a monastic order known for its strict discipline and obedience, and which originally constructed itself as a "company" of the soldiers of Jesus under the leadership of a "general." And such a positive attitude toward militarism is, perhaps, not surprising in a writer living under circumstances in which missionaries like himself were sometimes subject to the "Christian martyrdom" of death by torture, and who saw themselves as dependent for protection against such a fate not only on their own religious virtues but also to a large extent on the military deterrent forces of the French colonial government.

If there is any kind of idealization at work here, it is perhaps an idealization of Lescarbot's old argument for the necessity of "terror," generalized and enhanced into a paradigm of universal human virtue. But this seems to lead us rather far afield from romantic musings on the Noble Savage as a pure and gentle, simple child of nature.

6 Rousseau's Critique of Anthropological Representations

7. BEARSKIN AND BLANKET.
Jean-Jacques Rousseau highlighted the choice between animal skin and blanket raingear to challenge assumptions of the superiority of civilization over savagery. Postcontact Makah Indian whalers and fishermen chose to wear both (Swan 1868: 16).

We have seen that Marc Lescarbot fills two roles often ascribed to Rousseau—inventor of the Noble Savage concept and early proponent of anthropological science. We must ask, then, what is Rousseau's relationship to concepts of the "savage" and the foundation of a science of anthropology? First, he leaves no doubt that his construction in the *Discourse on Inequality* of a primordial man that he calls alternately "natural" and "savage" is a deliberate work of fiction.

> Let my readers not imagine that I flatter myself as having seen what
> I believe to be so difficult to see. I have launched several arguments, I

have hazarded several conjectures, less in the hope of resolving the question than with the intention of clarifying it and reducing it to its true form. It will be easy for others to go further down the same path, without it being easy for anyone to reach the end. For it is no light enterprise to separate that which is original from that which is artificial in man's present nature, and attain a solid knowledge of a state which no longer exists, which perhaps never existed, and which will probably never exist, yet of which it is necessary to have sound ideas if we are to judge our present state satisfactorily. (Rousseau 1755b: 68)

His explanation of the need for such a speculative enterprise proceeds from a critique of previous theories:

The philosophers who have examined the foundations of society have all felt it necessary to go back to the state of nature, but none of them has succeeded in getting there. . . . [A]ll these philosophers talking ceaselessly of need, greed, oppression, desire and pride have transported into the state of nature concepts formed in society. They speak of savage man and they depict civilized man. . . .

Let us begin by setting aside all the facts, because they do not affect the question. One must not take the kind of research which we enter into as the pursuit of truths of history, but solely as hypothetical and conditional reasonings, better fitted to clarify the nature of things than to expose their actual origin; reasonings similar to those used every day by our physicists to explain the formation of the earth. (1755b: 78)

In this appeal to the scientific imagination, it is certainly possible to perceive a mirror reflection of scientific endeavors such as Galileo's proceeding from a consideration of ethnographic reports to the projection of a hypothetical ethnographic fantasy to an attempt to imagine and "explain the formation of" the moon (Galileo 1632: 48–64). There is an interesting reversal here, though, in Rousseau's construction of an imaginary world: namely, that despite his declared intent to "set aside all the facts," Rousseau, like other writers of his time, looks at ethnographic information on "savages" for clues to the life of man in a "state of nature."

Unlike some of the more enthusiastic promoters of the Enlightenment ideal of perfection, but following in the critical humanist tradition of Lery, Montaigne, and others, Rousseau uses the "savage" as a source of information and ideas to critique aspects of civilized life that less critical writers would prefer to have left swept under the rug of progress. This is the usage that resulted in the popular stereotype that Rousseau promoted the myth of the "Noble Savage." In fact, Rousseau not only never uses the term "Noble Savage,"[1] but his conception of savagery is remote from any notion of natural moral goodness. For Rousseau, the savage "could not be either good or bad, and had neither Vices nor Virtues" (Rousseau 1755a: 66). Although lacking the noble or "sublime" virtues that only civilized minds can conceive, he was nevertheless "rather wild than wicked" (Rousseau 1755a: 78). Indeed, in Rousseau's construction, the savage was in some ways happier and more fortunate than civilized man precisely *because* he was not, and could not be, "Noble": lacking the abstract concepts of good and evil that civilization had invented, he was also spared the practical effects of socioeconomic and moral exaltation and degradation that developed alongside them.

For Rousseau, man in a state of nature was "placed by nature at an equal distance from the stupidity of brutes and the fatal enlightenment of civilized man" (Rousseau 1755b: 115), advanced far above the animals but possessing few of the qualities that would come with the advance toward civilization. His mind was unable to form abstract ideas (Rousseau 1755a: 81).

> His imagination paints no pictures; his heart yearns for nothing; his modest needs are readily supplied at hand; and he is so far from having enough knowledge for him to desire to acquire more knowledge, that he can have neither foresight nor curiosity. (Rousseau 1755b: 90)

With the evolutionary concurrence of a technological advance from stone to metal tools, a sedentary lifestyle, the beginnings of agriculture, the establishment of settled communities, the acquisition of personal property, and the appearance of differences in social roles and status, humans began to move out of the savage state of the hunter and started their advance toward civilization and its moral exaltation and ambiguities. With the rise of inequalities of wealth and power, class distinctions, and oppression of the weak and poor, suffering gives rise to yearning for lost freedoms and nostalgia for a golden age.

> Discontented with your present condition for reasons which presage for your unfortunate posterity even greater discontent, you will wish perhaps you could go backwards in time—and this feeling must utter the eulogy of your first ancestors, the indictment of your contemporaries, and the terror of those who have the misfortune to live after you. (Rousseau 1755b: 79)

But it is not possible to go backward in time; and Rousseau, for one, has no wish to do so.

> What then? Must we destroy societies, annihilate *meum* and [*tuum*] and return to live in the forests with the [Wolves and] bears? A conclu-

sion in the style of my adversaries, which I would sooner forestall than permit them to disgrace themselves by drawing. Oh you . . . who can leave your fatal acquisitions, your troubled spirits, your corrupt hearts and your frenzied desires in the midst of cities, reclaim—since it is up to you to do so—your ancient and first innocence; go into the woods and lose the sight and memory of the crimes of your contemporaries, and have no fear of debasing your species in renouncing its enlightenment in order to renounce its vices. As for men like me, whose passions have destroyed their original simplicity for ever, who can no longer nourish themselves on herbs and nuts, nor do without laws and rulers; those . . . who are convinced that the divine voice called the whole human race to the enlightenment and happiness of celestial intelligences; all those will endeavour, by the exercise of virtues . . . [to] respect the sacred bonds of the societies of which they are members; they will love their fellowmen and serve them with all their strength; they will scrupulously obey the laws . . . , but they will nonetheless despise a constitution . . . from which, in spite of their cares, there will always arise more real calamities than seeming advantages.[2] (Rousseau 1755b: 153–54)

Precisely because it is impossible to return to primordial innocence, it is impossible for the civilized and enlightened person to retreat to a state of unthinking, uncritical acceptance of any way of life, whether that of savagery or of civilization. The moral and intellectual advancement of civilized man demands an informed awareness and criticism of self and others; and this in turn requires a knowledge and critique of civilization and its possible or hypothetical alternatives, of what it is, might have been, and could possibly be. It is here that consideration of the differences between the artificial and the natural, between civilization and its imaginative and ethnographic alternatives, becomes mandatory.

But what, then, is the relationship between ethnography and the imagination? How much does Rousseau's evolutionary construction of the savage man of nature have to do with the "Savages" reported in travel literature on America and elsewhere? Rousseau certainly makes use of ethnographic writings in the construction of his fictional Savage. However, he also clearly distinguishes the so-called Savages of America from those he considers "true Savages":

> *Song* does not seem to be natural to man. While the Savages of America sing because they speak, true Savages have never sung at all. Mutes do not sing; they only produce a voice without permanence, a dull roaring pulled out of themselves by effort. . . . Infants shriek, cry, and do

not sing at all. The first expressions of nature have nothing in them of
the melodious or the sonorous, and they learn to sing as they learn to
speak, by imitating us. (1768: 83–84)

Leaving aside particularities of detail, the general principle emerges
clearly. The so-called Savages of America and elsewhere are not "true Savages" because they have advanced beyond the state of nature exemplified
by infants and mutes who neither speak nor sing; it is only "for lack of
having sufficiently distinguished between different ideas" that we can con-
fuse them. Rousseau does not share that confusion. For him, the songs and
language of the Indians and Europeans are not a part of nature, either
physical or human. They belong instead to another sphere, shared by the
non-Savage American Indians and civilized Europeans alike, the sphere of
society, learning, and culture.

Accordingly, Rousseau distinguishes the "savage peoples known to us"
from his hypothetical evolutionary construction of "true" savages in a
state of nature.

> Thus, . . . revenge became terrible, and men grew bloodthirsty and
> cruel. This is precisely the stage reached by most of the savage peoples
> known to us; and it is for lack of having sufficiently distinguished be-
> tween different ideas and seen how far these peoples already are from
> the first state of nature that so many authors have hastened to conclude
> that man is naturally cruel. (Rousseau 1755b: 114–15)

If one had "sufficiently distinguished between different ideas" there should
arise the necessity for constructing the state of "true savagery" as hypothetical, as a deliberate act of projective fiction. Considering "the savage
nations known to us," and seeing "how very far they already are from the
state of nature," the conclusion is inevitable that the time travel imagined
by some other eighteenth-century investigators of the science of man
(Degerando 1800; see also Fabian 1983: chap. 1) is impossible. "You will
wish perhaps you could go backwards in time," Rousseau remarks; but
ethnographic travel leads only to glimpses of peoples like "the Caribs, who
of all peoples existing today have least departed from the state of nature"
(Rousseau 1755b: 103). Obviously, the least departure is still a departure;
the Caribs are clearly not any longer in a state of nature, just as Europeans
and other peoples existing today are not.

In the end, such glimpses afford only a difference of degree rather than
kind, showing mainly that the images of natural man projected by theorists may be, as Rousseau (1755a: 83) charges, "diametrically opposite to
Experience." In making this charge, Rousseau echoes the classic Renais-

sance scientific critique of theories constructed without observed evidence, purely on the grounds of logical consistency; and he projects the "savage nations known to us" as providing a control against wild speculation and a dialectical contrast with experience-centered and potentially ethnocentric constructions of "civilization." It is in the construction of such a dialectic that anthropology plays a role.

When Rousseau begins his *Discourse* by observing, "The most useful and the least developed of all the sciences seems to me to be that of man" (1755b: 67), we might wonder what kind of usefulness he has in mind. It is easier to discern Rousseau's stance on the second point than the first, since so much of his discussion of anthropology in the *Discourse* has to do with its lack of development. For example,

> We know nothing of the peoples of the East Indies, visited only by Europeans eager to fill their purses rather than their minds. The whole of Africa with its numerous inhabitants, as remarkable in character as in colour, is yet to be studied. The entire world is covered with peoples of whom we know only the names, and yet we amuse ourselves judging the human race! (1755b: 160)

But the problem is not one of simple ignorance; rather, despite a long history of intensive exploration and ethnographic description by Europeans, little beyond ethnocentric misrepresentations has resulted.

> In the two or three centuries since the inhabitants of Europe have been flooding into other parts of the world, endlessly publishing new collections of voyages and travel, I am persuaded that we have come to know no other men except Europeans; moreover it appears from the ridiculous prejudices, which have not died out even among men of letters, that every author produces under the pompous name of the study of man nothing much more than a study of the men of his own country. . . .
>
> One does not open a book of voyages without finding descriptions of characters and customs, but one is altogether amazed to find that these authors who describe so many things tell us only what all of them knew already, and have only learned how to see at the other end of the world what they would have been able to see without leaving their own street, and that the real features which distinguish nations, and which strike eyes made to see them, have almost always escaped their notice. Hence that fine adage of ethics, so often repeated by the philosophistical throng: that men are everywhere the same, and since they all have the same passions and the same vices, it is pretty useless to seek to characterize different peoples—which is as reasonable as saying that one cannot distinguish Pierre from Jacques, since they both have a nose, a mouth and eyes. (Rousseau 1755b: 159–60)

If we recall that the *Discourse* similarly began with a critique of philosophical representations of natural man, we begin to perceive the underlying episteme that establishes Rousseau's unified approach to all the disciplines with which he is concerned and that serves as the best index of his special contribution to the rise of anthropology. In anthropology, as in his approach to other sciences, Rousseau's characteristic emphasis is on the construction of a critique of theories formulated in terms of a critique of representations. The critique is as characteristic of his approach to anthropology as it is to philosophy, or, for example, ethnomusicology.

> Most of these opinions are founded on the persuasion which we have of the excellence of our music. . . . To put the reader in a position to judge the diverse musical accents of the peoples, I have also transcribed in the Plate a Chinese melody taken from Father du Halde, a Persian melody taken from Sir [Jean de] Chardin, and two songs of the savages of America taken from Father Mersenne. One will find in all of these pieces a conformity of modulation with our music, which might arouse admiration in some for the goodness and universality of our laws, and in others might render suspect the intelligence or the accuracy of those who have transmitted these airs to us. (Rousseau 1768: 313–14)

Similarly, in addressing the currently much-debated question of the relationship of various species of anthropoid apes to men, Rousseau laments the lack of accurate observations by scientifically and philosophically sophisticated observers:

> If such observers as these were to assert of an animal that it is a man and of another animal that it is a beast, then I say we must believe them; but it would be excessively naive to accept the authority of uncultured travellers about whom one is sometimes tempted to ask the very question that they take it upon themselves to answer in the case of other animals. (1755b: 161)

If Rousseau's critique had remained at the level of negative criticism, it would have been considerably less influential in the rise of anthropology. However, it also includes an analysis of the causes of the problem.

> Individuals go here and there in vain; it seems that philosophy does not travel and that the philosophy of one nation proves little suited to another. The cause of this is obvious, at least in the case of distant countries. There are hardly more than four sorts of men who make long distance voyages: sailors, merchants, soldiers and missionaries. Now it

can hardly be expected that the first three classes should yield good observers, and as for the fourth . . . one must believe that they would not lend themselves willingly to researches that would look like pure curiosity and distract their attention from the more important labours to which they have committed themselves. (1755b: 159)

The problem had in fact already been noted in the attempts of Renaissance ethnographers to formulate a theory of observations; Pierre Belon (1553: 1:1a–1b), for example, had suggested virtually the same analysis in less detailed form as early as 1553. Now Rousseau, along with an analysis of causes, begins to develop suggestions as to how the lack of development of anthropology might be remedied.

> I have spent my life in reading relations of voyages. . . . I have never found two that have given me the same idea of the same people. In comparing the little that I have been able to observe with that which I have read, I have ended by setting aside the travellers, and regretting the time I have given to instructing myself by reading them, thoroughly convinced that in making every kind of observation, one must not read, one must see. (Rousseau, cited in Chinard 1913: 347–48)

In maintaining the primacy of observation over written authority, Rousseau once again echoes the classic critical stance of Renaissance scientists such as Galileo and Bacon—in fact, the same critical principle we find highlighted in the works of early ethnographers and ethnographic theorists such as Lery and Nicolay. The principle itself is implicitly a critique of theory and representations, and it was manifested as such in many observations cited both by scientists and ethnographers in refutations of particular theories. Given his broad understanding of the theoretical significance of the issue, we can only regret that Rousseau himself did not undertake ethnographic travels to other parts of the world. Perhaps we can imagine some of what might have resulted from such journeys by noting the richness of cultural observation in his narrative of his residence in Italy (Rousseau 1782–89: 269–96), his analyses of the "national" differences embodied in the contrast between French and Italian music, and the emphasis in so many of his works on the self-consciously unique identity of himself as a citizen of the republic of Geneva living in monarchical France. Personal self-awareness, anthropology, and ethnomusicology are strongly interwoven themes in his works, and there are grounds for inferring that his own travels, observations, and attraction to new and different people and their music were the primary sources that led him to reflect on "national," that is, cultural, differences and so stimulated his interest in the development of anthropological theory.

> I had brought with me from Paris the national prejudice against Italian music, but Nature had also endowed me with that fine feeling against which such prejudices are powerless. I soon conceived for this music the passion which it inspires in those who are capable of judging it correctly. (Rousseau 1782–89: 286)

The energizing confluence of passion and "correct"—that is, reflexively corrected—judgment enables the construction of the Rousseauian critique and its projection into ethnographic investigation, both of music and of culture. Less an *episteme*, in Foucault's (1970: xxii) sense of an epistemological field in which knowledge is grounded, than an *epistogen*, which generates it, the confluence of passion and reflexivized reason becomes a founding force rather than a fundamental framework of Rousseau's epistemology, and it moves him to situate himself in near-diametric opposition to the stereotypical Enlightenment project of a quest for "disinterested knowledge." We see the opposition, for example, in Rousseau's rejection of the mathesis (Foucault 1970: 56–57, 71–75) exemplified in the trend extending from Mersenne (1636) to Rameau (1760), of reducing music to tabularized mathematical representations based on universal physical "laws." For Rousseau, by contrast, the effects of music "come from nothing but experience, memory, the thousand circumstances which, retraced by the melody for those who listen, and recalling their country, their former pleasures, their youth, and all their ways of life, . . . it is not in their physical action that one should search for the greatest effects of sounds on the human heart" (Rousseau 1768: 314–15). Such a model, with its prominent foregrounding of emotional, experiential, and cultural differences, both follows from and logically requires a further pursuit of understanding through a direct, self-aware engagement with its diverse objects rather than through disengaged cogitations that facilitate the construction of universalizing tabularizations from analytically extracted bits of data.

Thus the convergence of "passion" and reflexive judgment led Rousseau to further analyses of the differences between French and Italian musics in relation to the ways of life with which each was associated, and in relation to the reactions that each produced in those who approached it from a different cultural background. This led to the critique of representations we have seen above and to the projection of problems and paths of investigation for understanding the nature and importance of "national" differences and their larger human implications. Similarly, his anthropological critique leads to a projection of new paths of investigation, centered in the role of the scientific observer of other peoples and cultures who will personally undertake anthropological research expeditions.

> We admire the magnificence of several men whose curiosity has made them undertake, or have undertaken, at great expense expeditions to the East with scholars and artists, to make drawings of ruins there or to decipher and copy inscriptions; but I find it hard to imagine why in a century which prides itself on its fine sciences, we do not find two well-matched men . . . who would sacrifice, in the one case twenty thousand crowns of his property, in the other, ten years of his life, so as to make a glorious voyage round the world in order to study, not eternally plants and stones, but for once men and customs; and who, after all the centuries that have been spent measuring and appraising the house, should finally decide that they would like to have knowledge of the inhabitants. (Rousseau 1755b: 160)

In fact, earlier writers such as Belon and Nicolay had suggested or implied the need for ethnographic voyages, and Rousseau himself praised the ethnographic achievements of traveler-ethnographers such as Chardin in Persia and the Jesuits in China. But all such voyages seemed to have been undertaken for mixed motives; and Rousseau goes beyond the other theorists in his call for a new kind of expedition devoted specifically and ex-clusively to anthropological research. Such a "glorious voyage" would re-quire a different kind of traveler than those who had produced the exist-ing ethnographies; a kind of traveler Rousseau believed had occasionally emerged as a happy accident of genius in the past, and might serve as a model for the deliberate cultivation of a present or future science.

> Shall we never see reborn those happy times . . . when a Plato, a Thales, a Pythagoras, impelled by an ardent desire for knowledge, un-dertook the most extensive voyages solely to instruct themselves, and travelled far in order to shake off the yoke of national prejudices, to learn to study men by their resemblances and their differences, and to acquire a universal knowledge which was not that of one century or one country exclusively, but being that of all times and all places, was, so to speak, the universal science of the wise? (Rousseau 1755b: 160)

Here is Rousseau's vision of anthropology: "the universal science of the wise." Such a science cannot be constructed using the methods of the past, whereby adventurous travelers produced narratives that would be reflected and speculated on by armchair philosophers. Rather, we must turn our imagination to the future, when we can hope for the appearance of a new kind of anthropological researcher, one whom later centuries would know as the fieldworker, and whose synthesis of theoretical expertise and direct observation of peoples in every part of the world is conceived by Rousseau as a philosophical traveler.

> Suppose a Montesquieu, a Buffon, a Diderot, a Duclos, a D'Alembert, a Condillac and other men of that stamp were to travel to instruct their compatriots, observing and describing as only they know how, Turkey, Egypt, Barbary, the Empire of Morocco, Guinea, the land of the Kaffirs, the interior and the East coast of Africa, the Malabars, Mogul, the banks of the Ganges, the kingdoms of Siam, Pegu and Ava, China, Tartary and above all Japan, and then in the other hemisphere, Mexico, Peru, Chile, and Magellan lands, not forgetting the Patagonias, true and false; Tucamen, Paraguay if possible, Brazil; finally the Caribbean islands, Florida and all the savage countries—the most important voyage of all, and the one that would have to be undertaken with the greatest possible care. Suppose that these new Hercules, on their return from these memorable journeys, then wrote at leisure the natural, moral and political history of what they had seen, we ourselves would see a new world spring from under their pens, and we should learn thereby to know our own world. (Rousseau 1755b: 161)

This, then, is the promise of anthropology: to see a new world, and one that would help us to know our own. Its present underdevelopment results from the ignorance and prejudice of projecting our own familiar world, instead, into our representation of the Other. The promise of a new world that exploration and discovery seemed to offer has resulted in the reproduction of old images in new settings; but the true New World remains undiscovered as long as it has not emerged into the minds of Europeans and others who remain trapped in the localized consciousness of old, familiar ideas and representations, of not knowing and appreciating its newer and vastly wider horizons. Rousseau can sense the excitement but cannot see the overall shape or specific features of this new world; for, given his own critique of representations, he knows himself bounded as much as anyone else by the old preconceptions that would inevitably distort any construction he might project of what lies beyond. Anthropology, the "universal science of the wise," will necessarily broaden those limiting horizons; but its own emergence lies in the future.

And finally, as for the future, we should note that Rousseau has a quite different conception of the place of the "savage" than Lescarbot and others who saw them as part of the past, doomed to physical or cultural disappearance. For Rousseau, if time travel is impossible and civilized persons must go ahead into the future rather than back into the past, so also the direction of "savage" nations must be forward rather than back. And Rousseau, unlike some others, is by no means convinced of the inevitable triumph of European civilization, or of the necessary disappearance of "savage" ways of life.

> It is an extremely remarkable thing that after the many years that Europeans have spent tormenting themselves to convert the savages of the various countries of the world to their way of life, they have not been able yet to win a single one. . . . Nothing can overcome the invincible repugnance they have against adopting our morals and living in our style. If these savages are as unhappy as it is claimed, by what inconceivable depravity of judgement do they refuse steadfastly to civilize themselves in imitation of us and to live happily among us, whereas one reads in a thousand places that Frenchmen and other Europeans have voluntarily found refuge among these peoples, spent their whole lives there without being able to leave such a strange way of life, and we see sensible missionaries tenderly lamenting calm and innocent days spent among those much despised peoples? . . . In fact, after a few observations it is easy for them to see that all our labours are directed towards two objectives only: namely, commodities of life for oneself and consideration from others. But how are we to imagine the kind of pleasure a savage takes in spending his life alone in the depths of the woods, or fishing, or blowing into a bad flute, not knowing how to produce a single note from it, or troubling to learn how to do so?
> . . . I remember among others the story of a North American chief who was brought to the Court in England some thirty years ago. A thousand things were put before his eyes in the search for a present that would please him, but nothing could be found which he appeared to like. Our weapons seemed heavy and incommodious to him; our shoes hurt his feet, our clothes constrained him; he rejected everything. Finally, it was noticed that having taken a woolen blanket, he seemed to enjoy wrapping it round his shoulders. 'You would agree at least,' someone promptly said to him, 'that this article is useful?' 'Yes,' he replied, 'it seems to me almost as good as an animal skin.' He would not have said even that if he had worn them both under the rain.
> (Rousseau 1755b: 168–69)

The "savage," too, is a critic, because he is also a thinking man; like the Europeans, he has left forever the simple state of nature and can no longer unthinkingly embrace whatever fate may give him. He may deliberately decide to accept the gift of the blanket, perhaps as much or more for the sake of cultivating friendly relationships with the givers, for investigating their foreign values and motivations, or for the aesthetic pleasure of experiencing newness and difference, as for its "usefulness." In the emerging world of mercantile colonialism, eventually he might even choose to buy the blanket. But he is unlikely to buy the whole accompanying package of European cultural superiority. Given the apparently declining likelihood of universal genocide, "savages" would continue to live while their ways of life would change, as human lives always do; but they would not inevitably and globally be replaced by European culture, as long as other peoples had any freedom at all to think and make choices concerning their own destinies.

How could one say more clearly or simply that the future belongs, in all its unknown variety, to both? There is no need to enhance the narrative, or to ennoble the "savage" by putting flowery words or philosophical concepts in his mouth. Rousseau has had his horizons expanded by a simple, even if vicarious, act of observation: he is delighted to show his understanding by emulating the Indian chief's concise discursive style. Rousseau knows a fellow thinker and a fellow man when he sees one. No wonder he celebrates the Indian's punch line by joining in with an appreciative tag line of his own!

But even so, Rousseau's sympathetic intention may have led him into factual oversimplification. Bruce G. Trigger (1985: 204) says of the seventeenth-century Montagnais: "They wore much French clothing, finding woolen garments more convenient than skin ones, especially in wet weather." Trigger's conclusion has to be drawn by inference from the Jesuit sources he cites, with their less specific remarks about mixing European and Indian clothing because "there is no article of dress, however foolish, which they will not wear in all seriousness if it helps to keep them warm" (*Jesuit Relations* 7:9). Yet it is certainly true that wool retains body heat when wet and dries more quickly than a skin that is thoroughly soaked, as could happen under prolonged rainfall. Thus, if Rousseau was correct in principle in casting his "wet blanket" on smug assumptions of European superiority, he was at least oversimplistic in his projection of ethnographic results into cold and rainy climates he had never seen. After all, blankets did become both a major commodity in the American fur trade and an important early index of culture change—not only in the Northeast but also later in the Northwest, where the wet-weather gear of the early postcontact Makah included a protective bearskin worn over the blanket! (Swan 1868: 16, 60; see fig. 7).[3] So perhaps Rousseau was not so mistaken after all.

Wet blankets aside, it is at least clear that Rousseau made various misjudgments, not only factual but also ethical, in his pursuit of the ideals that find expression in his works. In pointing out Rousseau's contributions to anthropology, there is no need to idealize or ennoble him. His own *Confessions* attest to his ignoble treatment of his contemporaries, particularly women and his own children.[4] His philosophical and personal commitment to Euro-Christian individualism seems at times to be carried to pathological extremes. Thus, for example, the most serious challenges to his construction of the fictional "state of nature" eventually came not from the ethnological discipline he envisioned—for the world of expanded horizons whose promise he saw necessarily led to a chaos of seemingly infinitely expanding horizons, opening out onto vistas of new and unforeseeable worlds. However, the convergence of research in disciplines he had barely foreseen—archaeology and ethology—would furnish evidence that, in the first case, humans of the remotest discernible periods had been social beings living in mutually interdependent communities, even before the emergence of sedentism and agriculture; while, in the second, studies of primate bands would suggest that human ancestors had been social even before the emergence of humans as a distinct species. Rousseau argued that man in the state of nature had no more need of society than monkeys or wolves; but it has been precisely the wolf pack and the primate band that have opened up some of the most interesting issues of animal society and its relation to human ancestry. But twentieth-century research has also led to work on problems such as territoriality and archaeological research on bands of Kalahari Bushmen where sedentization correlates with increasing property accumulation and separation, with implications of breakdown of social equality and close relations, all of which seem to reflect Rousseauian processes and to vindicate other aspects of his analysis. There is no simple assessment we could make of even the most speculative and seemingly time-bound of his theories. Which may be true of any significant or interesting theory whatsoever.

There may even be some justice, as Chinard claims, in believing that Rousseau's ideas are unoriginal, derivative of his readings of ethnographers. In asserting that "he has sinned not by an excess of imagination, but by an excess of documentation. . . . The success of Jean-Jacques comes precisely from the lack of originality of his ideas" (Chinard 1913: 357–58), Chinard sees Rousseau as a promoter of ideas of *le bon sauvage* derived from travel narratives—surely, as we have seen, a distorted and trivialized perception—and as having "sinned" in assuming that Indians and Europeans shared a common humanity such that the history of one could possibly relate to the other, a judgment that seems to reflect the dehumanizing assumptions of the racist ideologies that mushroomed in France in the decades before Chinard (Todorov 1993). Nevertheless, there may be some truth to Chinard's general point, in that not just Rousseau's ethnographic information but also aspects of his critique were anticipated by earlier writers.

We may see hints of anticipations of Rousseau's critique in some of the authors he cites, such as Chardin on Persia and the Jesuits on China, who certainly criticized distortions in earlier works. A more powerful precedent is John Green's *New General Collection of Voyages and Travels* (1745–47; often mistakenly attributed to Astley, its publisher). Throughout this collection, Green engages in a dialogue with his authors by developing a critique that prefigures many of Rousseau's points. For example, when one of Green's authors says of the Javanese, "Without Doubt, formerly, they were Man-eaters," Green responds, "It is strange the Author should suggest such a Thing, without shewing any Reason for it. It is questioned by many, if there are, or ever were such people in the World; notwithstanding the Reports both of the Antients and Moderns, which they say are groundless, putting this among the Number of the Fictions of Travellers" (Green 1745–47: 1:285–86). Again and again, in notes throughout four large volumes, Green inserts comments such as "This must be a Falshood owing to the Prejudices or Inattention of Travellers" (2:32); or "The Ignorance or Malice of *Europeans*, generally speaking, hath made them misrepresent the People of distant Countries, and pronounce them *Atheists;* when, upon Examination, often it would be found, that they had better Notions of God, as well as Morality, than their Defamers" (1:549). Green's critique is clearly prior to Rousseau's and more extensively detailed; Rousseau's, on the other hand, is more unified and theoretically generalized. Green's collection was actually one of Rousseau's main ethnographic sources, translated into French as the *Histoire général des voyages* (Prévost 1746–92). However, the French edition not only systematically omitted Green's critical notes but also sometimes, as in the reference to Javanese cannibalism, deleted the offending part of the original text as well (Prévost 1746–92: 1:416). Rousseau thus worked not only without access to Green's critique but also with censored texts lacking key elements that could have contributed to his own. In such a context, Rousseau's critique and analysis can only appear more original and creative.

In the end, the points I have weighed against Rousseau seem minor. Many stories could indeed be told of Rousseau, some positive, some negative, and some, as in his argument for the rights of animals, that would arouse conflicting positive and negative responses in different audiences. The story I extract here from his writings is the clearest account I can imagine of his relationship to my two main questions: the representation of the "savage," where his role is complex, and the construction of anthropology, where his critiques and projective constructions play an inspirational role. He is an original synthesizer, who brings out clearly the significance of what others had separately and individually hinted. Rousseau brings the world of cultural diversity together into a vision of analytic and critical human unity. It was this unity that a later, harsher, and less humanistic opposition would oppose through its generation of the myth of the Noble Savage.

III

DISCURSIVE OPPOSITIONS
The "Savage" after Rousseau

7 The Ethnographic Savage from Rousseau to Morgan

FIGURE 8. CAROLINE PARKER,
IROQUOIS ETHNOGRAPHER.
Gä-hah,-no (Caroline Parker), native
Seneca ethnographer and research
collaborator of Lewis Henry Morgan
(Morgan 1851: 148).

So far, we have not succeeded in tracing any convincing appearances of the Noble Savage in the century and a half after Lescarbot—and least of all, it would appear, in the writings of Rousseau. This seems to be a strange contradiction of long-held scholarly beliefs concerning the pervasiveness of Noble Savage representations throughout the period; but in fact the scholarly picture may be beginning to shift toward a new balance more consistent with the results of our search. For example, Gordon Sayre (1997: 124), in his study of representations of American Indians in French and English colonial literature, observes, "The unpopularity of the Noble Savage trope appears to have actually made it less common in seventeenth- and eighteenth-century texts. Critics of works containing some of what were once considered the most famous Noble Savages have declared that they are in fact not to be found there."

But the possibility remains of a reemergence of the Noble Savage after Rousseau. If, as the myth would have us believe, Rousseau had been instrumental in the creation or popularization of the Noble Savage concept, we might expect his work to stand as a kind of watershed between earlier, relatively more negative or at least neutral, and later, idealized and romanticized, views of the "savage." This is not the case, either in the ethnographic or the philosophical literature. The same ambiguities, the same oppositions, the same dialectic of vices and virtues continue to dominate the literature after Rousseau as had done so before him. If there are changes of tone and emphasis, they result from new kinds of geographic and interpretive interests, and the most evident change is toward a more negative evaluation. Continuing to take the ethnographic writings on the American Indians as the primary source, let us touch on some of the new directions that emerged after Rousseau.

In this and the following chapters of this part, I selectively sample a chronological progression of works from each of the various genres—travel-ethnography, science, philosophy, popular and political literature—relevant to understanding the process that gave rise to the myth of the Noble Savage. For each of these genres, I begin each sweep of the radar scope at or slightly before Rousseau's *Discourse* to avoid coming in too late on the action, after a "post-Rousseau" situation had already arisen, on which the *Discourse* might already be suspected to have exerted some influence.

Abstract considerations of ideal preferences for a uniform chronological sample must obviously give way to the availability of actual works useful to the project. Thus, depending on the subject of the chapter, a time lag of up to several decades may be required for establishing a "pre-Rousseau" baseline from which to proceed in examining changes in the representational approaches of later works. For example, in the science chapter, I go back to 1732 for a pre-Rousseau example of a work by a leading scientist that can be usefully juxtaposed with later works, including some that highlight the possibility of opposing interpretations of the same peoples, and so, by extension, the constructedness of scientists' interpretations.

Such an approach helps us to see more clearly, despite the great differences of method and subject matter reflected in the various disciplines, the underlying similarity of the ideological currents of increasing negativity that flowed together into the generation of the myth of the Noble Savage.

From this standpoint, each chapter contributes, in its own very different way, to a multifaceted reflection on the rising currents of racial negativity that increasingly suffuse the writings of every discipline during the period after Rousseau.

THE TWO MINDS OF CHARLEVOIX

Toward the middle of the eighteenth century, perspectives on the American Indians began to undergo a perceptible change. We can see the effects of the change even in the work of an individual writer such as Pierre F.-X. de Charlevoix (1682–1761), who embodies much of the complexity and ambiguity of changing European views of the "savage." Charlevoix was a Jesuit priest who lived and taught in Canada in the first decade of the century, returned on a royal exploration mission in 1720–22, and twenty-two years after his return completed the *History and General Description of New France* that he published together with a travel-ethnography, the *Journal of a Voyage to North-America*, consisting of letters represented as having been written during his expedition two decades earlier (Bannon 1962). Although the "letters" may never have actually been sent, and were undoubtedly reworked at the time of publication twenty years later, they are so different from the *History* in tone and in their evaluation of the Indians that they can best be considered as a separate work reflecting ideas and attitudes more characteristic of their nominal date of composition than the later period when the two works were published together.

In the *Journal of a Voyage to North-America* (1720–22), Charlevoix might seem at first glance to have projected the very epitome of the ennoblement of the "savage" in his frequent praise of Indian ways in contrast to European, and even in his deployment of the rhetoric of nobility itself. In his *History* (1744b), by contrast, oscillating between the polarities of court and colonial intrigues, on the one hand, and "edifying" narratives of missionary conversions and Christian martyrdoms in the face of lurid atrocities, on the other, Charlevoix appears as an unrelenting critic not of Europeans but of Indians; and "these Savages" is repeatedly and exclusively used as an epithet of condemnation. When we compare the *Journal* and the *History*, oppositions of contrasting rhetoric and evaluations present themselves so strongly and repeatedly that we would almost certainly, if we did not know their authorship, attribute them to two opponents in an intellectual-political debate. As it stands, we have to wonder whether the oppositions between the two works simply reflect a personal change, a shift from youthful optimism and enthusiasm to a more jaded maturity, or whether other factors might account for the difference. There are, in fact, several such factors that deserve our attention.

In the first place, Charlevoix was hardly a young, naive newcomer to America at the time of his 1720–22 travels, having already lived and taught four years in Canada a decade previously and now approaching his fortieth year. Rather, we might seek the source of his enthusiasm in his implication in a particular kind of professionalism, that of the secret agent. Charlevoix was engaged by the king ostensibly to investigate the condition of missions in the French colonies but actually to gather intelligence concerning possible transcontinental trade routes to the Pacific, without arousing the suspicions of the English, competitors of the French for control of North American trade, or of French critics of excessive expenditures by the Crown (Bannon 1962). In this role, he assumed the function of a long line of spy-ethnographers, from John of Plano Carpini (1248) to Nicolas de Nicolay (1567–68) and beyond, including the necessity of not divulging his true mission but instead giving a heightened prominence to his ethnographic descriptions. His ostensible audience for the public part of his mission was the French nobility, personified in the Countess de Lesdiguieres, the supposed addressee of his letters. For such an audience, he projected an enthusiasm that highlighted the wonders of the New World, including its inhabitants, and indirectly the wisdom of the Crown in promoting its exploration. Central to this project was an appeal to the interests and ideals of the nobility.

By contrast, when Charlevoix wrote the *History* in 1744, he was committed to the emergent scholarly professionalism of the Enlightenment, which placed a high value not only on the systematic tabularization of factual knowledge but also on a certain standard of objectivity and detachment. It is no accident that a number of twentieth-century scholars have seen this work as the first modern, that is, professional, history of French Canada (Bannon 1962). Charlevoix's particular professional commitment here is that of the historian; but more specifically, his project was a comprehensive history of the Jesuit missions, including other studies on Japan and Paraguay. The contrast of the *History* with the *Journal* becomes more understandable when we consider that, unlike the noble audience of the earlier work, there was no need to "sell" America or its inhabitants to the Jesuits. Their commitment to the Indian missions was foreordained and driven by stimuli other than personal enthusiasm expressed in the rhetoric of nobility.

But twenty years before the *History*, in the *Journal*, we find one of the more interesting cases of the rhetoric of nobility since Lescarbot. To be sure, much of it will be familiar from other contexts. For example: "His mien, the tone of his voice, and the manner of his delivery, though without any gestures or inflections of the body, appeared to me extremely noble and calculated to persuade, and what he said must have been very eloquent" (Charlevoix 1720–22b: 2:10). Although this is the familiar trait-ascriptive, aesthetic nobility seen in other writings, the "extremely noble" seems to promise a new, more positive or "romantic" viewpoint. But it turns out that the heightened intensity here is an artifact of the English translation, the French original being the weaker "me parurent avoir quelque chose de noble," "appeared to me to have something of the noble" (1720–22a: 5:381). Still, it is one of the apparently rather rare cases in which the word *noble* is actually used in a French ethnographic narrative; and there are more such instances throughout the book. Again, many of these have an air of familiarity: "one is called the most noble, the other the most ancient" (1720–22b: 2:23); "the noblest matron of the tribe" (2:24); "this nation . . . is however one of the noblest in all Canada" (2:47); "the husband of this woman not being noble" (2:262). These and other instances are almost without exception cases either of aesthetic nobility or of the familiar some-are-more-noble-than-others rhetoric of the nobility of distinction. But the single exception seems to present us with the most interesting case of all.

In a discussion of the "Character of the Indians of *Canada*" (1720–22b: 2:77 ff.), in which he begins with a complimentary description of their physical strength, sensual acuity, and the vivacity and "beauty" of their imaginations, Charlevoix offers this extraordinary assessment: "Most of them have really a nobleness of soul and a constancy of mind, at which we rarely arrive, with all the assistance of philosophy and religion" (2:83). Here at last we seem to have a construction of "savage" nobility that equals Lescarbot in its universal pervasiveness and essentialist definitive quality, as well as in the strength of its positive rhetoric and its framing in terms of a standard against which Europeans are found comparatively wanting. A closer examination reveals that this is not quite the case; for, at least with regard to the dimension of global pervasiveness, "most of them" falls a bit short of the universal nobility of either Lescarbot's model or the Noble Savage myth. So it seems that, even here, some are still nobler than others. Still, perhaps, as a statistical approximation of universality in what we are coming to see as a complexly ambiguous ethnographic world, "most of them" may be close enough to satisfy ourselves that we have at last found a sufficiently satisfactory instance of the elusive Noble Savage here in a work of the eighteenth century, where the myth says we should.

But once again, a closer look turns an apparently clear match into clouded ambiguity. What is Charlevoix referring to here? In the next few paragraphs, we find that his "nobleness of soul" refers to the bravery of the Indians facing torture and death (1720–22b: 2:83–85). In fact, Charlevoix's "nobility of soul" is exactly the same nobility of stoic heroism under torture praised by his Jesuit contemporary Lafitau, who, as we recall, was directly quoting from Lescarbot in his characterization of the "nobility" of the warfare complex among the Indians. We should not be surprised that the two Jesuits, colleagues in the Canadian mission in the early eighteenth century, should have emphasized the same subject, since there is other evidence that Charlevoix had been reading or having discussions with Lafitau: "The Huron language has a copiousness, an energy, and a nobleness, which are scarce to be found united in any of the finest we know" (Charlevoix 1720–22b: 2:299; cf. Lafitau [1724: 2:263]: "The Huron language is noble, majestic and more regular than the Iroquois dialects"). But, since we know that Lafitau based his discussion of the nobility of warfare on Lescarbot, we might ask whether Charlevoix did likewise.

And it turns out that Charlevoix had also been reading Lescarbot, and quotes him in the *Journal* as an authority on the Indians (Charlevoix 1720–22b: 2:21). Moreover, in the *History*, Charlevoix reveals himself not only as a reader of Lescarbot, but as one of his most ardent admirers.

> This author has collected with much care all that had been written before him. . . . He seems sincere, well informed, sensible, and impartial. (Charlevoix 1744b: 1:75)

> Marc Lescarbot, an advocate from Paris, a man of ability . . . had had a curiosity, quite unusual in men of his profession, to see the New World; and he was highly instrumental in putting and retaining things in this happy state. He encouraged some; he touched the honor of others; he won the goodwill of all, and spared himself in naught. He daily invented something new for the public good. And there was never a stronger proof of what advantage a new settlement might derive from a mind cultivated by study, and induced by patriotism to use its knowledge and reflections. We are indebted to this advocate for the best memoirs we possess of what passed before his eyes. . . . We there behold an exact and judicious writer, a man with views of his own, and who would have been as capable of founding a colony as of writing its history. (Charlevoix 1744b: 1:257–58)

Given Charlevoix's profound admiration for Lescarbot, we might expect to find further signs that Lescarbot has stimulated his use of the rhetoric of nobility. And, indeed, we find such evidence just where we might expect it, in the discussion of hunting: "Thus hunting is no less noble amongst these nations than war; and the alliance of a good hunter is even more courted than that of a famous warriour, as hunting furnishes the whole family with food and raiment, beyond which the Indians never extend their care" (1720–22b: 1:182).

Once again, when we encounter the strongest traces of the Noble Savage in the ethnographic literature, and particularly the rhetoric of nobility in French writing, it turns out that we are still hearing the reverberations of Lescarbot. As such, the echoes that come through to us in these later writers are inevitably weaker, vestigial resonances of the full force of Lescarbot's argument, so embedded in the ideology of its own time. Charlevoix, for example, continues the dialectic of virtues and vices to the point where it is clear that, even in 1721, his admiration for their good qualities is hardly unconditional.

> We must however agree that what we most admire in the Indians is not always to be attributed to pure virtue; that their natural disposition and their vanity, have a great share in it, and that their brightest qualities are obscured by great vices. These very men who appear to us so very contemptible at first sight, hold all the rest of mankind in the greatest contempt; and have the highest notion of themselves. The proudest of all were the Hurons, till success puffed up the Iroquois and inspired them with a haughtiness, which nothing has hitherto been able to tame, together with a brutal ferocity which always constituted their chief characteristick. (Charlevoix 1720–22b: 2:87)

Moreover, Charlevoix is attracted less to Lescarbot's idealization of feudalism than to the eighteenth-century attractors of liberty and equality, which he sees as strongly present in "savage" life, but not in such a way as to frame them in the rhetoric of nobility.

> In a word, these Indians are perfectly convinced, that man is born free, and that no power on earth has a right to infringe his liberty, and that nothing can compensate the loss of it: and it has been found a very difficult matter to undeceive even the Christians among them, and to make them understand how, by a natural consequence of the corruption of our nature, which is the effect of sin, an unbridled liberty of doing mischief differs very little from obliging them to commit it, because of the strength of the byass which draws us to it; and that the law which re-

strains us, causes us to approach nearer to our original state of liberty, while it appears to take it from us. (Charlevoix 1720–22b: 2:30)

Liberty, then, was problematic rather than paradigmatic, at least to someone with Charlevoix's commitment to obedience and discipline. As the Age of Revolution approached, crested, and shaded over into the Terror, Napoleonic imperialism, and conservative reaction, the idea of liberty would oscillate between positive and negative polar extremes, sometimes praised, sometimes condemned, but always charged with a certain amount of opposition and resistance to concepts and rhetorics of nobility. In the meantime, we find that the rhetoric of "savage" nobility retains its old Lescarbotian linkages to warfare and class superiority instead of rebonding itself to, or reframing itself in terms of, the emerging philosophical and political discourses of the eighteenth century. Liberty and nobility were, after all, a rather unlikely mixture, although we will again encounter their confluence, in an interpretation strangely reminiscent of Charlevoix, in one of the most famous works on the ethnography of the "savage" by Lewis Henry Morgan (see below).

As for Charlevoix's own apparent double-mindedness about the Indians in his earlier and later publications, we can now see that the apparent enthusiasm of the earlier *Journal* was never so single-minded as its isolated bits of Lescarbot-derived rhetoric of nobility might have led us to believe. There were always undercurrents of negativity and condemnation lurking beneath the surface optimism of its propagandistic facade; and, we might equally suspect, there remained currents of optimism and admiration hidden below the repeated epithets he later pronounced on "these savages" from the lofty chair of the ecclesiastical historian as he wrote the *History*. If not, after all, why publish the two works together, so that the tone of one counterbalances that of the other? And yet their opposition evokes a historical progression from a lighter to a darker time, in which each work speaks as its own contemporary witness; and their sequential juxtaposition delineates a vector leading toward progressively unhappier constructions of the "savage."

VANISHING SAVAGES, DIMINISHING NOBILITY

Recognizing that the vestigial and constantly diminishing echoes of Lescarbot's Noble Savage rhetoric linger most perceptibly in the Jesuit writings on the Canadian Indians of New France, we may wonder to what extent Charlevoix's growing pessimism about the Indians derived from his awareness of the increasingly problematic status of the New France colony and of the Jesuits themselves. Charlevoix certainly expresses considerable uneasiness about the former, as the colony was increasingly threatened by English competition; and, indeed, in the second decade after the publication of his *History*, New France would come to an end with the English conquest of Canada. But in the following decade, the Jesuits themselves would also disappear, first suppressed by legislation in the Catholic kingdoms of Europe and then dissolved as a religious order by papal decree. With the colony and the order went the policy of "Frenchifying" the Indians by assimilating them as near-equals in what was effectively a French-Indian confederation, recognizing and promoting their "good" qualities as a basis for the limited amount of political and religious tutelage they would need to share in the future development of what Lescarbot had conceived of as the new Golden Age in America.

Now, with Anglo-American dominance of the colonial enterprise uncontested, new policies and attitudes would arise in which the Indians, once useful allies in the struggles between rival colonial powers, had passed their usefulness and become obstacles to a process of expansion that did not include them. From such a standpoint, the growing perception of Indians as a "vanishing race" may have constituted wishful thinking; but it was a wish that could be hurried to practical realization, ideologically energized by a strongly negative shift in rhetorical constructions of the "savage." This shift appears most strikingly in the French travel-ethnographic literature toward the end of the century, as French travelers, now outsiders to the Euro-American enterprise, visited the domains of their new allies in the American Revolution and learned to see the Indians through their eyes. For example, François-Jean, marquis de Chastellux (1734–88), a scholar-soldier who had published widely acclaimed books on philosophy, poetry, and music, serving as a general of the French army sent to help the Americans in their revolution, visited the Iroquois borderlands in 1780 and described an Indian village and its residents:

> The Indian village Mr. Glen conducted me to is nothing but an assemblage of miserable huts in the woods, along the road to Albany. He took me into the hut of a savage from the Sault Saint Louis, who had long lived at Montreal and spoke good French. . . . In addition to the savage who spoke French, there was in this hut a *squah* (the name given to the Indian women), who had taken him as her second, and was bringing up a child by her first husband; two old men composed the remainder of this family, which had a melancholy and poor appearance. The *squah*

was hideous, as they all are, and her husband almost stupid, so that the charms of this society did not make me forget that the day was advancing and that it was time to set out. (Chastellux 1780–82: 1:208)

In this account, we seem to be hearing of a settlement of displaced Indians; but the narrative is as uninformative as it is unsympathetic. Here we certainly have nothing of the rhetoric of nobility, the Golden Age, or even the moderating balance of the dialectic of vices and virtues. Rather, we have only vituperative denunciation, apparently driven mainly by a visceral aesthetic reaction, insofar as we can guess at a cause beyond unthinking ethnocentric prejudice and aristocratic contempt for the poor. If the Indian's "good French" was taken advantage of for any meaningful communication, we do not hear of it; perhaps the soldier-philosopher, friend to Voltaire and member of the French Academy, was unable to think of anything to say? His own firsthand observations being limited to this momentary spasm of aesthetic-literary nausea, he goes on to represent the Indians according to his understanding of the viewpoint of "the Americans":

> The savages of themselves therefore would not be too much dreaded, were they not supported by the English and the American Tories. . . . But their cruelty seems to augment in proportion to their decrease in numbers; it is such as to render it impossible for the Americans to consent to have them longer for neighbors; and a necessary consequence of a peace, if favorable to Congress, will be their total destruction or at least their exclusion from all the country this side of the lakes. Those who are attached to the Americans, and live in some manner under their laws, such as the Mohawks in the neighborhood of Schenectady and a part of the Oneidas, will ultimately become civilized, and be intermingled with them. This is what every feeling and reasonable man should wish, who, preferring the interests of humanity to those of his own fame, disdains the little artifice so often and so successfully employed, of extolling ignorance and poverty, in order to win acclaim in Palaces and Academies. (Chastellux 1780–82: 1:208–9)

The last, of course, is a dig at Rousseau, whose complexly ambivalent discussion of "savagery" was viewed as an obstacle by other "feeling and reasonable men" who accepted that the outcome of European-"savage" encounters should rightly be the assimilation of some and the "total destruction" of others. Toward the end of the century, we see the rise of a number of such two-pronged attacks, on the "savages," on the one hand, and on Rousseau, seen as their defender, on the other. Such attacks would furnish an important part of the basis for the construction of the myth of the Noble Savage; although, of course, at the time there was no attempt to connect Rousseau with the rhetoric of nobility, as he had not used it and the myth itself did not yet exist. Perhaps the most interesting example of such an attack is to be found in the writings of C. F. Volney.

VOLNEY AND THE RUINS OF SAVAGERY

Constantin François Chasseboeuf, comte de Volney (1757–1820), born a member of the minor nobility, had achieved fame through his travel-ethnography of Egypt and Syria (Volney 1787), a work that set new standards for the inclusion of precise scientific and economic data in its description of foreign places. From this landmark of objectivist realism, he seemed to transport himself to the opposite extreme with the publication of the *Ruins* (1791), a visionary work that begins with a meditation on the crumbled architectural monuments of desert kingdoms, proceeds to a visitation by an "apparition," "phantom," or "genius" who reveals the secrets of social degeneration in the growth of stupidity and ignorance, and ends with an imagined "General Assembly of the Nations" where attempts to resolve differences and achieve progress are stymied by religious intolerance and "fanaticism." A great legislator appears to the assembled peoples and announces that one nation has resolved to lead them out of their impasse by constructing a new kind of society based on reason and the "Law of Nature," which is then laid out as a kind of cross between a legal constitution and a religious creed for all to follow. The vanguard nation that will lead the others is, of course, revolutionary France; and the legislator is no other than Volney himself, by now a deputy in the National Assembly. A severe blow to this visionary ardor came, however, when Volney was arrested, imprisoned, and narrowly escaped the guillotine; and he left France for America with considerable disillusionment.

> In the year 1795, I embarked at Havre for America, with all the dreary feelings that flow from the observation and experience of persecution and injustice. Saddened by the past, anxious for the future, I set out for a land of freedom, to discover whether liberty, which was banished from Europe, had really found a place of refuge in any other part of the world. (Volney 1803: v–vi)

But it seems that Volney's phantoms would follow to haunt him wherever he went. Although he had planned to settle in America, an impending crisis gave rise to anti-French hostility and charges that he was a spy, so that he "was obliged to withdraw from the scene" and return to Europe in 1798, disillusioned even more with the real results, if not the ideal principles, of societies that attempted to base themselves on freedom and equality. It was in the intervening three years when, torn between his embitterment with postrevolutionary France and his visionary hopes for achieving the perfect state of European rationality in postrevolutionary America, that he wrote his treatise "On the Indians or Savages of North America" (in Volney 1803, Appendix 6).

> My stay at Vincennes afforded me some knowledge of the Indians, who were there assembled to barter away the produce of their red hunt. . . . This was the first opportunity I had of observing, at my leisure, a people who have already become rare east of the Allegheny. It was, to me, a new and most whimsical sight. . . .
>
> The men and women roamed all day about the town, merely to get rum, for which they eagerly exchanged their peltry, their toys, their clothes, and at length, when they had parted with their all, they offered their prayers and entreaties, never ceasing to drink till they had lost their senses. . . . We found them in the streets by dozens in the morning, wallowing in the filth with the pigs. (Volney 1803: 352–54)

This encounter with the seamier side of frontier trade-fair revelry and debauchery was enough to satisfy Volney's urge for direct scientific observation. Although he had pioneered a participant-observation approach to ethnography in his earlier work on the Bedouins of Egypt (Volney 1787: 1:377 ff.), he decided to forgo the opportunity in America.

> I at first conceived the design of spending a few months among them, as I had done among the Bedwins; but I was satisfied with this sample, and those the best acquainted with them assured me, that there was no Arabian hospitality among them: that all was anarchy and disorder. . . . They dwell separately, in mistrust, jealousy, and eternal animosity. With them, what they want they have a right to, and what they have strength enough to seize is their own. Besides, as they scarcely made provision for themselves, a stranger would run the risk of being starved. (Volney 1803: 354–55)

Hospitality was, of course, after warfare, the most-discussed feature of Indian life in almost every existing ethnography; and whatever difficulties and dangers previous travelers and missionaries had confronted in living with Indians, starvation was hardly the most prominent. Volney's narrative can be read to suggest either that, having decided not to undertake direct personal observation of the Indians, he was forced to fall back on indirect, hearsay evidence from the white Americans who traded with, despised, and made war upon them; or, as evidence that, having previously heard and accepted hostile white viewpoints, he had already decided the Indians were not worth his attention. In any case, his further contacts with Indians were limited to casual observations and to a series of conversations in January and February 1798 with a Miami chief at Detroit.

For this, he required the services of a certain Mr. Wells, who had lived as a captive in an Indian village for "twelve or fifteen years," learning "many of their dialects" (Volney 1803: 374, 356). Wells is represented in the narrative as an unrelenting critic of Indian character and customs, whose authoritative status supplies the basis for Volney's own negative interpretations. It may well be that the former captive felt some resentment against his former captors and a need to show his fellow whites that he had not "gone native" during his years with the Indians; for he denounces whites who voluntarily choose to live with Indians as "shallow libertines, idle and capricious," prone to "licentious indulgences with the squaws" due to their "vicious minds" (Volney 1803: 372). Perhaps in a dig at Volney, who prides himself that "being a Frenchman . . . lessened that suspicion and distrust which these people are apt to entertain of strangers" (Volney 1803: 358), Wells adds that most such vicious-minded turncoats are "Canadians," that is, French (Volney 1803: 372). Volney cannot fully agree with the suggestion of French perversity, seeking instead an explanation in the universal childishness of mankind.

> Yet the preference of a savage life is less common among grown men than among the young. Americans, who have been carried off at an early age, have sometimes become attached to this life, because the liberty in which children are indulged of running and playing about is more agreeable to them than the restraints of schools. . . . [A] few days will give them habits of idleness and independence. These are the primitive inclinations of man, and he turns to them mechanically. (Volney 1803: 371–72)

The implication is that the Indians themselves were the captives of childish impulses, a charge that would increasingly be levied against them in the nineteenth century. Nevertheless, Volney is forced to agree that Wells's suggestion of French susceptibility to corruption by the allure of savage life was substantiated by what he himself had "already heard from men of sense and experience."

> I learned from all these persons, that the Canadians, or men of French descent, were much more apt to make this exchange, than the men of British or German blood. The latter bear a violent antipathy to the Indians, which is encreased by the cruelty these people exercise upon their captives. They have a particular repugnance to the Indian females, which the French have not. (Volney 1803: 371)

Thus perhaps Volney, no less than his translator, is concerned to demonstrate his own loyalty to the attitudes of Anglo-Saxon society, with its "violent antipathy" to and "repugnance" for the Indians, in which he finds himself also a potential object of suspicion and hostility. But, in any case, Wells's role as translator gave him considerable control over the shaping of the hearsay information from which Volney would construct his representation of the Indians and their way of life.

The third participant in the dialogues, the Miami chief Mishikinakwa, or Little Turtle, is far from the least interesting of the three. As the great war chief of the Miamis, he had led them to victories against American armies from 1780 until their surrender in 1795 (Callender 1978: 687), and then, having "had the wisdom to persuade his tribe to peaceable measures," he had lived among the whites long enough to accustom himself to wearing European-style clothing, acquired the ownership of a cow from whose milk his wife churned butter, and even traveled to the U.S. capital at Philadelphia to get help from the government and the Quakers in establishing agriculture among his people (Volney 1803: 356–57, 360–61, 378–79). Volney represents him as one who had carefully observed white customs and could comment thoughtfully on the differences between them and the Indians' way of life. Little Turtle even appears as something of an Enlightenment rationalist-environmentalist in his anthropological thinking, criticizing theories of Indian migrations from Asia (363) and asserting the environmental basis of human physical variety (362). He seems to stand as Volney's answer to Lahontan's Adario; and Volney also relies on his authority, as interpreted by Wells, for his construction of a negative image of the "savage."

What the disillusioned, expatriate philosopher actually learned from the defeated, displaced chief, as mediated by the repatriated captive translator, is this:

> Here we have an Indian, who, in spite of the prejudices of his education, of prejudices sanctioned by the ancient and universal habits and opinions of his countrymen, has had penetration enough to discover the essential basis of the social state in the cultivation of the earth, and in landed property: for there can be no regular cultivation without a stable right of property. (Volney 1803: 385)

A naked philosopher, indeed; and a worthy successor to Adario! Volney is nevertheless reaching rather far here, for Little Turtle, as cited by Volney (1803: 384–85) to support this conclusion, says nothing about property rights; his speech is rather about the whites' ability to sustain a greater population on a smaller agricultural land base than the Indians required for hunting. But Volney requires the inference about property rights to set up Little Turtle as his proxy for an attack on Rousseau.

> Let any one compare this sketch with the speculations of Rousseau, who maintains that the introduction of exclusive property was the first corrupter of manners, and who deplores that folly and infatuation which prevented the savage from pulling up the first stake, as a sacrilegious restraint upon his natural liberty. Let him consider to which the most credit is due; a man situated like Little Turtle, who has spent fifty years in the management of public affairs, in governing turbulent and jealous minds, with acknowledged skill and address, and has fully experienced the benefits and evils of both ways of life; or a humble individual like Rousseau, who never had the care of any public business, and knew not even how to manage his own; who, having created for himself an airy and fantastic world, knew as little of the society of which he was born a sequestered member, as of Indians.[1] (Volney 1803: 386)

If ever there was a case of the American Indian elevated to the state of a "naked philosopher" able to outshine his European philosophical counterparts, this is certainly it. Little Turtle, the seasoned manager of public affairs, the experienced traveler and comparativist thinker, far outshines the ignorant, incompetent, and mendacious leading light of French Enlightenment philosophy. Volney goes on to lament the sad waste of Rousseau's efforts.

> What a pity it is that this author embraced a bad cause, as his talents would have been proportionably more useful and successful in the cause of truth, and he might have had ample scope in declaiming against the genuine corruptions of society. If he had drawn a true picture of savage life . . . (Volney 1803: 387)

And he proceeds with a long list of might-have-beens:

> . . . he would thus have proved that civilisation is only that state of human society, in which persons and property are carefully protected. . . . He might have shown, that if civilised communities have vicious and depraved members, they are . . . merely vestiges and remnants of that barbarous condition from which all nations arose. . . . [H]e might have maintained that the arts . . . are proofs of civilisation, and indications of the prosperous conditions of a nation. Yet he might have produced examples from Italy and Greece, to show that these arts may flourish un-

der licentious democracy, and under military despotism, which are both
equally savage states. (Volney 1803: 388–89)

Etc., etc. The litany is a clear echo of Volney's introduction to his own book,
in which he constructs a similarly lengthy, rambling list of all the things
that he himself might have written about, if the circumstantial rise of
American-French hostilities had not prevented him from completing a
longer residence and more extensive research in the United States. Obviously, at this point in his life, Volney's imagination is dominated by regret-
ful contemplations on what might have been, weighed against the disappointments of what actually is.

But he is, at least, quite clear in his own mind that the antidote to savagery, revolutionary chaos, and "licentious democracy" is the sanctity of
property rights, a position that makes Rousseau a particularly apt emblematic embodiment of all that is wrong with the world. Rousseau represents
the threat of a regression to a savagery that menaces the very existence of
property, the basis of civilization endangered not only by "savages," misguided philosophers, and revolutionists but also by the communalistic tendencies of the common people of Europe.

> To the same cause are owing the poverty and rudeness of the people
> who inhabit the *commons* of Brittany. The evils produced by this state
> of things, in Great Britain, have been forcibly displayed by sir John
> Sinclair, to whose speculations on this subject I refer the reader. In
> Corsica, waylaying and murder has become, on this account, more fre-
> quent: the land being a desert, affords opportunities which otherwise
> would be wanting. The abolition of these common rights is the first
> step towards civilising this island. (Volney 1803: 397–98)

Here we see the appearance of a theme that will assume increasing
prominence in the nineteenth century and play an important role in the
rise of the myth of the Noble Savage: the threat to property ownership and
established privilege represented by the common people and their conse-
quent equivalence with savages as an antithesis to civilization. No wonder
that Volney does not couch his damnation of Rousseau and the savages in
terms of the rhetoric of nobility; for the danger they represent is embodied
in its very antithesis.

But what, then, does Volney's ethnographic research, based on secondary sources and the problematically mediated dialogues with his displaced war chief/philosopher of the Miamis, tell him about the nature of
"savage" life? He cites his secondary sources to evoke lurid descriptions

of scalping and tortures (Volney 1803: 401–2), in which he finds nothing "noble" but only further evidence of the "religious fanaticism" (403) on which he had blamed the universal decline of civilizations in the *Ruins*. "After this," he says, "let romantic dreamers boast of the mildness and purity of their man of nature" (402). He sees the parallel, noticed by others from Lescarbot through Lafitau and beyond, between the Indians and the classical societies of Greece and Rome (410 ff.); but for him, it has a darker significance than for his predecessors.

> A very interesting and instructive parallel might be drawn between the savage nations of America and the primitive states of Italy and Greece. It would dissipate a great number of illusions, by which our judgment is misled in the ordinary modes of education. We should be enabled to form just notions of the *golden age,* when men roamed about naked, in the woods of Thessaly and Hellas, feeding upon herbs and acorns. We should see, in the early Greeks, just such savages as those of America. . . . We should see the origin of that pride and ostentation, treachery and cruelty, sedition and tyranny, which the Greeks display, in every period of their history. . . . Since, of late, we have been seized with a passion for imitating these people, and regard their morals and manners, like their poetry and arts, as the models of all perfection, we should, finally, perceive that we are worshipping the spirit of a rude and barbarous age. (Volney 1803: 413–15)

As for the state of savagery itself:

> Thus it appears, that the virtues of the savage are reduced to mere courage in danger, to contempt of pain and death, and patience under all the evils of existence. These, no doubt, are useful qualities: but they relate to the individual himself, they centre in his safety or felicity, and have no relation to the benefit of others. They are indications of a life of danger and distress; a state of society so depraved, that its members look not for succour and sympathy to each other, but are driven, for solace, into despair or indifference. Of the aid or compassion they cannot procure they make themselves independent, and what they cannot get they learn not to wish, and when they cannot live they consent to die. . . .
>
>   More advantageous notions cannot reasonably be formed of Indian liberty. He is only the slave of his wants, and of Nature, froward and unkind. He has neither food nor rest at command. He must continually encounter fatigue, hunger and thirst, heat and cold, and every inclement vicissitude. His ignorance engenders a thousand errors and superstitions, unknown to civilised nations, of which his tranquillity is the hourly victim. (Volney 1803: 408–10)

Remembering Volney's elevation of his philosophical informant, Little Turtle, to a position of superiority over scholars of the French Enlightenment, we sense something of a rhetorical shift here. But this is the good news, Volney's peculiar, idiosyncratic approximation of the dialectic of virtues and vices. The bad news is a full frontal confrontation with the naked realities of "savage" life.

> The American *hunter*, who has daily occasion to kill and to eat the slain, by whom every animal is regarded as prey which he must be quick to seize, has imbibed, of course, an errant, wasteful, and cruel disposition. He is akin to the wolf and the tyger.—He unites with his fellows in troops, but not in fraternities. A stranger to property, all the sentiments springing from a family are unknown to him. Dependent on his own powers, he must always keep them on the stretch: and hence a turbulent, harsh, and fickle character; a haughty and untractable spirit, hostile to all men. He is constantly vigilant, because danger is ever present, and always ready to hazard a life which at best is held by so frail a tenure; he is equally indifferent to the past, which has been destitute of comfort and security, and to the future, from which there is nothing better to hope; and, lastly, he enjoys an existence concentering itself in the present moment. Such is the private, and from such is formed the national character. Always in want, yet thriftless; and always greedy, yet improvident, their situation leads them to extend their rights of hunting, and to encroach upon their neighbours. Hence a more warlike spirit towards strangers; while at home their imperfect ties, social and domestic, give birth to a democracy, turbulent and terrible, or, more accurately speaking, to a pure anarchy. (Volney 1803: 395)

Thus speaks the troubled refugee from the turbulence and terrors of the visionary hopes of democratic liberation that he had seen degenerate into anarchistic violence and bloodshed. No wonder his mind is constantly haunted by the images of dangerous, predatory beasts. What dreams Volney must have had. And the bestial imagery continues to dominate his construction of the nature of the "savage":

> They likewise resemble in having a mouth shaped like a shark's, the sides lower than the front, the teeth small, regular, white, and very sharp, like the tyger's. (Volney 1803: 364)

> They are reduced to subsist, like the wolf, on roots and the bark of trees. . . . When, after a long fast, they light on prey, a deer, bear, or buffaloe, they fall on it like vultures. (Volney 1803: 369)

> He is like those animals, who defend themselves with fierceness and obstinacy, when assailed in their last retreat. (Volney 1803: 403)

He further says:

> These men are in the state of wild animals, which cannot be tamed af-
> ter they have reached a mature age. The missionaries have been long
> ago convinced of this, and they all agree that this people can only be
> changed by taking them from infancy, nay, even from the birth, as we
> take birds we wish to discipline, from the nest. This passion for inde-
> pendence, that is, for doing nothing, is so strong among mankind, that
> the mechanics who adventure from Europe to America, if they have not
> skill to thrive pretty soon in the towns, generally apply their little
> earnings to buying a few acres in the country. . . . Cutting down trees
> being rather toilsome, they soon relinquish the task, and mingle with
> their labour the diversions of shooting and fishing. In short, they be-
> come half savages. (Volney 1803: 377–78)

Thus the hermeneutic circle reaches its closure with the reintroduction
of the "mechanics," the common people, who become the equivalents of
the beasts and "savages." We will hear more of this equivalence in the
coming century.[2]

MORGAN AND THE ENNOBLING EFFECTS OF EVOLUTION

American independence and rapid postwar expansion accelerated the processes of displacement and decimation of the eastern U.S. Indian populations, and the accompanying disruptions of their way of life, that had contributed to general acceptance of negative stereotypes such as the polemic
representations of Chastellux and Volney. Against the prevailing ideology
and practice of taming the wilderness, the "savage" seemed to be in a state
of inevitable decline or retreat. Indeed, the northeastern Indians, the original prototypes of the Noble Savage, could no longer be credibly represented as very "wild" at all; and, for those interested in the observation of
"savagery," interest shifted to peoples farther to the West. For the first half
of the nineteenth century, the greatest excitement focused on the discovery of the nomadic buffalo-hunting peoples of the newly acquired Louisiana Purchase territories, extending from the Mississippi across the Great
Plains to the Rockies.

In the decades of increasing negativity and declining ethnographic excitement after the middle of the preceding century, there was also a perceptible decline in ethnographic originality. In the late eighteenth and early
nineteenth century, we do not find the innovation, experimentation, and
exploration of new representational approaches that had so variously characterized the works of writers such as Lescarbot, Lahontan, or Lafitau. But

toward the middle of the nineteenth century, innovations once more began to appear in the ethnographic writings on the Indians. One such innovation was the participant-observation approach to ethnography emphasized by writers such as Charles Murray and George Catlin (see chap. 10 below). Another was the construction of a careful and systematic ethnographic program of research based on long-term acquaintance and collaboration with members of the group being studied, together with a sophisticated theoretical approach to anthropology. The outstanding example of this is the work of Lewis Henry Morgan (1818–81).[3]

Morgan, whose *League of the Ho-dé-no-sau-nee, or Iroquois* (1851) raised ethnography to a new height of professionalism, was a lawyer-ethnographer who combined ethnographic interests with a practical commitment to providing the Iroquois with legal and political support against corporate attempts to divest them of their remaining lands. Energized by this ideological commitment, he wrote his major ethnographic study with the explicit intent of evoking a more positive public attitude to the people he depicted (fig. 8).

> To encourage a kinder feeling towards the Indian, founded upon a truer knowledge of his civil and domestic institutions, and of his capabilities for future elevation, is the motive in which this work originated. . . . Born to an unpropitious fate, the inheritors of many wrongs, they have been unable, of themselves, to escape from the complicated difficulties which accelerate their decline. To aggravate these adverse influences, the public estimation of the Indian, resting, as it does, upon an imperfect knowledge of his character, and tinctured, as it ever has been, with the coloring of prejudice, is universally unjust.
>
> The time has come in which it is befitting to cast away all ancient antipathies, all inherited opinions; and having taken a nearer view of their social life, condition and wants, to study anew our duty concerning them. (Morgan 1851: ix–x)

In pursuing this project of the construction of ethnographic knowledge as an aid to resistance against ignorant prejudice and injustice, Morgan certainly makes more use of the rhetoric of nobility than the purveyors of negativistic stereotypes; but not in the way that the Noble Savage myth would lead us to expect. Many of Morgan's references to nobility are to the nobility of distinction, with its familiar "some are more noble than others" constructions.

> Notwithstanding the equality of rights, privileges and powers between the members of this body of sachems [chiefs], there were certain discriminations between them, which rendered some more dignified than

others. The strongest illustration is found in the Onondaga sachem, *To-do-dä'-ho,* who has always been regarded as the most noble sachem of the League. . . . Down to the present day, among the Iroquois, this name is the personification of heroism, of forecast, and of dignity of character; and this title has ever been regarded as more illustrious than any other, in the catalogue of Iroquois nobility. (Morgan 1851: 67–68)

In fact, Morgan is not an advocate of the general nobility of "savages." To understand his position, we must appreciate how much he shows himself to be the heir of the sociocultural evolutionists of the eighteenth century. As such, it is not surprising that his concept of the noble belongs to the last and highest evolutionary stage rather than the "savage" state that lies the closest to nature.

Modern political writers also recognize three species [of government], as laid down by Montesquieu: the despotic, the monarchical, and the republican. . . . The order of their origination suggests an important general principle; that there is a regular progression of political institutions, from the monarchical, which are the earliest in time, on to the democratical, which are the last, the noblest, and the most intellectual. (Morgan 1851: 129)

To a certain extent, the savage state of society, with its lesser development of constraining institutions, provided a high degree of individual and group freedom that could serve as a basis for movement toward the higher, democratic forms of social organization: "The spirit which prevailed in the nations and in the Confederacy was that of freedom. The people appear to have secured to themselves all the liberty which the hunter state rendered desirable. They fully appreciated its value, as is evinced by the liberality of their institutions" (Morgan 1851: 138).

However, for Morgan, as for his eighteenth-century evolutionist predecessors, peoples in a "primitive" state of nature were enslaved by it, deceived by the illusory appeal of its apparently unbounded individual freedom, with little hope of advancing to the more dynamic and mature kind of freedom that characterized institutional democracy of the higher stages.

There was, however, a fatal deficiency in Indian society, in the nonexistence of a progressive spirit. The same rounds of amusement, of business, of warfare, of the chase, and of domestic intercourse continued from generation to generation. There was neither progress nor invention, nor increase of political wisdom. Old forms were preserved, old customs adhered to. . . . The hunter state is the zero of human society, and while the red man was bound by its spell, there was no hope of his elevation. (Morgan 1851: 142–43)

The irony of this characterization of "the hunter state" as "the zero of human society" appearing in an ethnography of the Iroquois is, of course, that the Iroquois were not subsistence hunters but agriculturalists. Their hunting, like that of the Euro-Americans, was a secondary dietary supplement to their primary mode of subsistence. But Morgan needed an example of hunting peoples to support his own intellectual movement from a rather conventionally eighteenth-century evolutionary progressivist viewpoint toward his later, more fully developed evolutionary theories, in which the Iroquois would assume a place in the lower ranks of barbarism (Morgan 1877: 14, 118), a quantum step higher than the "savages" who were characterized by their exclusive dependence on hunting.

In the meantime, the flat-earth theory of reduction of all native Americans to "the hunter state" provided a useful, if fictionally distorted, point of departure for navigating the precarious terrain separating the apparent freedom of the Iroquois from that of Euro-American democracy, with its inherent claims to superiority.

> It would be difficult to describe any political society, in which there was less of oppression and discontent, more of individual independence and boundless freedom. The absence of family distinctions, and of all property, together with the irresistible inclination for the chase, rendered the social condition of the people peculiar to itself. It secured to them an exemption from the evils, as well as denied to them the refinements, which flow from the possession of wealth, and the indulgence of the social relations.
>
> At this point the singular trait in the character of the red man suggests itself, that he never felt the "power of gain." . . . This great passion of civilized man, in its use and abuse his blessing and his curse, never roused the Indian mind. It was doubtless the great reason of his continuance in the hunter state; for the desire of gain is one of the earliest manifestations of progressive mind, and one of the most powerful passions of which the mind is susceptible. It clears the forest, rears the city, builds the merchantman—in a word, it has civilized our race. (Morgan 1851: 138–39)

Thus what seems to begin as a celebration of Iroquois freedom, which we might be inclined to think would be natural in a proponent of early American democracy (Bieder 1986: 196 ff.), turns into an unfavorable comparison with the ambivalently compromised, but ultimately more highly exalted, progressivism of "civilized man." The critical evaluation of the "savage" state is reminiscent of Rousseau; but Morgan's less critical view of civilization places the two stages in a more unequal relationship. By comparison with the triumphant march of civilized progress, the Iroquois are impoverished and retarded, frozen in the childish gratifications of the past rather than leaping forward to shape and control the future.

Moreover, we see in this comparison the continuation of the process heralded by Volney by which the Golden Age would lose its glitter, receding into a tarnished mythological shabbiness by comparison with the emergent glories of the capitalist-industrialist age of the Gold Standard and the frontier gold rushes. Indeed, Morgan's fully developed evolutionary model of two decades later would project a symbolic reversal of the traditional Golden Age myth, with its regressive decline from an age emblematized by the "noblest" of metals, gold, through successively more degraded ages of silver, bronze, and iron. By contrast, in Morgan's (1877: 8 ff.) model, based in part on a modification and elaboration of the "Three Age" classification developed by European archaeological theorists, there would be a progressive ascent from ages (or in Morgan's terms, "ethnical periods") associated with stone technology to the semiprecious bronze and then finally to the highest stage, iron. The low point of Classical-Renaissance teleochronology had become the apex of the evolutionary imagination—and the gold had vanished from the ideal model. With it vanished the golden luster of the "savage" state of nature.

Nevertheless, the very existence of evolution showed that it was possible for humans to advance and develop toward a higher state. Whether they actually did so depended in part on their access and response to "ennobling" influences tending toward their elevation to higher stages of civilization and political democracy, whether such influences emanated from within their society or were imported from the outside. The Iroquois, in fact, had developed influences of this kind, and so, though they could not *be* "noble"—for the highest state of nobility belonged to the highest stages of sociocultural evolution and was therefore incompatible with the low stage of savagery—they could nevertheless embody traits and processes that partook of the ennobling quality of the civilizing influences that moved all peoples toward a higher stage of development.

> While, therefore, it would be unreasonable to seek those high qualities of mind which result from ages of cultivation, in such a rude state of existence, it would be equally irrational to regard the Indian character as devoid of all those higher characteristics which ennoble the human race. (Morgan 1851: 141)

Indeed, for Morgan, nobility appears to be not so much a state as a potentiality, one that gave impetus to an evolutionary vector leading to progressively higher stages of cultural development and ennoblement. What, then, are these "higher characteristics which ennoble the human race"? It turns out that some of them, at least, are characteristics of a special and exemplary branch of humanity.

> The ennobling and exalting views of the Deity which are now held by enlightened and christian nations would not be expected among a people excluded from the light of revelation. In the simple truths of natural religion they were thoroughly indoctrinated, and many of these truths were held in great purity and simplicity. Such is the power of truth over the human mind, and the harmony of all truth, that the Indian, without the power of logic, reached some of the most important conclusions of philosophy, and drew down from heaven some of the highest truths of revelation. (Morgan 1851: 155–56)

Once again we recognize the vestigial influence of the idea of the Golden Age, with its familiar rhetoric of comparative negation (they have no revelation, no logic) and its characteristic attribution of a "natural religion" that approximates and anticipates Christianity despite its institutional absence. In a way that reminds us of late Renaissance writers such as Lescarbot and Dryden, Morgan's rhetoric of ennoblement is constructed on a base of universalized ethnocentrism and projects a vector pointing in the direction of a kind of virtual Europeanization.

> Whatever excellences the Iroquois character possessed are to be ascribed, in a great measure, to their beliefs, and above all, to their unfailing faith in the Great Spirit. By adhering to that sublime but simple truth, that there was one Supreme Being, who created and preserved them, they not only escaped an idolatrous worship, but they imbibed a more ennobling and spiritual faith, than has fallen to the lot of any other unchristianized people. (Morgan 1851: 181)

In this projection of monotheism and Christianity to universal evolutionary potentialities, we see the influence of the Jesuit writers, particularly Charlevoix, who were Morgan's primary sources of historical material on the Iroquois and their neighbors. However, even though religion was an important dimension of Morgan's evolutionary theory, he also saw similar tendencies in the development of secular and political institutions resulting from the "ennobling" tendencies universally shared by members of all human societies.

> Of the comparative value of these institutions, when contrasted with those of civilized countries, and of their capability of elevating the race, it is not necessary here to inquire. It was the boast of the Iroquois that

the great object of their confederacy was peace—to break up the spirit of perpetual warfare, which had wasted the red race from age to age. Such an insight into the true end of all legitimate government, by those who constructed this tribal league, excites as great surprise as admiration. It is the highest and the noblest aspect in which human institutions can be viewed; and the thought itself—universal peace among Indian races possible of attainment—was a ray of intellect from no ordinary mind. (Morgan 1851: 92)

All in all, Morgan provides one of the strongest examples of the use of the rhetoric of nobility since Lescarbot. We might wonder whether, with his background readings into the history of the northeastern tribes, Morgan had in fact encountered Lescarbot's writings. Unfortunately, Morgan's list of bibliographic references is brief and incomplete; and the only historical source he cites repeatedly other than Charlevoix is, rather surprisingly, the widely criticized work of Lahontan, in which he finds descriptions of ceremonies that he considers accurate enough to cite in support of his own observations among the Iroquois. However, although he does not specifically cite Lescarbot, Morgan, in reading Charlevoix, would have encountered Charlevoix's overwhelming admiration for Lescarbot and may well have been moved to explore Lescarbot's work for himself.

Whether or not this is the case, Morgan clearly adopts a significant part of his rhetoric of nobility from Charlevoix, as he does other theoretical emphases. For example, his assessment of the religious and philosophical achievements of the Iroquois closely parallels Charlevoix's language; while his critique of Indian concepts of freedom resembles Charlevoix's own critique enough to be considered a secularized generalization of it. Given Morgan's theoretical and rhetorical dependence on Charlevoix, and Charlevoix's own admiration and adoption of the rhetoric of nobility from Lescarbot, Morgan may provisionally be considered not only a secularized descendant of the Jesuit ethnographic tradition but also the ultimate, even though indirect, heir of Lescarbot's rhetoric of savage nobility.

We might also wonder whether there is any significance in the occurrence of two of the strongest cases of the rhetoric of nobility by two writers trained professionally as lawyers, each pleading the case of the Indians' physical survival in the face of Euro-American expansion and overwhelming culture change. We will encounter yet another case of a lawyer-ethnographer with a similar political agenda, who also exemplifies an exceptionally strong use of the rhetoric of nobility, in chapter 10.

Like some other evolutionary-oriented writers, Morgan engages in a kind of ethnographic time shifting that is opposite to the kind of dehistoricizing that some readers of Fabian's (1983) innovative critique of ethno-graphic detemporalization tend to overgeneralize into a stereotype of all nineteenth-century anthropology. Like most post-Enlightenment progres-sivist writers, Morgan (1851: 169) assumes a fundamental dichotomy be-tween the dynamic progressivism of civilization and the static, unchanging conservatism of earlier stages: "The worship of the Iroquois, it is believed, has undergone no important change for centuries. It is the same, in all re-spects, at this day, that it was at the commencement of their intercourse with the whites."

However, in contrast to the model projected by some followers of Fabian's critique onto all anthropologists of the period, although Morgan does in-deed repeatedly refer to Iroquois traditions and customs as unchanging, he nevertheless usually describes them not in the ethnographic present but in the past tense—even including practices he himself had recently witnessed and knew to be ongoing, living customs (e.g., Morgan 1851: 210, 223). The choice of tense is deliberate, a consequence of Morgan's own evolutionary views, according to which Iroquois customs were already a part of the past, soon destined to be dead and gone.

> Their council-fires, so far as they are emblematical of civil jurisdiction, have long since been extinguished, their empire has terminated, and the shades of evening are now gathering thickly over the scattered and feeble remnants of this once powerful League. Race has yielded to race, the inevitable result of the contact of the civilized with the hunter life. . . . The Iroquois will soon be lost as a people, in that night of im-penetrable darkness in which so many Indian races have been en-shrouded. Already their country has been appropriated, their forests cleared, and their trails obliterated. The residue of this proud and gifted race, who still linger around their native seats, are destined to fade away, until they become eradicated as an Indian stock. We shall ere long look backward to the Iroquois, as a race blotted from existence; but to remember them as a people whose sachems had no cities, whose reli-gion had no temples, and whose government had no record. (Morgan 1851: 145–46)

The emblematic features of civil jurisdiction, like the existence of the In-dian tribes themselves, would nevertheless endure through the continual renewal of challenges to tribal sovereignty over the next century and a half. In this respect, Morgan's deficiency as a prophet stands in stark contrast to his excellence as an ethnographer. Despite his positive assessment of the ef-fects of "ennobling" influences on aspects of Iroquois character and society and despite his political and legal advocacy on their behalf, Morgan's overall projection of the Iroquois' future seems to differ little from the purveyors of negative stereotypes. We see here a confluence of the current of post-Enlightenment pessimism with the emerging tide of racially centered anthropological discourse that was to characterize the century, progressively eroding whatever positive or relativistic tendencies had existed in previous generations of writers. Perhaps somewhat paradoxically, it was this rising tide of raciocentric negativism that would soon give rise to the myth of the Noble Savage.

8   Scientists, the Ultimate Savage, and the Beast Within

HIBOU

BOUC

FIGURE 9. THE BEAST WITHIN. Atavistic bestiality in the European lower classes, depicted by Charles Le Brun, from Camille Flammarion's *Le Monde avant le Création de l'Homme* (1886: 813).

The ethnographic literature of the late eighteenth and early nineteenth century shows a pattern of convergences: on the one hand, of the "savage" and his counterpart, the common man of Europe; on the other, of their representations with increasingly negative valorizations and rhetorical images of bestiality. We will see similar patterns in the scientific and philosophical writings of the period. While the "savages" may have represented an external threat, weakening and vanishing as they were pushed back beyond the expanding frontier, the lingering and more dangerous enemy turns out to be the beast lurking within civilized society itself. The nineteenth century would develop as an era of hidden monsters awaiting their opportunity to emerge and destroy, the vampires and werewolves from within and the increasingly bestialized "savages" from without. Ethnographic and scientific representations would increasingly find evidences of animality and atavism in "savages" and lower classes alike. We see, for example, the animal embodied in the savage "lower races" of humanity in the work of the American racist anthropologists Josiah C. Nott and George R. Gliddon (1854: 458–59; 1857: 548), and in the lower classes of "our own white race" in the reemergence of Charles Le Brun's seventeenth-century beast-man images in Camille Flammarion's *Le Monde avant la création de l'homme* (1886: 812–15; see fig. 9).

Volney would be far from the only one to be haunted by phantoms and premonitions, as native rebellions abroad and working-class revolts at home reared up, bared their claws, and slashed at the foundations of established privilege and dominance. The threat called for ruthless countermeasures, on the ideological as well as the military front.

Negative rhetoric was a vital ideological implement of the war against native and lower-class resistance; and its deployment gave new value to a search for the lowest types of humanity, which could be used as a base to construct and define the image of all potential opponents in the emerging atmosphere of us-them confrontations. There had always existed a kind of contest among European travel writers to discover, or to appropriate the authority for representing, the world's worst people—if only for the added sales value of new descriptions that were more vividly shocking than any previously available. For much of the first two centuries of the Age of Exploration, the leading contenders had been the Caribbean and South American "cannibals" and the Khoisan peoples, the "Hottentots" and "Bushmen," of southern Africa. In the eighteenth and nineteenth centuries, new explorations, colonial settlements, and investments of energy in interests ranging from economic to intellectual, all combined to widen the field of candidates considerably. The Australian Aborigines, the Fuegians, the Fijians, the "Digger" Indians of the Great Basin, the Inuit, the Samoyed, the people of Kamchatka, and large numbers of African peoples were described by competing authors as the "lowest," "most savage," "most brutal," "wildest," "least human," "most degraded," "most degenerate," and even "most demented" forms of humanity.

It was an ongoing contest that needed no winner, for it validated itself simply by the reiterated application of its own assumptions and procedures. Somewhere out there, everyone knew, there *had* to be a people that would constitute the "specimen" or "type" of the "savage"—not, indeed, in the scientific sense of being in any way typical, for the qualities sought were the most extreme, the most deviant from all imaginable norms. Rather

than a scientific type, the contest was to define an ideal type that, by its
perfect deviancy from the ideal of European civilization, would serve to
define the "savage" in clear, absolute opposition to itself. In its intellectual
dimension, the search for the "lowest type" of man proceeded from the
theories of eighteenth-century sociocultural evolutionary progressivism,
which, as we have seen in Rousseau, posited a sequence of development
from the "savage" state of the hunter-gatherer through agricultural to
"civilized" urban societies. Thus, with a few exceptions such as the Fijians,
whom William Mariner (1827) and others had identified as the new type
of the cannibal, most of the energy devoted to this quest for the worst of
humanity was focused on hunting and gathering peoples, whom everyone
knew to be the "most savage." To those who played this game, its rules
and increasingly negative intensity made discursive linkages between
"savages" and "nobility" increasingly unlikely and problematic, since the
search for the ultimate savage led by definition to the lowest humans, those
most removed from the high and ennobling virtues of civilization.

But the negativistic turn of European discourse on the "savage" also
marked a significant break with eighteenth-century progressivism. If the
new rhetoric of degeneracy and degradation meant anything beyond surface appearances, it signified a degradation of European hope and optimism,
as we have seen in Volney. And the newer, darker perceptions, even though
they continued to be projected outward onto the non-European Other, did
not simply affect the evaluation of the North American Indian. After all, if
the creative ethnographic energy that had been expended on the Indians
had reached any kind of explicit or implicit consensus, it was the convergence of widely varying works in representing the Indians as too complex
and, in the cumulative results of ethnographic writings, too well known to
support simple, speculative, one-sided evaluations. Now the interpretations of other peoples began to change as well, and the change reached as
far as the boundaries of Europe itself.

EUROPEAN "WILD MEN": LINNAEUS'S
SENSE OF WONDER AND AN ACERBIC REACTION

Since the late Renaissance, when the concept of a "European" identity began to replace declining conceptions of "Christendom," the construction of
"Europe" had been recognized by its more reflective participants as problematic (Heylyn 1629: 27–29). Physically, the "continent" that existed as
a peninsular appendage of a much greater Eurasian landmass had uncertain
boundaries, the political and military consequences of which provided a vi-

FIGURE 10. SAAMI CAMP.
Reindeer herding camp of the Saami, late eighteenth century, as
depicted by Giuseppe Acerbi (1802: 2:107).

tal impetus for defining the limits of Europe, even as they clouded the quest
for clear and unambiguous results. Culturally, the construction of a European identity was achieved by setting up a tripartite contrast between the
"European," the "Oriental," and the "Savage"; but again, the problem was
determining where one ended and the other began. At the margins of Europe were, and are, the peoples whose identity was debated at the centers,
sometimes included, often excluded from the discourse and politics of Eu-
ropeanness: the Moors and the Basques, the Mediterranean island peoples,
the Irish, the Slavs, and the Saami or "Lapps" of northern Scandinavia
(fig. 10).

The Saami and their country had seemed so exotic that Heylyn (1629:
333) had been able to say of them that they "use to give worship and divine
honour all the day following to that living creature what ere it be, which

they see at their first going out at their doores, in a morning"—the same story that had been told of people in India by the great liar Mandeville, among others. Even in 1732, when the young naturalist Linnaeus (Carl von Linne, 1707–78) traveled through Lapland for scientific study and research, he felt he had entered an exotically different world.

> When I reached this mountain, I seemed entering on a new world; and when I had ascended it, I scarcely knew whether I was in Asia or Africa, the soil, situation, and every one of the plants, being equally strange to me. Indeed I was now, for the first time, upon the [Lapland] Alps! Snowy mountains encompassed me on every side. I walked in snow, as if it had been the severest winter. All the rare plants that I had previously met with, and which had from time to time afforded me so much pleasure, were here as in miniature, and new ones in such profusion, that I was overcome with astonishment, thinking I had now found more than I should know what to do with. (Linnaeus 1732: 1:283–84)

And the people of Lapland seemed no less exotic than its ecology.

> My companion was a Laplander, who served me both as servant and interpreter. In the latter capacity his assistance was highly requisite, few persons being to be met with on these alps who are acquainted with the Swedish language; nor was I willing to trust myself alone among these wild people, who were ignorant for what purpose I came. (Linnaeus 1732: 2:257–58)

Apprehension turned to desperation as Linnaeus found himself and his guide lost and hungry in this strange new world of "wild people"; and it was in this distressed state that he had his first encounter with a Saami woman.

> He was accompanied by a person whose appearance was such that at first I did not know whether I beheld a man or a woman. I scarcely believe that any poetical description of a fury could come up to the idea, which this Lapland fair-one excited. It might well be imagined that she was truly of Stygian origin. Her stature was very diminutive. Her face of the darkest brown from the effects of smoke. Her eyes dark and sparkling. Her eyebrows black. Her pitchy-coloured hair hung loose about her head, and on it she wore a flat red cap. She had a grey petticoat; and from her neck, which resembled the skin of a frog, were suspended a pair of large loose breasts of the same brown complexion, but encompassed, by way of ornament, with brass rings. Round her waist she wore a girdle, and on her feet a pair of half boots.
> Her first aspect really struck me with dread; but though a fury in appearance, she addressed me, with mingled pity and reserve, in the following terms:

> "O thou poor man! what hard destiny can have brought thee hither,
> to a place never visited by any one before? This is the first time I ever
> beheld a stranger. Thou miserable creature! how didst thou come, and
> whither wilt thou go? Dost thou not perceive what houses and habita-
> tions we have, and with how much difficulty we go to church?" (Lin-
> naeus 1732: 1:144–45)

The unexpectedly kind, churchgoing woman provided the hungry traveler
with fish and reindeer cheese (Linnaeus 1732: 1:147–48); and Linnaeus,
having moved beyond the culture shock of first appearances, went on to
write a work that was as much an ethnography as it was natural history.
Linnaeus begins to develop a strong curiosity about these unfamiliar people.

> I wondered, indeed I more than wondered, how these poor people
> could feed entirely on fish, sometimes boiled fresh, sometimes dried,
> and then either boiled, or roasted before the fire on a wooden spit. They
> roast their fish thoroughly, and boil it better and longer than ever I saw
> practised before. They know no other soup or spoon-meat than the
> water in which their fish has been boiled. If from any accident they
> catch no fish, they cannot procure a morsel of food. At midsummer
> they first begin to milk the reindeer, and maintain themselves on the
> milk till autumn; when they kill some of those valuable animals, and
> by various contrivances get a scanty supply of food through the winter.
> (Linnaeus 1732: 1:154)

And as he wonders, he begins to ask questions and to learn something
about the ecological and economic realities of their nomadic combination of
pastoralism and foraging.

> I wondered that the Laplanders hereabouts had not built a score of
> small houses, lofty enough at least to be entered in an upright posture,
> as they have such abundance of wood at hand. On my expressing my
> surprise at this, they answered: "In summer we are in one spot, in win-
> ter at another, perhaps twenty miles distant, where we can find moss
> for our reindeer." I asked "Why they did not collect this moss in the
> summer, that they might have a supply of it during the winter frosts?"
> They replied, that they give their whole attention to fishing in summer
> time, far from the places where this moss abounds and where they re-
> side in winter.
>   These people eat a great deal of flesh meat. A family of four persons
> consumes at least one reindeer every week, from the time when the
> preserved fish becomes too stale to be eatable, till the return of the
> fishing season. Surely they might manage better in this respect than
> they do. When the Laplander in summer catches no fish, he must either
> starve, or kill some of his reindeer. He has no other cattle or domestic

animals than the reindeer and the dog: the latter cannot serve him for food in his rambling excursions; but whenever he can kill Gluttons (*Mustela Gulo*), Squirrels, Martins, Bears or Beavers, in short any thing except Foxes and Wolves, he devours them. His whole sustenance is derived from the flesh of these animals, wild fowl, and the reindeer, with fish and water. A Laplander, therefore, whose family consists of four persons, including himself, when he has no other meat, kills a reindeer every week, three of which are equal to an ox; he consequently consumes about thirty of those animals in the course of the winter, which are equal to ten oxen, whereas a single ox is sufficient for a Swedish peasant. (Linnaeus 1732: 1:167–69)

When one asks questions instead of assuming the answer, as Linnaeus discovered, the answers may pose more challenges to preformed conclusions and comparative assumptions than to the subjects of the interrogation. Perhaps a few such experiences were enough to caution Linnaeus against assuming that Saami practices should follow the rationality of principles held by Swedish agriculturalists, or even urban-based scientists. As his questions lead him into new areas of discovery, his wondering expressions of scientific curiosity shade over into the wonder of an exciting, disturbing, and not fully comprehensible admiration.[1]

I could not help wondering how the Laplanders knew such of the herd as they had already milked, from the rest, as they turned each loose as soon as they had done with it. I was answered that every one of them had an appropriate name, which the owners knew perfectly. This seemed to me truly astonishing, as the form and colour are so much alike in all, and the latter varies in each individual every month. The size also varies according to the age of the animal. To be able to distinguish one from another among such multitudes, for they are like ants on an anthill, was beyond my comprehension. (Linnaeus 1732: 1:314)

Such moments of self-disclosure and admiration for his subjects are rare. For the most part, the ethnographic sections of Linnaeus's narrative, actually a journal of daily field notes, are full of detailed, precise descriptions of Saami customs and practices, virtually all in a matter-of-fact, neutrally scientific-descriptive tone. He seldom ventures into evaluations and judgments. But at the time, like the New World, Lapland was undergoing colonization by outsiders; and Linnaeus was not hesitant to express his criticism of oppression by his fellow countrymen in terms that show both sympathy and an appreciation of the humanity of the Saami themselves:

In the evening of the 1st of June we came to an island occupied by fishermen. . . . For this fishery these people pay no tax, neither to the crown nor to the native Laplander, who has free access to the water only when these adventurers have left it. Though he himself pays tribute for it, he dares not throw in the smallest net during the stay of his visitors; for, if they find any of his nets, they may throw them up into the high trees, as I was told they often had done. The poor Laplander, who at this season has hardly any other subsistence for himself or his family, can with difficulty catch a fish or two for his own use. (1732: 1:128–30)

Linnaeus compares this behavior with the treatment of the colonists by the Saami:

The colonists who reside among the Laplanders are beloved by them, and treated with great kindness. These good people willingly point out to the strangers where they may fix their abode so as to have access to moist meadows affording good hay, which they themselves do not want, their herds of reindeer preferring the driest pastures. They expect in return that the colonists should supply them with milk and flour. (1732: 1:131)

Although he continues to see some faults in them as individuals and as a group, and cannot accustom himself to some of their ways, still, all in all, Linnaeus's assessment of the Saami is strongly positive:

Ovid's description of the silver age is still applicable to the native inhabitants of Lapland. Their soil is not wounded by the plough, nor is the iron din of arms to be heard; neither have mankind found their way to the bowels of the earth, nor do they engage in wars to define its boundaries. They perpetually change their abode, live in tents, and follow a pastoral life, just like the patriarchs of old. (1732: 1:131–32)

And if this is only the age of silver, one step removed from the perfection of the Golden Age, in fact Linnaeus promotes them to the higher state later in his narrative:

The tranquil existence of the Laplanders answers to Ovid's description of the golden age, and to the pastoral state as depicted by Virgil. It recalls the remembrance of the patriarchal life, and the poetical descriptions of the Elysian fields. (1732: 2:132)

With this appearance of a mythic paradigm already well known to us from New World ethnography, we should not be surprised to encounter some very familiar language in this quite different ethnographic context. The rhetoric of comparative negation, defining the ethnographic Golden Age by a recital of features of civilization not found among the people under discussion, has a noticeable place in Linnaeus's representation of the

Saami. Even the fascination with nakedness, well known from the American tropics, but perhaps not entirely expected in an environment straddling the Arctic Circle, plays a part in the narrative:

> The inhabitants sleep quite naked on skins of reindeer, spread over a layer of branches of Dwarf Birch (*Betula nana*), with similar skins spread over them. The sexes rise from this simple couch, and dress themselves promiscuously without any shame or concealment. . . . The inhabitants, sixteen in number, lay there all naked. They washed themselves by rubbing the body downwards, not upwards. They washed their dishes with their fingers, squirting water out of their mouths upon the spoon, and then poured into them boiled reindeer's milk, which was as thick as common milk mixed with eggs, and had a strong flavour. Some thousands of reindeer came home in the morning, which were milked by the men as well as the women, who kneeled down on one knee. (1732: 1:126, 291)

Thus, although the Saami reversals of civilized European ways remained as disconcerting to Linnaeus as their diet and hygiene, given their general conformity to the norms of the Golden (or Silver) Age, it is no wonder that his overall assessment of them remained positive.

> I witnessed with pleasure the supreme tranquillity enjoyed by the inhabitants of this sequestered country. After they have milked their reindeer, and the women have made their cheese, boiled their whey to the requisite consistence, and taken their simple repast, they lie down to enjoy that sound sleep which is the reward and the proof of their innocent lives. (1732: 1:314–15)

Although Linnaeus reserves his use of the rhetoric of nobility for the forests and plants that are his chief scientific interest, he nevertheless presents a remarkably sympathetic view of a people widely considered, and criticized, as a savage antithesis to the European civilization whose geographic fringes they inhabited. Sixty-seven years later, another young traveler, the Italian Giuseppe Acerbi (1773–1846), would retrace Linnaeus's route through northern Lapland and come to a quite different evaluation.

Like Linnaeus, Acerbi was in his mid-twenties when he visited Lapland in 1799; and like him, Acerbi would pursue horticultural interests, albeit in a more modest way, later in life. He also shared something of Linnaeus's dual interest in natural science and ethnography, expressing the latter in the new discourse of sociocultural evolutionary progressivism:

> To the enlightened philosopher Lapland presents throughout subjects of reflection and contemplation. . . . In Lapland, the philosopher has an opportunity of studying among wandering tribes the first elements of

FIGURE 11. ACERBI'S DISCOVERY OF THE SAUNA.
Giuseppe Acerbi discovers the sauna as a source of scientific
data and sexual amusement in late-eighteenth-century
Finland (Acerbi 1802: 1:297).

social life; of society in its most ancient and primitive form. . . . What a
journey is that to Lapland, to a traveller from the South! (Acerbi 1802:
2:131)

Beyond these general resemblances, it is difficult to imagine two authors
more different than the Swedish student traveling under a grant from the
Royal Society, with his pervasive self-restraint and scientific neutrality,
and the self-financed Italian aristocrat, indulging his personal curiosity
with a sensualist emphasis on self-gratification and self-expression. One of
Acerbi's greatest delights on his northward journey through Finland was
his discovery of the sauna (fig. 11).

> Men and women use the bath promiscuously, without any concealment
> of dress, or being in the least influenced by any emotions of attach-
> ment. If, however, a stranger open the door, and come on the bathers
> by surprise, the women are not a little startled at his appearance; for,
> besides his person, he introduces along with him, by opening the door,

a great quantity of light, which discovers at once to the view their situation, as well as forms. . . . I often amused myself with surprising the bathers in this manner, and I once or twice tried to go in and join the assembly; but the heat was so excessive that I could not breathe, and in the space of a minute at most, I verily believe, must have been suffocated. I sometimes stepped in for a moment, just to leave my thermometer in some proper place, and immediately went out again, where I would remain for a quarter of an hour, or ten minutes, and then enter again, and fetch the instrument to ascertain the degree of heat. My astonishment was so great that I could scarcely believe my senses, when I found that those people remain together, and amuse themselves for the space of half an hour, and sometimes a whole hour, in the same chamber, heated to the 70th or 75th degree of Celsius. The thermometer, in contact with those vapours, became sometimes so hot, that I could scarcely hold it in my hands. (Acerbi 1802: 1:297–98)

Whoever is inclined to think of the quest for scientific data in terms of an austere, near-monastic detachment from sensual and emotional gratification ought to read Acerbi. But, leaving aside the temptation of critical debates over sexism versus a youthful playfulness sanctioned by his own culture, if Acerbi's actions deserve to be considered scientific observation, they hardly qualify as participant-observation. Like the English traveler Lady Mary Wortley Montagu (1716–18: 58–60) in Turkey earlier in the century, Acerbi may have been drawn to the bath by its sensual and erotic appeal, but he couldn't take the heat and never took off his clothes.

The sauna seems an apt metaphor for Acerbi's approach to ethnography. Whatever excitement he felt for the new world he had entered, his senses were shocked by its reality.

At length we began our march, each of our Laplanders with his load of baggage, one of them taking the lead, and the rest following one by one in single file. This was the first time during our whole journey that we had travelled in this manner, and we were wonderfully delighted with the singular appearance which our caravan made. . . . The pleasure we had in reviewing this procession was destroyed by the intolerable stench which these filthy Laplanders left behind them, when they began to perspire. (Acerbi 1802: 2:46)

And, overcome by a sensory shock he could not assimilate, Acerbi is carried away by a repulsion that reflects back not on his own perceptions but on the people he has come to study.

The persons and dress of these Laplanders, taken altogether, were the most filthy and disagreeable that it is possible to conceive. They held the fish they were eating in their hands, and the oil that distilled from it ran down their arms, and into the sleeves of their coats, which might be scented at the distance of some yards. (Acerbi 1802: 2:43–44)

Thus spatial metaphors of distance come to symbolize the distance of negativity that Acerbi constructs between himself and the Saami. The missionary Knut Leems, whose own ethnography Acerbi cites in an abridged translation, had provided a deeper reflection and a logical explanation of the problem.

Others again have asserted, with a greater appearance of truth and justice, that they had from nature an offensive smell. It must indeed be acknowledged, that there is a certain unsavoury rankness which attends the Laplander, more than is commonly found with the inhabitants of other countries; but this is not so much to be imputed to his natural temperament as to his mode of life, dwelling as he does in a hut or tent, in the midst of a constant smoke, and clothed in a dress which has imbibed quantities of dirt, grease, and train oil. (Leems 1767: 152)

So it seems that the missionary is able to deal with the sensory upset more elegantly and logically, to say nothing of fairly, than the philosophical traveler. What, then, are the kinds of philosophical insights that Acerbi was able to obtain in his travels? First of all, he could not help noticing some of the features of Saami society that had led Linnaeus to invoke the paradigm of the Golden Age.

Free by nature, their manner of living exempts them from the necessity of laws. They dwell in a country which cannot be inhabited by any other race of mortals. They feed their rein-deer with a vegetable rejected by every other animal. Their only society consists in the union of a few families drawn together partly by common wants, and partly by social affections: and when two such families with their herds, chance to meet on the same spot, there is land enough. . . .

There are no venomous animals in those rude countries; and as to men, they all live in the most perfect innocence. Here the necessity of government, for the distribution of justice, and the equal protection of the people, exists not. A small number of inhabitants, dispersed over immense tracts of lands, have little inducement to make aggressions on each other; and the general equality of condition that prevails, and above all, the constitutional feebleness of passion, and equanimity of temper, prevents not only infliction of injuries, but resentment. Though the Laplanders are defenceless, yet the rigours of their climate, and their poverty, secure them from invasion; and thus they exist without combination or protection, and without bending with submission to superiors. Here the melancholy examples, which exist in all histories, of the great tyrannizing over the meaner sort, are not to be found, nor the falsehood and perjury which generally prevail among rude and barbarous nations. (Acerbi 1802: 2:56, 104)

Nevertheless, application of the rhetoric of comparative negations from the Golden Age paradigm leads Acerbi to quite different conclusions than it had Linnaeus. Acerbi takes note of some of the same elements that Linnaeus had observed, such as the settlement of Finnish fishermen in Saami territory.

> Nature has done every thing for those people; and in proportion to her profuse bounty is their abominable indolence. The fishermen of the isle of Kintasari were . . . a Finnish colony established in Lapland. These inhabitants of Kintasari preserve all the original boldness of character, force, and activity, by which the Fins are distinguished; whereas the unsettled and wandering Laplanders are remarkable for sloth and dirt. (Acerbi 1802: 2:61–62)

By the time of Acerbi's visit, the colonizing and missionizing process Linnaeus had noted had run its course for two more generations. Unlike Linnaeus, who had defended the rights of the Saami against the colonists, Acerbi's contrast of the Saami and the Finnish colonists is almost identical rhetorically and substantively to the pejorative contrasts drawn between Indians and American colonists of the same period by writers such as Chastellux and Volney. Acerbi's decided preference for the colonists may have been, like Volney's, the semidetached judgment of a foreign observer; but it was hardly that of a neutral observer. And the dominant-subaltern dynamics of the colonial situation rendered Acerbi himself an object of suspicion in the eyes of the Saami: "The answers they made to our questions were not so frank and plain as might have been expected from such simpletons. The passions which so often make men of sense act like fools, sometimes give art and address to the most stupid" (Acerbi 1802: 2:54).

There is at least a kind of poetic justice in the suspicion and hostility of the Saami toward Acerbi, who, while concealing the deep contempt and hostility he felt toward them, had nevertheless to defend himself against their perceptions that he was somehow implicated in their oppression and subordination.

> It was not without extreme difficulty that we were able to persuade our Laplanders that we were neither kings, commissaries, nor priests, but only private individuals who were travelling from mere curiosity. The principle of curiosity, which exists only in cultivated minds, and

which is derived either from self-interest, in search of something that
may be advantageous, or from the pride of knowing more than other
men, or from a desire of comparing what is already known with some
object or objects not yet known—this principle is obviously too abstruse, and can in no wise enter into the head of a roving Laplander.
(Acerbi 1802: 2:56)

It seems, we might add, that the principle of curiosity is restricted by
definition to the rich, either the traveler himself or the urban society that
supports him, and excluded by definition from the outsider to this privileged group. For, by any open-minded definition, the Saami showed a
greater curiosity in trying to understand Acerbi and his motives than he
did in assuming he knew theirs. And assume he did.

> There did not appear to be any kind of rule or order among those
> people; no beginning of any thing, and no end. Their only regulator
> and guide seemed to be appetite and instinct. . . .
>   Laziness and stupidity were prominent in all the Laplanders did, in
> all that appertained to them. The only things that they were able ac-
> tively to perform, were to keep up an everlasting chatter, to smoke
> their pipes, to chew tobacco, and to drink brandy. (Acerbi 1802:
> 2:53, 59)

Acerbi's assumptions about appetite and instinct, laziness and stupidity,
were so overwhelmingly global as to effectively preclude any serious effort
at understanding; and from this point onward, he gives up the attempt.

> I will not tire my readers at present with any farther details on the
> manners and habits of those people. What has been already mentioned
> may suffice to give a tolerably just idea of their character and deport-
> ment. We were every instant on the point of losing all patience with
> them. But for want of geographical information, and from the need
> we had of them, we were, in a great measure, under their power, and
> therefore obliged to put up with all their stupidity, laziness, and beast-
> liness. (Acerbi 1802: 2:64)

Thus we witness the same closing of the circle as in Volney's contemporary account of the New World "savages"; for here the ethnographic
subjects are themselves the hired laborers on whom the dominant and authoritative party is hopelessly dependent, and within them lurks the ever-
present, ever-threatening beast. On the fringes of Europe itself, we begin
to sense something of the global scope of the fears and negativities that
would energize the ethnography of the new century.

DARWIN AND THE SAVAGE AT THE END OF THE EARTH

We might also compare Linnaeus's ethnographic picture of "wild men" with that of the leading naturalist of the next century, Charles Darwin (1809–82), in his voyage to the opposite end of the earth. At the same period in his life as Linnaeus had been when he journeyed to Lapland, Darwin encountered what to him was the apotheosis of the "savage" as the exploratory ship *Beagle* visited Tierra del Fuego at the southern tip of South America in 1833 and 1834. His first reaction is comparable to the culture shock of Linnaeus's first encounter with the Saami woman.

> It was without exception the most curious and interesting spectacle I had ever beheld. I could not have believed how wide was the difference, between savage and civilized man. It is greater than between a wild and domesticated animal, in as much in man there is a greater power of im-provement. . . . The party altogether closely resembled the devils which come on the stage in such plays as Der Freischutz. (Darwin 1839a: 228)

But at closer glance, there is something quite different from Linnaeus's reaction here, in that this is less of a naive first reaction, colored by ethno-centric experience, than one cast into a predetermined shape by prefor-mulated analytic models. To be sure, both project their representations in terms of European demonic-mythological imagery, in Darwin's case medi-ated by theatrical representations. But Darwin also superimposes the im-agery of animal domestication, our first indication that his narrative will be formulated in terms of the increasingly dominant bestialized image of the "savage"; and perhaps, in his case, foreshadowing the evolutionary con-nections he would later draw between humans and the animal kingdom.

Darwin's first reactions should forewarn us not to expect the rhetoric of nobility to play a part in his representation of these people. Describing an-other meeting with some Fuegians, he says:

> These were the most abject and miserable creatures I any where beheld. . . . These poor wretches were stunted in their growth, their hideous faces bedaubed with white paint, their skins filthy and greasy, their hair entangled, their voices discordant, their gestures violent and without dignity. Viewing such men, one can hardly make oneself be-lieve they are fellow-creatures, and inhabitants of the same world. It is a common subject of conjecture what pleasure in life some of the less gifted animals can enjoy: how much more reasonably the same ques-tion may be asked with respect to these barbarians. At night, five or six human beings, naked and scarcely protected from the wind and rain of

this tempestuous climate, sleep on the wet ground coiled up like animals. (1839a: 235–36)

There is almost nothing of the old dialectic of vices and virtues here. Typically for its time, the language is overwhelmingly negative in tone, alternating between uninhibited outbursts of aesthetic revulsion and the recurrent images of bestiality. We do, however, encounter some echoes of the rhetoric of comparative negation, although in Darwin's case it is hardly associated with evocations of the mythical Golden Age.

> The different tribes have no government or chief; yet each is surrounded by other hostile tribes, speaking different dialects, and separated from each other only by a deserted border or neutral territory: the cause of their warfare appears to be the means of subsistence. . . . The habitable land is reduced to the stones on the beach; in search of food they are compelled unceasingly to wander from spot to spot, and so steep is the coast that they can only move about in their wretched canoes. They cannot know the feeling of having a home, and still less that of domestic affection; for the husband is to the wife a brutal master to a laborious slave. . . . How little can the higher powers of the mind be brought into play: what is there for imagination to picture, for reason to compare, for judgment to decide upon?[2] to knock a limpet from the rock does not require even cunning, that lowest power of the mind. Their skill in some respects may be compared to the instinct of animals; for it is not improved by experience: the canoe, their most ingenious work, poor as it is, has remained the same, as we know from Drake, for the last two hundred and fifty years. (Darwin 1839b: 196)

Again, the comparison with animals. And bestializing representations continue throughout Darwin's discourse:

> One of our arms being bared, they expressed the liveliest surprise and admiration at its whiteness, just in the same way in which I have seen the ourang-outang do at the Zoological Gardens. (1839b: 189)

> The next morning . . . Jemmy's mother and brothers arrived. . . . The meeting was less interesting than that between a horse, turned out into a field, when he joins an old companion. There was no demonstration of affection; they simply stared for a short time at each other; and the mother immediately went to look after her canoe. (1839b: 201)

If the constant play of bestial similes, metaphors, and comparisons represents Darwin's protoevolutionary thinking, his rhetoric is very difficult to distinguish from other bestializers of the "savage," such as Volney or the

American racist anthropologists, who used similar language without any evolutionary concepts or intent. It is obvious in this and his later works that Darwin shared the general belief of nineteenth-century Europeans in their superiority over other peoples. Indeed, Marvin Harris (1968: 118 ff.) indicts "Darwin's racism" on the basis of Darwin's discussions in the *Descent of Man* (1871), written after, and partially in response to, the ascent of scientific racism to a position of dominance in British anthropology. Darwin's later discussions of race do show an unfortunate degree of accommodation with some of the ideas of the racist anthropologists; and his negative representation of the Fuegians would be used by those with overtly racist agendas as "scientific evidence" in support of their position, even playing a key role in the invention of the Myth of the Noble Savage (see chap. 17). Yet, as Darwin's ethnographic writings of 1839 show, he was far from being a simple racist. Speaking of the natives of Tahiti, he writes:

> They are very tall, broad-shouldered, athletic, and well-proportioned. It has been remarked, that it requires little habit to make a dark skin more pleasing and natural to the eye of a European than his own colour. A white man bathing by the side of a Tahitian, was like a plant bleached by the gardener's art compared with a fine dark green one growing vigorously in the open fields. Most of the men are tattooed, and the ornaments follow the curvature of the body so gracefully, that they have a very elegant effect. . . . The simile may be a fanciful one, but I thought the body of a man thus ornamented was like the trunk of a noble tree embraced by a delicate creeper. (1839b: 368)

Obviously, Darwin was no proponent of white superiority on the simple grounds of whiteness itself. And the rhetoric of aesthetic nobility is mirrored in a further comment on the Tahitians: "On the road we met a large party of noble athletic men going for wild bananas" (1839b: 377). Darwin's admiration for the Tahitians is occasioned, to a large extent, by his respect for their conversion to Christianity (1839b: 375–78), at a time when he was still considering a career as a Christian clergyman. But equally, it seems to have derived from his perception of their material happiness, the result of their transcendence of the "savage" state: "I was pleased with nothing so much as the inhabitants. There is a mildness in the expression of their countenances which at once banishes the idea of a savage; and an intelligence which shows that they are advancing in civilization" (1839b: 367–68).

In fact, it is not racial differences but perceived differences in relative states of evolutionary progress from savagery to civilization that energize

Darwin's critical and imaginative faculties. We see this in his comparison of the Tahitians and the Maoris of New Zealand:

> Looking at the New Zealander, one naturally compares him with the Tahitian; both belonging to the same family of mankind. The comparison, however, tells heavily against the New Zealander. He may, perhaps, be superior in energy, but in every other respect his character is of a much lower order. One glance at their respective expressions, brings conviction to the mind that one is a savage, the other a civilized man. (1839b: 384)

And even in his highly negative representation of the Fuegians, Darwin's criterion of evaluation is his perception of cultural, rather than racial, inferiority. Darwin's first sight of the Fuegians in their island habitat was not, in fact, his first experience with them; for the *Beagle* carried three Fuegians kidnapped or purchased on an earlier voyage who had spent several years in England and were now returning home. Darwin's reactions to these "civilized" Fuegians were generally favorable, and he goes into some detail discussing their intelligence and other "good qualities" (1839b: 187–88). Later, Darwin would write: "The Fuegians rank among the lowest barbarians; but I was continually struck with surprise how closely the three natives on board H.M.S. 'Beagle,' who had lived some years in England and could talk a little English, resembled us in disposition and in most of our mental faculties" (1871: 1:34).

But if their example showed the Fuegians, like other humans, to be capable of "domestication" and "improvement," their "savage" relatives showed the opposite extreme of what humans could be. Commenting on "Jemmy Button," one of the three Fuegians returning from England, Darwin says: "It seems yet wonderful to me, when I think over all his many good qualities, that he should have been of the same race, and doubtless partaken of the same character, with the miserable, degraded savages whom we first met here" (1839b: 188). Clearly, Darwin's perception of the inferiority of the Fuegians is not based on racial qualities, which in any case were obscured by the extent of variation he saw between one individual and another. Rather, it is based on his conviction of the inferiority of the state of savagery itself. In this conviction, he was a typical nineteenth-century heir of the sociocultural progressivist assumptions of the Enlightenment; and so, typically for holders of such assumptions, he reserves his use of the rhetoric of nobility for those he perceives to be the farthest removed from the state of the "savage."

The most problematic feature of Darwin's ethnography is not its racism but its ethnographic shallowness. Of course, the *Beagle's* sailing schedule, and Darwin's primary interest in and commitment to other scientific research subjects, did not allow for extended residence with a people or for participant-observation ethnography, if such an idea had even occurred to him. Nor did the company of his companions on the ship, with their military preoccupations and defensive hostility to the natives, encourage sympathy or even closer contact with the Fuegians. Darwin's attitude toward them must be seen, to some extent, as a reflection of his primary loyalty to the traveling community of his European military companions and their opinions.

> I was amused by finding what a difference the circumstance of being quite superior in force made, in the interest of beholding these savages. While in the boats I got to hate the very sound of their voices, so much trouble did they give us. . . . On leaving some place we have said to each other, "Thank Heaven, we have at last fairly left these wretches!" (Darwin 1839a: 241)

With little possibility of direct, much less participant, observation under the circumstances, Darwin tried the alternative method of primary-informant ethnography by interviewing Jemmy Button and the other Fuegian passengers during the long voyage but quickly grew frustrated with, as he put it, "their apparent difficulty in understanding the simplest alternative" (1839b: 189). Darwin's formulation of the problem is striking:

> Every one accustomed to very young children, knows how seldom one can get an answer even to so simple a question as whether a thing is black *or* white; the idea of black or white seems alternately to fill their minds. So it was with these Fuegians, and hence it was generally impossible to find out, by cross-questioning, whether one had rightly understood anything which they had asserted. (1839b: 189)

Perhaps the Fuegians were equally frustrated with the kind of thinking that insists on seeing the world in terms of black and white and demands that all questions be settled in terms of mutually exclusive choices between the "simplest alternatives." At any rate, Darwin, who knows as well as any European what can be expected of "savages," blames the difficulty of communication on their childishly undeveloped intellects and generalizes the defect to the rest of their people.

> An European labours under great disadvantages, when treating with savages like these, who have not the least idea of the power of fire-arms. . . . Nor is it easy to teach them our superiority except by striking

a fatal blow. Like wild beasts they do not appear in all cases to compare numbers; for each individual if attacked, instead of retiring, will endeavour to dash your brains out with a stone, as certainly as a tiger under similar circumstances would tear you. . . . We can hardly put ourselves in the position of these savages, to understand their actions. . . . [T]he fact of a body being invisible from its velocity, would perhaps be to him an idea totally inconceivable. . . . Certainly I believe that many savages of the lowest grade, such as these of Tierra del Fuego, have seen objects struck, and even small animals killed by the musket, without being in the least aware how deadly an instrument it was. (Darwin 1839a: 239–40)

How likely such a theory is, when Fuegians had already been in contact with Europeans and their weapons for three hundred years, is a question left open by Darwin's narrative; his only ethnographic evidence is a story of Fuegians who did not run away when a pistol was fired in the air (Darwin 1839a: 239). But, it seems, the only evidence Darwin was looking for was the minimum needed to justify the placement of the Fuegians in a predetermined taxonomic niche, the "savage slot" (Trouillot 1991) in the evolutionary hierarchy of cultures that had been under construction for nearly a century. Darwin, like a good naturalist, was collecting specimens—and, ethnographically, collecting peoples to serve as exemplars for a hierarchical ordering of living species that he still conceived, as late as the publication of the *Origin of Species* (1859a), in terms of the great chain of being. His account of the Fuegians, with its perceptions duly cut and tailored to fit their predetermined niche, stands as a reminder that great scientists do not necessarily make great ethnographers, although we might wish that, like Linnaeus, his interests and itinerary had been a little more open, to see what difference it might have made in his results.

To appreciate the extent to which Darwin's construction of the Fuegians represents a particularly negative extreme, we might consider part of a description of them by another traveler of the same period. Charles Wilkes, commander of the United States Exploring Expedition, who visited Tierra del Fuego a few years after Darwin, observes of some Fuegians, "They cannot endure a noise. When the drum beat, or a gun was fired, they invariably stopped their ears" (Wilkes 1844: 1:125). Later in his visit, he describes this encounter:

We were here visited by a canoe with six natives, two old women, two young men, and two children. . . . The expression of the younger ones was extremely prepossessing, evincing much intelligence and good humour. They ate ham and bread voraciously, distending their large

mouths, and showing a strong and beautiful set of teeth. A few strips of
red flannel distributed among them produced great pleasure; they tied
it around their heads as a sort of turban. Knowing they were fond of
music, I had the fife played, the only instrument we could muster. They
seemed much struck with the sound. The tune of Yankee Doodle they
did not understand; but when "Bonnets of Blue" was played, they were
all in motion keeping time to it. The vessel at this time was under way,
and no presents could persuade them to continue any longer with
us. . . . We found them also extremely imitative, repeating over our
words and mimicking our motions. They were all quite naked.

I have seldom seen so happy a group. They were extremely lively
and cheerful, and any thing but miserable, if we could have avoided
contrasting their condition with our own. (1844: 1:142)

We might wish that Wilkes's concluding point had occurred to other
ethnographic observers of the period; but Wilkes was an unusually perceptive and sensitive observer, who had devoted considerable effort to devis-
ing a code of conduct for his crew to avoid harming or offending indigenous
peoples they would encounter on their voyage. Wilkes also includes negative characterizations of other Fuegian groups and individuals, resulting in
a dialectic alternation between positive and negative imagery. Such a balance is achieved in Darwin's narrative mostly in comparing one "race" with
another, as his portrait of the Fuegians is primarily negative, with relatively little use of the sort of counterbalancing positive representations
found in Wilkes's description of them.

Darwin was able to draw two theoretical conclusions from his encounters with the Fuegians. One, as we might expect, is their place in the hierarchy of peoples.

I believe, in this extreme part of South America, man exists in a lower
state of improvement than in any other part of the world. The South
Sea Islanders of the two races inhabiting the Pacific are comparatively
civilized. The Esquimaux, in his subterranean hut, enjoys some of the
comforts of life, and in his canoe, when fully equipped, manifests much
skill. Some of the tribes of Southern Africa, prowling about in search of
roots, and living concealed on the wild and arid plains, are sufficiently
wretched. The Australian, in the simplicity of the arts of life, comes
nearest the Fuegian; he can, however, boast of his boomerang, his spear
and throwing-stick, his method of climbing trees, of tracking animals,
and of hunting. Although the Australian may be superior in acquire-
ments, it by no means follows that he is likewise superior in mental capacity; indeed, from what I saw of the Fuegians when on board, and
from what I have read of the Australians, I should think the case was
exactly the reverse. (Darwin 1839b: 209)

Thus Darwin makes his claim, although not an entirely unqualified one, to have discovered another leading contender in the contest to identify the world's ultimate savage, the lowest of the low. His doubts arise only from the inconvenience of his own observations of the undeniable "mental capacity" of the Fuegians, in comparison to the uncompromising denial of such capacity in the hearsay evidence available on the Australians. It might have been better if he had never seen or spoken with the people about whom he wrote; he certainly could have stated his case more strongly.

The other conclusion Darwin draws from his ethnographic foray is less predictable but still a reflection of his age:

> The perfect equality among the individuals composing the Fuegian tribes must for a long time retard their civilization. As we see those animals, whose instinct compels them to live in society and obey a chief, are most capable of improvement, so is it with the races of mankind. Whether we look at it as a cause or a consequence, the more civilized always have the most artificial governments. . . . In Tierra del Fuego, until some chief shall arise with power sufficient to secure any acquired advantage . . . it seems scarcely possible that the political state of the country can be improved. At present, . . . no one individual becomes richer than another. On the other hand, it is difficult to understand how a chief can arise till there is property of some sort by which he might manifest his superiority and increase his power. (1839b: 208–9)

Here, then, is the ultimate critique of the state of savagery: it is too egalitarian to permit the "improvement" of allowing some to accumulate property, wealth, and power at the expense of others. We have already heard this critique from Volney and Morgan; and we shall encounter it again in the anthropology of the nineteenth century, as it develops to play its part in giving rise to the myth of the Noble Savage.

SCIENTIFIC RACISM: LAWRENCE'S CONVINCING EVIDENCE

Darwin's racial negativism is neither an individual aberration nor a sign of political extremism but a simple reflection of the belief in white superiority and the inferiority of the "darker races" that pervaded European society and discourse, scientific as well as nonscientific, in the nineteenth century. As in Darwin's case, we see that European writers carried their prejudices with them, so that what appears in the travel-ethnographic literature to be rational assessment of non-European peoples and customs based on firsthand, ostensibly scientific "observation" was to a significant extent an artifact of the prefabricated racialist framework within which representations of the other were constructed. Indeed, it was possible to come to firm "scientific" conclusions about the inferiority of nonwhite peoples without ever "observing" them, as we can see in the work of one of the great early-nineteenth-century British comparative anatomists, William Lawrence. Lawrence's framing of the investigation of "moral and intellectual" differences between races leaves little doubt of his view of the nobility of "savages."

> If the physical frame and the moral and intellectual phenomena of man be entirely independent of each other, their deviations will exhibit no coincidence; the noblest characters and most distinguished endowments may be conjoined with the meanest organization: if, on the contrary, the intellectual and moral be closely linked to the physical part, if the former be the offspring and result of the latter, the varieties of both must always correspond. (Lawrence 1817: 324)

With the problem thus stated, we know what the solution will be. There is a rhetorical parallelism here between the arguments of the sociocultural-evolutionary progressivists of the previous century and this provisional framing of the opposition between "the noblest characters" and lower developmental forms; the social and cultural hierarchy, in fact, has simply been replaced by a somatic hierarchy. The mechanistic view of man has won out, because, as Lawrence explains it, one hierarchy is simply an index of the other:

> The different progress of various nations in general civilization, and in the culture of the arts and sciences . . . convince us beyond the possibility of doubt, that the races of mankind are no less characterized by diversity of mental endowments, than by those differences of organization which I have already considered. (1817: 324)

That is, temporal differences in "progress" are ultimately reducible to static, mechanistic differences in "endowments." Or, as computer programmers say, garbage in, garbage out. Once again, we notice the curious cultural artifact of a scientific discursive style that is claimed to be culture-neutral but nevertheless expresses itself in the language of a European-style absolutist, adversarial legal rhetoric in which cases are proven "beyond the possibility of doubt"—as if, perhaps, in preparation for passing a life sentence of penal servitude on the defendants, or worse? Let us follow the case further by hearing the presentation of the argument.

> The distinction of colour between the white and black races is not more striking than the pre-eminence of the former in moral feelings and in mental endowments. The latter, it is true, exhibit generally a

great acuteness of the external senses. . . . Yet they indulge, almost universally, in disgusting debauchery and sensuality, and display gross
selfishness, indifference to the pains and pleasures of others, insensibility to beauty of form, order, and harmony, and an almost entire want
of what we comprehend altogether under the expression of elevated
sentiments, manly virtues, and moral feeling. The hideous savages of
Van Diemen's Land, of New Holland, New Guinea, and some neigh-
bouring islands, the Negroes of Congo and some other parts, exhibit
the most disgusting moral as well as physical portrait of man. (Lawrence 1817: 325)

The reasoning will make perfect sense to anyone who accepts it as given
that the Negroes "exhibit the most disgusting . . . physical portrait of man."
If Lawrence reverses normal scientific and legal procedure in presenting the
verdict before the evidence, at least he does follow with some evidence. It
may be only secondhand, and thus inadmissible as hearsay in a court of law,
but the standards required by science to establish proof "beyond the possibility of doubt" may be less rigorous.

> PERON describes the wretched beings . . . as examples of the rudest bar-
> barism: "without chiefs, properly so called, without laws or any thing
> like regular government, without arts of any kind, with no idea of agri-
> culture, of the use of metals, or of the services to be derived from ani-
> mals; without clothes or fixed abode, and with no other shelter than a
> mere shred of bark to keep off the cold south winds; with no arms but a
> club and spear." (Lawrence 1817: 325)

Obviously, the time is past when symbolic alchemy could transform the
rhetoric of comparative negation into the dream of the Golden Age. This is
all the evidence Lawrence needs to forge ahead with a plea for the prosecu-
tion. By now, we need not be surprised that the target of his indictment is
someone far away from Van Diemen's Land.

> Their remorseless cruelty, their unfeeling barbarity to women and chil-
> dren, their immoderate revenge for the most trivial affronts, their want
> of natural affection, are hardly redeemed by the slightest traits of good-
> ness. When we add, that they are quite insensible to distinctions of
> right and wrong, destitute of religion, without any idea of a Supreme
> Being, and with the feeblest notion, if there be any at all, of a future
> state, the revolting picture is complete in all its features. What an
> afflicting contrast does the melancholy truth of this description form to
> the eloquent but delusive declamations of ROUSSEAU on the preroga-
> tives of natural man and his advantages over his civilized brethren!
> (Lawrence 1817: 325–26)

As in the case of Volney's attack on Rousseau (see above), Lawrence had certainly picked the right target. To maintain such virulent racist diatribes with impunity, the defenders of human equality would have to be discredited; and who more apt to epitomize them than Rousseau?

But then, as if the mention of the name had reminded him of the fanaticism of his own argument, Lawrence retreats into his particular version of the dialectic of virtues and vices, citing "brighter spots" in his dark picture—and goes so far as to use a word Rousseau never did: "There are some unconquered [American Indian] tribes equally conspicuous for the nobler attributes of our nature" (1817: 328). He puts the reference in its proper context by reiterating the inferiority of all dark races to whites, referring to the latter as "these nobler people" (1817: 330), and explains:

> In the white races we meet, in full perfection, with true bravery, love
> of liberty, and other passions and virtues of great souls; here only do
> those noble feelings exist in full intensity. . . . The spirit of liberty, the
> unconquerable energy of independence, the generous glow of patrio-
> tism have been known chiefly to those nobler organizations, in which
> the cerebral hemispheres have received their full development. (1817:
> 330–31)

The circular argument comes around again. So far, there seems little that is scientific in this massive outpouring of prejudices, supported by secondhand "observations" that confirm nothing so much as Rousseau's own critique of ethnographic representations. But Lawrence (1817: 33) finally returns to the language of science: "A fair comparative experiment has been made of the white and red races in North America; and no trial in natural philosophy has had a more unequivocal and convincing result."

Lawrence's point here is the decline of the Indians, as well known to the average Englishman as "the mighty empire founded by a handful of his countrymen in the wilds of America" (1817: 333). The passage provides a rather characteristic example of the tendency of scientific racism to naturalize genocide, constructing representations of the catastrophic colonial-induced declines of native populations in terms of "experiments" or "observations" of the outcomes of natural processes. To refer to this as an "experiment" is to cavalierly disregard all normal scientific concerns with issues of experimental controls and contamination, since one has hardly occurred independently of the other. Are all rapes and murders likewise "experiments" providing "unequivocal and convincing" proof of the inferiority of the victim? But once again, that wonderful conflation of scientific with legal discourse provides a solution: the confrontation of whites and Indians can certainly be characterized as a "trial," particularly if considered in light of its unique American form, the lynching.

In scientific racism, the racism was never very scientific; nor, it could at least be argued, was whatever met the qualifications of actual science ever very racist. How could higher or lower measurements of any physical feature confirm superior or inferior morality? Rather, the racism of popular prejudice was artificially joined to a scientific base—as forced a construction of unrelated and incompatible elements as P. T. Barnum's "Feejeean Mermaid," with its monkey torso joined to a fish's tail, or Piltdown Man's spurious assemblage of ape and human bones. Lawrence, indeed, was a minor player in this game of forced constructions, as was his fellow English anatomical racist-ethnologist, Robert Knox. Racism was a rapidly expanding international enterprise, pursued by many people other than scientists in Europe and America. The classic work that did the most to inspire the early growth of scientific racism in America, England, and elsewhere was, for example, written by Arthur de Gobineau (1854), who was an Orientalist and philologist rather than a natural scientist.

Still, it was in science where the biggest potential ideological gain for racism lay; and within a few years, the scientific racist enterprise would be pushed to new heights of sophistication by master players such as Paul Broca in France and Morton and Nott in America. The "American school" of racist anthropology was particularly influential in shaping some of the ideas and discourses that are examined in this study. The American racist school took its inspiration from the work of Dr. Samuel Morton (1799–1851), a Philadelphia doctor who conducted extensive measurements on the largest collection of American Indian skulls ever assembled and concluded that the American Indians were a distinct, indigenous race, unrelated to others (Morton 1839)—a conclusion later elaborated into an argument for "polygenesis," or separate origins of races conceived as distinct "species." Given a stronger political thrust by George Gliddon (1809–57), a British-American Egyptologist who used depictions of apparent racial "types" of blacks on Egyptian monuments to argue the permanence of racial distinctions, and Josiah Nott (1804–73), a Mobile doctor whose work with slaves led him to a theory of the nonviability of racial "hybrids," the school attracted adherents both in America and Europe (Nott and Gliddon 1854, 1857; see also fig. 12). The most famous of them was the Swiss naturalist Louis Agassiz (1807–73), whose shock at the appearance of Negroes after his move to America caused him, under the influence of Morton's theories, to incorporate distinctions between human "species" into his theory of contrasting geographic-ecological "provinces" (Agassiz 1854)—despite

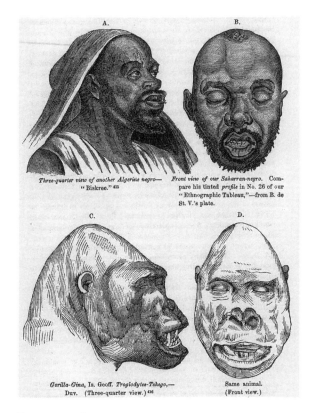

A.

B.

Three-quarter view of another Algerine negro—
"Biskree." [415]

Front view of our Saharran-negro. Compare his tinted *profile* in No. 26 of our "Ethnographic Tableau,"—from B. de St. V.'s plate.

C.

D.

Gorilla-Gina, Is. Geoff. *Troglodytes-Tshego*,—Duv. (Three-quarter view.) [416]

Same animal.
(Front view.)

FIGURE 12. SCIENCE AND THE SUBHUMAN.
Josiah Nott and George Gliddon's representation of blacks
as members of a subhuman race (Nott and Gliddon
1857: 548).

such glaring discrepancies as the conflict between Morton's insistence on the racial identity of North and South American Indians and the fundamental contrasts between animal species inventories in the North and South American ecospheres. The history and ideas of the American racists are covered in Stanton's *The Leopard's Spots*, and there is no need to deal extensively with them here. However, we will hear more of their names and writings as we pursue our study.

The claims of scientific racism to scientific legitimacy were not only rhetorical, but they rested to some extent on advances in quantitative data gathering, particularly in work as extensive and apparently carefully controlled as the cranial measurements of Morton and Broca. Yet contemporary efforts to replicate their data show that even their complex edifices of extensive measurements and data were erected on a warped scaffolding of popular racial prejudices that skewed and distorted their scientific results (Gould 1981). Given the problematic character of the "scientific" component in scientific racism, it would be unwise to concur too readily in assessments such as Stanton's (1960: 195–56) conclusion that the racists provided an important scientific contribution in anticipating major problems with Darwin's theories, having "been the guardians of a profound insight into nature which if borne in mind would have made the career of Darwinism more uniformly successful." If racists occasionally made correct guesses, we should not assume that it was necessarily for scientific reasons.

Likewise, we might do well not to accept on faith the racists' own often-repeated claims of disinterested support for a purely scientific theory of "polygenesis," or take too seriously the common folkloristic tendency to attribution of scientific legitimacy to virtually any writer who rhetorically opposed "scientific truth" to "religious dogma." While some scientific racist theory was polygenist or antireligious, as in Nott's and Gliddon's cases, some was not; and in both kinds of cases, the energizing juxtaposition of scientific pretension and racist preconception seems more fundamental than theories of origin or religious orientation. For example, an interesting case of a monogenist, pro-Christian form of scientific racism is the Swiss geographer Arnold Guyot's (1849: 240 ff.) theory of racially and sexually hierarchialized continents, in which the continents of the Southern Hemisphere, like the races that inhabit them, display signs of physical inferiority in comparison to their Northern counterparts:

> The continents of the North are more indented, more articulated; their contours are more varied. Gulfs and inland seas cut very deep into the mass of their lands, and detach from the principal trunk a multitude of peninsulas, which, like so many different organs and members, are prepared for a life, in some sort, independent. A great number of continental islands are scattered along their shores, and are a new source of wealth to them. . . . We have already seen that, in this respect, Europe and Asia present the most complicated structure, and the relative situations of the mountain chains and of their plateaus and their plains, exhaust, so to speak, all the possible combinations.
>
> The southern continents, on the other hand, are massive, entire, without indentations, without inland seas or deep inlets, scanty in articulations of every kind, and in islands. They are trunks without members, bodies without organs, and the simplicity of their interior structure answers to the poverty of their exterior forms.
>
> These differences are carried to the extreme in the Old World, where the rich border of peninsulas which deck the South of Asia and

of Europe, hanging like the ample folds or the fringes of a royal robe, form a striking contrast to the mean and naked lines of Africa and Australia. (1849: 242–43)

The abrupt about-face from a growing sense that the southern continents must have an acute case of penis envy for the prominently protruding "organs and members" of the northern to a sudden blush of modesty that cloaks the latter in royal robes while exposing the nudity of the former is probably necessary because Guyot must conceal the fact that the logic of his argument is no less twisted than his rhetoric. That the superior-inferior hierarchy of his anthropomorphized continents is an imaginative projection of a construction of human hierarchies is obvious enough; but when he moves on to represent the hierarchy of racial differences as a conclusion from, rather than a presupposition of, his geographic analysis, we find that the logic of one reverses the logic of the other.

> Let us take for a type of the central region of Western Asia, this head of a Caucasian. What strikes us immediately is the regularity of the features, the grace of the lines, the perfect harmony of all the figure. The head is oval; no part is too prominent beyond the others; nothing salient nor angular disturbs the softness of the lines that round it. . . . [I]n one word, all the proportions reveal the perfect harmony which is the essence of beauty. Such is the type of the white race—the Caucasian, as it has been agreed to call it—the most pure, the most perfect type of humanity.
>
> In proportion as we depart from the geographical centre of the races of man, the regularity diminishes, the harmony of the proportions disappears. (Guyot 1849: 255)

In the hierarchy of racialized continents, it was the complex angularity of projecting peninsulas and indented gulfs that served as a marker of superiority; but it seems that in the racial hierarchy, prominence, salience, and angularity are to be the marks of inferiority instead. The aesthetics of race reverses that of geography, even as it inspires and predetermines it. Indeed, Guyot's whole investigation is to be conducted on aesthetic principles that, although they may refer to physical features, are in fact based on no more objectively specifiable criteria than the selection of an arbitrary starting point.

> Thus, in all directions, in proportion as we remove from the geographical seat of the most beautiful human type, the degeneration becomes

greater, the debasement of the form more complete. . . . It results from this remarkable distribution of the races of man, that the continents of the North, forming the central mass of the lands, are inhabited by the finest races, and present the most perfect types; while the continents of the South, forming the extreme and far-sundered points of the lands, are exclusively occupied by the inferior races, and the most imperfect representatives of human nature. . . . The degree of culture of the nations bears a proportion to the nobleness of their race. The races of the northern continents of the Old World alone are civilized; the southern continents have remained savage. (Guyot 1849: 262–63)

Thus the racialized construction of geography leads us to yet another variant of the discursive opposition between nobility and savagery that developed after Rousseau, first in the cultural-evolutionary progressivism of social theorists and then in the biopolitical materialism of the scientific racists. Guyot's special variant could be described as geoaesthetic, insofar as it departs from the aesthetic centrality of his Eurocentric (or Caucasiocentric) starting point; but it also has another energizing principle so fundamental in nature that it both generates and resolves two major contradictions in Guyot's theory. The first contradiction is that, by Guyot's own logic, western and northern Europeans ought to have degenerated significantly by virtue of their considerable removal from the "centre of the races of man" in western Asia. This, Guyot admits, has occurred from a purely physical standpoint; but in compensation, "although . . . his features have less of regularity, of symmetry; but more animation, more mobility, more life, more expression. In him, beauty is less physical and more moral" (Guyot 1849: 256). Second, although purely geographic-ecological factors should dictate that man, like other creatures, ought to attain his greatest vitality and perfection in tropical zones, nevertheless, in the case of plants and animals,

> the degree of perfection of the types is proportional to the intensity of heat, and of the other agents stimulating the display of material life. The law is of a physical order.
>
> In man, the degree of perfection of the types is in proportion to the degree of intellectual and moral improvement. The law is of a moral order. (Guyot 1849: 264)

The moral, then, takes precedence over the physical in the case of man alone; and, as it turns out, it is the primordial power of the moral, rather than the merely physical, that ultimately shapes the aesthetic racial differences arising in different geographic environments. It is by means of consideration of the primacy of moral influences that Guyot constructs his unique theory of racist monogenist environmentalism.

> In speaking of man, we must not forget there are always two sides to consider; the one physical, the other moral. Western Asia is not only the geographical centre of the human race, but it is, moreover, the spiritual centre; it is the cradle of man's moral nature. . . . Now if man came from the hands of the divine Author of his being, pure and noble, it was in those privileged countries where God placed his cradle, in the focus of spiritual light, that he had the best chance to keep himself such. But how has he fallen elsewhere so low? It is because he was free, of a perfectible nature, and consequently capable also of falling. In the path of development, not to advance is to go back; it is impossible to remain stationary. . . . And what will come to pass if, separated from his God, and forgetting Him, he voluntarily stops the sources of the higher life, and moral life? Remote from the focus of tradition, where he might renew the temper of his faith, he remains unarmed in combat with that mighty nature that subjugates him; he yields in the struggle, and, vanquished, bears soon upon his figure the ineffaceable mark of bondage.
>
> Thus, perhaps, might one, I do not say explain, but conceive, the incontestable influence of each continent, and each region of the earth, on the physical forms, the character and the temperament of the man who dwells in it, and the degeneracy of his type in proportion as he is removed from the place of his origin, and the focus of his religious traditions. Renouncing moral liberty, which exists only in goodness, man gives to nature power over himself, submits to it, and thus are traced and distinguished, a race of Eastern Asia, an African race, an Australian race, a Polynesian race, an American race. (Guyot 1849: 266–68)

"Gives to nature power over himself"? Indeed, it would be possible to conceive the "scientific" racism of this (or perhaps any) period as a colossal warp in the intellectual mind-space continuum, with Guyot's theory constituting one of its most bizarre manifestations. And yet, were the opponents of the scientific racists, for example, Blumenbach and Prichard, any better in their efforts to bring science to the support of racial equality? After all, if we suspect that science in itself is incapable of proving superiority or inferiority, we would certainly be justified in questioning its capability for proving equality as well. The question is not easily resolved; and we might take note of Todorov's (1993) argument for treating racial issues in moral and political, rather than scientific, terms.

But as for the scientific antiracists of the period, at least we can observe, as in Prichard's case, that they were more honest than the racists in admitting the ambiguity of the results of investigations on both sides of the issue, and in raising the question of what could and could not be proved by the methods of physical science. In this, we might see them as the scientific analogues of those ethnographic travel writers who could be classified as "philosophical" because they raised questions not only about the meanings of observations but also about how those meanings could be constructed and interpreted.

9 Philosophers and Savages

FIGURE 13. UNCIVILIZED
RACES. The white man
teaches savages and
barbarians the benefits
of civilization and
Christianity, in J. G. Wood's
*The Uncivilized Races of
Men* (1871: 2:frontispiece).

In the philosophical literature of the eighteenth century we find that, just
as in the ethnographic literature, Rousseau's work does not form a watershed dividing more negative from more positive views of the "savage." If
anything, the opposite is true. But both before and after Rousseau, philosophical attitudes are often more or less simply marked by indifference,
neutrality, or ambivalence to the "savage," and by often strangely unreflective convictions of the superiority of European life and thought (fig. 13).
One example is provided by Giambattista Vico, whose *New Science* (1725)
has been recognized by various historians of anthropology (e.g., Harris
1968: 19–20, 27–28; Voget 1975: 46; Honigman 1976: 84–86, 108–9) as
influential in the development of anthropological thought.

Vico is one of the early contributors to the development of a widely accepted Enlightenment theory of sociocultural evolution, expressed at the time in terms of "progress," which postulated the development of human societies through a sequence of three or four stages from savagery to civilization. The theory would assume a more or less definitive form in the 1750s with its evolutionary stages grounded in patterns of subsistence: hunting as the basis of "savage" life, progressing upward into "barbarism" with the formation of pastoralist animal-herding societies, and advancing toward civilization with the emergence of societies based on agriculture and "commerce." Ronald Meek's *Social Science and the Ignoble Savage*, the most extensive study of the theory, identifies its early 1750s pioneers as Anne Robert Jacques Turgot in France and Adam Smith in Scotland (Meek 1976: 68). Rousseau, who promoted a three-stage theory of progress in the *Discourse on Inequality* in 1755, is identified as a possible co-inventor of the four-stage theory as well, depending on whether his formulation of it in the *Essay on the Origin of Languages* (1749–61?) is considered as dating from the 1750s or later. The theory would be further elaborated by Quesnay, Helvetius, Goguet, de Pauw, Dalrymple, Kames, Robertson, Ferguson, Millar, Falconer, and various other French and Scottish Enlightenment philosophical writers. Thus comparison of some of the theory's precursors before the publication of the *Discourse on Inequality*, such as Vico and Montesquieu, with Rousseau and with later sociocultural progressivist theorists provides a consistent baseline for assessing views of the "savage" before and after Rousseau's work.

For Vico, concerned with constructing his own model of sociocultural evolutionary progress that differed from other such models of the eighteenth century by its tripartite division into "Divine," "Heroic," and "Human" stages, the "savage" had no categorical significance in itself. Thus Vico's few references to the American Indians are as sources of comparative ethnographic data to support inferences drawn from Greco-Roman primary and Asiatic secondary cases: for example, Indian examples of "hieroglyphs" as heraldic insignia (Vico 1725: 163), heroic poetry (116, 158, 317), or "heroic natural law" (248). If the Indians are often associated with the "Heroic," we should note that this stage precedes the "Human" in Vico's teleochronology; and that, for him, the Indians are associated with the still more primitive "Divine" stage in rather uncomplimentary ways.

> The barbarians there feasted on human flesh (according to Lescarbot, *Histoire de la nouvelle France*), which must have been that of men who had been consecrated and killed by them. . . . So that, while the ancient Germans were beholding the gods on earth, and the American Indians

likewise, and while the most ancient Scythians were rich in so many golden virtues as we have heard them praised for by the writers—in these same times they were practicing such inhuman humanity! ... [w]e may conclude from all this how empty has been the conceit of the learned concerning the innocence of the golden age observed in the first gentile nations. In fact, it was a fanaticism of superstition which kept the first men of the gentiles, savage, proud, and most cruel as they were, in some sort of restraint by main terror of a divinity they had imagined. (Vico 1725: 178)

Thus Vico's savages are far from noble; and his use of the rhetoric of nobility is restricted to the class nobility of the higher stages of evolutionary progress and to its comparative correlates in other ethnographic contexts. The spears of the Indians, for example, are similar to those of European nobility (Vico 1725: 201). Although Indians in general are at far too low a stage to be noble, they show enough awareness of distinctions of status to have their own noble classes, like other human societies: "The custom of wearing the hair long was preserved by the nobility of many nations, and we read that one of the punishments of nobles among both the Persians and the American Indians was to pull one or several hairs from their heads" (Vico 1725: 188).

For other philosophers engaged in the construction of more standard and widely shared models of sociocultural evolution, "savages" occupied a fundamental stage in the ladder of progress. Nevertheless, they were not necessarily prominent in any particular theorist's work: depending on which evolutionary stages were given primary emphasis, the "savage" could be virtually ignored or given cursory treatment. Such is the case with Montesquieu's *Spirit of Laws* (1748), published seven years before Rousseau's *Discourse on Inequality*, in which, of the two great ethnological paradigm cases, the Oriental receives far more emphasis than the Savage, whose minor role is generally neutral or negative. Like Rousseau, Montesquieu is concerned with the hypothetical reconstruction of man as a solitary individual in a state of nature, before the formation of society.

Antecedent to all these laws are those of nature, so called because they derive their force intirely from our frame and being. In order to have a perfect knowledge of these laws, we must consider man before the establishment of society: the laws received in such a state would be those of nature.

... Man in a state of nature would have the faculty of knowing, before he had any acquired knowledge. Plain it is that his first ideas would be far from being of a speculative nature; he would think of the preservation of his being, before he would investigate its origin. Such a man would feel nothing in himself at first but impotency and weakness; his fears and apprehensions would be excessive; as appears from instances (were there any necessity of proving it) of savages found in forests, trembling at the motion of a leaf, and flying from every shadow.

In this state every man would fancy himself inferior, instead of being sensible of his equality. No danger would there be therefore of their attacking one another; peace would be the first law of nature. (Montesquieu 1748: 101–2)

For Montesquieu, as for other Enlightenment theorists of sociocultural evolutionary progressivism, the Savage is necessarily diametrically opposed to the Noble, since they stand at opposing poles of the evolutionary spectrum. We must wonder at the success of the Noble Savage myth in convincing so many scholars that widespread belief in such an antievolutionary notion as the Noble Savage is to be found in such an evolutionary age. If such were the case, it would be like finding religious tolerance to be widespread during the Crusades, or ecumenicalism during the religious wars of the Reformation. But, in fact, all the leading thinkers on sociocultural evolution who were to influence the development of anthropology seem to have remained consistent with their principles, and not to have compromised their progressivism with an opposing belief in anything so contradictory as a Noble Savage. If such an idea existed in the eighteenth century, we have to seek its origins elsewhere.

If there is anything like an official doctrine of the "savage" held by the Enlightenment philosophes associated with Rousseau, perhaps we should seek it in the great *Encyclopédie* (Diderot 1751–80) in which Diderot, d'Alembert, Rousseau, and the other major and minor philosophes collaborated. Louis de Jaucourt's short article "Sauvages," which deserves to be considered in full, begins with an evocation of the rhetoric of the Golden Age:

SAVAGES, n. m. plur. (*Mod. Hist.*) barbaric peoples who live without laws, without government, without religion, & who have no fixed habitation.

This word comes from the Italian *salvagio*, derived from [Latin] *salvaticus, selvaticus & silvaticus*, which signifies the same thing as *silvestris*, rustic, or having to do with the woods and the forests, because the *savages* ordinarily live in forests.

A great part of America is populated with *savages*, the majority of them ferocious, & who nourish themselves with human flesh. *See* ANTHROPOPHAGES.

Father Charlevoix has discussed in considerable length the manners and customs of the *savages* of Canada in his journal of a voyage in America, of which we have made use in several articles of this Dictionary.

SAVAGES, (*Mod. Geog.*) we call *savages* all the Indian peoples who have not submitted to their countries' yoke, and who live apart.

There is this difference between *savage* and barbaric peoples, that the first form small scattered nations which prefer never to unite with others, in place of which the barbarians often unify, & this occurs when one chief submits to another.

Natural liberty is the sole object of the policy of the *savages;* with that liberty, only nature and the climate exercise dominance over them. Occupied with hunting or the pastoral life, they do not burden themselves with religious observances, and do not adopt religions which require them.

There are found various *savage* nations in America, who because of the bad treatment they have experienced, still fear the Spaniards. Retreating into the forests and the mountains, they maintain liberty there, and find fruits in abundance. If they cultivate a scrap of land around their cabins, the corn comes first; and then hunting and fishing enable their access to a state of subsistence.

Since *savage* peoples do not make use of water channels in the places they inhabit, these places are filled with marshes where each *savage* troupe camps, lives, multiplies & forms a little nation. (1765: 29)

In Jaucourt's brief account, the rhetoric of nobility does not appear at all. The evaluation is ambivalent, with negative qualities such as ferociousness and cannibalism juxtaposed to positive features such as natural liberty and imagery of the Golden Age. In overall perspective, the article projects as classic a case of the dialectic of vices and virtues as we have seen in the ethnographic literature, with the generally neutral balance of positive and negative features lending little support to any argument that the article reflects a belief in the existence of the substantive Noble Savage.

Other articles in the *Encyclopédie* present more problematic features. Samuel Engel's article on American geography presents an interesting argument:

I believe the vast continent of North *America* to be inhabited by innumerable peoples, among whom several are very civilized. . . . One cannot say that *America* is peopled by barbarians, and that consequently the civilized peoples have come from elsewhere. Do we not all spring forth from the same stem? Are reason and genius not shared by all men, more or less? It is a matter of nothing but *culture*, like that of the earth. We see even in the ancient histories how the most fertile grounds have become sterile for lack of *culture,* and how good *culture* has given fertility to the most unrewarding soil. The Chinese, who are so ingenious and industrious, are not a foreign colony: they have created various inventions, such as gunpowder, printing, etc., before the Europeans. . . . Thus one becomes convinced that entire peoples, as civilized as they might be, have fallen by revolutions unknown to us into barbarity, and that others have emerged, conserved their customs, and advanced in the arts. Why should the Americans alone have been deprived of these advantages of nature? (1776: 360–61)

Engel's French term *culture,* of course, could be translated as "cultivation"; nevertheless, it seems to suggest more than just an etymological relationship to later anthropological concepts of culture. But it turns out that Engel is not one to follow through on his arguments. Although he proceeds logically from this passage to refute theories of a Chinese origin for the Peruvian civilization, he goes on to conjecture that the Chinese were indeed a "foreign colony" in Mexico, where, after linguistic and cultural changes during a residence of a thousand years or more, they provided the stimulus to the growth of Aztec civilization. Likewise, at the beginning of his essay, Engel goes to great length to establish methodological principles for differentiating accurate and inaccurate descriptions in travel writings— and then goes on to devote the greatest share of the article to a defense of Lahontan's geography of his voyage down the imaginary Long River.

Engel (1776: 358) admits, "No one believes that the Adario of Baron de la Hontan was ever a man of flesh and bone; one sees evidently that it was he himself: but the relation of his voyage need not be any less authentic, not having the same nature at all as his dialogues." Although he is able to cite supporting evaluations of the cultural advancement of some Indian groups from Charlevoix and others, his main evidence for the existence of "very civilized" peoples turns out to be based on the Gnacsitares, Mozemleks, and Tahuglanks living along the imaginary river, whom no one has seen since the time of Lahontan. If he does not adopt the rhetoric of nobility that Lahontan had applied to these peoples, neither does he provide a very convincing example of the application of Rousseau's notion of a critique of the representations of European travelers.

But the *Encyclopédie's* lead writer on America, Cornelius de Pauw, is nothing if not critical. De Pauw's critique, however, is not directed at the representations of European travelers but at the Indians themselves.

Among the peoples extending through the forests and solitudes of this world which have been discovered, it is not possible to enumerate more than two that have formed a species of political society. . . . Now, we see that which no one could even have imagined in America, where the people are incomparably less industrious and less inventive than the inhabitants of our hemisphere: above all, their indolence and their laziness have made a striking impression on the most attentive and the most enlightened observers. In the end, the stupidity that they show in certain cases is such that they appear to live, in the expression of M. de la Condamine, in an eternal infancy. (de Pauw 1776: 344)

There is certainly no possibility of finding the Noble Savage here, whether rhetorical or substantive. De Pauw's opinions are a philosophical derivative of the scientific theories of Buffon, who saw in the biology of the New World a collection of underdeveloped and inferior species, an idea that de Pauw partly adopted and partly modified into a theory of degeneracy. In the transition from science to philosophy, what remained constant was the attribution of inferiority in a temporocultural value hierarchy of racial dominance that grew increasingly stronger and more pervasive in the decades after Rousseau.

De Pauw, as one of the contributors to the development of the theory of sociocultural evolution after Rousseau, may be of interest for his theoretical elaboration of the stages of sociocultural development into more complex ranges of possibility (Meek 1976: 145–50); but he stands out even more for his spectacularly bleak depiction of the miseries of the savage state, particularly as exemplified by the American Indians. Yet none of the sociocultural progressivists after Rousseau projected a positive, or even a neutral, representation of savagery. Thus, for example, William Falconer, in his *Remarks on the Influence of Climate, Situation, Nature of Country, Population, Nature of Food, and Way of Life, on the Disposition and Temper, Manners and Behaviour, Intellects, Laws and Customs, Form of Government, and Religion, of Mankind* (1781) presented an excruciatingly detailed catalog (258–321) of the deleterious effects of savage life on character, morals, intellectual development, customs, government, religion, and various other aspects of those unfortunate enough to endure it—most prominent among whom, of course, were the American Indians. Whether we look at the effects of the French or the Scottish Enlightenment, we see little after Rousseau but increasing negativity expressed in projections of savage ignobility. But what else, after all, should we expect in an intellectual milieu in which the state-of-the-art theory of natural philosophy relegated the "savage" by definition to the lowest stage of progressive humanity?

Even in the circles closest to Rousseau, there is clearly no unanimity in the anthropology of the philosophes who contributed to the *Encyclopédie*. Those who collaborated with Rousseau, or wrote after him, certainly did not follow his party line on the evaluation of the "savage" or anything else. But in considering the diversity of their viewpoints, we can hardly ignore the distinctive viewpoint of the *Encyclopédie*'s editor in chief, Denis Diderot. Diderot's 1772 essay, *Supplément au voyage de Bougainville*, is often taken as the epitome of eighteenth-century portrayals of the Noble Savage (e.g., in Todorov 1993: 276–77). In examining it, we should note first that the discursive Noble Savage does not appear in it at all. Nowhere does Diderot refer to the Tahitians, his ethnographic exemplar of "savages" to set as a standard for critique of European society, as "noble." Where Robert Wokler's English translation has a Tahitian asking, "Is it wrong to submit to the most *noble* impulse of nature?" (Diderot 1772b: 69), the French original reads: ". . . l'impulsion la plus *auguste* de la Nature" (Diderot 1772a: 186; emphasis added). Likewise, when the translation shows the old Tahitian asking the French captain, "What more honest and *noble* sentiment can you put in the place of the one which we have inspired in [our young people] and which nurtures them?" (Diderot 1772b: 44; emphasis added), Diderot's French text says, "Quel sentiment plus honnête et plus *grand*" (Diderot 1772a: 126; emphasis added).

It should be noted that both references are to sexual impulses and feelings. But, issues of content aside, we see that once again we have encountered the curious predisposition to discursive nobility in English writing. The French translation of "noble" is *noble,* a word that does not appear in the *Supplément.* We do encounter at least one reference to *le bon sauvage,* where Diderot's interlocutor exclaims, "What! These people so simple, these savages so good, so decent" (Diderot 1772a: 131). But this results from a misinterpretation of Tahitian behavior by Diderot's naive interlocutor "A"; his wiser counterpart "B" quickly disillusions him and, together with the fictional Tahitians, supplies a more sophisticated characterization of "savage" character and motivations.

What, then, of substantive resemblances to the Noble Savage myth by adoption of the "romantic naturalist" perspective? John Hope Mason and Wokler consider Diderot's approach in the introduction to their collection of his writings, comparing Diderot's approach to "savages" with Rousseau's, and conclude that "neither man espoused the idea of a 'noble savage' which was so widely fashionable in the eighteenth century" (Mason and Wokler 1992: xviii). Likewise, Antoine Adam writes, "Diderot, one can be sure, had no sympathy for the chimera of primitivism and had no intention of lingering on the virtues of the noble savage" (cited in Sayre 1997: 125). But how can such a conclusion be possible, given some of Diderot's comparisons of Tahitian virtues with European vices?

> We are innocent and content, and you can only spoil that happiness. We follow the pure instincts of nature, and you have tried to erase its impression from our hearts. Here, everything belongs to everyone, and you have preached I can't tell what distinction between "yours" and "mine." . . . Leave us to our ways; they are wiser and more decent than yours. (Diderot 1772b: 42–43)

Here indeed is the classic language of the myth of the Golden Age, combined with the comparative critical dialectic of virtues and vices. But we should have learned enough from Lescarbot's use of a similar combination to avoid taking such language at face value, and instead turn to a closer look at Diderot's text. It turns out that resemblances to the Golden Age and Noble Savage myths are mainly found in the introductory and closing sections that frame Diderot's central project, one that certainly makes use of comparative critique but in a way quite different from either of the two myths.

Although Diderot pays lip service to ideas of nature and "natural" man, nature as such plays only the most token role as a backdrop to his Tahitian fantasy. We hear almost nothing of the beauties of this "tropical paradise"; Diderot's "nature" is rather individual human nature, and his "laws of nature" derive from the tensions between individualism and external constraints.

> We have no more in common with other human beings at birth than an organic similarity of form, the same need, an attraction to the same pleasures and a shared aversion to the same pains. These are the things which make man what he is, and which should form the basis of the morality suited to him. (Diderot 1772b: 67)

If we consider the extent to which mechanistic views of the natural world influenced the thinkers of the eighteenth century, then it should be more understandable to us that Diderot's concept of human "nature" is so far removed from the natural world that it is sometimes expressed in purely mechanical metaphors.

> I regard uncivilised men as a multitude of coiled springs, scattered and isolated. No doubt if two were to collide, one or the other [or both] would break. To overcome this difficulty, a person of profound wisdom and eminent genius assembled these springs into a mechanism; and

within that mechanism known as society all the springs were set in motion, recoiling one against the other, endlessly under strain. More were broken in one day under this regime of law than in a year as a result of Nature's anarchy. But what a crash! What devastation! What shocking destruction of the little springs took place when two, three or four of these huge mechanisms clashed with force! (Diderot 1772b: 73)

Thus it is hardly surprising that Diderot's imagined "savage" is far from being a simple and romantic child of nature. Rather, he is a cold and calculating economic machine, rationally computing the value of sexual relations to build up a pool of population resources so that he may have and control a force of women and children working to his ultimate gain. When Diderot's French chaplain asks, "But what about the powerful and delightful feelings of marital tenderness and paternal care?" the Tahitian responds:

In their place we've another which is altogether more general, energetic and durable: self-interest. . . . [T]ell me if there's any country in the world in which a father, unless held back by shame, wouldn't rather lose his child, or a husband his wife, than accept the loss of his fortune and the comforts of his life. . . . It's here that we take an interest in their upbringing, because in preserving them our fortune grows, while with their loss it is diminished. (Diderot 1772b: 63)

Thus the sexual freedom of the Tahitians is grounded in considerations quite distinct from those of sexual gratification and romantic love.

A child is a precious thing because it will grow up to be an adult. We thus have an interest in caring for it altogether different from that shown in our plants and animals. The birth of a child brings domestic and public joy. It will mean an increase of wealth for the hut, and of strength for the nation. It means another pair of arms and hands in Tahiti. We see in him a future farmer, fisherman, hunter, soldier, husband, father. (Diderot 1772b: 53)

And the standard for comparison of cultures, customs, and "laws" therefore follows.

Whether the ways of Tahiti are better or worse than yours is an easy question to settle. Has the land of your birth more people than it can feed: In that case your ways are neither worse nor better than ours. Can it feed more than it has? In that case our ways are better than yours. (Diderot 1772b: 48)

Obviously, Diderot's "savage" is less a creature of "romantic naturalism" than of masculine competitive sexual hegemony and rationalist economic exploitation. In this lies the true standard for his comparison and critique of Europeans.

> Would you like me to tell you a secret? But be sure to keep it to yourself. When you arrived, we let you have our wives and daughters. You were astonished, you showed such a gratitude that it made us laugh. You thanked us for having granted to you and your companions the greatest of all impositions. We never asked for your money, we didn't raid your possessions; we disdained your products; but our wives and daughters came to extract the blood from your veins. When you leave, you will have left your children; don't you think that this tribute levied upon your person, upon your very substance, surpasses all others? . . .
>
> More robust, more healthy than you, we have seen at first glance how you surpass us in intelligence, and immediately we selected some of our most beautiful girls and women to receive the seed of a race better than our own. It is an experiment we have undertaken, and one which might succeed for us. We have taken from you and your friends the only portion that we are capable of taking, and believe that, complete savages as we are, we also know how to calculate. (Diderot 1772a: 172–73)

Indeed, Diderot's construction of the motivation behind Tahitian sexual hospitality may not be all that far off the mark, if we accept Alexander H. Bolyanatz's (1996) recent analysis of them as "tacticians." But while Diderot's narrow focus on sexual-demographic economics causes him to omit the iron and other trade goods "taken" from the Europeans (Bolyanatz 1996: 43–44), which may after all have been more immediately advantageous than their reproductive profits, he does not omit to add a new element to the discourse on "savagery" that gives us a foreshadowing of issues that will arise in the next century. It may be that the morals of the Tahitians are superior to those of the Europeans; but there is no question of whose intelligence is superior or, in the final balance, which is the better "race."

10 Participant Observation and the Picturesque Savage

FIGURE 14.
OBSERVING THE
OBSERVER. George
Catlin painting
portraits in a Plains
Indian camp, observed
by members of the
tribe (Catlin 1841:
1:frontispiece).

As ethnographic interest in North American Indians shifted from the Northeast to peoples farther to the West in the first half of the nineteenth century, the greatest excitement arose from the discovery of the nomadic hunting peoples of the newly acquired Louisiana Purchase territories. Along with the new direction in ethnographic area focus came innovations in ethnographic method. One such innovation was the practice of what anthropologists would later call participant observation, that is, living for substantial periods with the people studied and taking part, as much as possible, in their way of life. To a limited extent, the approach had informed the writings of missionaries, traders, and others who had lived among non-European peoples to pursue their occupational goals, as well as captives whose participation was involuntary (e.g., Mariner 1827); but few had voluntarily undertaken it with the primary motivation of using it as a source of ethnographic information. We have seen that Volney had employed such a method to study the Bedouins in Egypt and had considered, but rejected, its use in America. Others, however, saw the advantages of such an approach as well; and by the 1830s it was applied to American Indian ethnography by Charles Murray and George Catlin (fig. 14).

MURRAY AND THE THEATRICAL SAVAGE

The Honourable Charles Augustus Murray (1806–95), a young Scots gentleman of independent wealth, while traveling in the United States in 1835, attended a Fourth of July celebration at Fort Leavenworth in the Kansas territory and encountered a visiting party of Pawnee Indians. He was fascinated by their appearance.

> I had already seen many Indians, but none so wild and unsophisticated as these genuine children of the wilderness. They entered the room with considerable ease and dignity, shook hands with us all, and sat down comfortably to cigars and madera. I was quite astonished at the tact and self-possession of these Indians, two-thirds of whom had never been in a settlement of white men before, nor had ever seen a fork, or table, or chair in their lives; yet, without asking questions, or appearing to observe what was passing, they caught it with intuitive readiness, and during the whole dinner were not guilty of a single absurdity or breach of decorum. . . .
>
> As we in our mirth sang one or two choral songs, we called upon our red brethren. They rose all at once; and I never shall forget the effect of that first Indian chorus which I ever heard. Each singer began, by strange and uncouth sounds, to work his mind and lungs up to the proper pitch of excitement; and when at full length their shrill and terrible cry rose to its full height, its effect was astounding, and sufficient to deafen a delicate ear. Then again they would allow their strain to fall into a kind of monotonous cadence, to which they kept time with inflections of the head and body, and again burst forth into the full chorus of mingled yell and howl. (Murray 1839: 1:253–55)

The overwhelming sensory effect was further intensified later that night, when Murray chanced on the Indian camp.

> In the midst of the encampment, the white tents of which showed like snow in the moonlight, were eight or ten large blazing fires, round which the savages were gathered in circles, roasting on rough sticks huge fragments of a newly-killed ox. The greater part of them were

naked, except the before-mentioned belt round their middle; and their dusky figures, lighted partially by the fitful glare of the crackling wood fire, seemed like a band of demons gathered round one of the fabled caldrons of necromancy. (Murray 1839: 1:255)

From these quasi-demonic necromancers, Murray receives his first taste of beef grilled to medium rare (or, as he says, "half-raw"); and by the next morning, he tells us, he had "formed a hasty, but determined resolution, of accompanying these Pawnees in their return to their nation" (1839: 1:256). Thus began a remarkable summer's odyssey in which he lived and traveled with the Pawnee in their summer hunting camp, joined with them in their buffalo hunt, and acquired firsthand experience that gives us one of the most vivid accounts of the everyday life of an American Indian people at the time.

As we might expect from this narrative of his first encounter, Murray's attraction to the Pawnee is more emotional than intellectual, more aesthetic than analytic. He is a sensationalist, in constant search of the greatest intensity of personal experience; and, in this, he and his narrative exemplify the romanticism of his age. There has been some tendency in the literature on the Noble Savage to equate "romanticism" with ennoblement, that is, to assume that to romanticize is to exalt and eulogize, ignoring or minimizing the tendency of romanticism to seek extremes of every kind from the highest to lowest, the most exalted to the most degraded of human emotions. For Murray, as for other romantics, the quest for aesthetic intensity also embraces the terrifying, the shocking, and the disgusting; and these dimensions play a significant role in constructing his representation of Pawnee life.

With his perceptions challenged by new, ever-changing experiences and acquaintances from one day to the next, Murray finds new things and new persons variously to praise and to condemn in his stay with the Pawnees. He admires their skill and their fortitude; he finds men to praise for their honesty and women for their beauty. Yet, the positive cases, the honest men (1839: 1:304) and the pretty girls (1839: 1:307), are always presented as exceptions to what he sees as the predominance of negative examples. In sum, the overall balance of his impressions of them is decidedly negative; and he comes to view his participant observation as a kind of triumph of undercover investigation that opens locked doors to expose some of the concealed, darker secrets of their true characters and lives.

> Every hour that I spent with the Indians, impressed upon me the conviction that I had taken the only method of becoming acquainted with

their domestic habits and their undisguised character. Had I judged
from what I had been able to observe at Fort Leavenworth, or other
frontier places, where I met them, I should have known about as much
of them as the generality of scribblers and their readers, and might, like
them, have deceived myself and others into a belief in their "high sense
of honour"—their hospitality—their openness and love of truth, and
many other qualities which they possess, if at all, in a very moderate
degree; and yet it is no wonder if such impressions have gone abroad,
because the Indian, among whites, or at a garrison, trading-post, or
town, is as different a man from the same Indian at home as a Turkish
"Mollah" is from a French barber. Among whites, he is all dignity and
repose; he is acting a part the whole time, and acts it most admirably.
He manifests no surprise at the most wonderful effects of machinery—
is not startled if a twenty-four-pounder is fired close to him,[1] and does
not evince the slightest curiosity regarding the thousand things that
are strange and new to him; whereas at home, the same Indian chatters,
jokes, and laughs among his companions—frequently indulges in the
most licentious conversation; and his curiosity is as unbounded and
irresistible as that of any man, woman, or monkey, on earth.

Truth and honesty (making the usual exceptions to be found in all
countries) are unknown, or despised by them. (Murray 1839: 1:303–4)

Despite the tone of dark accusation, Murray's discoveries do not seem all
that shocking. Is it really so awful that the Pawnee had a sense of humor,
or curiosity? But Murray's triumph in discovering what he considers a deliberate deceit, the concealment of their true character by "acting a part,"
derives in part from his own feelings of an underlying contest in which he
is himself obliged to constantly engage in role-playing.

In all my intercourse with the Pawnees, I made it a rule to humor their
prejudices, and to accommodate myself to their usages, however absurd. Moreover, I endeavored to make them believe that I could surpass
them in anything which I chose to attempt. (Murray 1839: 1:346)

Indeed, his feelings of antagonism are so strong that he attempts to rationalize them by biological speculations.

Nature appears to have divided the white from the red man by a species
of antipathy scarcely reconcilable with the benignity and sympathies
which are usually found in her provisions. An Indian infant cannot
endure the approach or sight of a white man, neither can the infant of
a white look without terror upon an Indian. In walking quietly through
the Pawnee camp, I have often found myself the innocent cause of the
cries and screams of at least twenty of these little alarmists, though
I may not have passed nearer than thirty yards from some of them.

> Nor is this most strongly-marked aversion confined to the human
> race: Indian horses cannot bear the smell of a white man. (Murray
> 1839: 1:280)

But fantastic musings on animal magnetism aside, the causes of uneasy
feelings between Murray and the Pawnee lay in more prosaic and familiar
political aspects of Indian-white contact.

> A council was held, but they carefully concealed their determination
> from me. . . . But of the measures which they adopted I remained in to-
> tal ignorance. Doubtless, they considered me somewhat in the light of a
> spy; for when I inquired . . . they either pretended not to understand,
> or made the sign of "mystery" or "silence," by placing the hand before
> the lips, and then extending it with the palm towards me. (Murray
> 1839: 1:333)

In simple terms, the foreign traveler, introduced and commended to the
safekeeping of the Pawnee by an Indian agent of the U.S. government, under the auspices of a claim of kinship to the great "grandfather" in Washington, appeared to the Indians as a newer and stranger kind of government
agent, and they accepted him in the role in which he was represented to
them. Nor was the representation far wide of the mark, questions of British citizenship notwithstanding; for Murray indeed moved in the highest
circles, receiving special courtesy and hospitality from the governor of
Canada and the chief justice of the United States, among other dignitaries
(Murray 1839: 1:88–89, 158–60). Returning to England, he addressed the
dedication of his book to Queen Victoria *from* Buckingham Palace. And in
1843 we find him at Windsor Castle, the household manager of the royal
family, at a visit by a touring delegation of Chippewa Indians who sang and
danced before the queen, "much to the apparent surprise as well as the
amusement of her Majesty." George Catlin, who arranged the visit, acted
as the Indians' interpreter; and Murray served as the official translator and
spokesman for the queen, expressing her gratitude and friendship to the
Indians (*ILN* 1843a: 401–2).

Clearly, Murray was a man with a reputation and a position to maintain;
and this undoubtedly had some effect on his defensive attitude toward the
Indians, as it did elsewhere in his travels. As a Scot, even though moving
in exalted circles, he belonged to one of the marginalized peoples of the
British kingdom, subject to romanticized projections and hints of connections to "savagery"; and, while expressing pride in his Scottish heritage, he
is careful to let readers know that his few words of Gaelic are not enough
to allow him to carry on conversations in it (1839: 1:126–27). He disasso-

ciates himself with expressions of "pity and disgust" from the "numerous and troublesome" Irish-Americans with their "prejudices" and "revengeful malice," who plot "scenes of destruction, blood, and revolution, which they hoped yet to see in Britain" (1839: 2:106). Murray cannot permit himself to be seen as less than completely loyal to England and its civilization; and he demonstrates his loyalty at every level down to his original contributions to the English language, claiming credit for such innovations as importing the word "appetizing" from France (1839: 2:62).[2] It is hard to imagine anyone less likely to admit to others, or to himself, that he had in any way "gone native."

But if Murray is in many ways a conventional and unphilosophical traveler, he is by no means an unreflective one. He looks at himself, the gentleman and once-elegant courtier adapted to the necessities of a nomadic hunting life, and wishes that the Indian he stands next to "could only give to the public as faithful a description of me as I have of him" (1839: 1:382). He takes a noticeable delight in his nondescript, ragged and dirty clothing, his belt hung with knives and pistols, and his tanned skin and face "disfigured by a pair of long mustachios" (1839: 1:382). At times the picture begins to verge on the surreal, as during his participation in a buffalo hunt, when he found himself thrown from his horse and alone on the prairie:

> From this prospect I turned to my actual state, sitting, as I was, on the ground, with my hands, arms, and face saturated and glued with blood; it was, indeed, too much, and I burst into an uncontrollable fit of laughter. I then began to think of the strange and varied notions of pleasure entertained by different men, and could not help questioning whether my Pawnee trip, voluntarily incurred, with its accompaniments, did not render the sanity of my mind a matter of some doubt. (1839: 1:397)

This is perhaps Murray's profoundest and most honest moment of insight in the whole journey, as he sits on the ground laughing at his own self-image, torn between irony and relativism, questioning the nature of "sanity" itself. There can be no doubt, even in some of the more artificially melodramatic parts of his narrative, that he sees himself changing at deeper levels than the physical appearances he constantly stresses. In one such moment, after two days of privation during a buffalo hunt, he finds himself at the scene of the kill.

> I reloaded my rifle, while the Indians cut him up with a speed which appeared to me, even among *them*, unexampled; indeed, they were nearly famished; and as they squatted on their hams round the huge

animal, and devoured large slices which they cut off yet warm, a *civilized* man might have doubted whether they were wolves or human beings. But *I* was no longer a civilized man—hunger had triumphed over the last traces of civilization—I received with thankfulness, and ate with eagerness, a good piece of the warm liver, untouched by fire, water, or salt, and I found it as agreeable to the palate, and as tender as any morsel I ever tasted. It must sound horrible to others, as it did to me a few weeks ago, but let none condemn me till he has been in a similar situation. (1839: 1:366–67)

The style is overblown, effusive, "romanticized"; and yet the concluding plea—"let none condemn me till he has been in a similar situation"—resonates for the Indians as well as for Murray, sunk into the self-revealing mirror of the contingencies of their experiential world as much as they are now reflected in the self-awareness of his own experiences. Murray sees himself reconstituted by the world he has chosen to enter, and his self-reconstruction dissolves the solid certainty of the self-concept he had known and embraced as the "civilized man," the superior antithesis of the "savage."

Or rather, it seems that logically this is what should have happened. But, in fact, despite such moments of reflection, his rhetoric retains a solidly negative thrust against the Indians. We wonder who is "acting a part" here. Could it be that participation in their life for a longer period than a single summer might have brought the seeds of reflexive self-insight to fuller fruition? Or is it just, as the Chippewa chief would tell him later at Windsor Castle that "Your wigwams are large, and the light that is in them is bright. Our wigwams are small, and our light is not strong" (*ILN* 1843a: 401)?

It goes without saying that Murray finds no nobility in the "savages." His use of the rhetoric of nobility is limited to noble forests (1839: 1:249), noble parks (1:260), and noble animals (1:122). The attractor that draws Murray to the Pawnee is not nobility but the picturesque. At his first sight of their camp, he says, "A more interesting or picturesque scene I never beheld" (1:277). In his first meeting with his host's family, he remarks, "If the features of the parties had not been so totally devoid of anything like beauty, the family-picture would have been as picturesque as it was interesting" (1:279). The scene of the Indians on the march between their nomadic camps "was picturesque in the extreme" (1:291); a chief's costume "was picturesque and in character" (1:381); and, watching the chief ride off with his followers, Murray says, "I could not help admiring the picturesque and warlike appearance of the warriors around him" (1:384).

FIGURE 15. THE PICTURESQUE "SAVAGE."
"Chippeway" pipe and tomahawk dances, from Charles Murray's *Travels in North America* (1839: 1:frontispiece).

The picturesque was a romantic aesthetic paradigm that became popular in the late eighteenth century as a broadening of previous aesthetic emphases on "the sublime," a category that embraced the awe-inspiring extremes of the sublimely beautiful and the supremely terrifying and sought to encompass the more inclusive intermediate ground of those things that combined visual and emotional attraction (Riffenburgh 1994: 11 ff.). Although Beau Riffenburgh (1994: 24) maintains that the subsequent rise of sensationalism in the nineteenth century "had to await the death of" the sublime and the picturesque as competing paradigms, in fact the category of the picturesque survived and flourished as the emblematic catchword of the romantic imagination, capable of encompassing every sensual-emotional effect from "sublime" exaltation to "sensational" degradation. Throughout the century, hundreds of works would appear on "picturesque" places and peoples—England, Egypt, India, China, America, the entire world—often lavishly and expensively produced, conceived in flights of originality and outrageousness, and united by a common appeal to the confluence of vision, sensation, and emotion. Here we see some of the most exalted, the most degraded, the most bizarre, and the most shocking treatments of the "savage"; and it is in a relatively early phase of this movement that Murray's work finds its place (fig. 15).

Murray's aesthetic of the picturesque embraces the whole range of romantic visual-emotional excitement. During a raid on the Pawnee camp by a war party, he writes:

> Standing thus quietly on the defensive, I had leisure to enjoy the wild beauty of the scene before me. The shrill and savage war-cry raised by a thousand voices—the neighing, struggling, and trampling of the excited horses, mingled with the howling of dogs, and the irregular firing of their guns, with which the Pawnees directed and cheered their warriors to the scene of action—formed a wild and exciting combination of sounds; while the groups of women and children gathered round the pale and expiring fires, and the tall dark figure of the old chief, standing with his arms calmly folded beside me, served admirably to fill the interesting and picturesque fore-ground. (1839: 1:330)

And, in fact, the visual-emotional impact of the picturesque could transcend the range of merely human emotion, as in Murray's description of a buffalo hunt:

> It was, indeed, one of the most picturesque sights I ever beheld, to see these hairy monsters rushing with headlong speed down the declivities, snorting, bellowing, and regardless of shouts or arrows; some rolling over lifeless under the shafts of their merciless persecutors; some standing still, with erect tail, blood-shot eye, and nostrils frothed with blood, waiting in vain for the crafty enemy to approach within reach of their dying rush; and others breaking through all opposition, and studding the most distant part of the landscape with black specks, which gradually diminished, and were at length lost to view. (1839: 1:387)

The awestruck appreciation of the grandeur of horror, blood, and death is a reflection and a reminder of what drew Murray to the Pawnees in the first place; and now we may sense some of the power of attraction that drew him to abandon, even if temporarily and hypercritically, the perceived superiority of civilization for the allure of the "savage." He will not state it directly but objectifies and dramatizes it in his comparison of two Indian tribes, as the Pawnee are visited by a neighboring people: "These men are more civilized than the Pawnees, and I believe affect to despise them; but in horsemanship, as well as in wild picturesque appearance and habits, they are very inferior" (1839: 1:341). Inferiority, it appears, is in some sense a relative thing after all, and not entirely determined by the contrast between savagery and civilization.

CATLIN'S AESTHETIC NOBILITY

Murray's representation of the picturesque had been entirely verbal, whereas George Catlin (1796–1872), his contemporary, used painting as his primary medium. But the difference between them was greater than simply the choice of representational medium. It seems entirely appropriate that in their meeting at Windsor Castle in 1843 Catlin acted as the spokesman for the Indians and Murray for the royal family; for, while Murray repeatedly represents himself in his ethnographic writing as a champion of civilization, Catlin is even more insistent on his own position as an advocate on behalf of the "savages." The dynamic tension generated by the interplay of, on the one hand, his use of verbal discourse as a secondary representational medium subordinated to his pictures and, on the other, his strongly articulated political agenda makes Catlin's work one of the most problematic and interesting that we have to consider.

Like Murray, Catlin is a devotee of the picturesque and a "romantic." The "romantic" ethos shows in the way that both writers represent their decisions to spend time living among the Indians as the result of unexpected, chance encounters of such a vividly compelling quality as to provide the impetus for a life-altering experience. In Catlin's case, he tells us, having abandoned a career as a lawyer to become a painter, he encountered "a delegation of some ten or fifteen noble and dignified-looking Indians, from the wilds of the 'Far West'" (Catlin 1841: 1:2), who had come to visit Philadelphia. The description, as a visceral reaction to a sudden and unexpected encounter, should certainly be read as "noble-looking and dignified-looking"—that is, as a reference to aesthetic nobility—since Catlin had no basis for a deeper assessment of the Indians' character. But on the basis of this first impression, he decided that he had found the perfect subject for his art.

> Arrayed and equipped in all their classic beauty,—with shield and helmet,—with tunic and manteau,—tinted and tasselled off, exactly for the painter's palette!
> In silent and stoic dignity, these lords of the forest strutted about the city for a few days, wrapped in their pictured robes, with their brows plumed with the quills of the war-eagle, attracting the gaze and admiration of all who beheld them. After this, they took their leave for Washington City, and I was left to reflect and regret, which I did long and deeply, until I came to the following deductions and conclusions.
> Black and blue cloth and civilization are destined, not only to veil, but to obliterate the grace and beauty of Nature. Man, in the simplicity

and loftiness of his nature, unrestrained and unfettered by the disguises of art, is surely the most beautiful model for the painter,—and the country from which he hails is unquestionably the best study or school of the arts in the world: such I am sure, from the models I have seen, is the wilderness of North America. And the history and customs of such a people, preserved by pictorial illustrations, are themes worthy the life-time of one man, and nothing short of the loss of my life, shall prevent me from visiting their country, and of becoming their historian. (Catlin 1841: 1:2)

In fact, the Indians' visit to Philadelphia occurred in 1822–23, and Catlin would depart for the West only in 1830, after arranging sponsorship and saving money and making preliminary portrait-painting visits to Indian reservations in the Northeast (Mooney 1975: 13 ff.). But having taken his time in making his decision, Catlin set out better prepared and with a far more enduring commitment than Murray, eventually covering a span of eight years in his travels to various peoples before publication of his first book, in 1841.

The world that Catlin entered in the Plains in the 1830s was not the pristine state of nature that he imagined. Transformed by the introduction of the horse after the Spanish arrival in Mexico three centuries earlier, the equestrian-nomadic Plains hunting cultures had become fully established only within the last century; and the economic prosperity he observed there, with its inevitable effects on features ranging from social hierarchy and warfare to the elaboration of richness of costumes, customs, and ritual, had been fundamentally altered by the Euro-American–Indian trade network, with its growing emphasis on the value of buffalo robes (for an overview of Great Plains history, see Fowler 1996). Even more radical transformations were in store as the result of the newly adopted policy of the U.S. government, after passage of the Indian Removal Act of 1830, to relocate all Indian tribes to the "Indian Territory" west of the Mississippi, where they competed for space and resources with existing Plains tribes and were subject to unprecedented and unregulated exploitation by invasive waves of white settlers and traders, a process Catlin chronicled with accuracy and uncompromising criticism.

Catlin, a keen observer of culture change in progress, developed precise observations and powerful critiques of the effects of Indian contact with white society. Nevertheless, his sophisticated and nuanced awareness of the details of culture change was subjected to an overall simplification by his temporoculturally induced preconception of a black-and-white dichotomy between the "wild" peoples in a "state of nature" that he imag-

ined he saw on the Great Plains and the "tame" peoples subject to contact with, and exploitation by, Euro-American society. In the latter case, his
descriptions and critiques of the harmful effects of dispossession, dislocation, and the alcohol trade bear comparison with Margaret Mead's (1932)
century-later critical study of the effects of culture change among the
Omaha, as well as with more recent critical works. But in the former case,
his perception of a pristine state of nature in Plains societies reflects an
anachronistic and antihistorical stance that derives, at least in part, from
his theoretical-methodological emphasis on the primacy of direct field
observation.

Catlin emphasizes repeatedly, "I am travelling . . . not to prove *theo-*
ries, but to see all that I am able to see, and to tell it in the simplest and
most intelligible manner I can to the world, for their own conclusions"
(1841: 1:206). He criticizes the armchair scholars who construct theories of the past history or origins of the Indians "whilst remaining at
home and consulting books, in the way that too many theories are supported" (1841: 2:236), and rejects on ideological grounds such theories
as "have been based upon the Indian's inferiority" (1841: 2:229). In Catlin's
view, not only should research be conducted by firsthand on-site observation, its primary goal should also be not to speculate about the dead
generations of the past but to describe the living people of the present—
not least because the ethical dimensions of ethnographic research demand a high priority for attempts to achieve justice for the living (Catlin
1841: 2:224 ff.).

Many of these points anticipate developments in the post-Boasian
theory and practice of fieldwork in the twentieth century. But, like some
twentieth-century ethnographers, Catlin also falls into a fairly common
fieldworker's dilemma, in which the concreteness of the actually present
becomes an obstacle to the comprehension of historical foundations on
which present structures are erected. In simple terms, it can be tempting
for a fieldworker to accept a pattern or process that obviously exists at the
moment of observation, as something that *is* characteristic of a people or
their way of life in a more essential and enduring sense. Catlin's radically
presentist empiricism, reinforced by the absolute binary opposition of the
primordially "wild" and the civilized "tame" that he and his contemporaries projected onto the cultural boundary of the "frontier," certainly lessened the likelihood of any critical reassessment of his preconception that
things as he saw them were as they had always been, unchanging "wild"
societies living in an equally unchanging world of "nature." And this de-

spite his vividly detailed observations of widespread, rapid, and fundamental changes in everything from native cultures to the plant and animal species of the physical landscape. Change was confined to the present and the future, rather than extending forward from the past.

Catlin describes his fieldwork activities in terms of participant observation: "mingling with red men, and identifying myself with them as much as possible, in their games and amusements, in order the better to familiarize myself with their superstitions and mysteries, which are the keys to Indian life and character" (1841: 1:3). He sees a need for comprehensive observation of the details of everyday life: "It is from the observance of a thousand little and apparently trivial modes and tricks of Indian life, that the Indian character must be learned" (1841: 1:102). Like Murray, he spent months traveling and hunting with Indians on the plains (1841: 2:43); he also lived in the lodges of the Mandan, exchanged paintings with one of their chiefs, attended their religious ceremonies, and discovered the liberating exhilaration of participating "naked" in their horse races (1841: 1:80 ff., 116–17, 155 ff., 198). Also like Murray, he regards firsthand observation and participation as providing a unique advantage.

> The reader will therefore see, that we mutually suffer in each other's estimation from the unfortunate ignorance, which distance has chained us in; and (as I can vouch, and the Indian also, who has visited the civilized world) that the historian who would record justly and correctly the character and customs of a people, must go and live among them. (Catlin 1841: 1:86)

But Catlin's participant observation leads him to conclusions diametrically opposed to Murray's. For example, on a "first contact" visit to a Comanche camp, he notes a reaction similar to one Murray had witnessed among the Pawnee.

> We white men, strolling about amongst their wigwams, are looked upon with as much curiosity as if we had come from the moon; and evidently create a sort of chill in the blood of children and dogs, when we make our appearance. (Catlin 1841: 2:64)

However, unlike Murray, he treats this as a rather matter-of-fact situation and is not drawn into biological speculations by it. We may also recall Murray's example of how participant observation led him to expose the deceit of the Indians' dignity, their "acting a part" to conceal the secret of their true character, tainted by such weaknesses as humor and curiosity. Catlin observes the same behavior:

> I have observed in all my travels amongst the Indian tribes . . . that they are a far more talkative and conversational race than can easily be seen in the civilized world. . . . No one can look into the wigwams of these people . . . without being at once struck with the conviction that small-talk, gossip, garrulity, and story-telling are the leading passions with them. . . . One has but to walk or ride about this little town and its environs for a few hours in a pleasant day, and overlook the numerous games and gambols, where their notes and yelps of exultation are unceasingly vibrating in the atmosphere; or peep into their wigwams (and watch the glistening fun that's beaming from the noses, cheeks, and chins, of the crouching, cross-legged, and prostrate groups around the fire; where the pipe is passed, and jokes and anecdote, and laughter are excessive) to become convinced that it is natural to laugh and be merry. . . .
>
> They live in a country and in communities, where it is not customary to look forward into the future with concern, for they live without incurring the expenses of life, which are absolutely necessary and unavoidable in the enlightened world. . . . With minds thus unexpanded and uninfluenced by the thousand passions and ambitions of civilized life, it is easy and natural to concentrate their thoughts and their conversation upon the little and trifling occurrences of their lives. They are fond of fun and good cheer, and can laugh easily and heartily at a slight joke, of which their peculiar modes of life furnish them an inexhaustible fund, and enable them to cheer their little circle about the wigwam fire-side with endless laughter and garrulity.
>
> It may be thought, that I am taking a great deal of pains to establish this fact, and I am dwelling longer upon it than I otherwise should, inasmuch as I am opposing an error that seems to have become current through the world; and which, if it be once corrected, removes a material difficulty, which has always stood in the way of a fair and just estimation of the Indian character. For the purpose of placing the Indian in a proper light before the world, as I hope to do in many respects, it is of importance to me—it is but justice to the savage—and justice to my readers also, that such points should be cleared up as I proceed; and for the world who enquire for correct and just information, they must take my words for the truth, or else come to this country and look for themselves, into these grotesque circles of never-ending laughter and fun. (1841: 1:84–85)

Although both Murray and Catlin regard their residence with the Indians as helping to overcome previous misunderstandings, where Murray finds deceitful theatrics, Catlin finds overtones of the Golden Age, together with a sharing of human qualities that he obviously considers worthy of admiration.

But the greatest difference in the two observers is Catlin's concern with "justice," which, along with the aesthetics of the picturesque, is a primary energizing force in his narrative. He repeatedly refers to himself as an "enthusiast" on the Indians' behalf; and indeed he is, repeatedly extolling their virtues and innocence of the crimes and character defects of which others have accused them and repeatedly denouncing the wrongs done by his countrymen against them.[3] "My heart has sometimes almost bled with pity for them," he says (1841: 1:61); but luckily for him, the myth of the "bleeding-heart liberal" would not be born until the next century.

For Catlin, neither art nor ethnography is a morally neutral enterprise. He says, "I find that the principal cause why we underrate and despise the savage, is generally because we do not understand him" (1841: 1:102). Ethnography, by increasing understanding, can aid the cause of justice; and this, for Catlin, is the highest value of ethnographic observation. He uses it to explain and defend such widely criticized practices as warfare and scalping, and says:

> If the reader thinks that I am taking too much pains to defend the Indians for this, and others of their seemingly abominable customs, he will bear it in mind, that I have lived with these people, until I have learned the necessities of Indian life in which these customs are founded; and also, that I have met with so many acts of kindness and hospitality at the hands of the poor Indian, that I feel bound, when I can do it, to render what excuse I can for a people, who are dying with broken hearts, and never can speak in the civilized world in their own defence. (1841: 1:239)

No more classic formulation of the principle of participant observation could be found than "I have lived with these people, until I have learned the necessities of Indian life in which these customs are founded"; and, as with many other participant observers, Catlin's knowledge energizes him into sympathy and defensive advocacy on his subjects' behalf. Elsewhere, Catlin acknowledges that the Indians can speak very well in their own defense and gives ample descriptions and examples of their eloquence. But his point is that they needed defenders within the society and system that was increasingly coming to dominate and oppress them. The role of defensive advocate that he assumes is quite in keeping with his earlier professional training and practice as a lawyer, as is his rhetoric of accusation and defense, guilt and innocence, mitigating circumstances, ownership, rights, and justice. Both rhetorically and substantially, there is much in Catlin's writing to evoke recollections of Lescarbot's legalist orientation. The crucial difference, of course, is that, unlike Lescarbot, Catlin never assumes the role of prosecutor but pleads only as an advocate of the defense.

What most strongly brings Lescarbot's work to mind, however, is Catlin's use of the rhetoric of nobility. For example, Catlin describes the purpose of his work in these terms:

> I started out in the year 1832 . . . inspired with an enthusiastic hope
> and reliance that I could meet and overcome all the hazards and priva-
> tions of a life devoted to the production of a literal and graphic delin-
> eation of the living manners, customs, and characters of an interest-
> ing race of people, who are rapidly passing away from the face of the
> earth—lending a hand to a dying nation, who have no historians or
> biographers of their own to pourtray [sic] with fidelity their native
> looks and history; thus snatching from a hasty oblivion what could be
> saved for the benefit of posterity, and perpetuating it, as a fair and just
> monument, to the memory of a truly lofty and noble race. (1841: 1:3)

And he goes on to say:

> I have, for many years past, contemplated the noble races of red men
> who are now spread over these trackless forests and boundless prairies,
> melting away at the approach of civilization. Their rights invaded,
> their morals corrupted, their lands wrested from them, their customs
> changed, and therefore lost to the world; and they at last sunk into the
> earth, and the ploughshare turning the sod over their graves, and I
> have flown to their rescue—not of their lives or of their race (for they
> are *"doomed"* and must perish), but to the rescue of their looks and
> their modes, at which the acquisitive world may hurl their poison and
> every besom of destruction, and trample them down and crush them to
> death; yet, phoenix-like, they may rise from the "stain on a painter's
> palette," and live again upon canvass, and stand forth for centuries yet
> to come, the living monuments of a noble race. (1841: 1:16)

Here, in this credal affirmation of belief in picturesque immortality, is by far the strongest, most global, and most pervasive linkage of the "savage" with nobility since Lescarbot himself. And it seems that Catlin shares Lescarbot's salvage-ethnography orientation, but with a particularly fatalistic twist, characteristic of his age, based on his anticipation of the Indians' impending doom. In fact, although Catlin seems assured in these passages of the physical elimination of the Indians, he is inconsistent on this, as on many other points. Although he is firmly convinced of the inevitability of white expansion into the remaining territories of the Indian peoples (Catlin 1841: 2:156–59), he vacillates between dire forebodings of the inevitability of genocide and surges of hope in which, like Lescarbot, he argues their good qualities, denounces white aggression and oppression, and pleads for clemency, justice, and fair dealings in the interest of their ultimate survival, arguing the virtues of the "savages" as a mitigating plea in the face of their threatened extermination.

Thus we might expect Catlin's rhetoric of nobility to serve as the voice of a kind of virtual character witness pleading the case for a reprieve from the harsh sentence that white society would pass on the Indians. But, in fact, very few of Catlin's references to nobility have to do with nobility of character, or even with the nobility of Indians in general. The passages just cited refer to the Indians as a "noble race"; but they comprise just three out of sixty of Catlin's uses of the term "noble" and its derivatives, without any indication of what the term means for him. Is this the essentially pure and exalted character of the uncorrupted children of nature, as posited by the Noble Savage myth?

As it turns out, Catlin actually does represent the Indians living beyond the western frontier of white civilization as possessing just such qualities—only he does not associate these qualities with the rhetoric of nobility.[4] Only three of his sixty "noble" references are clearly associated with character and moral qualities, all having to do with a single individual rather than with Indians in general (Catlin 1841: 1:212, 222, 224). And as for the problematic association of nobility and Indians as a race, Catlin only juxtaposes "noble" and "race" in one additional instance, where he refers to the Assineboines as "a fine and noble looking race of Indians" (1841: 1:54). The artist's eye is the energizing force behind the writer's pen: the nobility of race, as Catlin represents it, is an aesthetic nobility.

Aesthetic factors clearly play an important role in Catlin's representation of the "noble." It is not simply that the sublime or the picturesque is interchangeable with the noble in his discursive palette; rather, aesthetic beauty is a multidimensional quality that shades over into other value spaces, including the more positive and attractive ranges of the moral spectrum. On a classically cross-cultural level, the possibility of such a synaesthesia of value dimensions is an assumption underlying the widespread representation of heroes as young, richly dressed, and handsome; and in terms of the world in which Catlin moved, it represented a confluence of the artistic conventions of romanticism with the mode of scientific thinking that assumed the embodiment of intellectual and moral qualities in features of physiognomy.

Catlin transposed to the Indians the standard practices of Euro-American portraiture, framing individuals in their richest and most symbolically distinctive attire and surroundings—their "Sunday best" and "parade dress"—to let their outer beauty give expression to their inner beauty. Indeed, Catlin repeatedly refers to Indian costume and ornamentation in terms of insignia of office and the heraldry of coats of "arms"; and it is hardly surprising that the Indians he finds most "noble" are those with the richest and most decorative costumes, grounded in an economic matrix of relative prosperity. For other less fortunate Indians, such as the dispossessed tribes living under white domination and exploitation, or the "Flat Heads" (a term then used loosely to refer to various Plateau and Northwest Coast peoples), he has little to say about nobility:

> These are a very numerous people . . . living in a country which is exceedingly sterile and almost entirely, in many parts, destitute of game for the subsistence of the savage; they are mostly obliged to live on roots, which they dig from the ground, and fish which they take from the streams; the consequences of which are, that they are generally poor and miserably clad; and in no respect equal to the Indians of whom I have heretofore spoken, who live on the East of the Rocky Mountains, in the ranges of the buffaloes; where they are well-fed, and mostly have good horses to ride, and materials in abundance for manufacturing their beautiful and comfortable dresses. (1841: 2:108)

All "savages," then, are not equal, nor are they equally noble. Indeed, following the comparative paradigm that we have seen to dominate ethnographic writings since the rise of eighteenth-century sociocultural evolutionary progressivism, the most "savage" lifestyles—that is, those farthest removed from civilized advancements—are the least noble; and deficiencies of wealth and comfort play a significant role in evaluating them.

It will hardly be surprising, then, to find that among Catlin's references to nobility, the second-largest group, more than one-third of the total, are concerned with the nobility of distinction and the exaltation of one individual or group over another. Plains Indian societies, among whom Catlin did most of his ethnographic studies, all had greater or lesser emphasis on distinctions of wealth and status hierarchies; and his own direct participant observation awareness of their hierarchy was continually reinforced by the inevitable insistence of the Indians that he paint his portraits in order of rank, beginning with chiefs and shamans, progressing to warriors, and finishing with low-ranking individuals, if not omitting them entirely. As the highest-ranking individuals were generally the most elaborately dressed and ornamented, yet another stimulus was furnished, this time arising from observation of the Indians' own beliefs and practices, that reinforced the perception of a correlation between picturesqueness and external beauty, on the one hand, and culturally attributed superiority of character and moral qualities, on the other. In a discursive praxis in which "chief" becomes the term most frequently juxtaposed with "noble," it is easy to appreciate that although for Catlin the Indians may all be equally children of nature, they are by no means equally noble: some are clearly more noble than others.

But the nobility of distinction is still only the second-largest category of references to the "noble" in Catlin's work. If we ask what comprises the largest class, the answer may be somewhat unexpected: nearly half of the uses of the rhetoric of nobility in his book refer to the nobility of non-human objects and beings. Among them are "noble" features of the land-scape—scenes, hills, ridges—and even objects such as a "noble pair of pistols" (1841: 2:151), and "noble" animals, including eagles, horses, and especially buffalo. There can be no question, given the mixture of animals, inanimate objects, and artifacts, that nobility necessarily implies any con-nection with morality, ethics, or character—or, for that matter, given the domesticated horses and pistols, with wildness or nature. The only kind of "nobility" that all these objects can have in common is a nobility of aes-thetics and distinction that sets them off from similar objects by their picturesque appearance, or by other kinds of uniqueness that create a sub-jective sense of heightened value to an interested perceiver.

Sometimes it seems that man and animals are equally noble, and some-times the latter come out ahead.

> Nature has no where presented more beautiful and lovely scenes, than those of the vast prairies of the West; and of *man* and *beast*, no nobler specimens than those who inhabit them—the *Indian* and the *buffalo*. . . . It may be that *power* is *right*, and *voracity* a *virtue;* and that these people, and these noble animals, are *righteously* doomed. (Catlin 1841: 1:16; emphasis in original)

If nobility is not restricted to humans, its human manifestations are like-wise not restricted to "savages." The hearts of the Indians, Catlin main-tains, are "of a human mould, *susceptible* of all the noble feelings belong-ing to civilized man" (1841: 2:83; emphasis in original). Catlin makes it clear that nobility is a universal human capacity that can find expression in any people:

> The very use of the word savage, as it is applied in its general sense, I am inclined to believe is an abuse of the word, and the people to whom

it is applied. The word, in its true definition, means no more than *wild*, or *wild man*; and a wild man may have been endowed by his Maker with all the humane and noble traits that inhabit the heart of a tame man. (1841: 1:9)

Thus it is appropriate that just as Catlin painted portraits of both Indians and whites in the same "romantic" style (Catlin 1841: 2:79, 151), so also he speaks of members of both peoples as "noble." For example: "The Captain is a gentleman of high and noble bearing, of one of the most respected families in Philadelphia, with a fine and chivalrous feeling" (1841: 2:87).

Just as he does when speaking of Indians, Catlin grounds his rhetoric of white nobility on picturesque aesthetics and distinctions of social status, which form a dual foundation for the construction of an evaluation of character. It is these distinctive features, rather than a shared racial constitution or participation in the "wild" lifestyle of the "children of nature," that ennoble certain individuals or groups of Indians. The "wild" Indians are not noble because of their wildness; rather, nobility acts as a counterforce against the more negative energies of "savage" life: "Even here, the predominant passions of the savage breast, of ferocity and cruelty, are often found; yet *restrained,* and frequently *subdued,* by the noblest traits of honour and magnanimity" (1841: 1:60).

Thus, although Catlin finds many examples of aesthetic and status nobility among the relatively more unacculturated western Indians whom he considers "wild," he also finds instances of nobility among more acculturated groups living in close proximity to white society. Although he repeatedly laments the poverty and alcoholism endemic among such groups, he admits that "there are many noble instances to the contrary" (1841: 2:255). Instead of being associated with the preservation of "savage" ways or the "state of nature," these instances of nobility mostly have to do with the adoption of a "civilized" lifestyle and, above all, Christianity: the Indians who do not succumb to demoralizing and life-threatening despair constitute the "striking and noble exceptions . . . who have followed . . . their Christian teachers" (1841: 2:245). Watching one such teacher, a converted Kickapoo chief preaching a Christian sermon, Catlin "was singularly struck with the noble efforts of this champion of the mere remnant of a poisoned race" (1841: 2:98).

In overall balance, Catlin's rhetoric of nobility is generally grounded in picturesque aesthetics, individual uniqueness, and status distinctions; but in detail, it is complex and multifaceted and at times apparently contradictory. In some cases, it leads to constructions that appear indistinguishable from the myth of the Noble Savage; in other cases, to those that seem its direct antithesis, as in the attribution of nobility to Indians who have abandoned their "savage" ways to become "civilized" and Christianized. Given such apparent contradictions, it is worth noting that Catlin never actually uses the term "noble savage." His rhetoric of nobility flows on a different vector from his discourse on the communal innocence and purity of life in the state of nature, however much the two may tend to converge in a few discussions of some individual cases.

What renders Catlin's narrative particularly interesting and problematic is his use of language. He warns us about it:

> And if some few of my narrations should seem a *little too highly coloured,* I trust the world will be ready to extend to me that pardon which it is customary to yield to all artists whose main faults exist in the vividness of their colouring, rather than in the drawing of their pictures. (1841: 1:5; emphasis in original)

To call Catlin's language "highly coloured" is an understatement; and even to say "purple prose" would fail to do it justice. Sometimes quiet and subdued in tone, often precise and realistic in detail, it unexpectedly flares out in blazing technicolor bursts, pulsating in every hue and shade, aggressively confronting the reader with its high-intensity energies. Here is an excerpt from Catlin's description of the annual religious ceremony of the Mandans:

> Oh! *"horrible visu — et mirabile dictu!"* Thank God, it is over, that I have seen it, and am able to tell it to the world. . . . I shudder at the relation, or even at the thought of these barbarous and cruel scenes, and am almost ready to shrink from the task of reciting them. . . . I entered the *medicine-house* of these scenes, as I would have entered a church, and expected to see something extraordinary and strange, but yet in the form of worship or devotion; but alas! little did I expect to see the interior of their holy temple turned into a *slaughter-house,* and its floor strewed with the blood of its fanatic devotees. (1841: 1:155–56; emphasis in original)

He goes on to describe parts of the ceremony as "shocking," "disgusting," "ridiculous," "horrid," and "sickening." He quotes mythological narratives associated with the ceremony, observing:

> Such are a few of the principal traditions . . . and I have given them in their own way, with all the imperfections and absurd inconsistencies which should be expected to characterize the history of all ignorant and

superstitious people who live in a state of simple and untaught nature. (1841: 1:180)

Such a statement could hardly be construed as a romantic affirmation of belief in the nobility of the wild and simple children of nature. And he goes on to refer to the Mandan as "an ignorant race of human beings" with "ignorant and barbarous and disgusting customs" (1841: 1:183, 182).

Now it must be remembered that the Mandan were Catlin's favorites, the people he spent the longest and most intimate time with, and the ones he singles out for the most glowing praise of all the peoples he describes. Is the negativism of these passages, then, another manifestation of the old dialectic of vices and virtues we have seen in ethnographic writings from Lescarbot onward? In part, yes, insofar as Catlin's narrative necessarily is shaped by historical vectors flowing from earlier ethnographic writings; but in terms of his deliberate rejection of dependence on such writings in favor of exclusive reliance on personal experience and direct observation, it should be seen more in terms of his attraction to the aesthetics of the sublime and picturesque.

The gloomy shades of negativism found here and elsewhere in Catlin's work are the darker colors of a discursive palette, from which he selectively chooses to paint the most strikingly dramatic representations of which he is capable. His discourse is constructed exactly like his painted imagery, with selected dramatic highlights of the brightest and the darkest imaginable colors accenting a softer range of subtler, more "natural" shades, overlaid on a strongly outlined draftsmanship that ranges from exquisitely precise beauty of line to occasional slightly misshapen, disproportionate forms. But it is the accenting with flashes of vivid color that dominates and enlivens his representations, whether iconic or discursive (fig. 16).

In keeping with the "romantic" aesthetic, both pictorial and verbal media demand a range of expression from the brightest to the darkest shades of coloring and human emotion, a feature of the aesthetics of the sublime that sometimes tends to push the overall effect in the direction of sensationalism. The "shocking," the "disgusting," the "ridiculous," the "horrid," and the "sickening" are some of the darker shades available for creating representations of the picturesque "savage" from Catlin's discursive palette. The "noble" is one of the brighter colors he uses. Neither the darker nor the brighter elements can be isolated from the overall picture he constructs without severe distortion of their representational significance.

Nor can the verbal narrative be considered in isolation from the pictorial narrative of the sequentially arranged scenes and portraits to which

FIGURE 16. THE COLORFUL "SAVAGE."
George Catlin's vivid use of color highlighting,
as in his portrait of an Oto chief, is reflected in
his prose discourse (Catlin, reproduced in
Prichard 1843: 405).

it is subordinated to serve as a kind of extended caption, and as a synaes-
thetic frame to attract and focus the viewer's attention on the pictorial representations that stand at the center. Given the immediate sensual appeal
of the color highlights in the paintings themselves, the verbal-narrative
frame must incorporate correspondingly vivid accents of discursively colored highlighting to adequately reflect and enhance the strength and intensity of the pictorial images. It is not that we shouldn't take Catlin's
verbal representations "seriously"; but, considering their special use as
secondary enhancements of primary representations in another representational medium, we also should not make the mistake of treating them as
ordinary-language formulations to be analyzed like those of other ethnographic writers.

Simply put, a term like "noble" in Catlin's discourse has a coloristic
function that gives it a different kind of representational value, and calls
for a different mode of critical treatment, than we would accord to the
discursive and logical values of the same term when we encounter it in

other ethnographic writings. All discourses of nobility are not equal or interchangeable.

And yet the intensity and extensiveness of Catlin's use of the rhetoric of nobility may have helped to pave the way for the construction of the myth of the Noble Savage. Although his linkages of the "savage" with nobility are far from the kind posited by the myth, he nevertheless does invoke the image of the "noble" far more than any other ethnographic writer, and so may have stimulated the interests and oppositional energies of the faction that ultimately brought the myth into being. Remembered today primarily as an artist, he is automatically relegated to a subaltern and insignificant status in the anthropology that Margaret Mead (1975) once characterized as a "discipline of words." Moreover, since we also tend to think of him, perhaps primarily because of his technicolor prose style, as an ethnographic popularizer, it is easy for us to underestimate the degree to which he was recognized as a serious ethnographic researcher after the publication of his book, or the ways in which he influenced other anthropologists of the period. For example, James Cowles Prichard, the leading theorist of British ethnology in the first half of the nineteenth century, not only reproduces ten of Catlin's portraits in his *Natural History of Man* (1843: 388–415) but also cites him a half dozen times as a source of ethnographic information. Given this kind of influence in anthropological circles, it would be more accurate to think of Catlin as a pioneer in visual anthropology and the theory and practice of participant observation than simply as a painter and popularizer of ethnographic subjects. But given Catlin's political commitment to the advocacy of Indian rights, his influence would inevitably be short-lived, as antagonistic forces arose in anthropology over the next two decades to challenge the rights and ultimately even the humanity of non-European peoples. It was their influence, and not that of Catlin and other defenders of native rights, that would give rise to the myth of the Noble Savage.

11   Popular Views of the Savage

FIGURE 17. "DOG-EATERS."
Sensationalized image of the ritual eating of a dog in the Nuu-chah-nulth
(Nootka) Wolf Ritual, from J. G. Wood's *The Uncivilized Races of Men*
(1871: 2:1367).

Among the important sources of popularized images of the "savage" in
the various "aftermarket" enterprises that drew on the productions of ethnographic writing, we cannot fail to take notice of the considerable influence of literary fiction. After all, much of the scholarship on the Noble Savage has focused on fictional genres, in which the presence of "savage" heroes
in an aesthetic context of emerging "romantic" sensibilities would seem to
provide prima facie evidence for the growing popularity of Noble Savage
figures in the century after Rousseau. However, although it may conceivably be the case that novels, plays, and poetry contain a greater proportion
of positive representations of the "savage" than other written genres, still,
over against the enumeration of cases of "romantic naturalism" cited in a
work such as Fairchild's 1928 work, *The Noble Savage*, we have counter-

balancing inventories of cases reflecting the growing negativism of the period, such as given by Louise K. Barnett in *The Ignoble Savage* (1975). Nor are negative representations peculiar to American literature of the period. For example, in 1832 the popular English weekly, *Penny Magazine*, published a poem by Cowper titled "Civilized and Savage Life," which begins:

> Blest he, though undistinguished from the crowd
> By wealth or dignity, who dwells secure,
> Where man, by nature fierce, has laid aside
> His fierceness, having learnt, though slow to learn
> The manners and the arts of civil life.
>
> His wants indeed are many; but supply
> Is obvious, plac'd within the easy reach
> Of temp'rate wishes and industrious hands
> Here virtue thrives as in her proper soil;
> Not rude and surly, and beset with thorns,
> And terrible to sight, as when she springs
> (If e'er she springs spontaneous) in remote
> And barb'rous climes, where violence prevails,
> And strength is lord of all; but gentle, kind,
> By culture tam'd, by liberty refresh'd,
> And all her fruits by radiant truth matur'd.
>
> War and the chase engross the savage whole;
> War follow'd for revenge, or to supplant
> The envied tenants of some happier spot;
> The chase for sustenance, precarious trust!
>
> His hard condition with severe constraint
> Binds all his faculties, forbids all growth
> Of wisdom, proves a school, in which he learns
> Sly circumvention, unrelenting hate,
> Mean self-attachment, and scarce aught beside . . .
>
> (PM 1832: 69)

If the positive and negative tendencies in literature of the period are not equally balanced, it is difficult to avoid forming a preliminary impression that the romanticizing of European characters far outweighs any similar treatment of "savage" characters and that negative representations of the latter are more prevalent and stronger in tone than positive ones. Indeed, Barnett (1975: 90 ff.) categorizes the great majority of instances of sympathetic Indian characters in nineteenth-century American fiction not in terms of the generalized Noble Savage but rather in terms of the stereotype of the exceptional individual "good Indian"—whose function, she points out, is to act in dramatic opposition to the more numerous "bad Indians" and to show the superiority of white heroes and their way of life, contact with which has generated the atypical "goodness" that sets him off from his "bad" compatriots. Generally, "the Indian was by definition . . . a completely ignoble being" (Barnett 1975: 87). Nevertheless, she argues for the existence of Noble Savage representations by giving the term a far more restricted definition than it usually receives.

> Although in the aggregate, either as bands raiding the pioneer home-steads or as whole tribes making war on the whites, Indians in the frontier romance usually belong to the bad Indian stereotype, the noble savage concept maintains an uneasy coexistence with the bad Indian image. . . . [T]he Indian was by definition a scalper and murderer of whites, a completely ignoble being. To find him otherwise without repudiating their commitment to white civilization, authors had to create a fictive situation which partially antedated white-Indian conflict: in isolation, in his Edenic wilderness, the Indian could be approved of as a noble savage, certainly inferior to whites, but suited to the simple and in some ways attractive life of the forest. . . . The easiest way to pay homage to the noble savage without disrupting the plot mechanism was to praise Indian virtues as a phenomenon of the past. (Barnett 1975: 86–88)

In fact, since no fiction of the period actually featured Indians in isolation from the expanding white civilization that provided the primary interest for contemporary audiences, such "noble savages," if they existed (Barnett provides only one example employing the rhetoric of nobility), occupied a very minor, contingent, and problematic place in the literature. Barnett explains the problematic nature of their roles:

> Because the frontier romance is really about whites, isolation cannot be complete nor can fiction [*sic*] be avoided totally. When the issue is joined, the noble savage is suddenly changed into the enemy: white authors naturally support their white characters and the values they stand for against the Indian. . . . Although portraying the Indian as a noble savage in some past period of time is not in itself illogical, in practice the necessary compression of time often results in an overly sudden transformation: the worthy aborigine of one page becomes the howling savage of the next. (1975: 87, 89)

Thus even the supposed "noble savage" of this restricted definition reveals himself as a contingently generated special instance of the nobility of distinction: constructed by time-shifting backward into an Edenic or Golden Age dreamtime, he is brought back to earth by the necessary awakening to the realities of present conflicts, in which all Indians are ignoble by definition. Dramatic stereotypes of "good" and "bad," in other words, have simply been temporalized into serial manifestations in a single character, distinguished from himself only in his successive states. And the necessary dramatic outcome negates the illusory nobility: "Indians exist in the frontier romance primarily to be killed by whites. . . . The Indians' nobility ultimately resides in their death" (Barnett 1975: 28, 37). Barnett also maintains the existence of a second limited type of Noble Savage representation, that of the "good tribes" that sometimes stand in opposition to "bad tribes." But this is simply a pluralization of the "good Indian / bad Indian" stereotype; and in any case, would be only another instance of the nobility of distinction.

Overall, the existence of extensive scholarship on the Noble Savage in literary fiction, including high-quality work such as Barnett's study, allows us to see how problematic the concept is, despite its unquestioning acceptance by many critics and despite the positive representations of "savage" characters by a considerable number of authors. On the one hand, it would be surprising if the writers of a "romantic" age had not romanticized "savages," as they did all the other subjects of their books. On the other hand, we need to look carefully at whether the ways in which they did so differed in any significant way from their romanticizing of "civilized" characters, and, in particular, to what extent their treatments of particular "savage" characters did or did not support ennobling generalizations about man in a state of nature. After all, as we have seen in comparing the "romantic" ethnography of Murray and Catlin, romanticism can tend toward the enhancement of negative as well as positive representations. But, in fact, a critical survey of the vast field of literary fiction would far exceed the limits of this work and lead too far from its primary focus. We will have to be content with a brief consideration of a single novelist who, perhaps more than any other literary figure, has become associated with the myth of the Noble Savage.

CHATEAUBRIAND IN THE WILDERNESS

The name of the French novelist François-Auguste-René de Chateaubriand (1768–1848) appears over and over again as a kind of ongoing background motif for many of the literary investigations of the Noble Savage theme (e.g., Fairchild 1928; Chinard 1913). Some might think it strange that the work of such a respected literary figure should be included here in a chapter on "popular" views of the savage, even in an age when we are increasingly inclined to accept that popular arts can also be great art, and vice versa. But, in fact, Chateaubriand's work, in addition to its high status in elite literary circles, was indeed popular in the most commonly accepted sense of the term. For example, Irving Putter, one of the translators of *Atala*, says,

> Few books in France have met with the success which greeted *Atala* in 1801. Within a year of its publication it boasted five French editions, and its success spread rapidly abroad as Spanish, Italian, German, and English translations appeared in quick succession. Overnight Chateaubriand was catapulted from obscurity to the heights of the literary firmament, where he remained for the rest of his life as a star of the first magnitude. It was hardly necessary to read the book to know about Atala, her lover, and Father Aubry; their waxen images stood like little saints in the stalls along the Seine, reproductions hung in the inns, their likenesses were used to adorn brass clocks or dinnerware, and the characters were represented on the stage. (1980: 1)

Chateaubriand's work occupies an interestingly complex place in the literature of the "savage," covering the spectrum from travel-ethnography and autobiography to literary fiction and religious propaganda. All of these works and genres draw on one another, with some episodes, narratives, and even entire works recast and reframed as parts of others. For example, the "Indian" novel *Atala* (1801) was incorporated both into *Génie du Christianisme* (1802) and *Les Natchez* (1826), while material from a travel journal supposedly completed and lost following Chateaubriand's return to Europe, and rediscovered only years later, is incorporated not only in his *Travels in America* (1827) and *Memoires d'outre-tombe* (Memoirs from beyond the Tomb; 1848–50) but also in his fictional works, to which Chateaubriand sometimes refers the reader for factual descriptions omitted from the travel-ethnographic and autobiographical works. In this blending of genres, Chateaubriand thus presents a particularly problematic case of the relationship of ethnography to other forms of imaginative discourse.

For many, Chateaubriand has become one of the archetypal ennoblers of the savage, and a primary witness in the indictment of Rousseau. For example, Richard Switzer, the translator of his *Travels in America*, says,

> Throughout the eighteenth century there had been frequent visitors from France to America, and in harmony with the ideas of the *philosophes*, the Noble Savage had grown to become one of the fundamental concepts concerning the new world. The freedom from all restraints of

society, the lack of contamination of man's innate good nature through the evils of the city, coincided perfectly with the other theories of the new generation of thinkers. But . . . America was full of disappointments for the young traveler. . . . The Indians are cruel and dirty instead of being the Noble Savages they should be. Thus, America as Chateaubriand portrayed it, was much more a product of his reading and his imagination than of his actual visit. (1969: xi, xix)

Except for the last sentence, as we shall see, the reality is considerably more complex. Chateaubriand, to be sure, gives a vividly disconcerting description of one of his first encounters with American Indians, framed in terms of an ironic reference to Rousseau:

> It is already known that I was fortunate enough to be received by one of my compatriots on the frontier of solitude, M. Violet, dancing master among the savages. His lessons were paid for in beaver skins and bear hams. "In the midst of a forest, there could be seen a kind of barn; I found in this barn a score of savages, men and women, daubed like sorcerers, their bodies half naked, their ears slit, ravens' feathers on their heads and rings in their noses. A little Frenchman, powdered and curled as in the old days, with an apple-green coat, brocaded jacket, muslin frill and cuffs, was scraping on a miniature violin, having these Iroquois dance Madelon Friquet. M. Violet, speaking to me of the Indians, always said, 'These gentlemen Savages and these lady Savagesses.' He congratulated himself on the lightness of foot of his students: indeed, I never saw such capers. M. Violet, holding his little violin between his chin and his chest, would tune up the fatal instrument; he would cry in Iroquois, 'Places!' and the whole troop would jump like a band of demons."
>
> It was a rather strange thing for a disciple of Rousseau to be introduced to primitive life with a ball given for Iroquois by a former kitchen boy of General Rochambeau. We continued on our way. (1827: 22–23)

In regard to Chateaubriand's perception of Rousseau, Todorov (1993: 284) remarks, "At this point Chateaubriand is thinking in terms borrowed from Rousseau, although he commits the usual error of interpretation by identifying the man of nature with contemporary savages." We recall Rousseau's own insistence that the American Indians and other contemporary "savages" were not to be confused with his fictional man of nature. Still, the episode is delightful, unforgettable, and seems to provide the perfect illustration of Switzer's characterization. Unfortunately, as Switzer (1969: 212) himself informs us, "This episode seems almost certainly imaginary. No trace of an authentic 'M. Violet' has ever been found." Is the story simply a *conte violet*, or improbable tale? Or is the similarity between the reddish *rousseau* (red-haired) and *violet* a color key to suggest a hidden identity for the old-fashioned music master with his miniature violin (similar to the one played by Rousseau's music teacher father), powdered and curled and wearing an apple green coat like Rousseau in one of his portraits (Cranston 1982: cover), and showing an exaggerated respect to "savages"? Although we now think of Rousseau as a philosopher or a writer, his principal means of support was his work as a copyist and music teacher.

Not only M. Violet himself is problematic, however; for despite the many weird and varied instances of cross-cultural musical contact reported in the ethnomusicological literature on the American Indians, formal instruction in ballroom dancing is not one of the kinds generally known to occur. The bizarre uniqueness of the report nevertheless gives it a certain plausibility; it is just strange enough that it *might* have happened. But even on ethnographic grounds, Chateaubriand's account seems problematic. Lewis Henry Morgan, author of the classic Iroquois ethnography, who paid great attention to costume, mentions and shows pictures of people wearing earrings (1851: 386, bks. 1 and 2 frontispieces), which perhaps accounts for Chateaubriand's "slit ears" remark. He does not refer to or depict nose rings. He does, however, mention white feathers rather than raven feathers in dance headdresses, remarking, "This feather, which was usually the plume of the eagle, is the characteristic of the Iroquois head-dress" (Morgan 1851: 264). And if the Iroquois costumes are problematic, the ridiculously anachronistic getup worn by M. Violet himself seems rather too neatly tailored to fit a polemic construct; as Don Herzog (1998: 475) remarks, "In the earlier eighteenth century the dancing master was as much an exemplary figure of contempt as is the hairdresser after the French Revolution."

All in all, we would do well to take seriously the opening sentence of Switzer's (1969: xi) introduction to Chateaubriand's *Travels:* "To look upon Chateaubriand as a source for authentic information about the America of 1791 would be folly." We might gain some appreciation of the problematic nature of Chateaubriand's descriptions by considering part of his description of Niagara Falls, the one site in the American "wilderness" that critics agree he almost certainly visited and observed firsthand.

> The eastern branch falls in dismal gloom, calling to mind some downpour of the great flood. . . . Eagles, drawn by air currents, spiral down into the depths of the chasm, and wolverines dangle by their supple

tails from the ends of low-hanging branches, snatching the shattered corpses of elk and bears out of the abyss. (Chateaubriand 1801b: 79)

Quite a feat for the cocker spaniel–sized wolverines, with their tails that, however supple, were most certainly not prehensile! With such descriptions to his credit, it is no wonder that later generations have looked to Chateaubriand as a literary artist rather than as a scientific observer; and it is in his avowedly fictional works that many have seen him as a promoter of Noble Savage imagery. *Atala,* the first and most famous of Chateaubriand's Indian novels, does at first glance appear to justify such an impression. Without invoking the rhetoric of nobility, it does indeed portray its Indian hero and heroine as embodiments of the loftiest romantic ideals, doomed ultimately to a tragedy that is inexorably brought on by the purity of their love. And beyond the distinctions of individual heroism, there is at least one hint of natural exaltation of an Indian people as a whole. Chactas, the Natchez hero taken prisoner by a hostile tribe, reflects,

> Prisoner though I was, I could not help admiring my enemies during those first few days. The Muskogee, and particularly his ally the Seminole, breathes joy, affection, and contentment. His gait is nimble, his manner open and serene. He talks a great deal and fluently. His language is harmonious and smooth. Not even old age can rob the sachems of this joyous simplicity. Like the aged birds in our woods, they continue to blend their ancient songs with the fresh melodies of their young offspring. (Chateaubriand 1801b: 24)

But if anyone is inclined to take this as a bestowal of noble status on savage man in a state of nature, Chateaubriand leaves no doubt that such is not his intention. In the preface to the first edition of *Atala,* he states,

> Moreover, I am not at all, like M. Rousseau, an enthusiast for the Savages; and . . . I do not at all believe that *pure nature* is the most beautiful thing in the world. I have always found it extremely ugly, when I have had occasion to observe it. (1801a: 8)

Commenting on the prepublication controversy that the announcement of *Atala* had generated, Chateaubriand says, "They had perhaps calculated that it had to do with a partisan affair, and that I would have a great deal of bad things to say in the book about the revolution and the *philosophes*" (1801a: 11). Indeed he would, if not directly, at least allegorically. It does not take any great imagination to see in the description of a people represented as one who "breathes joy, affection, and contentment," whose "gait is nimble," whose "manner [is] open and serene," who "talks a great deal and fluently," and whose "language is harmonious and smooth" (Chateaubriand 1801b: 24) another people much closer to home than the Muskogees and the Seminoles. Similarly, we might reflect on the speech of the Natchez hero Chactas, as he awaits his coming execution by this charming and articulate people: "Men must be pitied, my dear son! Those very Indians whose customs are so moving, those very women who had treated me with such tender concern, now were calling loudly for my execution" (Chateaubriand 1801b: 35–36).

Again, it does not take a great act of imagination to see Chactas as the embodiment of a patronizingly paternalistic member of the French nobility, reflecting with horrified irony on the screaming crowd as he is carted off to the guillotine. When Chactas escapes death, he and Atala flee into exile and wander, as Chateaubriand himself did in the years of the Terror, aimlessly and helplessly in the wilderness. Perhaps it is in this sense that Chateaubriand's claim that *Atala* was "written in the wilderness and in the huts of the Savages" (1801a: 5) may be reconciled with the opinion of critics that it was mainly written after his return to exile in England: for had not the Revolution made all the world a wilderness, and revealed the Savage hidden in every person? Chateaubriand affirms the connection in the concluding paragraph of the novel:

> Hapless Indians whom I have seen wandering in the wildernesses of the New World with the ashes of your ancestors, you who showed me hospitality in the midst of your misery, today I could not return your kindness, for, like you, I wander at the mercy of men, and, less fortunate than you in my exile, I have not brought with me the bones of my fathers! (1801b: 82)

Chateaubriand, like Volney, was a victim of the Revolution, and in a more tragic way: rather than just property and position, he had lost several close members of his family to the guillotine. It was after this loss that he turned away from revolution to Christianity. Thus, like Volney, we find him emblematizing and attacking Rousseau as the personification of the philosophes who had unleashed the dark forces of savagery. In his failure to unequivocally establish the superiority of *société policée* over the ways of "savages," Rousseau had committed a far greater transgression than simply defend an exotic people: he had given aid and comfort to a deadlier enemy, the bestial presence of the savage lurking within the repressed instincts and the disenfranchised classes of Europe itself.

But so far it would appear that we have been looking merely at a slightly refurbished project of Drydenesque antirevolutionary dramatization, using a contrived tragedy of exceptionally "noble" characters in Indian dress to plead the case for the restoration of a truly noble social hierarchy as an antidote to revolutionary savagery. If such a project seemed useful to Dryden, writing in a postrevolutionary age of restoration in which an already reestablished order of dominance required only ideological and aesthetic reinforcement, it must have seemed altogether too wishfully unsubstantial to the French exile, writing in a time of revolutionary chaos and dislocation. Chateaubriand required a more complex solution, one that involved conquest of the wilderness itself, and taming of the savage to reimpose civilized order on a desolated world.

As Chactas and Atala wander in exile in the wilderness, they witness many scenes of great natural beauty, running the full gamut of romantic aesthetic sensibility from the picturesque to the sublime (Chateaubriand 1801b: 39, 46). Amid the picturesque beauties of nature, they discover the beauty of their own irresistible sexual attraction; and during a cataclysmic thunderstorm, they make the cataclysmic discovery of their own symbolic brother-sister relationship through a Spanish colonist who had been Chactas's adoptive and Atala's biological father. The theme of unconsummated brother-sister attraction pervades Chateaubriand's life and fiction; and he gives it vivid expression in the novel:

> At these words a cry escaped me which rang through the solitude, and my ecstatic outbursts mingled with the din of the storm. Clasping Atala to my heart I cried out between my sobs: "O my sister! . . ." This fraternal affection which had come upon us, joining its love to our own love, proved too powerful for our hearts. . . . Already I had caught her in my arms, already I had thrilled to her breath and drunk deep of love's magic on her lips. With my eyes lifted heavenward, I held my bride in my arms by the light of the flashing thunderbolts and in the presence of the Eternal. Nuptial ceremony, worthy of our sorrows and the grandeur of our passion! Glorious forests, waving your vines and leafy domes as curtains and canopy for our couch, blazing pines forming the torches of our wedding, flooded river, roaring mountains, O dreadful, sublime Nature, were you no more than a device contrived to deceive us, and could you not for an instant conceal a man's joy in your mysterious horrors? (1801b: 46)

By now, the dangers of untamed nature have become not only apparent but positively life-threatening as well. Atala, already weakened by her exile and by the struggle of sexual attraction against her Christian principles, is almost killed by a thunderbolt; and it becomes clear that some kind of refuge must be found. Miraculously, one appears in the ringing of a church bell and the appearance of an old Catholic priest, who takes the young Indian couple back to live in his missionary settlement. Here is revealed the solution to the threat of the wilderness and savagery.

> We went on to the village. There the most charming harmony of social and natural life prevailed. In a corner of a cypress grove, in what had once been the wilderness, new cultivation was coming to life. Ears of grain were swaying in golden billows over the trunk of a fallen oak, and the sheaf of a summer replaced the tree of three centuries. Everywhere the forests were delivered to the flames and sending dense clouds of smoke up in the air, while the plow went its slow way among the remains of their roots. Surveyors with long chains went about measuring the land. Arbitrators were establishing the first properties. The bird surrendered its nest, and the lair of the wild beast was changing to a cabin. Forges were heard rumbling, and the falling axe was forcing the last groans from the echoes as they expired with the trees which had served as their refuge.
>
> I wandered in delight amid these scenes, and they grew even lovelier with the thought of Atala and the dreams of joy gladdening my heart. I marveled at the triumph of Christianity over [savage life]. I could see the Indian growing civilized through the voice of religion. (Chateaubriand 1801b: 54–55; emended from 1801a: 111)

As Chateaubriand says, he is no great enthusiast of savages, or of nature. Nature, it seems, is to be subjected to an uncompromisingly ecocidal attack; and the treatment of the Indians, subject to the "triumph" of a foreign authority, would likewise fit the twentieth-century definition of cultural genocide. Chateaubriand may have been sincerely convinced that the good intentions of those who sought to civilize the "savages" would be met with appreciation as readily and unproblematically forthcoming as the approval of the enlightened Chactas. And he may well have adopted, like Chastellux and Volney in their American travels during the same period, the aggressively expansionist attitude of the Euro-American colonists to both nature and the Indians. Nevertheless, it would be naive to assume that Chateaubriand's story is "really" about America, or that the themes and issues it evokes are situated in the local landscape and ethnoscape.

For example, we might look more closely at the construction of Chateaubriand's "Indian" characters. Chactas, he tells us,

> is a Savage whom one supposes to have been born with genius, and who is more than half civilized, since he knows not only the living but also the dead languages of Europe. He can thus express himself in a mixed style, suited to the line he walks between civilization and nature.

> This has given me the great advantage of making him speak as a Savage
> in the depiction of customs, and as a European in drama and narration.
> Without this, it would have been necessary to abandon the work: if I
> had always adhered to the Indian style, *Atala* would have been Hebrew
> to the reader. (1801a: 8)

We have encountered this argument before in the fictional constructions
of "savages" by Lahontan and Diderot. But, in fact, Chactas is more than
a mixture of Indian and European. For example, the part of his life when
he had been "held prisoner in the galleys of Marseilles through a cruel injustice" (1801b: 20) and later traveled in France before returning to America was a story told of certain Canadian Indians by both Lahontan and
Charlevoix. But the story of his being raised by an adoptive white "father"
and then appearing one day in native costume to give back his European
clothes and announce his return to the wilderness (1801b: 23) was a widely
told story of a young Hottentot man in South Africa. Chactas seems to be a
montage of parts from the heroic and ethnographic literatures, constructed
in such a complexly arbitrary way as to seem almost a kind of ethnographic
Frankenstein's monster.

Atala, the heroine, is even more problematic. Chactas first meets her as
the daughter of a Muskogee-Seminole chief and then later discovers she is
half European, child of a Spanish father and an Indian mother. When she
dies of self-administered poison, rather than choose to break her Christian
vow of virginity out of love for Chactas, he reveals further unexpected details about her:

> Toward evening we took up the precious remains and brought them to
> an opening of the grotto facing northward. . . . In her dazzling white
> cheeks blue veins were visible. . . . Many times as the morning breeze
> played through Atala's long tresses, a golden veil was spread before my
> eyes. (1801b: 72–73)

At this emotional moment of climax of the novel, it does not appear to be
an Indian woman, or even the daughter of Spanish and Indian parents, that
Chateaubriand has in mind. Some of his editors and translators have suggested that the dazzling white cheeks and golden tresses belonged to
Chateaubriand's French mistress; but it seems possible to imagine in her
place a woman with whom Chateaubriand confesses to pursuing an affair
during his exile in England, or even perhaps his problematically beloved sister. At any rate, it seems that Atala is even less Indian than Chateaubriand
claims her to be, if not less than he ultimately makes her appear.

Chateaubriand tells us in his *Memoirs from beyond the Tomb* that Atala is based on a real woman whom he met when, after canoeing down the Ohio and Mississippi, he set out to explore the Southeast, or "Florida," which he locates along the banks of the Ohio:

> At a moment when we were least expecting it, we saw a flotilla of canoes come out of the bay. . . . They landed on our island. They carried two families of Creeks, one Seminole, the other Muskogee. . . . The Indian women who disembarked near us, the issue of a mixture of Cherokee and Castilian blood, were tall. Two of them resembled the creoles of Santo Domingo and the Île-de-France, but golden and delicate like the women of the Ganges. These two Floridian girls, cousins on the father's side, served as my models, the one for *Atala,* and the other for *Céluta;* only they surpassed the portraits I have drawn in that variable and fugitive truth of nature, in that physiognomy of race and climate which I was unable to render. They had something of the indefinable in the oval visage, in the shaded tint where one could believe one was seeing a light orange smokiness, in the hair so black and so soft, in the eyes so large, half hidden beneath the veil of two satiny eyelids which would slowly open; in short, the double seductiveness of the Indian and the Spanish woman. (1848–50: 1:331)

Chateaubriand spends the day in lovestruck admiration, watching the two girls work, sing, "pray," bathe, and finally, awaking from a nap, finds them feigning sleep with their heads on his shoulders. The idyll is forcibly interrupted when the Indian men gallop through the camp on horses, stampeding an unlikely mixed herd of cows and buffalo, and a "half breed" (*bois brûlé,* "burnt wood") and a Seminole man sweep the girls up on their horses and ride off with them.

> The devil who had carried off the Muskogee maidens, I learned from my guide, was a *Bois brûlé,* in love with one of the two women, who had become jealous of me and had resolved, with a Seminole, the brother of the other cousin, to take away my *Atala* and *Celuta.* The guides unceremoniously referred to them as *painted women* [prostitutes], which was a shock to my vanity. I felt myself even more humiliated since the *Bois brûlé,* my preferred rival, was an emaciated crane-fly, ugly and black, possessing all the characteristics of those insects which, according to the definition of the Dalai Lama's entomologists, are animals whose flesh is on the inside and bones on the outside. The solitude appeared empty to me after my misadventure. . . . I hastened to quit the wilderness, where I had been reawakened since my two companions fell asleep in my night. I do not know if I have rendered to

them the life which they gave me; at least, I have made the one a virgin, and the other a chaste wife, in expiation. (1848–50: 1:338–39)

A beautiful, richly evocative story; and, as Maurice Levaillant (1948: 1:333) informs us, one for which no valid argument has been advanced to show that Chateaubriand invented it. Even so, its impossibility seems hard to ignore. Chateaubriand almost certainly never came within four hundred or five hundred miles of the Muskogee (Creek)-Seminole homeland in Georgia, Alabama, and Florida (Switzer 1969: xvii–xviii); and an encounter with a mixed Creek-Seminole-Spanish party on the banks of the Ohio in 1791 seems as unlikely as the mixed population of cattle and buffalo, cranes, turkeys, and pelicans inhabiting the island where he met them. It is just possible that Chateaubriand, recovering from an arm broken at Niagara Falls, managed to enter the Ohio Valley during the two or three months remaining before his return to Europe, even if he could hardly have paddled a canoe down the Mississippi to the Gulf of Mexico and returned to the East Coast in that time. And it is certainly possible that he met mixed-ancestry Indian-white prostitutes somewhere and used them as models for characters. But the source for Atala, given Chateaubriand's explanatory tale, remains problematic: she could hardly have been who, where, and when he says she was, nor in the end could he.

Chateaubriand's most problematically constructed character, it turns out, is himself. And understandably so, lost as he was in the wilderness of revolutionary exile, adrift in a torrent of savage currents of human emotions and actions, grasping alternately for moorings in revolutionary ideology, Christianity, government bureaucracy, expatriate resistance, and, most successfully, in the construction of fictive characters and their stories. The credibility of stories and their characters hangs partly on threads of continuity; and for Chateaubriand, the radical reversal of identities from atheist revolutionary ideologue to neoconservative Christian apologist virtually demanded a sequence of plot developments to account for the transition, dramatized by conflict between the emergent Christian self and the unmasked villainous adversaries, the philosophes. Thus the construction of Rousseau becomes a necessary appendage of Chateaubriand's construction of himself, allowing the projection of a chronology of developing conflict between the younger "disciple" and the mature Christian; while the construction of the "savages" from whatever blend of observation, secondary source readings, and the imagination provides the continuity needed for the conflict to develop. Rousseau and the Indians are thus necessary components for projecting a self that will only be fully revealed—

or fully obscured—by the voice that speaks through the *Memoirs from beyond the Tomb.*

Regarding the trip to Louisiana and "Florida," Chateaubriand cites the manuscript that he says he wrote following his return to England, lost for many years, and later recovered:

> Immediately after the descriptions of Louisiana in the manuscript come some extracts from the *Travels* of Bartram, which I had translated with a fair amount of care. Mixed in with these extracts are my corrections, my observations, my reflections, my additions, my own descriptions. . . . But in my work, everything is much more close-knit, so that it is almost impossible to separate what is mine from what is Bartram's, or even to recognize it frequently. (1827: 59)

Indeed, the ambiguity of self-recognition pervades the whole corpus of Chateaubriand's Indian narratives, for he incorporates into his representations of himself and his subjects elements drawn from the whole range of writers who served as his sources. Their names are all familiar to us: Cartier, Champlain, Lahontan, Lafitau, Charlevoix—and, perhaps not surprisingly, Lescarbot (Chateaubriand 1848–50: 1:311). Although it is a fascinating exercise to untangle the strands of their various thoughts and words woven into Chateaubriand's works (see Chinard 1932), one of the least rewarding aspects of such an enterprise is to pursue the rhetoric of nobility in Chateaubriand, for it is barely in evidence, dependence on Lescarbot notwithstanding. There is, however, one current that lends itself to a more satisfying investigation.

> There are two equally faithful and unfaithful ways of painting the savages of North America: one is to speak only of their laws and their manners, without entering into details of their bizarre customs and their habits which are often disgusting to civilized men. Then all you will see will be Greeks and Romans, for the laws of the Indians are grave and their manners often charming.
>
> The other way consists in representing only the habits and customs of the savages, without mentioning their laws and their manners; then you will see only the smoky, filthy cabins to which retires a kind of monkey endowed with human speech. (Chateaubriand 1827: 81)

This passage introduces a systematic survey of Indian ethnography, arranged according to a list of categories derived from Lescarbot and incorporating data from all the authorities Chateaubriand cites as sources. The passage frames his ethnographic catalog neither in terms of a romantic idealization nor in terms of a polemic denigration of the Indians. Rather, it promises a continuation of the time-honored dialectic of virtues and vices, but framed in a critically and culturally self-aware perspective reminiscent of nothing so much as the critical stance of Rousseau. And Rousseauian themes continue to emerge throughout the section.

> Almost always the state of nature has been confused with the primitive state; from this mistake has come the misconception that the savages had no government, that each family was simply led by its chief or its father, that a hunt or a war occasionally united the families in common interest, but that once this interest was satisfied the families returned to their isolation and independence.
>
> Those are notable errors. Among the savages there are to be found all the types of governments known to civilized peoples, from despotism to republic, passing through monarchy, limited or absolute, elective or hereditary. (Chateaubriand 1827: 155)

The point of departure is borrowed directly from Rousseau: that we are wrong to label as "savages" contemporary peoples who have advanced beyond the hypothetical state of nature. The corrective is a promise, enabled by the advances in ethnographic knowledge since Rousseau's time, to replace the conjectural stereotype with documentation of cultural variety and complexity. This is exactly what Rousseau's critique had called for; and the conclusion Chateaubriand draws from it is accordingly Rousseauian in nature:

> The Indian was not savage; the European civilization did not act on the pure state of nature; it acted on the rising American [Indian] civilization; if it had found nothing, it would have created something; but it found manners and destroyed them because it was stronger and did not consider it should mix with those manners.
>
> Asking what would have happened to the inhabitants of America, if America had escaped the sails of navigators, would no doubt be a vain question but still curious to examine. . . . Putting aside for a moment the great principles of Christianity, as well as the interests of Europe, a philosophical spirit could wish that the people of the New World had had the time to develop outside the circle of our institutions. . . . A civilization of a nature different from ours could have reproduced the men of antiquity or have spread new enlightenment from a still unknown source. (1827: 178–79)

This is the voice of the mature Chateaubriand, speaking more than a quarter century after his supposed renunciation of Rousseau and return to Christianity. It concludes an ethnographic discussion that, while oversimplified and constructed from bits and pieces borrowed from many sources, nevertheless presents a credible attempt at a compilation framed by a critical awareness of historical development and change. Parts of it, such as the comparison of political systems and the discussion of contemporary political and cultural changes, represent original contributions to ethnological analysis, if not to ethnographic observation. All this seems entirely in accord with Rousseau's vision of the kind of ethnographic results desirable from the anticipated contributions of the philosophical traveler. If Chateaubriand had renounced the fictive Rousseau that he had constructed as a dramatic counterfoil to his own fictive self, he seems to have moved closer to a true discipleship in the ethnographic enterprise that Rousseau had projected in his own writings.

POPULAR ETHNOGRAPHY AND THE SAVAGE

Popular representations of the "savage" from the late eighteenth through the first half of the nineteenth century reflect the same tendencies we have seen in the ethnographic, philosophical, and scientific literature; but the reflections are often magnified and distorted by appeals to emotion and sensationalism. Some sense of the emerging public view of the "savage" in the mid-nineteenth century, with its complex mixture of indifference, ambivalence, and predominant negativity, can be gained from works of popular ethnography, such as James Greenwood's compendium, *Curiosities of Savage Life* (1863–64).

> The young English gentleman of modern times, whose mind, by culture and example, has become properly balanced, whose talents are wrought to their finest, whose sense of honour is extreme, and whose pride of ancestry is beyond speech—whose organs of sight and sound and taste are educated to exquisite fineness—whose claims, in short, to be considered a perfectly civilized being are indisputable—could scarcely, if he tried, succeed in realizing, for his contemplation and instruction, a perfect Savage: a wild uncultivated barbarian, whose mind would be a desert but for rank unwholesome weeds which are indigenous to the soil, and which are watered by his superstitious tears, and kept green by precious memories of those renowned men his father and grandfather, a being whose sympathies are bounded by the skin that covers him; whose carcase is often an evil to the eye, and ever unpleasant to the nose; who has, for manly trust and hope, the sorry substitute of suspicion and quaking fear; and whose mistrust of life is only exceeded by his mistrust of death, which he dreads like fire.

As already observed, he—the modern young English gentleman—could not realize such a picture if he tried; but, unless I am much mistaken, he does not try. Without risking an expression of his opinion on the subject, he has settled to his private satisfaction that the forest-haunting, clothes-eschewing, arrow-poisoning, man-devouring, bona fide Savage, is a thing of the past. . . . [But] curious as it may seem, dear young English gentleman, it is true. Savage life is still vigorous. When you rose from your snowy bed this morning, tens, nay, hundreds of thousands of men, women, and children, more or less in the condition of the savage above described, rose from couches of grass, and rushes and reeds, and bamboo withes, and from nest-like hammocks slung among the upper branches of lofty trees, and from rat-like burrows in the earth. . . . While we this very morning were profiting by the wholesome bath and its appurtenances, the brush and towel, whole nations were oiling and daubing their swart skins, and painting their ugly faces green, or scarlet, or light blue, or—as was the case with some of the American Indians and the Friendly Islanders—all these colours at once and a few others, according to the prevailing fashion. While we exercised the sanitary tooth-brush, savage molars and incisors were being dyed jet black, the file in a few instances being brought into operation that the said masticators might preserve their needle-like sharpness; a few ivory or fish-bone spikes stuck through the ears, and through the nose, and among the appalling shocks of wool, with a few iron or copper rings attached to the wrists and ancles, and a something for decency sake slouched about the loins, completing the toilet.

While we sat down at our well-ordered breakfast tables, legions of our savage brethren were devouring the flesh of the elephant, and the shark, and the ponderous manatee, and the nimble monkey, together with insects that fly and insects that creep, and grubs that live at the roots of the woods. Nay, the dark truth must be spoken, in certain of the earth's gloomy places man flesh was this morning bought and cooked and eaten; and, inasmuch as it is considered by these monsters proper and toothsome diet, will probably be cooked and eaten many a morning yet to come. True, the repulsive custom is now eradicated, or nearly, from among many whilom thorough-going cannibals, as with the Figians and the New Zealanders, but in certain parts of Africa it is common enough. The Fan tribe of Equatorial Africans may be mentioned as an example. The last European traveller who traversed their country, on approaching a Fan town, met an old lady with well filed teeth returning from "market," and carrying a joint of "man" with as little concern as a butcher's boy would carry a shoulder of mutton. However, I will say no more about cannibalism at present. Goodness knows, there will be more than enough to say about the abominable business before this volume is many chapters old.

But, alas! there is little to be gained by putting off the evil day. Were savage life like civilized, did it have its sunny as well as its gloomy side, one might hover about the pleasant bits, and at a merry grindstone whet one's pen for terrible encounters to follow; but in the life of a savage, from his birth to his burial, there is nothing to regard with real gladness: plenty that is odd and grotesque and provocative of laughter, but nothing abidingly funny, or that does not crumble to ashes beneath the weight of reflection. (Greenwood 1863–64: 1:1–3)

The heavy weighting of sensationalism, negativity, and bourgeois ethnocentric complacency in this introduction provides a fair indication of the approach of the entire work, and of the popular prejudices it mirrors. Nevertheless, Greenwood will revise his opinion later to embrace a less bleak view of savagery: "The assertion that from first to last there is nothing pleasing in savage life, was, on second thought, too sweeping. . . . [T]here are several happy exceptions" (1863–64: 1:7). Indeed, as Greenwood pursues his subject, he is drawn again and again into relativistic comparisons.

Man a smoking animal—That "all men are brothers" is in no way so forcibly shown as by the universality of tobacco smoking. No god, true or false, is so constantly worshipped as the "pernicious weed." Neither creed, nor colour, nor grade, has bearing on the question. The Emperor of France smokes, so probably does the Archbishop of Canterbury, and his holiness the Pope; so does the Hottentot and the cannibal Osheba of Central Africa, and the war-whooping warrior of the Black-feet nation. Each provides a sanctuary for his idol in shape of a box or a bag or a pouch, and each has his censer or pipe in which he makes burnt-offering; each derives from the act the same gratification, and, however much the fashion of the pipe and the quality of the tobacco may differ, of the six curling wreaths that float skyward, it would be impossible to distinguish that of the savage from that of the Emperor. As a smoker, the painted Blackfoot is the equal of the head of the politest nation in the world.

It would be hardly too much to assert that in the matter of tobacco-smoking, the Blackfoot, in common with the rest of his North American Indian brethren, may claim superiority to civilized folks, in as far as piety is preferable to pastime. Of the sacred origin of tobacco the Indian has no doubt. (1863–64: 1:116)

"A quiet pipe" would seem to be equally unappreciated among the chief of the savage tribes inhabiting South Africa; indeed, if the natives of Damara Land may be taken as a fair sample of South African smokers, the custom there may be said to take the maddest and most fanatical form it is possible to conceive, and one that more nearly than any-

thing else approaches—shall the humiliating thing be said?—the deliberate drinking-bouts common to "young bucks" and even elderly
gentlemen of a quadrupedal turn, in civilized England in the past century. (1863–64: 1:125)

Such comparisons occur repeatedly in Greenwood's work; and, moving beyond a Lescarbot-like dialectic of opposing virtues and vices of "savages"
and Europeans in which the overall balance remains neutral, he reaches
peaks of strongly positive appreciation of aspects of "savage" life such as
folklore and mythology. But some relativist inclinations notwithstanding,
Greenwood's views are driven by the attracting powers of popular prejudice, on the one hand, and the choice of biased ethnographic authority, on
the other, into an overwhelmingly negativistic mode of representation.
Relying on an eclectic mixture of a few generally sympathetic, sometimes
appreciative observers such as Catlin and Livingstone, greatly overbalanced
by a host of ideologically hostile missionaries, tactically hostile colonial
military commanders, sensationalist travel writers such as Ida Pfeiffer,
who seems never to have met a "savage" she didn't find disgusting, Captain Reid's "curious book concerning odd people" (1:339), and such ethnographic authorities as Burton and du Chaillu, the darlings of racist anthropological ideologues such as James Hunt (see chap. 14), Greenwood erects
his construction of the "savage" on corrupted ethnographic-rhetorical
foundations.

> When all was ready for the trial, I went down to look at the doctor, who
> looked literally *like the devil.* I never saw a more ghastly object. He had
> on a high headdress of black feathers. . . . A number of strips of leopard
> and other skins crossed his breast, and were exposed about his person,
> and all these were charmed and had charms attached to them. . . . To
> complete this horrible array, he wore a string of little bells around his
> body. He sat on a box or stool before which stood another box contain-
> ing charms. . . . He had a little basket of snake-bones, which he shook
> frequently during his incantations, as also several skins to which little
> bells were attached. Near by stood a fellow beating a board with two
> sticks. (du Chaillu, quoted in Greenwood 1863–64: 1:74–75; emphasis
> in Greenwood)

In fact, the ethnographic description, if materially colorful, presents an
ethically neutral subject that in no way supports the emotional intensity of
its rhetorical framing. Such narratives are more sophisticated than many
others in which racial animosity leads to ethnographic absurdity:

Turning from the Abyssinian to our little friend the Bushman native of Australia. . . . Travellers all—ancient and modern, laymen and church-men—with scarcely a single exception, hold up the poor little Bush-man as altogether the most contemptible being holding human shape. Even Mr. Moffat, the most charitable of missionaries, is compelled to express his opinion of the bushman in the following terms:—[1]

"Their manner of life is extremely wretched and disgusting. They delight to besmear their bodies with the fat of animals mingled with ochre, and sometimes with grime. They are utter strangers to cleanli-ness. . . . Their huts are formed by digging a hole in the earth about three feet deep, and then making a roof of reeds, which is, however, in-sufficient to keep off the rains. Here they lie close together like pigs in a sty. They are extremely lazy. . . . They are total strangers to domestic happiness. . . . They take no great care of their children, and never correct them except in a fit of rage, when they almost kill them by se-vere usage. . . . Tame Hottentots seldom destroy their children except in a fit of passion; but the Bushmen will kill their children without remorse. . . . There are instances of parents throwing their tender offspring to the hungry lion who stands roaring before their cavern, refusing to depart till some peace offering be made to him. . . ." (Greenwood 1863–64: 1:376–77)

If the overwhelming negativity, intensified by racial invective and sim-iles of bestiality, is not enough to arouse our suspicions, perhaps the trans-position of the South African Bushmen and the roaring lions to the deserts of Australia will warn us against taking such "charitable" representations on faith. Greenwood's narrative, serving as a bridge between prejudiced ethnographic observers and a prejudiced reading public, presents a perplex-ingly volatile mix of relativism and radically negativistic diatribe.

Whatever unfavourable opinion civilized folks may hold concerning the business of the lives of certain savages, it is certain that they—even the most brutish and furthest removed from our standard of what mankind should be—are of a different way of thinking, at least if in-ference may be drawn from the scrupulous attention that is paid to the performance of the various ceremonies considered necessary to a young man's induction to the rights and privileges enjoyed by the rec-ognized "men" of the nation. The aboriginals of Australia are a striking illustration of this. Cowardly as the fox, treacherous as the wolf, de-praved to the very lowest in his passions and desires, with no better abiding place, or scarcely, than the wombat scratches for himself in the earth, and with a language composed of guttural snortings and clacks and clicks of the lips and tongue, yet is he a stickler for the hereditary observances of his tribe, and would resolutely set his hideously dirty face against an infringement of them. (Greenwood 1863–64: 1:88)

Although both his rhetoric and the substance of his dismal evaluation of savagery strongly resemble those of the creator of the Myth of the Noble Savage (see chap. 17), Greenwood does not make use of the term. His uses of the term "noble" are those already familiar to us from the ethnographic literature: "Whatever may be the origin of this barbarous custom, the scalp constitutes in some sense the armorial bearings of the Indian warrior, a title of nobility which receives a new quartering from every fresh victim" (1863–64: 1:44). Here, as elsewhere in his narrative (e.g., 1:134, 164), Greenwood's "nobility" is the nobility of rank, a social distinction that raises the outstanding "savage" above his ordinary compatriots. He does, however, raise the issue of the "child of nature," without invoking the rhetoric of nobility.

> *The Savage considered as a child of nature*—At first sight it would seem hard to show a greater anomaly than an unthinking instinct-obeying nation of savages consenting to be controlled and governed by a fellow barbarian . . . ; and the said anomaly is the more striking when the savage is viewed as the vulgar view him,—as a free-born "child of nature," intolerant of rule, and guided in all his behaviour by certain instinctive high-souled sentiments, and vast powers of mind, that require only cultivation to fit their possessor for the achievement of all that ever was yet successfully attempted by man. This, however, is very far from the fact. Without doubt, and as we have only to refer back to our own ancient barbarism to be convinced, the germ of perfect manhood lies in every savage, but like the ore of gold and iron, the true metal lies deep, and to free it from dross and make its lustre apparent is a process neither easy nor rapid. Again, like golden ore, in which the precious deposit shows here and there with a sheen that undoubtedly reveals its presence, does the savage's mind manifest its existence in fitful flashes and glimmerings, that, alas! only reveal to him what a helpless wretch he is. . . . If he is a little man, any man a trifle bigger coming his way may strip him, seize his wife and children as slaves, knock him on the head, and appropriate his hut . . . : what then remains to be done, but to combine for the good of the common weal. (1863–64: 2:1–2)

Greenwood's negativist argument is hardly suggestive of nobility. But if he is clearly not a believer in the myth of the Noble Savage, he is equally clearly not a believer in the emerging mythology of race as the fundamental cause of human differences. Despite the work's obvious affinities with the attitudes and assumptions of overtly racist writings, race as such plays no essential part in Greenwood's construction of the "savage." When, after nearly two hundred pages, he finally brings himself to explicitly discuss the issue of race, he dismisses it with a humorous comment on schoolboy prejudices and an extended quotation from Dr. Winterbottom, one of the promoters of the settlement of Sierra Leone by freed African slaves:

> If, as an intelligent writer observes, the human race be divided into species merely from their colour, it must necessarily follow that, if the negroes form a specific class because they are black, those of an olive and tawny complexion must form another class, because they are not white, and from the same cause the Spaniards and Swedes would form two distinct species of men.
>
> Children of the same family in Europe very frequently are of different complexions, some being fair and others brown; the same variety occurs in Africa, independently of any admixture of white blood, and while some are of a jet black, others are sometimes only a dark brown. . . . The very striking difference of colour between the African and European is merely superficial, and resides in a part so extremely delicate as to require the skill of the anatomist to detect it. (1863–64: 1:194–95)

We might compare this with an overtly racist popular ethnographic compilation of the same decade, *The Natural History of the Human Races* (1869), by John Jeffries, an exponent of the views of the American racist anthropological school of Morton, Nott, Gliddon, and Agassiz. "The noblest study of mankind is man," writes Jeffries (9); and for him, that study centers on showing "the perfections, purity and superiority of the White Man" (9) and proving that the "forced Equality of Races is a system of tyranny intolerable in civilized governments that cannot be sustained upon any principle of political economy, law or morals" (8–9).

We find that, although Jeffries writes in support of white supremacy and black inferiority, he takes a more complex stance on American Indians, sometimes denouncing their "savage" cruelty, often defending them against "wrongs" done to them by Europeans. However, even in expressing admiration for their bravery and their great leaders, he does not refer to them as "noble." His uses of the word are all those we are already familiar with from the ethnographic literature, references to members of governing elites, the "large retinue of nobles" at Montezuma's "palace" (291), and ascriptions of aesthetic traits that distinguish one individual or group from others: "The Caribs are . . . a noble looking people" (303) or "He was clothed in a long garment, and had a noble beard" (304). In an ethnologically confused passage, he links nobility to a people's character:

As a nation the Apaches are among the most widely disseminated of
the American race. The Navajos, one of the largest tribes west of the
Rocky Mountains, belong to this family. They do not compare with the
natives of Missouri and Mississippi, being ill-formed and emaciated
and undignified, lacking those ennobling traits of character witnessed
in the Iroquois and Mobilians. (275)

But this trait ascription is clearly a case of "some savages are nobler than
others," rather than "savages are noble." Only once does Jeffries seem to
make an unqualified, global assertion about the nobility of an entire people:

Whilst the other great nations of New England have all virtually passed
from earth, a few hundred of the Narragansett descendants of the great
Canonicus and Miantonomoh still survive to witness the prosperity of
the descendants of the noble white men whom their ancestors had fed
and protected over two hundred years ago. (231)

These examples of popular ethnographic literature do not support the
notion of a general perception of "savages" as "noble" by the British or
American public. Indeed, negative representations are far more widespread; and a reader is struck by how much more common are attributions
of bestiality than nobility (fig. 17).

In his curious book concerning odd people, Captain Reid mentions a
tribe of Indians called Yamparico, or root digger, inhabiting the great
desert between the Nevada and the Rocky Mountains. . . . "Digger,"
says the Captain, is of a dark brown or copper colour. He stands about
five feet in height—often under but rarely over this standard—and his
body is thin and meagre, resembling that of a frog stretched upon a
fish-hook. The skin that covers it—especially that of an old Digger—is
wrinkled and corrugated like the hide of an Asiatic rhinoceros—with a
surface dry as parched buck-skin. His feet, turned in at the toes—as
with all the aborigines of America—have some resemblance to human
feet; but in the legs this resemblance ends. The lower limbs are almost
destitute of calves, and the knee-pans are of immense size—resembling
a pair of pads or callosities, like those upon goats and antelopes. The
face is broad and angular, with high cheek-bones; the eyes small, black,
and sunken, and sparkle in their hollow sockets, not with true intelligence, but that sort of vivacity which may often be observed in the
lower animals, especially in several species of monkeys. (Greenwood
1863–64: 1:339)

Again, we find a piling on of images of bestiality that reflects a growing
tendency in late-eighteenth- and early-nineteenth-century ethnographic
writing. Noting that neither Greenwood nor most other users of such im-

agery were evolutionists, we might conclude that the images were used simply as part of a project of degradation by dehumanization. Indeed, this seems to be the case for the racists and so-called polygenists like Nott and Gliddon.

But for some others, the case is not so clear. Bestiality and "nobility" in fact may be part of the same package, a construction of subject populations as resources to be managed and exploited by a process of colonial "domestication," as we will see when we turn to the representation of "savage" peoples by colonial administrators.

And where we do find attributions of nobility, they occur not in the context of representations of the "simple child of nature" who stands as an object for simultaneous reproach of, and emulation by, civilized man. Rather, the nobility seen in savage contexts is of a surprisingly familiar kind. Consider, for example, Greenwood's (1863–64: 2:88 ff.) treatment of the adventures of Sir James Brooke, a British adventurer who received the title Rajah of Sarawak from the sultan of Brunei and spent years battling pirates and other "savage" peoples of the region. Greenwood describes Brooke's antipirate forays in his native-built boat, the *Jolly Bachelor*, with high enthusiasm and boyish envy; and, when the struggle between equally fierce and implacable enemies ends in the slaughter of the pirates, he gives us this conclusion:

> Detestable, however, as is the trade of war, especially when carried on from mercenary motives, it is hard for us, with so much of the salt of the sea in our blood, to regard these savage Dayak rovers without something very like sympathy. Certain it is that they possess the chief elements of a great people, perseverance, courage, and a restless yearning for adventure—much the same sort of folks, dear reader, as those from which you and I sprang. But our freebooting ancestors were heroes and led by heroes, say you. Well, here is a Dayak hero, pictured by one who is himself a hero [Brooke]—a true British man of war, and one little likely to over estimate valour, or to mistake it on the score of sentimentality.
>
> "Among the mortally wounded lay the young commander of the prahu, one of the most noble forms of the human race; his countenance handsome as the hero of oriental romance, and his bearing wonderfully impressive and touching. He was shot in front and through the lungs, and his end was rapidly approaching. He endeavoured to speak, but could not. He looked as if he had something of importance to communicate, and a shade of disappointment and regret passed over his brow when he felt that every effort was unavailing and that his manly strength and daring spirit were dissolving into the dark night of anni-

hilation. The pitying conquerors raised him gently up and he was seated in comparative ease, for the welling out of the blood was less distressing, but the end speedily came; he folded his arms heroically across his wounded breast, fixed his eyes on the British seamen around, and casting one long glance at the ocean—the theatre of his daring exploits, on which he had so often fought and triumphed—expired without a sigh." (1863–64: 2:94)

Here, we recognize, is nothing more than Dryden's old characterization of the universal heroic nobility of the brave and uncompromising leader, a nobility of distinction of the superior individuals who are found in every society, standing head and shoulders above their fellow men. The concept is as feudal as the construction of its personifications is necessarily theatrical; heroes are inevitably handsome, as their physical appearance is a reflection of their inner nature. Of course they must exist among every enemy, even the most savage, for their nobility validates our own; what glory and nobility could we attain to by the mere slaughter of subhuman beasts or ignoble cowards? If anyone needed the Noble Savage, it was not the ethnographer or the philosopher of human equality but those who required a worthy adversary to validate and glorify their own conquering exploits.

12   The Politics of Savagery

FIGURE 18. POLITICAL IMBALANCES. Dutch emissaries kneel before the king of Congo in 1642, in a political power imbalance that would be strongly reversed by the growing colonial enterprise of subjugation of "savage" and "barbaric" peoples (Ogilby 1670, reprinted in Green 1745–47: 3:257, pl. 23).

That all discourse of "savage" peoples is essentially political should be obvious enough to require little comment. The term itself is oppositional, demanding a counterbalancing term such as "domesticated" or "civilized" to charge it with polarized discursive energy; and, historically, all such oppositions were projected toward their definitive construction within the globalizing enterprise of colonial expansion and domination. Application of the label "savage" created a point of polarity that enabled manipulative control of any subject to which it was attached in the system of colonial politics; just as, for example, application of a label such as "convicted sex offender" in a legal system enables, indeed requires, particular controlling manipulations that would not be possible in the label's absence. Similarly, to label a people "savage" enabled particular, more totalizing control moves that were not possible in political interactions with established states such as the Chinese or Ottoman Empire. Dealing with "civilized" or even "semi-civilized" state societies required diplomacy and negotiation, at least as preliminary steps toward the legitimation of warfare as a final option (fig. 18). Dealing with "savages," by contrast, required simpler and more direct steps toward conquest, control, territorial extirpation, and, in some cases, extermination.

This dynamic partly accounts for the growing negativity of connotations of the term "savage" and the expansion of the sphere of its application to a successively wider range of peoples in the nineteenth century. For, as the colonial system reached its peak of expansion, penetration to previously untouched areas was required for continued growth, while greater negativity called for increasingly severe corrective action against the designated offenders. Ethnographic, scientific, philosophical, literary, and popular writings all played a useful role in enabling the expansion of colonial control, as long as they contributed to the growing generalization and negativization of representations of the "savage"; and they all reaped the benefits of access to colonial resources such as new travel and research opportunities, new "specimens" and objects of description, new ideas, new images, new sensations, and new points of departure for flights of the imagination. Such imports enriched Europe as much as, or perhaps more than, the material goods shipped back from the colonies; and the profits to be gained from an investment of creative energy in the construction of representations of the "savage" were the direct result of the expansion of political control that such constructions helped to facilitate.

If, in this sense, all discourse on "savages" was generally political, there is a more specifically political range defined by the interaction of "savage" peoples with European political institutions. Virtually the entire sphere of intersection of "savages" with European politics was bounded by the area of colonial expansion and administration. In any given colony, on a day-to-day basis, philosophical considerations of "savages" in general ranked far below the need to deal with quite specific peoples with specific names, territories, and problems. Thus questions of "savage" nobility were as irrelevant as they would no doubt have seemed unrealistic to any busy administrator who might be urged to take the time to consider them. Insofar as administrators analyzed the character of the peoples they dealt with, it was by the quick, visceral generalizations—one group was docile, another warlike, a third untrustworthy—that facilitate control, rather like riders assessing the aggressiveness or docility of different horses before getting on for the ride. Or, perhaps, the characters of other kinds of livestock, depending on the uses to be made of them. As John Crawfurd, who served as a British colonial governor in Java and Singapore, put it,

> The Dutch have been fond of comparing the Javanese to their own favourite animal the buffalo, and denounce them as dull, sluggish, and perverse. Both the man and the animal, I believe, are calumniated. It would be more just to observe, that the Javanese, like his buffalo, is slow, but useful and industrious, and, with kind treatment, docile and easily governed. (1820: 1:43)

The characters of individual livestock species, or even of individual horses, could indeed be circumstantially important; but as for horses in general, well, everyone who dealt with them knew what a horse was. Similarly, everyone dealing with colonized peoples knew what savages were: people who needed the controlling hand of civilization, laid on lightly or harshly according to circumstantial differences. Otherwise, there was little need to ponder their characters. Indeed, on the larger, philosophical and policy levels, even the tactically important circumstantial differences between specific peoples became insignificant. Once again, we may consider Crawfurd's words:

> In delineating these characters, I shall consider the most civilized races only, for the habits of the mere savages of all climates are nearly assimilated, for the influence of physical and local circumstances on the character of our species, does not become obvious and striking until society has made considerable advances. (1820: 1:7–8)

We could easily multiply instances of similarly indifferent or more hostile statements by colonial administrators. It needs only a moment's reflection on the nature of the colonial system to understand why they must necessarily outweigh more positive representations. But, as with ethnographic writings, negative representations are relatively uninteresting, and it is enough for us to note their existence before moving on to the more interesting positive cases. Positive representations exist because colonial administrations, too, had their "philosophical travelers" (including Crawfurd, as we will see later); and colonial systems at higher levels of organization had to deal with political critics and supporters who were very likely to raise philosophical questions.

This became increasingly likely as the system expanded and abuses continued to mount. After all, it may well be, as Rousseau had suggested, that the very fact of growth in size and complexity of sociopolitical systems offers more opportunities for corruption; but when the system is one designed in the first place for the express purpose of facilitating control and exploitation of some humans by others, then corruption and abuses must be the inevitable result. Once such abuses are called to public attention, they give rise to adversarial discourses of accusation and defense. And in such a context, as Lescarbot had foreseen, questions of character are relevant to the construction of guilt, innocence, and the appropriate level of severity for acts of discipline and control. In such moments, discourse on the character of "savages" is drawn into the foreground because of its clear and practical political value.

Critiques and debates generated by abuses of colonial power had arisen sporadically ever since Las Casas's (1542/1552) denunciation of Spanish atrocities against the Indians in the sixteenth century. One of the most important of these debates developed in England during the first half of the nineteenth century, as the final push toward institutionalization and expansion of the colonial system was met by the formation of institutionalized opposition to colonial abuses. This opposition eventually crystallized into two dissenting organizations, the Anti-Slavery Society and the Aborigines Protection Society, each the institutional focus of larger and more diffuse political movements. The two, although formally separate and to some extent focused on different issues, were linked not only by founding inspirations and membership drawn largely from the Quaker movement but also by a common emphasis on universal human rights and defense of the non-European victims of European dominance and exploitation. The antislavery movement would generate a wave of political support that crested with the legal abolition of slavery in British territory by an act of Parliament in 1833. The same wave would carry the concerns of the aborigines' protection movement into other actions in Parliament, including the "Address of the House of Commons to the King, passed unanimously July, 1834," which stated,

> That his Majesty's faithful Commons in Parliament assembled, are deeply impressed with the duty of acting upon the principles of justice and humanity in the intercourse and relations of this country with the native inhabitants of its colonial settlements, of affording them protection in the enjoyment of their civil rights, and of imparting to them that degree of civilization, and that religion, with which Providence has blessed this nation. (Aboriginal Committee 1837: 3)

The phrase "civil rights" is an important key to understanding the significance of the message. "Civil rights" are not the same thing as "human rights" or the "rights of man," as the universalizing philosophical language of public debates over European-aboriginal relations would frame the issue. Instead, "civil rights" are more narrowly and legalistically conceived as those shared by all citizens or subjects of a common polity rather than by all mankind; and the validity of the expression assumes the legitimacy of the polity. In other words, Parliament framed the issue from the outset in terms of an affirmation of the unquestioned legitimacy of the colonial system, within which "native inhabitants" were guaranteed "protection in the enjoyment of their civil rights" only insofar as they submitted themselves to subjection by the system. Parliamentary debate was to be clearly limited to the discovery and correction of abuses within the system and was not to extend to the question of whether the system itself constituted an abuse of more fundamental rights.

That question, however, was beginning to be asked outside of Parliament. The Quaker William Howitt, in his *Colonization and Christianity: A Popular History of the Treatment of the Natives by Europeans in All Their Colonies* (1838), denounces the slave trade as "indeed the dreadful climax of our crimes against humanity" and bemoans the fact that "from Africa to America, across the great Atlantic, the ships of outrage and agony have been passing over, freighted with human beings denied all human rights" (501–2). His concerns thus find more universal scope than the narrower focus on civil rights favored by the parliamentarians. But Howitt also applies those concerns to a broader geographic and humanitarian scope than to slavery or to Africa:

> All other wrongs are but the wrongs of a small section of humanity compared with the whole. The wrongs of the Negro are great, and demand all the sympathy and active attention which they receive; but the numbers of the negroes in slavery are but as a drop in the bucket compared to the numbers of the aborigines who are perishing beneath our iron and unchristian policy. The cause of the aborigines is the cause of three-fourths of the population of the globe. The evil done to them is the great and universal evil of the age, and is the deepest disgrace of Christendom. (1838: 506–7)

Having taken up "the cause of three-fourths of the population of the globe," Howitt sets out to critically examine the entire history of European colonialism, beginning with the discovery of the New World by Columbus.

> But the fortunes of Columbus were no less disastrous. Much, and perhaps deservedly as he has been pitied for the treatment which he received from an ungrateful nation, it has always struck me that, from the period that he departed from the noble integrity of his character;

butchered the naked Indians on their own soil, instead of resenting and redressing their injuries; from the hour that he set the fatal example of hunting them with dogs, of exacting painful labours and taxes, that he had no right to impose,—from the moment that he annihilated their ancient peace and liberty, the hand of God's prosperity went from him. His whole life was one continued scene of disasters, vexations, and mortifications. Swarms of lawless and rebellious spirits, as if to punish him for letting loose on this fair continent the pestilent brood of the Spanish prisons, ceased not to harass and oppose him. (Howitt 1838: 41)

The vision of Columbus beset by swarms of vengeful spirits is certainly more surprising than the denunciation of Spanish atrocities, long a staple of British Protestant anti-Spanish and anti-Catholic polemic. But Howitt, as it turns out, is far from a stereotype jingoist or sectarian propagandist; he finds strong praise for Jesuit missionaries who treated Indians in humanitarian ways, and reserves his strongest condemnation for his own countrymen who did not. As he says in his preface,

The object of this volume is to lay open to the public the most extensive and extraordinary system of crime which the world ever witnessed. It is a system which has been in full operation for more than three hundred years, and continues yet in unabating activity of evil. . . . National injustice towards particular tribes, or particular individuals, has excited the most lively feeling, and the most energetic exertions for its redress,—but the whole wide field of unchristian operations in which this country, more than any other, is engaged, has never yet been laid in a clear and comprehensive view before the public mind. (1838: vii)

The goal, then, is not a critique and corrective of particular abuses but a devastatingly uncompromising indictment of the colonial system itself as "the most extensive and extraordinary system of crime which the world ever witnessed." The "crime" extends through three centuries and the colonial enterprises of a number of European powers; but Howitt presents the greatest share of his evidence, viewed in the most strongly critical terms, in an attack on British colonial abuses. In his conclusion, he remarks,

Many are the evils that are done under the sun; but there is and can be no evil like that monstrous and earth-encompassing evil, which the Europeans have committed against the Aborigines of every country in which they have settled. And in what country have they not settled? It is often said as a very pretty speech—that the sun never sets on the dominions of our youthful Queen; but who dares to tell us the far more

horrible truth, that it never sets on the scenes of our injustice and op-
pressions! (1838: 500–1)

That this was a radically unpopular viewpoint in Victorian England goes
without saying; and indeed, it would take another century, a Gandhi and a
mass of popular resistance movements, and a complete restructuring of the
world's political-economic order to create a hearing for a fundamental critique of colonialism and bring the system to its formal end. But for the
time we are considering, however radical and isolated Howitt's critique
may have been, it raises an interesting question. That is, given the claims
of the Noble Savage myth, ought we not to expect to find belief in the
Noble Savage embodied in precisely such a radical viewpoint as Howitt's,
with its radical critique of Europeans and its equally radical defense of the
rights of "savages"?

In fact, this is not the case. Howitt, in amassing evidence for his indictment of colonialism, does quote a few instances of the rhetoric of nobility
applied to "savages" by others, in the usual problematic ways; but he reserves almost all of his own uses of the rhetoric of nobility for Europeans.
This usage takes two forms. The first is negative, to cite nobility as something denied to or abandoned by Europeans, as exemplified in Howitt's
Columbus quote above, or in remarks such as "The Americans proclaimed
themselves not noble, not generous, not high-minded enough to give that
freedom to others which they had declared, by word and by deed, of the same
price as life to themselves" (Howitt 1838: 387). The second usage is positive, in which nobility is the distinguishing characteristic of those who exemplify the true spirit of Christianity to the natives, both by their words
and by their deeds. For example, in commenting on Quaker-Indian relations in Pennsylvania, he says, "What a noble testimony is this to the divine
nature and perfect adaptation of Christianity to all human purposes; and
yet when has it been imitated? and how little is heard of it!" (1838: 364).

For Howitt, nobility resides in Christian principles, not in the state of
nature. What savages in such a state are like can be seen from the effect that
Christianity has on them.

> But where the missionaries have been permitted to act for any length
> of time on the aboriginal tribes, what happy results have followed. The
> savage has become mild; he has conformed to the order and decorum of
> domestic life; he has shewn that all the virtues and affections which
> God has implanted in the human soul are not extinct in him; that they
> wanted but the warmth of sympathy and knowledge to call them forth;

he has become an effective member of the community, and his productions have taken their value in the general market. (Howitt 1838: 504)

Thus, although savages may possess virtues, they lie dormant, at best non-
extinct, until awakened and "called forth" by the ennobling influence of
Christianity. Among other advantages, this leads to economic profit; and,
indeed, Howitt devotes considerable energy to an attempt to persuade his
readers that respecting the human rights of savages is an economically
profitable investment:

> The idiocy of the man who killed his goose that he might get the golden
> eggs, was wisdom compared to the folly of the European nations, in
> outraging and destroying the Indian races, instead of civilizing them.
> Let any one look at the immediate effect amongst the South Sea Island-
> ers, the Hottentots, or the Caffres, of civilization creating a demand for
> our manufactures, and of bringing the productions of their respective
> countries into the market, and then from these few and isolated in-
> stances reflect what would have been now the consequence of the civi-
> lization of North and South America, of a great portion of South Africa,
> of the Indian Islands, of the good treatment and encouragement of the
> millions of Hindustan. Let him imagine, if he can, the immense con-
> sumption of our manufactured goods through all these vast and popu-
> lous countries, and the wonderful variety of their natural productions
> which they would have sent us in exchange. (1838: 504)

Whether Howitt himself accepts the bottom-line importance that plac-
ing this argument in his conclusion implies, or whether he is simply using
it to broaden his appeal to readers with different priorities, it does address
one of the fundamental issues underlying the debates over colonialism, human rights, and the character of "savage" peoples. The question of the economic effects of colonial policies was certainly one of the main factors that
led Parliament in 1835 to establish the Select Committee on Aboriginal
Tribes, which took testimony over a period of two years and issued its final
report in 1837. The committee's report begins:

> The situation of Great Britain brings her beyond any other power into
> communication with the uncivilized nations of the earth. We are in
> contact with them in so many parts of the globe, that it has become of
> deep importance to ascertain the results of our relations with them, and
> to fix the rules of our conduct towards them. We are apt to class them
> under the sweeping term of savages, and perhaps, in so doing, to con-
> sider ourselves exempted from the obligations due to them as our fel-
> low men. (Aboriginal Committee 1837: 1)

A promisingly self-aware, self-critical beginning, and one that shows that the committee, despite its more narrowly mandated focus on civil rights within a colonial system whose legitimacy was a foreordained conclusion, was at least willing to consider larger human issues. Chaired by an antislavery activist, Thomas Buxton, the committee invited testimony from human rights activists as well as government and military officials (Kass and Kass 1988: 267 ff.). The testimony included accounts of British atrocities as vivid as any in Howitt's indictment of colonialism (indeed, the committee report was to furnish one of Howitt's primary sources), among them a description by a missionary of a massacre of Samoan natives with a conclusion that resembles one of Catlin's more colorful statements: "Our hearts almost bleed for the poor Samoa people" (Aboriginal Committee 1837: 27). As in Catlin's case, we might note that the rhetorical impact of such a statement was relatively minor and straightforward, as the myth of the "bleeding-heart liberal" would not appear for another century. But other features of the committee testimony had more immediate rhetorical and political significance.

One such feature was the rhetoric of nobility. This made its appearance in the testimony before the committee as early as May 9, 1836, when Dr. Thomas Hodgkin, a founder of both the Aborigines Protection Society and the Ethnological Society of London, testified that the Indians of Canada were losing their "pristine noble character" as a result of colonial oppression (Kass and Kass 1988: 267–68). The phrase, which does not appear in Hodgkin's own ethnological writings, was certainly derived from the nature of his testimony as an "expert witness" before the committee, that is, at that stage in his life entirely an "armchair" ethnologist, whose role was to convey what he had learned from extensive readings in the ethnographic writings of others. We have no way of knowing how far back into the ethnographic literature on the Canadian Indians he had searched to find the phrase, whether to Charlevoix or even Lescarbot himself. But his testimony is almost certainly the source for the statement later written into the section of the committee report dealing with Canadian Indians: "All writers on the Indian race have spoken of them in their native barbarism as a noble people" (Aboriginal Committee 1837: 6). If we still do not quite have the exact expression "the Noble Savage," here we have a level of substantive generalization that reaches a stronger form, in this official government report, than any we have seen in the ethnographic literature.

The rhetoric of nobility had also begun to appear in the political debates over expansion and Indian removal in the United States, as noted by

Henry R. Schoolcraft, U.S. government Indian agent, ethnologist, and defender of the removal policy (Bieder 1986: chap. 5) who, in his 1857 report
to Congress on the results of his nationwide ethnographic investigation
commissioned to supply information for Indian policy planning, tried to
situate it in its proper context:

> Those who pronounce the Indian a "noble race," only mean some
> gleams of a noble spirit, shining through the thick moral oxydation of
> barbarism. The exaltation of thought that sometimes bursts out from
> him is ennobling, because it represents in him a branch of original hu-
> manity—of man in ruins. . . . In any comprehensive view of the trans-
> ference of civilization into the boundaries of savages, we must regard it,
> in every phasis, as a contest between two bitterly opposing elements.
> The one aiming to advance by the peaceful arts of the loom and plough;
> the other, by the tomahawk. It was ever as much a conflict of principle
> against principle, as of race against race. It was not the white man
> against the red man, but of civilization against savageism. It is a war of
> conditions of society. . . . [A]nd, as in all conflicts of a superior with an
> inferior condition, the latter must in the end succumb. The higher type
> must wield the sceptre. This is true in a moral as well as in a political
> sense. The prophet announces that the nation and kingdom that will
> not serve the Lord shall perish. It is a useless expenditure of sentimen-
> tal philanthropy to attribute the decadence of the Indian race to any-
> thing else. When the fiat had been uttered, "Thou shalt live by the
> sweat of thy brow," the question was settled. We sympathize with him,
> truly, but we do so with our eyes open. (Schoolcraft 1857: 27–28)

Schoolcraft is surely correct in pointing out the partial, contingent nature of the rhetoric of nobility in the political debate; and he reflects the
spirit of the times, even if from a fairly extreme fundamentalist perspective, in situating it in a context of a crypto–holy war imagined as irreconcilable conflict between superior and inferior "states of society" in which
the "inferior" side was doomed to "perish." As he shifts confusingly between the roles of ethnologist, colonial apologist, and religious zealot, it
is easy to lose sight of the origin of his opposition to constructions of savagery in terms of nobility as being grounded in his ethnology as much as
in his politics and religion; but indeed, neither in America nor in England
were ethnologists to be found among the primary exponents of the rhetoric of savage nobility. Thus in the hearings of the Aboriginal Committee in
London, the firsthand, direct testimony on the nobility of "savage" peoples
did not come from ethnologists but from the military and political leaders
of the colonial hierarchy. For example, Colonel George Arthur, governor of
Tasmania, said,

> Undoubtedly the being reduced to the necessity of driving a simple, but
> warlike, and, as it now appears, noble-minded race from their native
> hunting-grounds, is a measure in itself so distressing, that I am willing
> to make almost any prudent sacrifice that may tend to compensate for
> the injuries that the government is unwillingly and unavoidably made
> the instrument of inflicting. (Aboriginal Committee 1837: 14)

In fact, the rhetoric of nobility here is used in the context of impending
genocide, as the Tasmanians were one of the most widely recognized cases
at the time of a people perceived as undergoing physical extinction through
the aggressions of European colonists.

Strangely enough, then, where we find the strongest moves toward the
reemergence of the discourse of the Noble Savage, it is not among the
philosophical critics of the Enlightenment, or the first theorists of anthropology, but among the soldiers and colonial governors of the British Empire. But is this, after all, so surprising? Who else were the inheritors of
Lescarbot's dream of legitimate conquest and domination, tempered by at
least limited firsthand acquaintance and human contacts with their subject
peoples? And should we really be surprised that at least a few among them
developed, like Lescarbot, enough scruples to make the plea that even if it
were right for "savages" to be conquered and their cultures destroyed, it
was going too far to exterminate the people themselves? Indeed, in such a
context, it seems only right that some of them had recourse to Lescarbot's
old discursive linkage of savagery and nobility to make their plea for clemency; for they were the inheritors of his colonialist project, and the discourse of savage nobility had always been rooted in such projects.

Nor is it surprising that in the report, along with the rhetoric of nobility, we also find the rhetoric of domestication.

> Besides the subjugated Hottentots, there were other Africans of the
> same or of kindred tribes, who were early designated under the term
> Bushmen, from their disdaining to become bondsmen, and choosing
> rather to obtain a precarious subsistence in the fields or forests. From
> their fastnesses, they were apt to carry on a predatory warfare against
> the oppressors of their race, and in return were hunted down like wild
> beasts. . . . The Aborigines who did not become domesticated (as it
> was called) like the Hottentots, seeing no chance of retaining or recov-
> ering their country, withdrew into the interior as the whites advanced.
> (Aboriginal Committee 1837: 31)

The idea that "wild" or "savage" native peoples were to be brought to
a state of "domestication" was widespread in the rhetoric of both racist

anthropology (see below) and colonial administration. It was a logical extension of the recurrent use of metaphors of bestiality applied to "savage" peoples, extending the usage to become a conceptual tool of colonial management. Implicitly, the various peoples that colonial administrators had to bring under their control were conceived by analogy to a herd of livestock, some with better and some with worse qualities, that a gentleman farmer might profitably manage and blend to produce a better mix for the future, once he had worked out the hierarchical ordering of positive and negative resources contained in the individual members of the herd. Similarly, by identifying qualities and constructing a differential hierarchy of subject peoples, some more "noble" than others, the principles of animal husbandry could be employed by knowledgeable colonial administrators to manage subject populations by balancing their individual qualities off against one another, in much the same way that identification of a "noble" stallion could be used to produce an improved and more profitable strain of livestock.

It is in this spirit of preserving a useful resource for colonial management and not out of any idealistic desire to ennoble "savages" in general that the language of the colonial administrators and their London superiors occasionally highlights the rhetoric of nobility. Indeed, the conclusion of the committee report hardly suggests a belief in the essential nobility of savages: "We have had abundant proof that it is greatly for our advantage to have dealings with civilized men rather than with barbarians. Savages are dangerous neighbours and unprofitable customers, and if they remain as degraded denizens of our colonies, they become a burthen upon the state" (Aboriginal Committee 1837: 59).

What, then, is to be done to prevent further atrocities, and still forestall the danger of degradation of the "savages" and undue burdens to the state? One logically and ethically imaginable possibility, of course, might be to apply the force of British law to British subjects, controlling their depredations in such a way as to protect the rights of the "savages" to live as they chose on their own lands. But this, after all, would simply leave them in the state of "dangerous neighbours and unprofitable customers," an obviously unacceptable solution. And hence the committee's recommendation to Parliament for a course of action to remedy the abuses revealed in its investigation: "We have next to express our conviction that there is but one effectual means of staying the evils we have occasioned, and of imparting the blessings of civilization, and that is, the propagation of Christianity, together with the preservation, for the time to come, of the civil rights of the natives" (Aboriginal Committee 1837: 59–60).

The phrase "for the time to come" is an interestingly ambiguous qualifier to attach to the preservation of their civil rights; but these, it seems, are even more ambiguous. Whatever those rights may have been, they apparently did not include freedom of choice, freedom of religion, or freedom from blessings. The "savages" were to be doubly blessed by being transfigured into both pious Christians and profitable customers, a transfiguration achieved through the sacrament of subjugation. No matter if this particular sacrament might have been harder to swallow than its preachers believed: at least it was more palatable than the alternative choice of extinction, even with the possibility of canonization to wear the halo of "nobility" in the afterlife. It was, after all, man's immemorial burden (and glory) to have to walk a hard and narrow path between beasthood and sainthood; and savages were clearly closer to one extreme than the other. In such circumstances, blessings were few and far between, perhaps the more so when doled out by committees of Parliament; and anyone in a position so unenviable as that of savages had to take what they could get.

IV

THE RETURN OF THE
NOBLE SAVAGE

FIGURE 19. SAVAGE DEGRADATION.
"Punishment for killing fetish snakes" in Dahomey, from James
Greenwood, *Curiosities of Savage Life* (1863–64: 2:293).

13 Race, Mythmaking, and the Crisis in Ethnology

FIGURE 20. THE AZTEC LILLIPUTIANS. Popular and scientific representations of the "Aztec Lilliputians": (above) "The Aztec Children" from *Illustrated London News* (23, July 9, 1853, 12); (below) "Maximo" and "Skull of an Idiot" from the *Journal of the Ethnological Society* (1856: 4:137).

But now our mystery seems only to have deepened. The Noble Savage disappears after Lescarbot and Dryden and does not reemerge in Rousseau. We do find a tendency appearing among some late-eighteenth-century writers, particularly those such as Volney and Chateaubriand who suffered under the French Revolution, to single out Rousseau as an emblematic representative of those who had advocated and unleashed the forces of "savagery" on European civilization. But even in their strongest condemnations of him, we do not find any accusations of Rousseau's promotion of a belief in the Noble Savage, suggesting that neither the concept of savage nobility nor the myth of Rousseau's invention of it had yet emerged into general discourse.

Furthermore, as the events of the Revolution receded into the historical background and racial polemic increasingly dominated the discursive foreground, antisavage rhetoric became both stronger and more generalized in ways that seemed to render increasingly unlikely either the chances of emergence of a belief in savage nobility in general or its particular association with Rousseau. Thus, for example, a generation after the Revolution, an anonymous writer in the popular *Penny Magazine* stated,

> There has seldom probably been a period in which persons have not been found, who, from what they saw on a cursory view, were inclined to consider the savage state of man in many respects preferable to the civilized. But there never was a period in which this opinion found advocates so many, so zealous, and so able, as about the middle of the last century. It is not our intention to enter into the question. This is not necessary now, when the opinion is only met with occasionally, in some book of fiction; and is at present only regarded as one of the infatuations to which the human mind seems almost periodically subject. (PM 1834: 99)

Here we certainly find no rhetoric of savage nobility, and only the vaguest suggestion of multiply authored positive evaluations of the savage state, long since discredited. The Noble Savage seems as elusive as ever, even when we might expect to find growing awareness and discussion of it. We have seen evidence that the full-blown myth was in existence by 1865, when Lubbock refers to it; but the various possible connections we have examined in the century between Rousseau and Lubbock have proved inconclusive. Where, then, does the myth come from?

So far, each of the possible sources we have considered in examining the rhetoric of nobility in the ethnographic and derivative literatures has proven unsatisfactory in one way or another. We might consider the possibility that the sum total of all the occurrences of the various kinds of rhetorics of attributive, contingent and individual nobility, all the cases of literary romanticizing of "savage" characters, and all instances of qualified defensive praise of oppressed peoples together constitute overwhelming circumstantial evidence for a widespread belief in the existence of the Noble Savage, even if no exact link between his rhetorical and substantive representations can be clearly identified. But this, too, is unsatisfactory. It would be like saying, if we did not know of Darwin, that all references to the linkage of man and beast in the Great Chain of Being, all the bestial metaphors applied to "inferior races," and all anthropomorphized animal fables added up to circumstantial evidence for a widespread belief in the theory of evolution. The myth of the Noble Savage is a highly specific construct, combining specific rhetorical and substantive components. The specific combination of these components must necessarily have come from somewhere, even if we have not yet identified its source.

ANTHROPOLOGY AND NINETEENTH-CENTURY RACISM

We might then look for the emergence of the Noble Savage myth in the work of anthropological defenders of the humanity and rights of non-European peoples such as Friedrich Blumenbach, who investigated and strongly upheld the humanity of African peoples in the heated debates that accompanied the rise of antislavery movements toward the end of the eighteenth century. Again, we might seek it in the work of James Cowles Prichard, the leading theorist of the antislavery, antiracist discipline of ethnology, and of the Ethnological Society of London that grew out of the Aborigines Protection Society and later gave rise to the Royal Anthropological Institute.

But in either case, we would again be disappointed: the Noble Savage does not appear in such contexts. In looking for it there, we fall into the trap of once again assuming the reality of a fiction deliberately constructed to mislead us. The Noble Savage was associated only in the most marginal and problematic way with the defense of human unity and equality. In fact, the most serious promoter of anything like the myth of the Noble Savage may have been the racist anthropologist Luke Burke, who, however, in the absence of the myth as late as 1848, found it necessary to formulate his theory of the "Early Condition of the Primitive Races" in terms of the older myth of the Golden Age.

> All the individuals of each primitive race were essentially alike in structure, and natural disposition, and . . . all had the same tastes, the same wants, the same modes of thought and feeling. . . . Consequently, the primitive social condition of each race was that of a community, having all things in common. . . .
>
> As all races were originally placed in circumstances exactly accordant with their nature, the primitive condition of mankind was one of great happiness also. . . . [A]ll the members of a primitive race were, to each other at least, gentle, benevolent, and just. Consequently, the primitive condition of the aboriginal races was likewise one of peace and innocence. . . . As a primitive race . . . was, in wants and physical structure, in exact relation with external circumstances, its members, consequently, were exempt from most of the ordinary causes of disease and malformation, and generally speaking, maintained their health and vigour to the natural term of their existence. . . .

> For these various reasons, therefore, the primitive races of mankind, while they continued pure, and in their native localities, were no more subjected to moral or physical evils than any other portions of the animal kingdom. . . . The period, therefore, of the isolation of the primitive races, was a golden age of peace, innocence, and happiness, in which physical evils were few and slight, and moral evils almost unknown. (Burke 1848: 139–40)

This chilling evocation of the old myth of humanity's happier past, reconstructed as a new, sinister myth of a golden age of racial segregation, should furnish us with a warning of what we will encounter in pursuing our quest into the time of emergence of a formal anthropological discipline in the nineteenth century. At least it provides us with a clue that, if we wish to find the origin of the Noble Savage myth, we should look into the works of advocates of racial inequality and hierarchical domination. For the myth appears to have been introduced by a racist faction in the Ethnological Society of London, in a political coup to divert the society from the ideological orientation it had maintained since its origins in the antiracist, pro-human rights movement.

I use the term "racism/-ist" here and throughout the following discussion with some ambivalence. Few terms in late-twentieth-century discourse have been more broadly, indiscriminately, and heatedly applied to so many diverse objects of reference; and few, perhaps, have been rendered so ambiguous as a result. "Racism" has been used to label not only actions and ideas launched against racially constructed targets with overtly negative or hostile intentions and consequences but also, by some, any idea or action, whatever its original motivation or goal, that inadvertently produces racially sensitive side effects, or might be capable of producing them, or could conceivably be imagined to have such a capability. Arguments and programs promoting racial equality can be and have been denounced as racist.[1] Such usages hardly seem compatible with the suffix *-ism*. Given the extreme inflation of its potential field of reference, the term has become almost entirely devalued for any serious communicative use beyond emblematic evocations of allegiance to the usage of one or another partisan discursive community. Indeed, some thoughtful observers, including Stocking (1987) and Todorov (1993), prefer the term "racialist" in reference to race-centered scientific ideologies. Todorov (1993: 90), for example, distinguishes "racism" and "racialism" as applicable, respectively, to action and ideology, arguing, "The ordinary racist is not a theoretician. . . . Conversely, the ideologue of race is not necessarily a 'racist' in the usual sense: his theoretical views may have no influence whatsoever on his acts."

But still, even if we grant such a separation as an abstract theoretical possibility, it is at least problematic to assume that there were or are real persons in the complexly embedded communicative-political matrix of nineteenth- and twentieth-century European and American urban intellectual communities who actually managed to attain such an ideally Cartesian retreat into the thinking self so as to succeed in completely divorcing ideologies from their culturally and politically enabled connotations and consequences. Moreover, if such persons did exist, the figures discussed here were not among them. Anthropologists such as Luke Burke, Robert Knox, James Hunt, John Crawfurd, and Kenneth R. H. Mackenzie not only promoted the centrality of race as a scientific ideology but also, on the evidence of their own words, openly advocated consequences ranging from the subjection of "inferior" races to slavery to outright genocide. In such company, "racialist" is simply too weak and pretty a term to do its subjects justice; they require clearer and more accurate characterization.

Indeed, it may be more problematic that I refer to some of the opponents of racist anthropology as "antiracist." Avowed racists, after all, could sometimes stand in opposition to one another, and even to important racist beliefs and doctrines. Thus, for example, neither Crawfurd's later opposition to Hunt (see chap. 18) nor his explicit denial of the principle of black inferiority altered his fundamental stance in favor of racial hierarchy and domination. And given the pervasive influence of racism in Victorian society, there is abundant proof that racist ideas and discourse infected members of every political and ideological faction, including some of the most ardent exponents of equality and liberal politics (see, for example, Herzog's [1998: 283–323] extensive sampling of racist invective from both conservative and radical writers). In such a context, it should not surprise us that even those programs and discourses that most strongly maintained the universality of human rights, and opposed racial domination, were to a greater or lesser extent significantly compromised by patronizing condescension and prejudiced inconsistencies. But even so, all such caveats notwithstanding, we cannot understand the dynamics of the politics of racism during the period without recognizing its reactionary nature, its oppositional stance in relation to a powerful and threatening counterforce arising from the growing advocacy of equality and human rights. To the extent that this conflict played itself out in debates over the scientific and political legitimacy of racial hierarchies, it seems necessary to foreground this conflict in terms of opposition between racist and antiracist adversaries, ideas, and discourses—however problematic such labels may appear when judged by twenty-first-century standards. And, in particular, if we wish to understand the origin and meaning of the myth of the Noble Savage, we must directly and unequivocally confront its implication not only in the construction of a scientific ideology of racial differences but also in the oppositional dynamics of the struggle between the advocates of human rights and their adversaries, the proponents of a scientific-political program of racial domination that acted as a vitalizing force underlying the construction of the myth.

Understanding the emergence of the Noble Savage myth requires consideration of its place in the broader context of the anthropological and sociopolitical forces of the time. Anyone who wishes to know something of the intellectual and institutional development of anthropology in the mid-nineteenth century needs to consult George Stocking's historical studies (esp. Stocking 1971, 1973, 1987), with particular attention to the developing conflict between the Ethnological Society of London and its offshoot, the Anthropological Society, from the late 1850s through the 1860s (Stocking 1971; 1987: chap. 7). In the following discussion, I briefly sketch the historical context and highlight events and issues passed over or differently interpreted by Stocking, who nevertheless provides the basis that makes this discussion possible.

The Ethnological Society had been founded in 1843 as a scholarly offshoot of the Aborigines Protection Society, with its roots in the Quaker antislavery movement.[2] The organizational force behind the Ethnological Society was Thomas Hodgkin, a medical doctor and Quaker activist, who founded the society and undertook much of the work required for its survival in the 1840s and 1850s. But the inspirational and intellectual power behind the society, and the science of ethnology in general, was Dr. James Cowles Prichard. Prichard, like Hodgkin, was a medical doctor, whose *Researches into the Physical History of Man* (1813) ultimately led him to conclude that physical evidence of relationships and differences between human "groupes" was inconclusive and that the focus of ethnology could more reliably be centered in philological studies of linguistic relationships and in his newly invented field of "psychological ethnology," that is, cultural anthropology (Prichard 1843: 486–546). Prichard's antiracist enterprise led him in the first edition of *Researches* to a protoevolutionary hypothesis of modification of races, in which "Adam was a Negro" from whose descendants white and other races developed as secondary offshoots.

Stocking (1973: lxv ff.) correctly points out that, perhaps in part due to racist criticism, Prichard dropped this contention from later editions; but this did not stop him, in his last major work, from including a comment that black is, after all, "the finest colour that could be selected for a human being" (Prichard 1843: 149). Prichard's leadership in anthropological theory was unassailable during his lifetime; and, as racist opponents rushed to seize the opportunity afforded by his death in 1849, they were all forced to formulate their theories in terms of explicit responses to his.

Despite the tenaciousness of Prichard's opposition to racism and slavery and that of the society that embodied his approach, both were forced to compromise with growing racist strength. Prichard's compromise was to gradually modify his definition of ethnology to situate it largely in terms of a study of the past (Prichard 1848: 231), which laid it open to the charge of constituting a mere subfield of the study of man. This in turn reflected a more fundamental compromise inherent in the emergence of the Ethnological Society itself: that is, abandonment of the ethical motivation of helping to ensure the survival of non-European peoples for the neutral "scientific" goal of gaining knowledge about them. If the "savages" themselves would soon be nothing more than dead relics of the past, then so would their science be a science of the past and of the dead. And this forced ethnology into the salvage-ethnography mode that the most extreme racists found to be proper and acceptable for a scientific model, as shown by an address by James Hunt to the Anthropological Society:

> I may . . . inform you of a plan brought before the Council only this year for making a collection of authentic portraits of some of the most available African tribes . . . , but we found that this alone . . . would absorb more than a year's entire income; we were therefore compelled to relinquish the idea of obtaining the portraits of African races in this manner. Shall we allow them to pass away without making an effort to preserve for our own and our descendants' use some record of their form and features? Shall the form of a river or the height of a mountain be investigated at the expense of thousands of pounds, while the form and height of such fleeting objects as men and women be lost for ever, through our apathy? (Hunt 1867a: liv)

Late-twentieth-century critics of anthropology's supposed historical commitment to "preservationism" often are unaware of the historical role of racist ideologues such as Hunt in pushing a salvage-ethnographic orientation on the discipline. Hence they ignore or obscure an important underlying issue inherent in the word *preservation* itself: what difference does it make if, when we see a man drowning, instead of throwing him a life preserver to save his life, we choose instead to take his picture to "preserve" the memory of what he looked like? Such was the contextual issue of the rise of anthropology in a paradigm shift from ethically charged to avowedly neutral scientific representational foundations; and the complexities and ambiguities of this shift provide the background for consideration of the rise of a new racist anthropology in the 1850s and the role of the Noble Savage in its construction. Let us consider some elements of this series of developments.

ETHNOLOGY AT THE THRESHOLD: 1854–1858

In the year 1854 ethnology stood at the threshold of radical shifts in anthropological and political orientations. First of all, as the president of the Ethnological Society noted in 1854 (Brodie 1856: 294–95), it was a time of growing importance for ethnology, both intellectually and politically. Dramatic proof of the latter was given that same year in Nott and Gliddon's *Types of Mankind*, in Nott's narrative of an American political event that had occurred a decade earlier:

> Our colleague, G. R. GLIDDON, happened to be in Washington City, early in May, 1844 . . . at which time Mr. [John] Calhoun, Secretary of State, was conducting diplomatic negotiations with France and England. . . . Mr. Calhoun stated, that England pertinaciously continued to interfere with our inherited Institution of Negro Slavery. . . . Mr. Calhoun declared that he could not foresee what course the negotiation might take, but . . . was convinced that the true difficulties of the subject could not be fully comprehended without first considering the radical difference of humanity's races. . . . Knowing that Mr. Gliddon had paid attention to the subject of African ethnology; . . . Mr. Calhoun had summoned him for the purpose of ascertaining what were the best sources of information in this country. . . . He soon perceived that the conclusions which he had long before drawn from history, and from his personal observations in America . . . were entirely corroborated by the plain teachings of modern science. He beheld demonstrated . . . that it behoved the statesman to lay aside all current speculations about the origin and perfectibility of races, and to deal, in political argument, with the simple facts as they stand.
>
> What, on the vital question of African Slavery in our Southern States, was the utilitarian consequence? . . . Strange, yet true, to say, although the English press anxiously complained that Mr. Calhoun had intruded *Ethnology* into diplomatic correspondence, a communication

from the Foreign Office promptly assured our Government that Great
Britain held no intention of intermeddling with the domestic institutions of other nations. Nor, from that day to this, has she violated her
formal pledge in our regard. During a sojourn of Mr. Calhoun, . . . we
enjoyed personal opportunities of . . . receiving ample corroborations
illustrative of the *inconvenience* which true ethnological science might
have created in philanthropical diplomacy, had it been frankly introduced by a CALHOUN. (Nott and Gliddon 1854: 50–52; emphasis in
original)

Nott's account highlights many of the conceptual, rhetorical, and political elements of a surging tide of anthropological racism: the opposition of
"speculation," usually stigmatized as the outgrowth of narrow-minded religious dogmatism clinging to outmoded myths of human brotherhood and
equality, to the discoveries brought to light by "modern science" through
its neutral observations of "simple facts," which would reveal the fallacies
of, and ultimately destroy, "philanthropical" enterprises. As Stephen Jay
Gould (1981: chap. 2) points out in his attempted replication of some of the
"objective" measurements of American racist anthropological research of
the period, biases grounded in preconceived racial opinions introduced distortions into the data to the extent that the research results were essentially
a reflection of circular reasoning. But, more than this, they were a political
reflection of the kind of supposed neutrality that is primarily intended to
neutralize the opposition. The neutrality sought was the exclusion of the
ethics of "philanthropy" and human rights from anthropological representations; with these safely excluded, the science could neutrally reflect the
facts of life in a world in which the forces of slavery and racial oppression
were pervasively dominant.

Or at least they were for the moment, for the push for the new anthropology was also driven by an undercurrent of fear. The formal abolition of
slavery in the 1830s had posed the first threat to white dominance; but
British racists could console themselves with the success of their colonial
dominions, and with the hope that American slavery still provided an example of the coming decline of "philanthropy" in the English-speaking
world. With the increasing political crises of the mid-1850s—for example,
the Kansas-Nebraska Act, upsetting the Missouri Compromise that had
contained the expansion of American slavery, was passed in 1854; and both
the "Indian Mutiny" or "Sepoy Rebellion" against British colonial power
in India and the Dred Scott court case that would bring the question of
slavery in America to near the point of civil war occurred in 1857–58—it

was also a time of growing interethnic polarization in which perceptions and representations of non-European peoples took on heightened intensity. This polarization charged ethnology with potentially significant political force.

And for anthropologists, the decade 1850–60 was also a time of unprecedented opportunities for contact and observation of non-European peoples. Although there is considerable truth to the perception that this was an age of armchair anthropology dealing with secondhand information from travelers' reports, it was nevertheless no longer simply true (if it ever had been) that ethnologists had never seen any of the people they studied. The Crystal Palace and the Great Exposition of 1851 had brought unprecedented numbers of native peoples from all corners of the world for public display, and these displays soon spread outward not only to the exhibition halls of London but also to the Ethnological Society itself. Anyone who attended the society's meetings would have the opportunity to see and hear Eskimos, Africans, American Indians, Asians, Pacific Islanders, and other non-European peoples presented for examination, sometimes for dialogue, and occasionally represented by non-European scholars presenting their own educated viewpoints. In the city at large, the opportunities were even more numerous. During a single week in 1853, simultaneous exhibits were advertised of "Zulu Kafirs" at St. George's Gallery in Hyde Park (*ILN* 1853a: 6) and of the "Aztec Lilliputians" at the Hanover Square Rooms (*ILN* 1853b: 6). During the later part of the year, London had simultaneous exhibits of the "Aztec Lilliputians," the "Zulu Kaffirs," the Australian Aborigines, and the "Earthmen" (supposed cave-dwelling Bushmen), all of whom were the subject of a comparative paper by R. G. Latham at the British Association for the Advancement of Science (Latham 1853) and articles in the popular press (*ILN* 1853h: 226).

Ethnology was no longer just a small and rather esoteric science; it had also become a popular entertainment industry. P. T. Barnum, the American showman and self-styled "Prince of Humbugs," arranged for traveling shows of groups of American Indians in London, sometimes in partnership with the artist-ethnographer George Catlin (Barnum 1855–89: 1:399). He sponsored the exhibition of a Chinese family at the Crystal Palace during the Great Exposition (1:401) and dreamed of assembling a traveling exhibition that would be "nothing less than a 'Congress of Nations'—an assemblage of representatives of all the nations that could be reached by land or sea." He continued, "I meant to secure a man and woman, as perfect as could be procured, from every accessible people, civilized and barbarous, on the face of the globe. . . . Even now, I can conceive of no exhibition which would be more interesting and which would appeal more generally to all classes of patrons" (1:318–19).

Barnum's "Grand Ethnological Congress of Nations," also known as the Ethnological Congress of Savage and Barbarous Tribes, would have to wait another thirty years for its realization (Kunhardt, Kunhardt, and Kunhardt 1995: 296–97; Saxon 1989: 307 ff.). But in the 1850s "ethnological" shows of non-European peoples were increasingly popular and profitable. Admission prices for these exhibitions ranged from one to five shillings, and profits were augmented by the sale of "descriptive books."

Such shows were often highly successful: the "Zulu Kaffirs" had a run of several months; and the promoters of the "Aztec Lilliputians" reported an audience of "upwards of three thousand persons" in the first two days (*ILN* 1853e: 22). Some of the success in the latter case was due to the enterprise of the promoters in arranging feature newspaper articles (*ILN* 1853d: 11–12) and even a presentation of the "Aztec" children to Queen Victoria, who was reported to have "examined" them (*ILN* 1853c: 7) and to have been "so interested . . . that she remained with the 'Aztecs' for nearly an hour, and before their departure expressed herself much gratified with their visit" (*ILN* 1853d: 11). In fact, the ethnological craze had reached Buckingham Palace at least a decade earlier, at the time of the founding of the Ethnological Society of London, when visiting Sauk and Fox Indians had been invited for a visit and performance of their famous war dance (*ILN* 1843a, 1843b).

But as the case of the "Aztec Lilliputians" shows, the mid-nineteenth century was also a time of great anthropological hoaxes (fig. 20). Introduced by a romantic story of their capture in a lost city of Aztec priests in remote jungles of Central America by the only survivor of an ill-fated exploring expedition, the "Aztec" children remained prominent in the press throughout much of 1853, despite a growing controversy surrounding them (Donovan 1853: 43–44; *ILN* 1853f: 66; *ILN* 1853i: 307). In spite of papers given at a special meeting of the Ethnological Society in July (Cull and Owen 1853) and at the British Association in September (Latham 1853), presenting overwhelming evidence that they were congenitally deformed "idiot" children of ordinary Salvadorans of Hispanic descent rather than Aztecs or "representatives of any peculiar human race" (Cull and Owen 1853: 136), their popularity with the London public continued to grow, and they played every night to crowded theaters (*ILN* 1853g: 144). By September a reporter declared, "Of the Aztecs, readers have heard enough" (*ILN* 1853h: 226); but readers would hear yet more in coming months and years. In May 1854 Cull would complain that, despite the demolition of the "Aztec" myth by himself, Owen, and Latham, and even though Latham had been appointed head of the ethnological department of the "New Crystal Palace" at Sydenham, nevertheless,

> I am informed that it consists chiefly of a series of casts and models, coloured after nature, of the varieties of man, and I regret to hear that models of the wretched little idiots exhibited in London last year as Aztecs are placed there. They are not types of any race. I hope the other examples are actual types of mankind. (Cull 1854: 297)

Cull goes on to make some prophetic observations about the popular appeal of representations of obvious physical differences between races, as compared with the subtler aspects of the human mind that cannot be as easily displayed or made to appeal to the uninformed imagination. The Aztecs certainly had popular appeal; no less a showman than Barnum was exhibiting them "as specimens of a remarkable and ancient race in Mexico and Central America" during a visit by the Prince of Wales to New York in 1860 (Barnum 1855–89: 2:515; Kunhardt, Kunhardt, and Kunhardt 1995: 143, 150–51). Better-informed and more critical thinkers could see through the deception; Tylor (1863: 28), for example, referred dismissively in 1863 to "the wretched malformed Red Indian children that drew crowds of sightseers in London, not long ago." And yet, as late as January 1867, the "Aztecs" were still in the news: the *Daily Telegraph* reported a gala marriage ceremony between the brother and sister. This prompted an anonymous "Traveller in the New World" to write to the *Anthropological Review* complaining that Britain's leading anatomist, Owen, had been "lugged in" to furnish a (possibly spurious) speculation as to the nonincestuous nature of the union, and stating his own opinion, supported by a French colonial writer, of the ethnicity of the "Aztecs" as a "Zambo-Mulatto breed" of African Americans (*AR* 5 [1867]: 252–53).[3]

All these lessons were not lost on politically astute, ambitious, and unscrupulous observers, who were willing to allow their political programs to influence their scientific ethics. Ethnology had become a growth industry whose appeal to the imagination privileged visceral stimulation and traditional prejudice over scientific investigation, to the extent that ethnological hoaxes and myths could sell better and persist longer than ethnological facts. It was a promising field for anyone willing and able to exploit its weaknesses and potentials; and James Hunt was such a person.

Hunt gives us his own perspective on the crisis in ethnology in 1854:

> Fourteen years ago, a Fellow [i.e., Hunt] of the present Anthropological Society of London became a student of the writings of Knox and Law-

rence. Soon afterwards he became personally acquainted with the great modern British philosophical anatomist and physiologist [Knox], whose cruel history has yet to be written. It is necessary for us to go back to this period, because at that time were commenced the labours which finally produced this Review. At that date (1854), anthropology in England was at an extremely low ebb. Prichard was dead, Lawrence was silent, Knox was an outcast, Crawfurd took no part, and was not even a member of the only body which then existed in England for the cultivation of any portion of anthropological science. The Ethnological Society, which had been started ten years before, was in a dying condition. It only held seven meetings in the year, and these were but thinly attended. So scarce were original papers, that the meetings were not unfrequently eked out by the reading of extracts from books of travels. (Hunt 1868a: 432–33)

Ethnology was balanced on the threshold between institutional extinction and transformation, with the only alternative to its death being a radical change of direction to move it along with the swelling currents of new developments. Hunt resolved to push it over the edge.

14 Hunt's Racist Anthropology

FIGURE 21. "THE NEGRO"
AS A NATURAL SLAVE.
"The Negro" displays his
inferiority in his slouching,
sensual avoidance of the work
of loading cotton bales, as represented by John H. van Evrie in
*White Supremacy and Negro
Subordination* (1861b: 308), a
prime source for James Hunt's
racial theories.

James Hunt (1833–69) had developed an interest in ethnology by 1854, when, at the age of twenty-one, as he tells us, he "became a disciple" of Dr. Robert Knox, promoter of the doctrine that "race is everything in human affairs." He may have become active in the Ethnological Society at the same time, as John Beddoe (1870: lxxx), who was a member then, remembered Hunt as having joined the society in 1854; but the official records show Hunt's election as a member in 1856 (*ESL Minutes*, July 2, 1856, 216). He rose quickly in the society's ranks to become its secretary in 1859, and then in 1863 he led a breakaway faction to found the rival Anthropological Society of London, where he reigned as president, director, and editor until his death at age thirty-six in 1869 (Beddoe 1870: lxxix–lxxxiii; see also Hunt 1868a: 432 ff.). Stocking (1987) gives an incisive outline of Hunt's anthropological career and assessment of his character, focusing on the pugnacious racism that Hunt flaunted as a newer and better anthropological paradigm to oppose the antiracist heritage of Prichardian ethnology, attacked by Hunt as outmoded, unscientific, and tainted by association with religious doctrines and philanthropy. As Hunt described it,

> We had, unfortunately, different ways of showing our interest in mankind. There was a large and influential party in this country, who desired that the world should be governed on philanthropical principles. Another party, unfortunately not quite so large, would like the world to be governed on scientific principles. (1867b: 15)

Clearly, Hunt's "interest in mankind" was a "scientific" orientation that he saw as standing in direct opposition to "philanthropic" politics in the struggle to determine how "the world should be governed." Hunt's own political orientation is all too clear from his writings.

> The opponents of comparative anthropology may be enumerated under different general heads. As an illustration, I will take . . . persons suffering from what I will call respectively the religious mania, and the rights-of-man mania. . . . This disease afflicts alike statesmen, philosophers, and men of science. It is apparently produced in early manhood from having thoroughly assimilated in their mind the one gigantic assumption of absolute human equality, which is generally known under the title of rights of man. . . . This assumption of human rights is often the mainspring of action, and in such cases persons become what are called philanthropists—holding a sort of mongrel philosophy, like that of which Ben Johnson speaks . . . "a kind of mule that; half an ethnic, half a Christian."
>
> This assumption of human equality was first heard of in the latter half of the last century, and since then it has been industriously taught in our universities; and at the present day it has become a part and parcel of the systems of political economy on which we rear our legislators. The mischief done by those suffering from rights-of-man mania is incomparably greater than any other. In politics these persons are necessarily and logically radicals. The late Henry Thos. Buckle imbibed this assumption from its great modern teacher, Jeremy Bentham; and his work, which was rendered nearly useless to science on this account, is, I understand, about to be edited by one who exhibits one of the worst phases of this disease. I allude to Mr. John Stuart Mill, the son of the late private secretary to Jeremy Bentham. (Hunt 1867a: lviii–lix)

Jeremy Bentham (1748–1842), the Utilitarian philosopher, was a highly influential figure in the movement for social reforms, extension of educational opportunity beyond a narrowly restricted elite, and a more secularized society. Adrian Desmond (1989: 25–41, 373–78) gives a useful overview of his influence in "Radical" politics and the development of a protoevolutionary science. Bentham's better-known follower, John Stuart Mill (1806–73), exhibited "one of the worst phases" of the rights-of-man disease in his opposition to slavery and the oppression of women and his advocacy of democracy and equality.

> The case of Mr. Mill is perhaps the most painful ever recorded. It demonstrates to what absurdities the greatest minds may be driven when thus afflicted. Human equality once accepted, drives the philosopher madly forward, he knows and cares not whither. There is no such thing as a science of comparative anthropology; and all who dare deny that all men are equal, are exposed to much the sort of abuse which Mr. Abernethy applied to the teaching of Mr. Lawrence. We can only answer with the latter gentleman, "When favourite speculations have been long indulged, and much pains have been bestowed on them, they are viewed with that parental partiality, which cannot bear to hear of faults in the object of its attachment. The mere doubt of an impartial observer is offensive; and the discovery of anything like a blemish in the darling, is not only ascribed to an entire want of discrimination and judgment, but resented as an injury." (Hunt 1867a: lx, citing Lawrence 1817: 7)

Hunt's attraction to Lawrence's scientific racism caused him to ignore, or perhaps to attempt to conceal from others, the political implications of Lawrence's work. In fact, in the Abernethy-Lawrence debate, Lawrence had promoted a science that saw life developing from material rather than mystic forces; he was attacked by Abernethy, his former teacher, not only for impiety but also because such doctrines were welcomed and reproduced by political factions who attacked divinely sanctioned authority and privilege and promoted democratic and egalitarian reforms (Desmond 1989: 117–21, 255–57). Lawrence himself was an enthusiastic advocate of freedom and democracy, which he saw exemplified in American society.

> If we cannot repress a sigh when we see men of peaceful pursuits thus torn from their native soil, and driven into foreign climes, let us rejoice, not only for them, but for all mankind, that such an asylum for the victims of power and oppression exists; that there is, not a spot, but a vast region of the earth, lavishly endowed with nature's fairest gifts, and exhibiting at the same time the grand and animating spectacle of a country sacred to civil liberty; where man may walk erect in the conscious dignity of independence . . . and enjoy full freedom of word and action, without the permission of those combinations or conspiracies of the mighty, which threaten to convert Europe into one great state prison. The numerous people, whose happiness and tranquility are so effectually secured by the simple forms of a free government . . . may

reach in our lives as gigantic a superiority over the worn-out despotisms of the old world, as the physical features of America, her colossal mountains, her mighty rivers, her forests, and her lakes, exhibit in comparison with those of Europe. (Lawrence 1817: 26–27)

Moreover, Lawrence (1817: 184) was a proponent of the unity of human races in a single species and as such was a favorite of Hunt's most hated ethnological adversary, Prichard (1844–51: 1:vii), as Prichard was in turn cited (in both Latin and English) with strong approval by Lawrence (1817: 167, 348).

Thus, in citing Lawrence as his model, Hunt has hijacked the rhetoric of the reformers, and in fact is using the martyrdom of Lawrence to attack the egalitarian politics that Lawrence's work supported. But such forced appropriations of progressive rhetoric were a common trick of the politics of reactionary scientific ideologues; Desmond gives many similar instances in *The Politics of Evolution.* Hunt was an avid practitioner of this and other techniques of political infighting, and his targets are all too predictable.

> I shall do in the future as in the past, and, whenever I have a chance, shall endeavour to show that human equality is one of the most unwarrantable assumptions ever invented by man. Nay, the deduction from comparative anthropology will not enable me to stop here, but I shall have to proclaim that the theories of socialism, communism, and republicanism find not a fact in anthropological science to support such chimeras. (Hunt 1867a: lx)

Likewise, Hunt's political affinities were entirely predictable.

> I shall not be accused, I hope, of holding undue conservative opinions when I go still further . . . and declare my emphatic opinion that the existence of a well-selected hereditary aristocracy in any country is more in accordance with nature's laws than those glittering trivialities respecting human rights which now form the stock-in-trade of some professors of political economy, and many of our politicians. . . . There is much reason to believe that peculiarities are hereditary, and if a judicious use is made of this knowledge by those who are interested in the matter, then will all cavil be answered respecting the status of any well-selected hereditary aristocracy. (Hunt 1867a: lxi)

Indeed, in another article, Hunt envisions hierarchy as a metaphysical, almost mystical, quality of the structure of the physical universe itself.

> Nature is a grand hierarchy of cosmic and telluric organisms. Her suns rule their subordinate planets, surrounded again by their subject satellites. The vegetable and animal kingdoms are a succession of organic

stages, separated, as Swedenborg would say, by "discrete degrees."
While at the very apex of this pyramid of form and function, we find
regal man, the virtual king of the earthly sphere. And are we to suppose that this hierarchical arrangement ceases here; that there are no
innate and hereditarily transmissible diversities among men? Reason
as well as fact revolts at so absurd a conclusion. (Hunt 1866: 116)

Thus it is hardly surprising that, for Hunt, the great struggle between
hereditarian privilege and egalitarianism should have been acted out in the
drama of the slavery conflict; or that, as the conflict stirred the feelings and
consciences of other scholars, Hunt should have been drawn into the conflict as a defender of the scientific "truth" of racial superiority.

Even scientific men were sometimes afflicted with the disorder. He
heard, only on passing through London, that a very eminent anatomist
had had another attack, and actually gone and joined the Jamaica committee (laughter).[1] This was Professor Huxley; and it was said that
he intended to propose that they should prosecute M. du Chaillu for
shooting gorillas (laughter). Were there distinct races of men now existing? how could each of these races have the greatest amount of mental and physical happiness? Mr. Bright . . . said two nights ago he believed whatever might be defective in the Irish people came not from
race. . . . That was Mr. Bright's doctrine, started by Jeremy Bentham,
and although based on a groundless and unwarrantable assumption, it
was supported by such eminent political economists as S. Mill, Herbert
Spencer, and Goldwin Smith. Against these closet philosophers we have
experience on the other side, and the testimony of every traveller, from
Herodotus to Baker. He differed from one of the views of the president.
He did not think we had any evidence to prove that all races were capable of civilisation properly so called. Take only one instance. Up to
this time there was no evidence that the Australian aborigines could be
civilised. The question was—is there race? The same argument that
Mr. Bright would apply to the Irish Mr. Mill applies to the Negro, or
any other race. (Hunt 1867b: 17)

"Is there race?" Many late-twentieth-century anthropologists would
answer no: in the scientific sense, there is no such thing. Race is a popular
and political myth that privileges superficial bundles of obvious phenotypic
traits over the complexities of underlying genotypes, where similarities
and differences do not group into neat packages corresponding to the popular images of "races." Racist myths are constructed, in other words, by the
same logic that leads children to see bats as birds and whales as fish. Yet
Hunt strove his mightiest to make race the basis of anthropological science.

Hunt was committed to the politics of reification of nonexistent entities. And this commitment, more than concrete disagreements over political policy, may have been the deepest source of Hunt's vitriolic denunciation of skeptics such as John Stuart Mill (see below). But practical political policy was nevertheless a driving force in Hunt's scientific stance, particularly in his opposition to other writers on anthropology with whom his ostensible quarrel was over theoretical issues such as Darwinian evolutionary theory.

> There are certain dark figures moving about on this planet which produce entirely opposite effects on Professor Huxley and myself. These bodies act as disturbing forces on the harmony which ought to exist between us. Professor Huxley cannot yet bring himself to believe that I can hold my views on the negro without being influenced by the slaveholding interest; and I cannot yet convince myself that he can be a good, sound anthropologist, when he allows his name to be associated with those who wish to persecute a man for successfully putting down a negro revolt. (Hunt 1867a: xlviii–xlix)

Hunt's best-known piece of anthropological scholarship is the long paper, "The Negro's Place in Nature" (1863c), which he gave before the Anthropological Society in November 1863. Stocking (1987: 251), pointing out that the title was an obvious paraphrase of Huxley's *Evidence as to Man's Place in Nature* (1863), observes, "Hunt's paper was a compendium of anatomical, physiological, and psychological evidence and opinion that might well stand as archetypical of the traditional racist view of blacks." In fact, one reason it might do so is because of its lack of originality. The paper's claim to scientific legitimacy is its assembly of quotations, often at great length, of negative descriptions and evaluations of "the Negro" by anatomists and physical anthropologists from England (Lawrence, Knox), France (Pruner Bey, Broca), and America (Morton, Meigs, Nott). Hunt carefully selects these authorities to represent the most negative scientific expressions of racial evaluation available; where dissenting authors such as Prichard or Blumenbach are mentioned, it is only in passing, to ridicule or discredit their opinions.

As a compendium of scientific polemic, the article stands as a kind of manifesto of an international racist science, one of Hunt's goals for anthropology. But it presents no evidence that Hunt himself had ever conducted any research on black people, or, indeed, even so much as met any. For firsthand observations of living blacks, he relies on the most prejudiced of African travelers such as Richard Burton and Paul du Chaillu and on American pro-slavery polemicists such as Dr. John H. van Evrie. The last of these is particularly important, for he is one of two hidden authors of a substantive basis and agenda concealed in the review-of-the-literature surface form of Hunt's paper. One of these hidden authors, Hunt reveals in a footnote, is the German physical anthropologist Franz Ignatz Pruner Bey, a leading "upholder . . . of a certain brand of Aryanism" in the Anthropological Society of Paris (Schiller 1979: 140); for the paper incorporates a full translation, omitting only the introduction, of his 1861 memoir on the Negro (Hunt 1863c: 49). Thus Hunt appropriates the authority of the most up-to-date physical anthropological investigation of his subject available, but in an article under his own byline rather than a translation under the name of the original author. In so doing, he gives his article the air of an original scientific contribution that implies a solid basis for its otherwise questionable value judgments and conclusions.

The second hidden author is the American racial polemicist, John H. van Evrie (1814–96), who was "blatantly and openly an anti-Negro propagandist, perhaps the first professional racist in American history" (Fredrickson 1971: 92), and author of *Negroes and Negro "Slavery": The First an Inferior Race; the Latter Its Normal Condition* (van Evrie 1861a). Van Evrie had encountered some difficulty in finding a publisher for this work.

> A few years ago, the writer of this had prepared a work on the American Races, and asked the trustees of the Smithsonian Institution— founded to spread knowledge among men—to publish it at the same time that a Dr. Baird asked them to publish a work he had prepared on American Snakes, and they preferred the latter! This well illustrates the ignorance and foolishness of the learned world in regard to this subject. (van Evrie 1869: 97)

Van Evrie was forced to publish the work himself, but it eventually found admirers. Hunt cites van Evrie's book repeatedly throughout the article; but over and above the specific passages cited, van Evrie seems to provide the structural and motivational model that shapes Hunt's article, as well as many of the items of "factual" data that Hunt offers on his own authority without citing other sources. For example:

> There is a peculiarity in the Negro's voice by which he can always be distinguished. This peculiarity is so great that we can frequently discover traces of Negro blood when the eye is unable to detect it. No amount of education or time is likely ever to enable the Negro to speak the English language without this twang: even his great faculty of imitation will not enable him to do so. (Hunt 1863a: 22–23)

This would appear to be a paraphrase, condensed and rearranged, of a discussion by van Evrie.

> God has endowed him with a capacity of imitation, and he is enabled to apply it to such an extent that those ignorant of the negro nature actually offer it as a proof of his equal capacity! But with all his power to thus imitate the habits and to copy the language of the white man, it is not possible that a single example can be furnished of his success. . . . But no actual or typical negro will be able—no matter what pains have been taken to "educate" him—to speak the language of the white man with absolute correctness. . . . Each race or each species, as each and every other form of life, is in perfect harmony with itself, and therefore the voice of the negro, both in its tones and its structure, varies just as widely from that of the white man as any other feature or faculty of the negro being. Any one accustomed to negroes would distinguish the negro voice at night among any number of those of white men by its tones alone, and without regard to his peculiar utterances. (van Evrie 1861b: 111–13)

It is not, however, in Hunt's recapitulation of specific "facts" from van Evrie that his dependence is revealed, or even in their general agreement on significant points in the inventory of the markers of Negro inferiority. Van Evrie, like Hunt, is a secondary compiler of racist arguments, so much of their catalog of traits of inferiority must be expected to overlap. Thus, if they share an emphasis on the permanence of racial "types" (Hunt 1863b: 29 ff.; van Evrie 1861b: 136 ff.), or the infertility and eventual nonviability of mixed-race offspring (Hunt 1863b: 24 ff.; van Evrie 1861b: 146 ff.), both have borrowed their arguments from Gliddon's racial analysis of ancient Egyptian iconography and Nott's speculations based on faulty census data and his own medical work with Southern slave populations (Nott and Gliddon 1854, 1857; see also Stanton 1960). On the other hand, Hunt and van Evrie's shared emphasis on points such as the resemblance of the Negro's anatomical characteristics to those of the ape (Hunt 1863b: 7 ff.; van Evrie 1861b: 96 ff.), or on insisting that the accomplishments of educated Negroes represent cases of "improvements" brought about by the mixture of white "blood" in "mulattos" rather than indications of the abilities of "pure Negroes" (Hunt 1863b: 36 ff.; van Evrie 1861b: 163 ff.), is a repetition of arguments common to a wide selection of racist authors of the period, simple racial stereotypes lacking any originality (fig. 21).

It is, rather, in Hunt's framing and highlighting of van Evrie's racial polemicist rhetoric that he reveals how it has shaped his own agenda. From the second page of his article onward, Hunt replicates van Evrie's rhetorical strategy of marking words such as "slave," "slavery," and "slave trade" with ironic quotes each time he is forced to use them; or he uses van Evrie's alternative trick of prefixing the terms with "so-called." Beginning his article with a disingenuous denial that he means to lend support to pro-slavery arguments, he ends with a ringing defense of the institution whose existence he denies, all wrapped up in an appeal to a disinterested scientific truth. The underlying agenda, rhetorical strategy, and selection of details of the argument follow van Evrie throughout, with such adaptations as are necessary to disguise an abridgment of popular political propaganda as a scientific treatise. Van Evrie was so pleased with Hunt's adaptation of his own arguments that, following Hunt's death in 1868, he would publish an obituary titled "Death of the Best Man in England," eulogizing Hunt as "the best man of his generation" and mourning his death as "a great loss to England, to Christendom, to all mankind" (van Evrie 1869: 97). Some of "mankind" might have disagreed.

Hunt's voluntary, if disguised, dependence on van Evrie says a great deal about his subordination of scientific professionalism to propagandistic expediency. If Hunt has fundamental disagreements with van Evrie's political radicalism, a radicalism that finds the most important justification for slavery in what van Evrie sees as its essential role in providing a foundation for white egalitarianism and democracy, or with van Evrie's constant appeals to the will of God, he never brings their differences out into the open. For Hunt, the political agenda and strategy are all-important, and nothing must be allowed to weaken them. Hunt is engaged in creating a monster, built on the skeleton of Pruner Bey's physical anthropology, fleshed out by pieces from a scrapbook of racist anecdotes, and animated by a fervent belief in a system that van Evrie would later call "white supremacy" (van Evrie 1861b: title page), lent increased energy by van Evrie's crudely disingenuous satirical rhetoric. It was a construction that succeeded at least in attracting widespread attention, if not in inspiring unquestioning belief among all the anthropological and other scientific leaders of the period.

Hunt's most comprehensive attack on the politics of "philanthropy" comes in an unsigned 1866 *Anthropological Review* article, "Race in Legislation and Political Economy" (1866). Hunt (1866: 126) characterizes Mill and the defenders of human rights as "noble" in their motivations but misguided in what he sees as their one-sided tendency to explain human differences by environmental and educational factors: "And thus we are brought to the great question of political and individual liberty contemplated from the ethnic stand-point. Now it need scarcely be said even to the tyro in anthropology that this is pre-eminently a question of race as well as culture."

The terminology is interesting as a foreshadowing of later anthropological debates over questions of race versus culture, even though Hunt uses the term here in its pre-Tylor sense of "cultivation." But perhaps the most interesting rhetorical feature of the article is the way in which it lambastes the advocates of equality and human rights with a veritable lexicon of invective terminology: abominations, absurdities, a priori, assumption, astray, beg the question, blind (blinded, blindness, etc.), blissful ignorance, bookish, captive, chaos, childishly, closet, code, codification, communism, compulsion, concatenation, condemnation, conform, confound, contradiction, contempt, convict, creed, dangerous, darkness, daydream, deaf, defeat, defiance, deficiencies, denying, desperate, despotism, disregarding, dogma, dread, egregious, empyrean, enthroned, erroneous, error, evil, exposed, extreme, facile, fail, fallacies, fallacious, false, fatal, faulty, fervour, foolish, grave, gravest, grossest, groundless, groundlessness, habitual, hasty, helplessly, horrors, humiliation, *idola*, ignorance, ignorant, ignoring, impossibilities, incalculable, incautious, inconvenient, indifference, infantile, inferior, infirmity, intruded, inveterate, leaps, lofty, marvelous, melancholy, mischief, misconceptions, misled, mistakes, mistaking, mortification, negation, neglect, offensively, omission, opposition, oracular, overstepped, palpable, perilous, perversity, pet phrases, pity, preconceived, preconception, prejudgment, prejudices, propagandism, pseudo-philanthropy, reductio ad absurdam [*sic*], sad, savagism, self-contradictory, shameful, simple, sinister, speculations, stupendous, subservience, superficial, transparent, tyranny, undoubting, undue, unpleasant, unsafe, unwarranted, unwise, vague, and warning him off, among other more complex phrases and expressions.

Viewing this article alongside "On the Negro's Place in Nature," we might wonder whether Hunt's hatred was more intense for nonwhite races or for their white political defenders. In fact, the former of the two is the more problematic. As with many other racial polemicists, there is no apparent reason to explain Hunt's antagonism toward the Negro. Nothing in the writings by and about him suggests that he had any more direct experience with blacks than most other Victorian "gentlemen." He was confronted by an opponent of African descent when he gave a trial run of "On the Negro's Place in Nature" at the British Association for the Advancement of Science (Hunt 1863b); characteristically, Hunt responded to logical arguments with insults and invective. Although Hunt would have had opportunities to meet black travelers, servants, and others from time to time in London, the British Association debate was the only such face-to-face meeting that seems to have made a strong enough impression on Hunt and others to be worthy of specific mention. Certainly, we have no indication of other instances of opposition, conflict, or negative experiences that would explain Hunt's animosity toward the Negro.

It would be naive to assume that racial hatred is a logical process, or that a rational cause could be found for all its appearances. Nevertheless, the apparent lack of any experiential base for Hunt's racism is consistent with the assumption that the "Negro" of his polemics is a symbolic figure standing at the surface of something deeper and more significant, a kind of icon constructed in a virtual reality by means of which other kinds of targets and more powerful currents of forces in the real world can be manipulated and controlled. For the existence of such targets is plainly obvious in his writings.

Hunt willingly revealed the principles of his own political tactics and strategy. They need hardly surprise us.

> In the meantime, however our duty is plain. If we cannot, by a *coup d'etat*, obtain additional strength, we must try a more certain, and, perhaps, more successful plan.
>
> It has been said by one of England's greatest anthropologists, Robert Knox, . . . that the theory of race was despised in this country because it ran counter to the theories of historians, statesmen, theologians, and philanthropists—whom he describes as "impostors all". . . . Dr. Knox, however, was neither the first nor the last who has seen the antipathy manifested by historians, theologians, statesmen, and philanthropists, to the theory of race; nor did his peculiar style do much to remove this antipathy. We live in different times. At present we fight with facts rather than with sarcasm or invective. (Hunt 1867a: xlix, lviii)

But sarcasm and invective are glaringly apparent in nearly every page of Hunt's writings and speeches. Instead of being tactically opposed to "facts," they are simply rhetorically packaged as facts and surreptitiously bundled into claims of scientific objectivity. Nor did Hunt shy away from arousing antipathy; on the contrary, he willingly invited it: "Abuse, too, they would, no doubt, receive, but he could give his assurance, from personal experience, that it would do them no harm. The more their Society was abused the more immediate would be its success" (Hunt 1867b: 18).

Although Hunt's overriding concern was race and its political implications, his only firsthand anthropological research experience appears to have been archaeological rather than physical or ethnological. His one lasting contribution to anthropological theory was his conception of it as an encompassing field of study that included physical, archaeological, cultural, linguistic, and other studies (Hunt 1863a). But except for his political attachment to inequality, slavery, and racial dominance, it is a frustrating exercise to try to trace Hunt's ideas. Despite his combative advocacy of notions such as polygenism, separate human species, and the like, he seems to have formed no real opinions or convictions that could not change to suit the changing requirements of his political program. For example, although he unceasingly advocated craniological measurements as an index of relative racial intelligence, when he realized the latest and best figures available to him showed the Negro in the middle of human populations, with an equal number of "races" above and below, Hunt retreated: "But we now know that it is necessary to be most cautious in accepting the capacity of the cranium simply, as any absolute test of the intellectual power of any race" (Hunt 1863c: 13). Thus, like a lawyer who withdraws an objectionable question after having planted the idea in the jury's minds that there is something solid behind his insinuations, Hunt was able to claim the high ground of scientific objectivity for a preordained conclusion unsupported by the facts. Similarly, he was quite prepared to avow his polygenist faith one moment, to disavow it the next, and, perhaps most truthfully, to deny that it had any real importance.

> Anthropology offers . . . nothing to support Darwinism. . . . A fundamental objection to the application of Darwinism to anthropology is to be found in the fact that it is supposed to support a unity of the origin of mankind. (Hunt 1867c: 118)

> To the monogenist, of whatever sort, we have had to say, yours is an assumption unsupported by fact, reason, or analogy. To the polygenist we have to say, your hypothesis . . . is the most reasonable. (Hunt 1867a: lvii)

> The hypothesis of "many originally created species" is equally without foundation. (Hunt 1863a: 10)

> Let us leave the discussion of such a subject as the origin of man to those who like to waste their time and energies on so profitless a subject. (Hunt 1867a: lxvi)

Indeed, all that did seem to have real importance was the tactical struggle to assert racial supremacy; and, rather than ideas, Hunt provides the ideal case for a study of rhetoric.

Like his ally in the takeover of the Ethnological Society, John Crawfurd, Hunt favored a mythmaking rhetoric that delighted in the generation of ideological phantoms.

> There was unfortunately existing in this country a disease, said to be quite incurable, produced by systematically ignoring facts. It was wonderful, and at the same time melancholy to see the eccentricities, absurdities, and irrationalities, by which men are led when they refuse to accept a well-established fact. When persons are once afflicted with this disease, you can no longer reason with them. Facts they treat with utter contempt. He did not allude to those like himself who condemned cruelty to any race, but to those unfortunate persons who suffer from a disease which was termed negromania (loud laughter). Persons suffering from it treated with the utmost contempt all who differed from them. (Hunt 1867b: 17)

As was often the case with Hunt, the item that excited such loud laughter was unoriginal. Hunt had borrowed it from the title of another American racist polemic, John Campbell's 1851 work, *Negro Mania: Being an Examination of the Falsely Assumed Equality of the Various Races of Man* (cited in Hunt 1863c: 2). What was typical of Hunt was its characterization as a "disease"; for much of Hunt's rhetoric was quasi-medical. Hunt had begun, but never completed, medical studies, opting instead to pursue a career of promoting his father's proprietary cure for speech disorders. Although widely respected as a speech therapist, medically he was a semi-educated quack; and his rhetoric is driven by a highly charged ambivalent oscillation between pseudomedical fantasy and purposive manipulation of language.

> In the first place, it appears to me that a large majority of the opponents of the theory of race may be divided into two great parties. . . . My reflection on this subject has led me to think that the cause of the antipathy to even admitting the existence of comparative anthropology, is alone to be discovered by the medical psychologist and the cerebral physiologist.
> The opponents of comparative anthropology may be enumerated under different general heads. As an illustration, I will take the two largest classes who exhibit the greatest antipathy to that science. . . . Those who have had an opportunity of examining persons suffering under religious mania, cannot but have been struck with the large number of cases which have exhibited symptoms of arrested brain-growth. Those who have watched the development of youth, must have observed certain physical signs, which I need not here enumerate, which accompany those persons who suffer to any appreciable extent from religious mania. I believe that all attempts to cure religious mania, when it is combined with either arrested brain-growth, or early closing of one or more of the sutures, have proved utterly abortive. Nor do all persons who suffer from religious mania exhibit this antipathy to

comparative anthropology. In this it differs from those whom I would describe as suffering from what I believe to be an incipient form of disease, or at least mental idiosyncracy, called, for the want of a better name, rights-of-man mania. . . . Persons of the greatest ability, eloquence, and mental power, are afflicted with this disease. It is always however accompanied by more or less defective reasoning power, and often by a want of harmony between the organs of sense and expression,—between the brain and the face. This assumption of human rights is often the mainspring of action, and in such cases persons become what are called philanthropists. (Hunt 1867a: lviii–lix)

Again and again, Hunt would coin new terms as he developed his art of pseudomedical diagnostic invective. Behind his satire, we catch glimpses of a fantasy image of himself in the role of the great medical discoverers of the century, laying bare the symptoms, etiology, and treatment of one new disease after another.

Those afflicted with this disease sometimes made the most absurd charges against persons which they could not prove, and which were incapable of proof. It was a very terrible disease, and consequently a very long word had to be invented in order to give some slight idea of its awful character. This disease was called ANTHROPOLOGICOPHOBIA (laughter). Some persons suffering from it, whenever they see the word anthropology, give a very loud bark, others a suppressed growl, while if they see a live anthropologist, they not only bark and growl, but sometimes attempt to bite (laughter). He hoped that not many persons would be afflicted with this disease in Manchester, for he could assure them that anthropologists were very dangerous, some thought very wicked animals, for when they were attacked they defended themselves (laughter and loud cheers). (Hunt 1867b: 18–19)

Hunt's rhetoric was reported—at least in his own unsigned reports in the journals he edited—to have invariably produced the same responses; and, we sense, it appealed to the same faction among his listeners. He was incapable of reaching out, like Crawfurd, through the generation of sophisticated rhetorical-mythological constructs that could catch the imagination of a wide and varied audience. Hunt remained fixated at the level of undergraduate dormitory-party humor, with its crude appeal to the simple instincts of those already fully committed to its underlying assumptions and unable to imagine any alternative way of seeing the world.

When Hunt tried to appropriate myths generated by others, he was equally crude and obvious. For example, we read in the first volume of *Anthropological Review:*

Abolition of Slavery.—The following remarks are forwarded to us by a correspondent, who states that it is a *verbatim* report of a speech delivered at a meeting of a young men's debating society in October last, to advocate the abolition of slavery. We rely fully on the veracity of our correspondent, and give insertion to such a curious *morceau*, which we fear, but too truthfully exhibits the ignorance which exists in this country respecting negro slavery.

"Mr. Chairman, the proof which I wish to prove this evening is, that it will be for the universal good that the Southern or Free States should conquer the Northern or Slaveholding States; for slavery, to all honest hearts and Christian men, must be an abomination; but above all other Slaveholding States, the Northern States of America have been held up to the execration of the world for their abominable conduct towards, and their atrocities committed on, the wretched Hindoos whom they have so villainously enslaved. But we hope now that retribution is at hand, and the brave Southern general McClellan, who is now at the doors of New York clamouring for admittance, and his coadjutor, President Jefferson Davis, will soon burst the bonds that have so long ground down the unfortunate Brahmins, and bound them in chains and fetters in New York dark dungeons and in the 'dismal swamps' of Toronto, and restore these unfortunate members of society to that preeminence in the social scale of humanity that they have so long been deserving of. Their social life, and the high cultivation that those highly gifted members of the human race have attained to, is too well known to need any further argument upon it. Then, when at length New York and Montreal have yielded to McClellan, the commerce of the New World will again be open to the Old, then Europe once more will be able to export cotton to America, and America in turn will be able to export to Europe, wine, frankincence, and myrrh!" (*AR* 1 [1863]: 182)

This adolescent satire repeatedly beats the reader over the head with heavy markers of its own absurdity; it is so obviously constructed as a lampoon of the antislavery position that it could hardly be taken otherwise. But Hunt manages to repackage it as a truthful depiction of the ignorance and stupidity of the real advocates of equality and human rights. The recursive crudity shows a metasophomoric vapidity seldom attained in professional writing, and must have made a strong impression on some of the intellectual leaders who had initially been led to the society by Hunt's charisma. No wonder their eventual breaks with him were so decisive (Stocking 1987: 248).

15   The Hunt-Crawfurd Alliance

FIGURE 22. FAIR AND DARK RACES. John Crawfurd's illustration of superior and inferior races in Indonesia shows both "savage" Papuans and relatively more "civilized" Balinese as childlike compared to Europeans (Crawfurd 1820: 1:17).

Hunt's ambition, as apparent in his words as in his actions, was to be the leader in creating a racist anthropological science that would serve as the ideological basis for an attack on ideas and political policies associated with human rights. Writers on the period have tended to focus on his most obviously successful accomplishment, the foundation of the separate Anthropological Society of London in 1863 and the opposition of its racist orientation to the traditionally antiracist orientation of the Ethnological Society. His equally successful accomplishment of engineering a revolutionary takeover of the Ethnological Society of London and turning it in a new racist direction has gone largely unnoticed in the scholarly literature.

Today both the journal and the World Wide Web home page of the Royal Anthropological Institute point with some pride to origins in the Aborigines Protection Society and the Ethnological Society of London, evoking an image of both societies' reputations as opponents of racism, slavery, and oppression. The image is correct as far as it goes, but the reality is more complex. Hunt's takeover succeeded for several years in turning the Ethnological Society from its formerly antiracist position to a pro-racist orientation, and afterward severely compromised its ability to serve as an effective organizational opposition to the avowedly racist Anthropological Society throughout the remaining years of its existence. The ideological crippling of the Ethnological Society, in turn, had a significant bearing on the nature of the discipline that would result from the merger of the two societies in the 1870s. Thus the successful takeover and transformation of the Ethnological Society demands more detailed consideration than it has received so far.

Given the mismatch we have already seen between Hunt's ambitions and his political and rhetorical abilities, we see that Hunt needed an ally capable of reaching out to a broader and more respectable audience. He found that ally in John Crawfurd (1783–1868), a former colonial diplomat and author of a respected natural history/ethnography of Indonesia (Crawfurd 1820), as well as works on Southeast Asian languages. Crawfurd had begun his career as a doctor, turned quickly to colonial politics and diplomacy, conducted diplomatic missions to Thailand and Vietnam, and served as governor of British colonies in Java and Singapore. After his retirement from the colonial service, having found "that [his] moderate fortune render[ed] [him] perfectly independent" (Crawfurd 1834), he decided to run for Parliament but was unsuccessful in election campaigns both in London and in his native Scotland. He ran as an "advanced radical" (*DNB* 1908: 5:61), or, as some twenty-first-century Americans might say, an ultraliberal. His surviving campaign literature reveals a platform that included universal suffrage without poll taxes or fees, secret balloting, elimination of regressive taxes that "rest with an unequal, and unjust pressure upon those classes of society that are the least able to bear its weight," reduction of military expenditures and perquisites for officeholders, free trade, elimination of monopolies, increasing the availability of public education, nationalization of church properties, and freedom of religious dissenters from taxation to support a state church (Crawfurd 1834).

The last point may have played better in Scotland than in London, but the overall platform was apparently too radical to gain him election in either venue. Crawfurd would wait to enjoy political success for another two decades, and then find it in a totally different arena: by his election to the vice presidency of the Geography and Ethnology Section of the British Association for the Advancement of Science. It may have been this late victory that reawakened the frustrated political aspirations of twenty years earlier and stimulated his entry into the political intrigues that were to transform the Ethnological Society. By all available evidence, he certainly enjoyed his late discovery of the world of scientific politics.

Despite Crawfurd's high qualifications as a distinguished gentleman and ethnological scholar, and although there were probably some in the society's leadership who would agree even with some of his more liberal political positions, he was nevertheless looked on with disfavor by the Prichardian and Quaker elements of the Ethnological Society because of his racist views. Crawfurd's attitudes to racial differences had been apparent since his earliest publications. In his first major ethnographic work, the *History of the Indian Archipelago* (1820), he took race as the starting point for his first chapter, observing, "There are—an aboriginal fair or brown complexioned race,—and an aboriginal negro race" (Crawfurd 1820: 1:14; fig. 22). He went on to say of them:

> There are two aboriginal races of human beings inhabiting the Indian islands, as different from each other as both are from all the rest of their species. . . . The brown and negro races of the Archipelago may be considered to present, in their physical and moral character, a complete parallel with the white and negro races of the western world. The first have always displayed as eminent a relative superiority over the second as the race of white men have done over the negroes of the west. All the indigenous civilization of the Archipelago has sprung from them, and the negro race is constantly found in the most savage state. That race . . . is necessarily least frequent where the most civilized race is most numerous, and seems utterly to have disappeared where the civilization of the fairer race has proceeded farthest, . . . just as the Caribs, and other savages of America, have given way to the civilized invaders of Europe. (1820: 1:17–18)

Although the assertion of "superiority" of the "fair" over the darker races gives the appearance of the most blatant white supremacist prejudice, in fact Crawfurd's attitude to color differences was more complex. For example, later in the chapter, he remarks, "The complexion is generally brown, but varies a little in the different tribes. . . . The Javanese, who live most comfortably, are among the darkest people of the Archipelago; the wretched Dayaks, or cannibals of Borneo, among the fairest" (1820: 1:20).

Even if Crawfurd found the superiority of one race over another convincing, for him it was not a simple matter of black and white, or darker and lighter. Or so it seems at some times in his writings, while at other times he seems drawn to a simpler, more polarized view of white superiority versus dark inferiority. The oscillation between apparently contradictory viewpoints continued throughout Crawfurd's career and became a factor in the political maneuvers that developed as he and Hunt struggled for institutional leadership, as we will see below.

Crawfurd, although a prejudiced observer, was nevertheless an acute and inquiring one. His ethnography shows not only considerable accuracy and insight but even enough sympathy for and fairness to his subjects to balance some of his more negative opinions. He continues the time-honored dialectic of virtues and vices, adding the intermediate category of "weaknesses" to accommodate qualities he does not consider negative enough to qualify as actual vices (Crawfurd 1820: 1:49). Indeed, he does not even consider hereditary racial differences to be the only, or even the primary, determinant of superiority and inferiority of different peoples but rather gives primary emphasis to ecological resources such as the availability of domesticable animals and edible plants in explaining the rise of some peoples out of a "savage" state. And yet, even if Crawfurd's racial views were more moderate than those of many of his contemporaries—including some, like Hunt, who were already members of the Ethnological Society—they must still have been disturbing to the Prichardian leadership, if only because of Crawfurd's apparently unquestioning acquiescence to what he seemed to represent as the natural outcome of contact between superior and inferior groups:

> The East Insular negro is a distinct variety of the human species, and evidently a very inferior one. . . . Some islands they enjoy almost exclusively to themselves, yet they have in no instance risen above the most abject state of barbarism. Whenever they are encountered by the fairer races, they are hunted down like the wild animals of the forest. (Crawfurd 1820: 1:24–26)

Given his propensity for making such remarks, it seems no wonder that Crawfurd was not a favorite of the leadership of the Ethnological Society.

> Prior to Mr. Crawfurd's occupying the presidential chair, his views on certain scientific subjects had been far from popular with a faction of Quakers, who, headed by Dr. Hodgkin, were then dominant in the Society; and neither friendly nor respectful were the terms in which Mr. Crawfurd and his opinions were spoken of. (Hunt 1868a: 433)

Hodgkin, we recall, was the founder and main organizational mover of the society, who by default had assumed the chief leadership responsibility after Prichard's death for maintaining its antiracist, antislavery orientation, inspired by the ideological forces of Prichardian ethnology and Quaker activism. The distaste of the Prichardian-Quaker leadership of the society for Crawfurd, and his usefulness to Hunt, certainly rested on his embracing a substantial portion of the racist agenda, from an endorsement of racial hierarchy and domination to an apparent conditional readiness to support outright genocide. For example, in response to a paper by A. R. Wallace at the British Association,

> Mr. Crawfurd said . . . As to the Maories of New Zealand, they were a very different race. . . . We had done a great deal for these Maories, and had treated them on terms of equality. We had civilised them from their abominable savagery, and made Christians of them, and some, though they had plenty of land, would not let us have any of it; but if they resisted a superior race, they must be taught that they must give way, and he did not care, if they resisted us, what became of them. . . . Mr. Wallace briefly replied, and said, that with regard to the Maories, Mr. Crawfurd had enunciated a doctrine with which he would find but few sympathisers in that room. (Crawfurd 1864a: 334)

Belief in the innate superiority of Europeans and the inferiority of other "races," together with a commitment to activist promotion of the implementation of appropriate measures to preserve the dominant-subordinate relationship between them and to neutralize all forces of resistance to such a program, was the first and foremost feature of what Hunt and Crawfurd had in common. Both saw ethnology/anthropology as capable of lending crucial "scientific" support to such a program; and hence their scientific-political agendas placed a high priority on discrediting ethnology's Prichardian heritage of racial egalitarianism, by polemically associating it with religious—in particular, Quaker—defenses of human unity that could be conveniently denounced as antiscientific, ignorant, and outmoded superstitions. More problematically, they partially shared positions that asserted the nature of human races as biologically separate species, a belief that Crawfurd only gradually adopted, and polygenism or the separate origin of human races, a position that Hunt would alternately affirm, deny, or dismiss the scientific importance of, according to the shifting demands of political expediency.

Crawfurd's acceptance of the idea of human races as constituting distinct species may, in fact, have only developed under the influence of his association with Hunt. As we have seen in the citations above from his 1820 ethnographic writing, Crawfurd had earlier maintained that the "fair" and "dark" races were, despite their differences and hierarchical inequality, nevertheless only distinct varieties of a single human species. He shows evidence of a change of belief, still apparently tentative, in a paper presented to the British Association for the Advancement of Science in 1858 and repeated at a meeting of the Ethnological Society in 1859:

> Whether these races constitute distinct species of a single genus, or mere varieties of a species, is a question difficult, and perhaps impossible, to determine. . . . [T]he result of their union is invariably a fertile offspring. To judge by the analogy of the lower animals, this would make the races of man mere varieties of a species, such as exist in some of our domesticated animals. . . . Man, indeed, differs so widely in essential attributes, mental and physical, from even the most highly organized of the lower animals, that any comparison between him and them for the purpose of classification must be deceptive. . . . Man, then, belongs to an exclusive category, and for the purpose of classification, the analogy of the lower animals may only mislead; so that practically, the races may be considered as distinct species. (Crawfurd 1858: 79)

A decade later, in a debate with John Lubbock over Darwin's theories, Crawfurd's disbelief in the unity of the human species would be expressed in far less tentative terms (see below). His hedging on the issue here, at the time when he and Hunt were first beginning to forge their political alliance, suggests that they were attempting to reach an accommodation of ideas and rhetorical stance that would facilitate their alliance in the attempt to take over the leadership of the Ethnological Society.

Beyond these points of agreement, they were very different individuals, with differences that rendered their alliance problematic and ultimately untenable. Hunt was a fanatical proponent of a strict biological determinism in which race was the irreducible solution to every question of every human difference; whereas Crawfurd took a contingent and conditionalist standpoint on the relative importance of racial heredity as one element among many, including environment, ecology, availability of plant and animal species suitable for domestication, ease of movement and communication, and other factors in the generation of differences between one or another society's way of life. Hunt's professional emphasis, as a medical school dropout, was always on physical anthropology, while Crawfurd's, as a doctor-turned-colonial-diplomat, was more characteristically on politics, economics, and especially on language and the discipline of philology. In this last respect, Crawfurd remained closer to the orientation of the

Prichard-Hodgkin school of ethnology, with its pronounced philological and cultural emphases, than to Hunt and his followers.

The background in colonial diplomacy likewise shaped Crawfurd's tendency to focus on issues defined within the context of British imperialism. Hunt, by contrast, had a more internationalist outlook, shaped by an awareness of the growing international popularity of racist anthropological views once considered characteristic of the "American school" of Morton, Nott, Gliddon, and Agassiz but now finding support in the writings of European racist anthropologists such as Luke Burke in England and Paul Broca in France. Thus, as Burke had reached out to collaborate with Gliddon in spreading racist dogma across national borders, so also Hunt actively sought the cooperation of Burke and Broca in uniting the strands of national racisms and encouraged the growth of similar racially focused movements in Spain and other countries. Crawfurd, perhaps in part because of his inability to ally himself with the American slaveholders, maintained a less internationalist, more British-centered orientation.

Indeed, Crawfurd's denunciation of slavery, a point noted by Stocking (1987: 252) and others in contrasting the Crawfurd-led Ethnological Society with Hunt's Anthropological Society, was the strongest substantive disagreement between them, even though one of Crawfurd's main arguments against slavery was that it degraded white slave owners (Crawfurd 1859a: 160–61). Hunt's defense of slavery took a characteristically rhetorical turn: as we have seen, he imitated the American race propagandist John H. van Evrie in flatly and sarcastically denying that such a thing as slavery existed, even while arguing in its favor (Hunt 1863c: 2, 54 ff.).

Political-scientific rhetoric constituted perhaps an even more significant field of difference between them than any substantive issue. To cite one obvious example, Hunt's polemics, perhaps understandably for a young scholar in his mid-twenties, continuously stressed the newness of racism as opposed to the old, outmoded belief in racial equality. Crawfurd, by contrast, was not only willing but took a gleeful delight in demolishing any idea, old or new, that contradicted his opinions. When they both found it necessary to set themselves in opposition to Darwin's evolutionary theory, with its racially threatening implications of human unity of origins, Hunt could think of no more original or effective strategy than to recycle his old anti-Prichardian rhetoric, casting "Darwinism" in the image of yet another irrational, superstitious, quasi-religious belief, opposed to the scientific empiricism of racist anthropology (Hunt 1867c). The approach was as unsuccessful as it was unimaginative and unbelievable. Crawfurd, as we shall see, fought back with a more creative and colorful rhetorical strategy that, for a time, succeeded in gaining him the status in the national press of one of the leading anti-Darwinian critics.

They must have been an odd couple of allies: the seventy-five-year-old colonial diplomat, universally praised for his good manners and with a constant eye for pleasing "the ladies," and the brash twenty-five-year-old promoter of a proprietary treatment for speech impediments, with his love of invective, insult, and misogyny. For Crawfurd, at least, a key to the viability of the relationship emerges from his *Times* obituary:

> Of singularly simple and unostentatious bearing, few were more able, and certainly none more ready, to impart sound information to those who sought his advice and assistance. A self-made man, he showed none of that jealousy which sometimes makes self-made men believe that kind of creation ended when they were made. In society, ever hale and hearty in body, ever fresh and vigorous in mind, he seemed to be of no age in particular, but in some sort to belong to all, and thus men of a younger generation both loved and respected him; for they felt that near him they would find warm shelter, not cold shade, that any merit they might have would be fully appreciated, and that they would receive from the mellow octogenarian a sympathy and consideration for all shades and phases of opinion and thought, too often wanting in circles where men of science seem to meet rather as antagonists pitted against each other in an arena than as fellow-soldiers bound to combat ignorance and error to the death. (*LT*, May 13, 1868, 5)

Hunt found exactly this kind of warm support from Crawfurd. In Crawfurd, at least at the beginning, Hunt also found what he thought he recognized as a useful resource to be exploited.

16 The Coup of 1858–1860

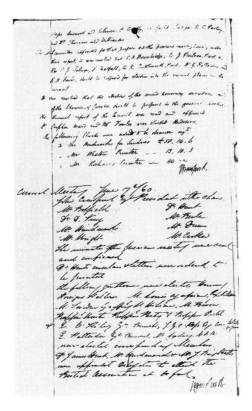

FIGURE 23. THE TRIUMPH OF ANTHROPOLOGICAL RACISM. Crawfurd's ascension to the presidency of the Ethnological Society is emblematized in the *Minutes* by the changeover to Hunt's flamboyant secretarial handwriting. Crawfurd signed the minutes at midpage and bottom (*ESL Minutes*, May 24– June 7, 1860).

We have already seen Hunt's depiction of the pitiful decline of the Ethnological Society from 1854 onward. Now we must consider his description of the events of 1858 and the crisis that led to the transformation of the society:

> At the anniversary meeting of 1858, this utter indifference came to a culminating point—the meeting consisting of but six members, the President Sir James Clark, three officers, and two other members! Nor was even this extremely select gathering by any means unanimous in sentiment, a vote of thanks to the President and Council failing to find a seconder. (Hunt 1868a: 433)

The anniversary meeting, usually held in May of each year but in 1858 postponed twice and finally held on June 30, was designated in the society's bylaws as its major business meeting, when election of officers occurred. The *ESL Minutes* (May 5–June 23, 1858, 244–46) contain no information on the meeting beyond the postponement of the date; and the official news report of the meeting submitted by the society to the *Athenaeum* (July 3, 1858, 21) mentions only Sir James Clark's presiding and the election of officers, with no public hint of any crisis. Thus we have only Hunt's testimony suggesting the crisis produced by the disastrously small attendance at the 1858 meeting, and his hint of the crucial role it played in the transformation of the society. However, Hunt is surprisingly inaccurate in his chronology of other events related to this period. For example, in one statement Hunt seems to say that Crawfurd's election to membership in the society and nomination for president took place as early as 1857 (Hunt 1868c: clxxi), while in a more clearly formulated chronology, he dates the society membership of Crawfurd and Knox, together with Crawfurd's presidential nomination and election, in 1858 (1868a: 432). But the *ESL Minutes* show all these events as occurring in 1860 (*ESL Minutes*, April 12, 1860, 258; November 21, 1860, 261; May 24, 1860, 259). Thus Hunt's later reconstructions of the chronology differ from the contemporary record by two to three years; and, in the same article and paragraph in which Hunt describes the disastrous meeting of 1858, the other events he mentions as linked to it in the same year are described in contemporary records as occurring two years later.

It would seem likely, then, that the disastrous meeting, like other events that Hunt describes as having taken place in 1858, might have actually occurred in 1860; but, in fact, it turns out that this is not possible. If the disaster occurred during Sir James Clark's presidency, the latest possible date is 1859; and the 1860 meeting marked the beginning of Crawfurd's presidency, identified by Hunt as the beginning of the society's recovery from the disaster. The meeting, then, must have taken place in either 1858 or 1859. As we will see, there is circumstantial evidence of a leadership crisis in the society in connection with both years' meetings. Nevertheless, the evidence for a crisis in 1858 is so compelling that we are justified in proceeding from the supposition of Hunt's accuracy on this point; for even if the disastrously small attendance occurred in 1859, events in the months following the 1858 meeting make it clear that a revolutionary change had occurred, one that can only be explained by the assumption of pressures resulting from some particularly catastrophic development. Hunt's account is the only satisfactory explanation of what occurred later, even if corroborating evidence is lacking and he gives only the barest clues as to either the chronological facts or their political significance.

In the absence of more concrete information, then, we must fall back on an analysis of the dynamics of the Ethnological Society's internal politics as played out against the larger political processes of the period. The general political atmosphere of the time was certainly conducive to the generation of racially focused crises, as the Indian Mutiny, or Sepoy Rebellion, of 1857 had raised interracial tensions to a new peak of intensity and left the defenders of racial equality and human rights in a state of virtual paralysis.

> Such wars could not help but have a cumulative effect upon the way in which the British public regarded the coloured peoples under their rule, and in the course of the years, these "natives" came to be thought of as bloodthirsty savages. . . . This view was almost ineradicably fixed upon the collective mind of the British public by the events of the Indian mutiny of 1857. Day after day, the newspapers told stories of massacres of British women and children. . . . The Whig parliamentarian and historian, Thomas Babington Macaulay, wrote in his diary, in June 1857: "The cruelties of the Sepoy natives have inflamed the Nation to a degree unprecedented within my memory. Peace Societies, Aborigines Protection Societies, and societies for the reformation of criminals are silent. There is one terrible cry to revenge. . . ." (Semmel 1962: 20–21)

It was during this crisis, in May–June 1857, that the Ethnological Society took the unusual step of rescheduling its annual business meeting in a smaller room because "there was no reason to suppose that more than twenty Fellows would assemble on that occasion," and of scheduling in its place "an Extra-ordinary Meeting at which a certain number of Ladies Tickets should be issued" in an attempt to counteract the declining attendance at its meetings (*ESL Minutes*, May 6, 1857, 234). The crisis would continue to worsen in the coming year.

We must also note that for the Ethnological Society in particular, the likelihood of an internal political crisis was particularly great in 1857–59, when Thomas Hodgkin, who had zealously guarded the welfare of the society and guided its leadership in adherence to the Prichardian-Quaker antiracist heritage, was mainly occupied with planning and undertaking trips to the Holy Land and to Rome, in company with Sir Moses Montefiore, to give aid and assistance to oppressed Jewish communities and individuals (Kass and Kass 1988: 459–74). During the 1858–60 crisis, he was also preoccupied with concerns such as fund-raising for the resettlement of repatriated African slaves (480 ff.) and with the politics of reforming the University of London's charter (470)—the latter during the period of the disastrous 1858 Anniversary Meeting, when he was absent from the society's council meetings from May through July (*ESL Minutes*, May 5–July 14, 1858, 244–47).

With Hodgkin otherwise occupied, and absent from England and the society for months at a time, the society was particularly vulnerable and its leadership dangerously disorganized. It was during Hodgkin's absence in 1858 that the council, perhaps in a misguided attempt to maintain a low profile during the national outbreak of antinative sentiment, took the unprecedented steps of twice postponing the Anniversary Meeting from its normal May date to successively later dates in June—and then of deciding not to advertise the meeting in the newspapers but instead to send a privately printed circular to the members (*ESL Minutes*, May 5–June 23, 1858, 244–46). When the council adjourned its June 23 meeting until 7:30 P.M. on the evening of June 30 to consider last-minute questions before the Anniversary Meeting that same evening, it resolved to reconvene the adjourned meeting "without giving any further notice of it"—in effect assuring that members absent the previous week would also miss the meeting on June 30. In retrospect, these were fatal errors that set the society up for the disaster that followed; and we can only wonder at whose instigation, and for what reasons, the council was persuaded to follow such a disastrous course. On a more mundane level, we might also wonder who took responsibility for distributing the meeting announcements and how many members actually received them.

What happened at the meeting itself must be inferred from an analysis of the interplay of political tensions and the Ethnological Society's procedures as encoded in its bylaws. What were the implications of the small attendance at the meeting and the failed vote of thanks? Because four of the six present were officers of the society, they could neither move nor second a vote of thanks to themselves. Thus the motion would fail if only one person were present who did not even vote in opposition but would simply abstain from providing the necessary second to the motion.

But the motion's failure, even though such an eventuality had not been foreseen or dealt with explicitly in the society's bylaws, nevertheless would certainly be perceived by any politically aware British gentleman as equivalent to the failure of a Parliamentary vote of confidence. It would effectively produce a constitutional crisis that would call the legitimacy of the existing leadership into question. Thus a minority of only two persons, one playing an ostensibly supportive role by moving the vote of thanks and the other simply remaining silent, could undermine the existing leadership of the society and create a crisis of revolutionary potential.

Hunt describes the meeting from the perspective of an eyewitness; and we can hardly doubt that he, an energetic participant over the last two years and soon to move into the society's leadership circle, was one of the members present. He was not an officer at the time, and so must have been one of the two eligible to vote on the resolution of thanks. Knowing his opinions, ambitions, and strong opposition to the previous antiracist leadership and considering the dynamics of the vote, we cannot escape the implication of a deliberately manipulated crisis.

Hunt himself later said: "If we cannot, by a *coup d'etat*, obtain additional strength, we must try a more certain, and, perhaps, more successful plan" (1867a: xlix). The remark has enough of a tone of wistful regret to suggest that he spoke from personal experience of what a coup could and could not accomplish. In the best Victorian fashion, then, let us fall back on conjecture and hypothesize that a "coup" was deliberately engineered and executed during and after the 1858 meeting. If so, we can hardly see Hunt in the role of the passive nonseconder of the motion of thanks. He would almost certainly have been the one to show his loyalty and responsibility to the society by moving thanks to its officers and allowing his lone friend and ally to scuttle the motion by remaining silent.

But what did Hunt have to gain in a revolt by a minority of two? Even if he actually succeeded in provoking a constitutional crisis, he and his friend would still be outvoted by the three council members who possessed Prichardian-Quaker loyalties. Indeed, the official record shows the previous leadership remaining in power, under the continuing presidency of Sir James Clark, for the following year. However, if Hunt's goal at this point was not to immediately displace but rather to destabilize and delegitimize the existing leadership in preparation for a later decisive action, his strategy succeeded admirably. There is ample evidence to show that the 1858 crisis precipitated a series of radical changes in the coming months, such that the hypothesis of a coup in process of execution appears extremely likely.

Hunt would have required support in engineering a coup, and perhaps the most likely ally was Charles Robert des Ruffières, who would later follow Hunt into the leadership circle of the breakaway Anthropological Society. Ruffières, despite his membership on the councils of both the Ethnological and the Anthropological Society, was an obscure figure who seems never to have given papers, and whose only publication was the one-paragraph "Report on the Failure of the Amalgamation Scheme" for reuniting the Ethnological and Anthropological societies in 1868, affirming his total agreement with what Hunt had already said (Ruffières 1868). From the scanty evidence available, Ruffières's main role in both societies would seem to have been that of serving as Hunt's ally. He had been nominated as a member of the Ethnological Society's council just before the disastrous 1858 meeting (*ESL Minutes*, May 26, 1858, 245), and, although not yet elected, had participated in the council's planning session immediately before the meeting, when the decision not to advertise had been made. He would thus have been in an ideal position to pass information on to Hunt, and even to help in setting up the crisis—for example, we might conjecture, by expressing his inability to second the vote of thanks because of his own involvement in the council's actions? At any rate, Ruffières would preside at the council meeting in the coming year, when Hunt was appointed to the honorary post of auditor (*ESL Minutes*, April 28, 1859, 252)—a step that normally preceded election to the council itself—and had himself named to the nominating committee that proposed Hunt for election to the council a month later (*ESL Minutes*, April 28–May 26, 1859, 252–53).

For the rest of 1858, the society's leadership made sporadic efforts to deal with the crisis and recoup its losses. Sir James Clark, the president, did not attend another meeting until the end of October. In the meantime, the council began efforts in July and August to resume publication of their journal, which had not appeared for two years (*ESL Minutes*, July 14–August 4, 1858, 246–47). In late October, with Hodgkin and the president both present for the first time since February, the council attempted to reestablish a stable and predictable schedule for both its own meetings and those of the general membership—the first Thursday and the third Wednesday of each month, respectively. However, the leadership itself appeared unable to resolve its own problems of stability and continuity, with the president again absent from December until March and Hodgkin absent from March until November 1859 (*ESL Minutes*, December 2, 1858–November 10, 1859, 249–55). During this period, the coup moved decisively toward realization.

By early 1859, with the president again absent for three months, there are clear signs of the leadership beginning to lose control. In September 1858, while the Ethnological Society had been inactive, John Crawfurd had given a paper, "On the Effects of Commixture, Locality, Climate, and Food on the Races of Man," at the annual meeting of the British Association for the Advancement of Science. Later that year Crawfurd began to take an active part in discussions at the Ethnological Society meetings (*Athenaeum*, December 25, 1858, 840) and continued to take part in 1859.

SCIENTIFIC/SOCIETIES/Ethnological.—*Jan. 19.*—Dr. Hodgkin in the chair.—The Hon. Secretary read a paper "On the Popular Poetry of the Maori," by W. B. Baker. . . .—In the discussion on this paper, Admiral FitzRoy gave an account of the New Zealanders and their ethnological characteristics and traditions from his own observations.—The Rev. W. Ellis made some interesting remarks on the poetry of the Polynesian islanders in general, and especially on that of the natives of the Sandwich Islands, of which he gave some examples and made a comparison between it and that of the Maori.—Mr. Crawfurd stated his own opinions as to the origin of the inhabitants of the different groups of the islands of the Pacific Ocean. (*Athenaeum*, January 29, 1859, 155–56)

As Crawfurd was not then a member of the society, he would have had to attend the meetings as the guest of a member, almost certainly Hunt. In this official press report submitted by the Ethnological Society, FitzRoy, captain of Darwin's ship *Beagle*, based his remarks "on his own observations," and Ellis, the well-known missionary-ethnographer of Hawai'i, "made some interesting remarks"; Crawfurd, on the other hand, merely "stated his own opinions." The subtle but unmistakable difference in treatment (probably attributable to the secretary, Thomas Wright) tends to support Hunt's contention that some of the society's leadership held attitudes to Crawfurd that were "neither friendly nor respectful." But shortly afterward, in February 1859, the council invited him to present the British Association paper at the next public meeting of the Ethnological Society (*ESL Minutes*, February 3, 1859, 250).

Given the unfavorable attitude toward Crawfurd and his ideas on the part of the council leadership, we can only wonder at what opposition was raised to the invitation and what arguments and pressures prevailed against them. It might have been argued, for instance, that Crawfurd, a recognized scientific leader and the vice president of the British Association's Geography and Ethnology Section (BAAS 1859: xxvii), certainly deserved a hearing on a subject central to the society's interests and that his established prestige might help to restore the flagging attendance at the society's meetings. Then again, there is a possibility that misrepresentation played a role in securing the invitation; for the title of the paper as approved in the society's minutes was simply "On the Influence of Climate, etc., on Race" (*ESL Minutes*, February 3, 1859, 250). In this form the title has the innocuous appearance of reflecting the long-established interests of Prichard and other longtime members of the society; and some may even have imagined they were voting in favor of a presentation that would accord with what until now had been the ideological mainstream of the society's leadership. If so, they would be quickly disillusioned.

Crawfurd's paper was, in fact, an anti-Prichardian manifesto. Beginning with a broad sketch of human physical diversity, he quickly moved to the construction of a racial hierarchy expressed in terms of a series of comparisons of the "mental endowment" of various races, set up as contrasts of superiority to inferiority, with the superiority of Europeans serving as a standard for the measurement of the relative degree of inferiority of all the others (Crawfurd 1858: 76–79). Having disposed of the possibility of racial equality, he went on to deal with the question of whether human beings constituted a single species, concluding that "practically, the races may be considered as distinct species" (Crawfurd 1858: 79).

Having constructed this anti-Prichardian framework, Crawfurd then proceeded to his main topics: "commixture," which a few years later would begin to be called "miscegenation" (Croly, Wakeman, and Howell 1864), locality, climate, and food, all taken as factors for explaining the differences he maintained in racial "endowments." Commixture with a superior race led to improvement, and with an inferior, to degradation; while commixture of equal races produced "mongrel" or "bastard people" like the English (Crawfurd 1858: 80 ff.). Only commixture could alter the physical features of races, which were otherwise fixed and immutable; but physical features and hereditary traits were in any case only partial determinants of relative superiority or inferiority. The other factors—climate, locality, and food—could in fact take precedence over heredity in raising or lowering racial status; only under ideally equal conditions would hereditary differences result in evidence of the superiority of one race over another, while physically identical races showed wide disparity under differing conditions (Crawfurd 1858: 77, 85 ff.).

Here, the Prichardian-oriented members of the Ethnological Society must have breathed a sigh of relief, for Crawfurd, as a career colonial administrator, shared with the missionaries the belief that a race could be "improved" by altering the conditions under which they lived. They must also have found the shock of his overall framework mitigated to some extent by his stress on the importance of philological research for investigating the history of relations between races (Crawfurd 1858: 82 ff.), an emphasis equally stressed, even if in pursuit of diametrically opposite ends, by Prichard and his followers in the society.

Still, the reactions must have been strongly mixed, for Crawfurd's explicitly and fundamentally racist framework was a radical point of departure for the society. It certainly would have attracted a new and different audience, and so helped to arrest the alarming decline in attendance and interest; but the gain in attendance would have come at the expense of a radical shift in ideological orientation of those who attended the society's meetings.

Nevertheless, the council persisted on its new course, giving yet stronger indications of how far the crisis had pressured it into acting against its own inclinations. The following month, the council invited Dr. Robert Knox to present a paper on another seemingly innocuous subject, "Observations on the Assyrian Marbles, and on their place in History and in Art" (*ESL Minutes*, March 3, 1859, 250). If Crawfurd may have been a relatively unknown quantity to some of the society's members, Knox could hardly have escaped his own notoriety. Having attained the reputation of a brilliant lecturer in comparative anatomy at the University of Edinburgh, he was implicated as the main purchaser of corpses from the notorious murderers Burke and Hare (Richardson 1987: chap. 6), and subsequently losing his teaching license, he became a wandering apostle of an embittered racist pessimism (Richards 1989; Desmond 1989: 79–80, 388–89, 424–25). Hunt (1868a: 433) tells us that Knox had applied for membership in the Ethnological Society in 1855 but had been "black-balled"; and now, suddenly, he was invited by the council to address the society!

Knox's paper (1859) adhered closely to its promised subject, one that must have seemed less threatening than Crawfurd's; but in some ways, it must have been even more disturbing. Knox began with a citation of his own work on race and then proceeded to an analysis of racial portrayals in Assyrian art that used art as evidence for the racial inferiority of the Assyrians, and by extension, all non-European races.

> But admitting that in architectural designs the strictly Oriental, the African, or the Coptic mind far excelled all European races, there exists a gulf between those races which nothing can bridge over. The gulf I allude to is the contempt for truth and the acceptance of conventionalism in its place by all Oriental races. . . . The Coptic artist was a caricaturist: hence his drawings cannot be trusted. Of the beautiful they were profoundly ignorant; truth in nature they despised; a national conventionalism filled the minds of the race, shutting out for ever all hopes of progress, for no nation or race can ever make progress in fine art whose minds are unsuited to discover the beautiful, and who accept of falsehoods for truth. . . . In whatever way Assyrian art originated, if it did not originate with the race (which in my own opinion it did), it received from it those profound modifications which the element of race stamps on mankind. Nature had denied to the race the perception of the beautiful, in the absence of which high art cannot exist; in lieu thereof

they substituted, as other races have done, conventionalities, derived from those ever varied and endless varieties in circumstances and accidents forming the basis of art within the trammels of conventionalism—the basis in fact of what is called national taste. The art became Assyrian, and as such, Oriental and theatrical, antagonistic not to the Assyrian nature, but to the nature of a higher gifted race whose aim in art was truth and beauty. (Knox 1859: 150–51, 153)

If there were some in the audience who would have been predisposed to agree with Knox's aesthetic hierarchy, they may have been uneasy with his analysis. And they might have been still more disturbed by other aspects of his discussion.

> Thus all their figures, man, woman, and child, are carved after one model, a model displaying the coarse anatomy of the *interior* structures of the body, of all sights the most abhorred by those on whom nature has bestowed a love of fine forms and of the beautiful. In their sculptures the Assyrians displayed even the *skeleton* forms of the feet, forms which . . . nature constantly endeavours to conceal, and successfully conceals in all her finest productions of humanity. To display skeleton forms on the surface is to bring prominently into view those hideous shapes of the interior which nature has so carefully concealed. In all fine forms of sculpture a skeleton-shaped foot . . . is to display to the spectator those emblems of decay and of dissolution from which all men of correct taste turn with aversion. (Knox 1859: 151; emphasis in original)

Coming from the master dissector of human corpses, who had once mesmerized students in "Edinburgh's largest anatomy class" (Desmond 1989: 388), talk of "the coarse anatomy of the *interior* structures of the body" as "those hideous shapes of the interior" and "those emblems of decay and of dissolution" must have seemed, to say the least, a bit bizarre. Did it reflect the twisted guilt of the man whose dissection table, even if unknowingly, had been the chief market for Britain's most notorious serial killers? At any rate, the Ethnological Society Council, at its next meeting, saw fit to pass a resolution "that the following Notice should be printed in the forthcoming part of the Society's papers—'As the subjects which come within the scope of Ethnology necessarily admit of differences of opinion, the Society is not to be considered as advocating the opinions expressed in any particular paper printed in the volumes of its Transactions'" (*ESL Minutes*, April 7, 1859, 251). The disclaimer, in the face of the council's continuance of the new policy of inviting racist papers, is the best proof we have of the capitulation of the previous leadership to the inexorable force of a racist coup in progress; for the next month's paper would complete an unbroken three months' run of racist presentations at the society's meetings. At the same meeting in which it published the disclaimer, the council invited a return engagement by Crawfurd with an entirely new paper—the one, in fact, in which he created the myth of the Noble Savage, which we will return to in the following chapter.

Crawfurd's Noble Savage paper was presented on April 20, 1859, a week before the council would select Hunt as auditor and just over a month before it would endorse him for election to council membership (*ESL Minutes*, April 28–May 26, 1859, 252–53). The last paper of the 1858–59 "season" before the Anniversary Meeting was John Beddoe's presentation, "On the Physical Characteristics of the Jews" (1859). The paper was a relatively neutral, straightforward enumeration of measurements and observations, with little of the racist coloration that tinged the papers of Knox and Crawfurd; but it is still quite possible that Beddoe was another of Hunt's allies in the society. Beddoe (1910: 209) tells us, "[It was only] late in the sixties when I began to be interested in what might be called the politics of anthropology," offering as proof of his political naïveté an incident from the later warfare between Crawfurd's Ethnological Society and Hunt's secessionist Anthropological Society:

> Indeed, on one occasion, when I attended a dinner of the principal supporters of the Anthropological [Society] . . . I was a little annoyed at the merriment which some of what I thought serious and weighty propositions occasioned, until I found out that I had been throughout using the obnoxious term *ethnological*, though in perfect innocence. (Beddoe 1910: 209–10)

Despite his perfect innocence, or perhaps because of it, it seems entirely possible that Beddoe, who in 1859 was a member of the Ethnological Society Council, and who would follow Hunt into the Anthropological Society and ultimately succeed him as its president, might have been attracted strongly enough by Hunt's promotion of physical anthropology to lend him politically "innocent" but tactically valuable support in the takeover of the Ethnological Society. At any rate, Beddoe's paper continued the run of racially focused papers through a fourth month, so that virtually all of 1859 up to the Anniversary Meeting had been dominated by the new racial emphasis. Hunt's agenda had come to dominate the society; and now, at the annual elections, Hunt was to take an official place among its leadership by election to the council.

In retrospect, it seems clear that the stage had been set for the coup that would soon be consummated and that various actors were being tried out for the leading role in the drama. Hunt tells us that he became "a student" of Knox in 1854 and that he became acquainted with Crawfurd in 1858. Crawfurd, a previous member of the Ethnological Society, fellow of the Royal Geographic Society, and since 1857 vice president of the Geography and Ethnology Section of the British Association for the Advancement of Science (BAAS 1858: xxvii; 1859: xxvii), clearly possessed the qualifications, respectability, and connections with the scientific establishment that Knox so obviously lacked. Furthermore, while even Hunt could recognize the political liabilities evoked by Knox's confrontational style (Hunt 1867a: lviii), Crawfurd's diplomatic charm and personal warmth were so strong as to arouse positive reactions even from his opponents. If Hunt would have preferred Knox, he could certainly live with Crawfurd as an acceptable compromise; and in the end, so, too, could the council leadership, as they showed the following year. But in 1859 they mounted one last effort to defeat the racist onslaught.

If the poorly attended 1858 meeting had been a disaster, the 1859 Anniversary Meeting was to be an even greater one. First of all, the date was misadvertised as May 18, when Beddoe gave his paper on the Jews (*Athenaeum*, May 14, 1859, 651); but the council did not even meet to select candidates for the election until May 26 (*ESL Minutes*, May 26, 1859, 253). The Anniversary Meeting would have been held the following week, most likely on Wednesday, June 1. As in the case of the 1858 meeting, the actual date of the 1859 meeting was not advertised, which may have led to attendance problems like those of the previous year, with further exacerbation of the already precarious political situation.

But in planning the Anniversary Meeting, the council faced new difficulties and dangers. Sir James Clark, following the Ethnological Society's unofficial two-term rule, planned to resign the presidency at the end of his second term in May. His prolonged, repeated absences from meetings during the year shows such a lack of involvement after the 1858 meeting as to suggest that he may well have wished to be rid of the responsibility even sooner. Hunt offers a curious appreciation of Clark's role during this period:

> It would be wrong to conclude this part of our subject without a passing notice of Sir James Clark, Bart., who was President of the Society before Mr. Crawfurd. *We do not hesitate to assert that no president of any scientific society ever performed his duty more conscientiously than did this distinguished physician.* (1868a: 433; emphasis added)

Knowing Hunt's contempt for the society's pre-Crawfurd leadership and the active role he played in unseating them, Hunt's praise seems unlikely. Could it be that Clark's conscientious performance of his "duty" consisted in his recognition of the handwriting on the wall and a gracious exit, without lending his prestige to efforts to support a lost cause, or perhaps even supporting Hunt's elevation to the council in an attempt to forge a reconciliation between him and the old leadership? But in any case, Clark had been largely a figurehead president chosen for his social position (he was Queen Victoria's personal physician), who, like John Conolly, his predecessor, never published an ethnological paper in the society's publications.

We recall that Hunt's attack on the society's leadership attributed its "decline" chiefly to lack of productivity: "So scarce were original papers, that the meetings were not unfrequently eked out by the reading of extracts from books of travels" (1868a: 433). Indeed, in contrast to the dynamic Crawfurd, who had presented two papers at the British Association's last meeting and two at the Ethnological Society in three months, Clark would most likely have seemed almost irrelevant to the society's main interests. Crawfurd must have presented an appealing solution as far as some of the members were concerned; and any credible opposition would have to center on a candidate who was not only socially respectable but ethnologically productive as well. At the May 26 meeting, the council endorsed a candidate who met both requirements.

> It was resolved, that Admiral FitzRoy should be requested to accept the presidency, and that, with this view, he should be considered as having been at this meeting of council reelected a member of the Society. And that the present President, Sir James Clark, should be placed on the list of vice-presidents. (*ESL Minutes*, May 26, 1859, 253)

Admiral FitzRoy, the commander of Darwin's *Beagle* expedition and now the head of a government bureau in London, had presented an ethnological paper to the society in May 1858 that would become the first article in its new series of publications (FitzRoy 1858). FitzRoy's article, based on naive reflections on visceral but still firsthand observations made during his voyages, was a mix of prejudiced assumptions of white superiority, diffusionist speculations, and affirmations of biblical piety so fundamentalist in character that they must have embarrassed the sophisticated Quaker ethnologists in his audience. Still, his point was the rapid development of varieties of the human race rather than the essential separateness of races conceived as mutually alien species; and this, along with his undoubted respectability, may have recommended him as a viable candidate to the embattled leadership of the Ethnological Society. Unfortunately, the choice proved to be unsuccessful.

What happened at the Anniversary Meeting the next week is unclear. The *ESL Minutes* for this period contain no information on the meeting, and the 1859 meeting is the only one from 1857 through 1861 for which no report was published in *Athenaeum*. But we can infer from the results that the meeting was a disaster, not only from the fact that no report of it was submitted for publication, but even more from the events that followed. The ESL Council held another meeting the week after the Anniversary Meeting, in the minutes of which FitzRoy is not even mentioned. Instead, we read:

> The honorary secretary having stated that Sir J. Emerson Tennent had finally resigned the presidency, it was unanimously resolved that, the duty of filling of the vacancy for the year having devolved upon the Council, Sir James Clark should be requested to remain in the office of president during another year. (*ESL Minutes*, June 9, 1859, 253–54)

FitzRoy had either declined the presidency or been rejected by the society, whether because of his intellectual weaknesses or his unwillingness to accept the makeshift construction of a status in the society that would allow him to assume its leadership, or for other reasons that are unclear. Sir James Emerson Tennent, a knighted politician and civil servant whose book on Ceylon was just published that year, was an equally respectable alternative and definitely an intellectually more viable candidate. The book (Tennent 1859), a two-volume study encompassing natural history, geography, history, and ethnography, met with enthusiastic reviews, and probably with an equally enthusiastic reception among those members of the society who appreciated its avoidance of the racial emphases that pervaded so many contemporary ethnographic writings.

Tennent seems exactly the kind of candidate the society leadership would have fallen back on in the event of the collapse of the FitzRoy nomination; but, obviously, the Tennent alternative had also failed disastrously. The clear proof of the fiasco is the wording of this brief passage in the minutes. Tennent had not simply declined the nomination before the election, he had "resigned the presidency"; and the action of the council in reinstating Sir James Clark would only have been legal under the society's bylaws in the case of a vacancy occurring after an election (*ESL Regulations* 1855: Article 5). The fiasco was, in other words, that Tennent had actually been elected president in the panic following the collapse of the FitzRoy nomination and had "finally" resigned barely a week later, perhaps because no one had had enough time in the quickly developing crisis to ask him if he was willing to serve. Tennent's name does not appear in any list of ESL presidents, and his term in office is by far the shortest on record.

With the double failure of the FitzRoy and Tennent nominations, the Ethnological Society leadership must have appeared particularly incompetent and discredited. Meanwhile, Crawfurd's ascendancy continued, as he seemed to exhibit inexhaustible energy. At the meetings of the British Association, he presented no less than three papers, at least one of which extended beyond the confines of Section E, the Geography and Ethnology Section, into the Statistics Section. He also chaired a day of sessions in Section E. Of the papers he presented, only "On the Importance of the Domesticated Animals" became partly incorporated into an eventual larger composite publication in the ESL *Proceedings*, along with other papers presented at the Ethnological Society and the British Association, while the analyses he presented to the Ethnological and Statistical sections of the British Association of the effects of gold discoveries in North America must remain objects of conjecture.

Crawfurd returned to the Ethnological Society to present a paper at its monthly meeting in January 1860. Meanwhile, the run of papers focused on physical and racial subjects had continued in November and December. The leadership appears to have conducted a cold war against Crawfurd, freezing him out of the official reports of the meetings. None of his papers from 1859 through the first half of 1860 were reported or commented on in the official reports of the meetings, beyond a bare listing of their titles and a single remark that the "Noble Savage" paper of April 1859 was "very long." Even Knox had received better treatment, with at least a sentence or two in the official reports reflecting the ethnological content of his papers presented to the society. The lack of recognition accorded Crawfurd by the society's leadership must have been a negative reflection of his growing appeal to its changing membership.

But by now the Hunt-Crawfurd bandwagon was rolling forward with irresistible momentum. Hunt was proposed as joint honorary secretary by the council on March 13, 1860 (*ESL Minutes*, March 13, 1860, 257). On the day his acceptance was received by the council, on April 12, John Crawfurd was proposed as a member of the society (*ESL Minutes*, April 12, 1860, 258). On May 10 Hunt was named to the nominating committee to create the annual "house list" of candidates endorsed by the council for election at the annual meeting (*ESL Minutes*, May 10, 1860, 258–59). Two weeks later the council approved the committee's recommendation that the candidate for president should be Crawfurd (*ESL Minutes*, May 24, 1860, 259).

Eight years later, Hunt described the change: "Whilst [the Ethnological Society was] in a state of utter depression, the late lamented Mr. John Crawfurd, in the year 1858, became a Fellow of the Society, and was nominated as President on the same day. From this time may be dated the renaissance of the Ethnological Society" (1868a: 432). Here, as elsewhere, Hunt's dating may be off, but he cannot be far amiss in his statement of the facts or their implications. As we have seen, Crawfurd's approval as a fellow by the council did indeed come on the same day as Hunt's acceptance of the secretaryship; and if Hunt's absence that day prevented him from voicing a nomination at the meeting, it was less than a month later that he was named to the committee that selected Crawfurd to be the next president. With Crawfurd in the president's chair, he and Hunt were able to almost instantaneously stack the society's council and membership with the most notorious racists in England.

> Both President [Crawfurd] and other officers worked energetically in its behalf, and their joint labours soon resulted in financial improvement and marked progress throughout. . . . It may be mentioned also, as a further example of the state of scientific feeling thirteen years ago, that the late *Dr. Robert Knox was, in the year 1855, proposed an ordinary Fellow of the Society, and black-balled! He was, however, elected in 1858 an Honorary Fellow,* to the horror and indignation of the Quakers. (Hunt 1868a: 433; emphasis added)

Again, Hunt's chronology is off, but his facts may be close to the mark. The only indication that any attempt had been made in 1855 to make Knox a fellow of the society is an ambiguous note in the *ESL Minutes* for February 7, 1855, that "letters were read from . . . Dr. Knox," with no further mention of contents, discussion, or vote. Hunt had described himself as a "student" of Knox since 1854; but Hunt himself did not become a member until 1856. If Knox had been "proposed" as a member in 1855, who had nominated him? Considering that the actual date of Knox's membership was 1860 rather than 1858, is it possible that the failed nomination was attempted in 1857, when the society's membership crisis was already becoming evident and the leadership apparently at a loss as to how to counteract it? Was the failure of the nomination the event that suggested the necessity of a coup against the existing leadership?

Whatever the chain of events, it is unmistakably clear that by 1860 a revolutionary change had occurred, wresting control of the society out of the hands of "the Quakers." The election of Knox by the new controlling faction was certainly not the only event that struck them with "horror and indignation."

> It was in the autumn of 1859 that a prospectus was first drawn up of a quarterly journal . . . and *both Dr. Knox and Mr. Crawfurd promised their active support and co-operation. Shortly after an application was made to Mr. Luke Burke,* who, in 1848, edited the Ethnological Journal, to enter into the scheme. (Hunt 1868a: 433; emphasis added)

As always, we must question Hunt's chronology here. If, as on various other points, he is off by two years, the journal prospectus would belong to 1861, the year after Crawfurd was elected president, rather than 1859. In fact, the "Special Statement" issued by the society under Crawfurd's signature on March 19, 1861, mentions publication plans for both a volume of "Transactions" and a "Journal" (Crawfurd 1861c: 2). Still, the 1859 date seems quite plausible. There is no reason why the *Journal* could not have been envisioned as a publication independent of the society, a ploy later used by Hunt in his simultaneous publications of Anthropological Society "Memoirs" and "Journals" and the nominally independent *Anthropological Review,* all in fact edited and controlled by himself.

Crawfurd, as we have seen, had been actively participating in society meetings since late 1858, and Knox not only gave papers but also took an active part in discussions at the society's meetings in 1859 (*Athenaeum,* December 3, 1859, 744), both apparently under Hunt's sponsorship. With the addition of Burke, later also to be elected to the society's council, it is by no means unlikely that as early as 1859 the four most notorious racist anthropologists in England were planning the publication of a journal that would pose severe competition to the publications of the society, of which Crawfurd, Knox, and Burke were not yet officially members. The threat of such formidable competition may have given Hunt just the edge he needed to force the capitulation of the society's leadership to adopt his agenda; and, seen in this light, the leadership's acquiescence to the three months' run of racist papers by Knox and Crawfurd in 1859 seems less inexplicable. The papers were, in fact, a preview of the planned journal and a foretaste of the inevitable victory of the racist alliance.

As to how the revolution came about, Hunt gives us a further piece of revealing information in his memorial resolution for Crawfurd.

> The PRESIDENT [Hunt] remarked that he but expressed the general feeling of the Society when he said how deeply they all deplored the death of that gentleman. . . . It was fifteen years since he first became ac-

quainted with him; and eleven years ago, when connected with the
Ethnological Society, *he had proposed Mr. Crawfurd as the President
of that Society.* Since that time they had been working together, and
he never knew a man who evinced more enthusiasm and who took
as much interest in the science. During the first five or six years that
Mr. Crawfurd was President of the Ethnological Society, he (Dr. Hunt)
had been associated with him as the secretary of the Society; and during the whole period, though at times apparently opposing each other,
they never had a quarrel nor had an unfriendly word passed between
them in private, but, on the contrary, they were the best of friends.
(Hunt 1868c: clxxi; emphasis added)

Hunt's chronology here displays the usual inconsistencies with the
contemporary record but is consistent with the political dynamics of the
takeover of the society. Hunt's retroactive calculations of absolute dates
from 1868 backward are impossible: Crawfurd was not a member in 1857,
eleven years earlier; and Hunt resigned the secretaryship in 1863, when
he left to found the Anthropological Society of London, only three years
into Crawfurd's presidency. On the other hand, the internal chronology of
relative dates is entirely consistent. Hunt tells us that he had known Crawfurd for four years, since he joined the society (in 1856) when he nominated Crawfurd for president (in 1860), and that their relationship lasted
"five or six years" (from 1856 until Hunt took steps to form the competing
Anthropological Society in late 1862). Above all, he confesses that he himself was the one who promoted Crawfurd's election as president.

Thus was the coup brought to fruition. At least by early 1860, and perhaps as long as a year earlier, the racist takeover of the society was a fait ac-
compli, awaiting only the elections of 1860 to provide official validation.
Crawfurd was formally elected a member on April 18, 1860, at the same
meeting where Hunt was appointed joint honorary secretary (*Athenaeum,*
April 28, 1860, 585) and the principal players were in place to assume their
new roles.

However, the Prichardian leadership managed to mount a final act of resistance that, ineffectual and quixotic though it may have been, still constituted a poignant evocation of the society's grounding in the Aborigines
Protection Society and the quest for human equality. Stocking (1971: 372)
suggests that after the foundation of the Ethnological Society in 1843,
"those who entered the ESL had decided it was a good idea to separate hu-
manitarianism and ethnological research," pointing out that the "minutes
of the Society's Council . . . are singularly lacking in discussion of any issues of a specifically humanitarian character." In fact, they are lacking in

discussion of any substantive issues whatever. Nevertheless, on May 16, 1860, with Hodgkin in the chair in place of the president,

> the Chairman introduced a Lady Diplomatist, who came to England to represent the grievances of the North American Indians. She spoke very clearly and concisely, and said she had been deputed to come to England by a large council of all the tribes of British North America. The Indians, she said, were not looked upon or treated as human beings. An Act, passed in 1857, by the Canadian Government, deprives them of the power of holding any land. They are insulted and treated like brutes; and she had now come to England to ask for help for her oppressed people, and she felt like a child going amongst lions. (*Athenaeum*, May 26, 1860, 724)

The "Lady Diplomatist's" reversal of the metaphor of bestiality was indeed concise, and even elegant, but must have fallen on a majority of deaf ears. Two weeks later Crawfurd was elected president of the society. The change was emblematized stylistically as well as substantively in the *ESL Minutes*, when at the first meeting where Crawfurd presided, the secretarial hand changes dramatically from Wright's cribbed jottings to Hunt's flamboyant copperplate (fig. 23).

17 The Myth of the Noble Savage

FIGURE 24. PARADIGMATIC SAVAGES.
Natives of Tierra del Fuego as the ultimate in savage degradation, from
J. G. Wood's *Uncivilized Races of Men* (1871: 2:1163).

The same issue of *Athenaeum* that announced Crawfurd's first lecture
to the Ethnological Society also advertised P. T. Barnum's final series of
lectures in London, "MONEY MAKING and HUMBUG" (*Athenaeum*,
February 12, 1859, 225–26).[1] Barnum, reputed author of the aphorism
"There's a sucker born every minute" and self-styled "Prince of Humbugs," had made his fortune in his 1840s "Tom Thumb" tour of England
and Europe, exploiting connections with, among others, Charles Murray,
George Catlin, and, above all, the press (Barnum 1855–89: 250–53, 399;
Fitzsimmons 1970: 83–89). Now, having been ruined by falling for others'
swindles, he had returned to make another fortune by lecturing British
audiences on the public appeal of "humbugs" and their potential usefulness for achieving success. Advertisements for his highly successful and
profitable lectures quoted favorable reviews in the British press, reviews
that praised features such as their "racy anecdotes, apt illustrations, good
sense, and worldly wisdom of a thoroughly straightforward character" and
referred repeatedly to their apparent strong appeal to the "ladies" in the

audience (*Athenaeum*, January 15, 1859, 85; January 22, 1859, 117; February 26, 1859, 288).

The month after Barnum left London, another lecturer would reproduce these features of his style so closely that the descriptions of Barnum's reviewers would apply equally to him. We might wonder whether John Crawfurd had been among the thousands inspired by Barnum, since his "humbug," although foisted on a much smaller audience, nevertheless had far more enduring success than any hoax Barnum had ever perpetrated. In any case, whether Crawfurd actually sat in Barnum's audience or not, it seems appropriate to consider the shift in his rhetorical style and career that began after February 1859 as part of the general process of Barnumization that transformed British showmanship during the period (Fitzsimmons 1970: 164 ff.). For Crawfurd, abandoning the restrained, serious style of his earlier lectures in favor of a Barnumesque foregrounding of blunt language, vivid imagery, humor, and an appeal to the "ladies" would create a humbug that would live until the end of the next century.[2]

So, finally, it is time for us to return to the question of when and how the Noble Savage reentered the theoretical discourse of anthropology. It appears to have been reintroduced by Crawfurd, soon to be elected president of the Ethnological Society of London, in a paper, "On the Conditions Which Favour, Retard, or Obstruct the Early Civilization of Man," presented to the society on April 20, 1859,[3] and published in 1861 in the society's *Transactions* (Crawfurd 1859a). The paper is represented in the *Transactions* as the first recorded pronouncement of Crawfurd's presidency, a problematic issue to which we will return shortly. But as so represented, it seems to stand as a kind of inaugural address, an announcement of the overthrow of the old ways and the ascendancy of a new anthropological racism and, above all, of a new supporting mythology.

The substantive focus of Crawfurd's paper is a virtual reiteration of the points made in his February presentation to the Ethnological Society (Crawfurd 1858):

> The conditions which favour, retard, or obstruct the early civilization of man are, the physical and intellectual character of the races of man, the character, auspicious or inauspicious, of the localities in which the races are found, the presence or absence, the abundance or paucity, of animals capable of domestication, or of useful plants suitable for cultivation, as well as the intercommunication of rude tribes with nations that have already made some advance in social progress. (Crawfurd 1859a: 159, 177)

For the April paper, the list was somewhat more specific, with domesticated plants and animals emphasized over the less specific category "food" and a new emphasis on intercommunication between peoples replacing the February paper's attention to climate, now subsumed under the characteristics of localities. Above all, racial differences now received the explicit highlighting that had been concealed under the term "commixture" in the title of the earlier paper. And yet virtually all of the substantive points of the April paper had been made, in slightly revised order or under slightly different headings, in the February lecture. The outstanding difference between the two papers is not substantive but stylistic; and in the later paper, Crawfurd employs a radical departure from his previous rhetorical style to construct, vividly and unforgettably, a foundation myth for the emergence of a newly racialized anthropology.

Crawfurd's myth is grounded in both visionary experience and scriptural citation. For the visionary experience, he cites a description of the savage by Sir Humphrey Davy "in the form of a vision, partly fictitious, and partly founded on an actual dream."

> A dim and hazy light, which seemed like that of twilight in a rainy morning, broke on my sight, and gradually a country displayed itself to my view, covered with forests and marshes. I saw wild animals grazing in large savannahs, and carnivorous beasts, such as lions and tigers, occasionally disturbing and destroying them. I saw naked savages feeding upon wild fruits, or devouring shell-fish, or fighting with clubs for the remains of a whale, which had been thrown upon the shore. I observed that they had no habitations—that they concealed themselves in caves, or under the shelter of palm-trees, and that the only delicious food which nature seemed to have given to them was the date and the cocoa-nut, and these were in very small quantities, and the object of contention. I saw that some of these wretched human beings that inhabited the wide waste before my eyes had weapons pointed with flint or fish-bone, which they made use of for destroying birds and fishes that they fed upon raw. But their greatest delicacy appeared to be a maggot or worm, which they sought for with great perseverance in the buds of the palm. (Davy, cited in Crawfurd 1859a: 154–55)

If this "vision," part dream and part fiction, established a suitably garish Barnumesque frame for the construction of the myth that would follow, it must also have surprised the audience of ethnologists used to hearing quite different kinds of narratives at their meetings. They would certainly have been reassured by Crawfurd's return to a more comfortably familiar discursive mode, the citation of ethnographic narratives, among which one stands out as a scriptural citation that establishes the second part of the myth's supporting framework. The source is already familiar to us; it is part of Darwin's description of the natives of Tierra del Fuego (fig. 24):

> I could not have believed how wide was the difference between savage and civilized man. It is greater than that between a wild and a domesticated animal, inasmuch as in man there is a greater power of improvement. Among the central tribes, the men generally possess an otter skin, or some small scrap about as large as a pocket handkerchief, which is barely sufficient to cover their backs as low down as their loins. This is laced across their breasts by strings, and, according as the wind blows, it is shifted from side to side. But these Fuegians in the canoe were quite naked, and even one full-grown woman was absolutely so. It was raining heavily, and the fresh water, together with the spray, trickled down her body. In another harbour, not far distant, a woman, who was suckling a recently-born child, came one day alongside the vessel and remained there, whilst the sleet fell and thawed on her naked bosom and on the skin of her naked child.
>
> These poor wretches were stunted in their growth, their hideous faces bedaubed with white paint, their bodies filthy and greasy, their hair tangled, their voices discordant, their gestures violent without dignity. Viewing such men, one can hardly make oneself believe they are fellow-creatures, and inhabitants of the same world. It is a common subject of conjecture, what pleasure in life some of the lower animals can enjoy. How much more reasonably the same question may be asked with respect to these barbarians. At night, five or six human beings, naked and scarcely protected from the wind and rain, sleep on the wet ground, coiled up like animals. Whenever it is low water, they must rise to pick shell-fish from the rocks; and the women, winter and summer, either dive to collect sea-eggs, or sit patiently in their canoes, and with a baited hair-line jerk out small fish. If a seal is killed, or the floating carcass of a putrid whale is discovered, they are feasts. Such miserable food is assisted by a few tasteless berries and fungi. (Darwin, cited in Crawfurd 1859a: 176)

As it turns out, in Crawfurd's construction there is no difference between vision and scripture, between dream, fiction, and scientific observation. They carry the same message, painted in the same viscerally repugnant forms and garish colors; and their agreement in tone and content seems to empower an imaginary field with currents of negative energies, within which the myth of the Noble Savage can be projected.

Crawfurd proceeds to construct the myth on the dual foundation provided by the Davy and Darwin citations, using them to lead into, respectively, a preliminary misquote of Dryden and a concluding misinterpretation of Rousseau. Thus, first of all, Davy's fictionalized dream provides the visionary foundation for the invocation of Dryden and the resurrection of the Noble Savage but in a discursive mode radically transformed from Lescarbot's and Dryden's original constructions of it two centuries earlier.

> The first men were undoubtedly very miserable beings; fortunately, however, without being, in the absence of any object of comparison, aware of it. Dryden thus describes such a savage:
>
> > "I am as free as Nature first made man,
> > When in the woods the noble savage ran." [4]
>
> I cannot set much value on the freedom of the being who was liable to be knocked on the head by the first stronger man he met, for the sake of the possession of a dead rat or a cocoa-nut; nor can I conceive anything noble in the poor naked, crouching creature, trembling with cold and starving from hunger. (Crawfurd 1859a: 159)

Then, in the paper's conclusion, Crawfurd uses the Darwin citation to set up his punch line, invoke another well-known name, and fill in the missing half that would complete the myth as we know it.

> Such savages as I have now been describing, are the men whose condition was envied by a very eloquent but very eccentric philosopher of the last century; but I imagine a week's residence—even a night's lodging with the Fuegians would have brought Jean Jacques Rousseau to a saner conclusion. Meanwhile, I think I may safely congratulate you that you are not the red men of Terra [sic] del Fuego, but civilized white men and accomplished women, the humblest amongst you having the power of enjoying more of the comforts and pleasures, physical and intellectual, of life, than the proud lords of a horde of ten thousand barbarians. (Crawfurd 1859a: 159, 177)

Here, at last, is the myth we have been seeking. How to begin to develop a critical understanding of it? One could, of course, problematize the concluding appeal to Victorian modernist upper-class complacency in the relative assessment of "comforts and pleasures," to say nothing of their quantitative significance in the evaluation of qualities such as nobility and freedom. The present, after all, is a spatial as well as a temporal construction, a kind of recessively reflexivist time travel that contributes an extra dimension of idealization to the negation of the exotic. But to dwell on these or other substantive issues would miss the point of the myth's construction as a rhetorical rather than as a substantive project, one designed to give voice to an argument deliberately concealed in the form of its own construction.

For example, who were the "savages" whose nobility the myth purports to disprove? As we have seen, the term had long served as a generic label for "wild" or "uncivilized" peoples, paradigmatically exemplified by the American Indians. With the new ethnographic discoveries of the late eighteenth and early nineteenth century, its ethnographic focus had broadened to include peoples from various parts of the world, with new emphases on Africans, Maoris, and other Oceanic peoples and the inhabitants of Tierra del Fuego—the last group, as represented through Darwin's raciocentrically negativist portrayal, being Crawfurd's own choice of a paradigm case to represent the miserable state of the savage (Crawfurd 1859a: 175–77). But as we will see, the apparent emphasis on the Fuegians conceals an offensive aimed at a much broader range of targets. Crawfurd had more important "savages" in his sights.

We have also seen that in the century before Crawfurd's paper the term "savage" had acquired increasingly negative connotations, even as it acquired an increasingly precise technical definition in theoretical writings. That is, with the growing popularity of Enlightenment theories of "progress" or sociocultural evolution, the "savage" state of society represented the earliest, and the lowest, stage in man's ascent from hunter-gatherer life to pastoralism, agriculture, and eventual civilization. Thus "savage" had become increasingly synonymous with "hunter-gatherer," even if there was still a tendency among some writers to apply the term to tribal subsistence agriculturalists as well as hunters. In such cases, it seems likely that for convinced hierarchialists, subsistence agriculture, as opposed to surplus agriculture, was simply too economically unproductive and uncivilized to deserve the name, or to be taken as a serious departure from the other subsistence lifestyle, hunting, with which it was often found in close proximity. Some vagueness could be tolerated, as long as the term remained centered in hunting and the "lowest" state of progress; the vagueness would simply allow for inclusion of more "savages" at the lowest end of the hierarchical scale than would a stricter definition.

In any case, Crawfurd's choice of the Fuegians for his primary ethnographic example would seem both scientifically unobjectionable and strategically sound. They were indeed hunter-gatherers; and, because they would appear as among the lowest of the low if viewed in terms of their technological and material "progress," they would be well suited to generate almost a visceral evocation of feelings of scorn for any rhetorical juxta-

296 / The Return of the Noble Savage

position of exalted language. But, after all, evoking scorn for a few groups of "savages" defined in the narrowest technical sense of the term would hardly be a major gain for the racist agenda. What, then, is the point of the construction of the myth?

Crawfurd gives a barely perceptible sign, at least to the modern reader, of his broader intentions by inclusion of the strikingly humorous but otherwise seemingly innocuous phrase, "possession of a dead rat or a cocoanut," in his framing of the first part of the myth. Actually, the "cocoa-nut" was a readily recognizable keyword in the anti-Negro, pro-slavery racist invective of the period. Thomas Carlyle, for example, in his "Occasional Discourse on the Nigger Question" (1849), repeatedly refers to the "cocoa-nut" as the emblematic sign of the Negro's racially determined laziness and willingness to be satisfied with finding subsistence in even the crudest gifts of nature, unless inspired to more "noble" ambitions by the lash of the slave master. Rendered equivalent by juxtaposition to the dead rat, the intention is obviously to evoke the most vivid possible disgust and scorn for the widest possible range of racial targets. Crawfurd achieves this by a kind of linguistic shell game in his last sentence, where his punch line, set up in terms of an opposition between the "red men of Terra del Fuego" and "civilized white men and accomplished women," makes use of the concealing device of its exaggeratedly complimentary syntactic formulation to slide in a new contrast with "the proud lords of a horde of ten thousand barbarians."

By sneaking his barbarian horde through the rhetorical gates, Crawfurd has not only raised a specter of menace to which he transfers the scorn generated by the harmlessly pitiful Fuegians but also considerably raised the political stakes. "Barbarians," as distinct from "savages," included agriculturally based societies of every conceivable type, increasingly, in the racial invective of nineteenth-century colonialism, even those urbanized and literate non-European state societies that had previously been considered "civilized." The opposition now was simply between "civilized white" society and all others, while the extension of the scorn generated by the original hyperbolically absurd juxtaposition of "noble" and "savage" translated logically—but with great emotional intensity—into a denial of the possibility of attribution of good qualities to any people who were not white. The trick was so neatly done that it was not likely to be noticed, much less criticized. Yet, once carried off, the effect of having demolished the illusion of savage nobility once and for all, to the discredit of any and all unspecified but obviously inferior claimants of undeserved respect, was so self-convincing and self-perpetuating that the original creation of the myth could be left behind and the mere repetition of the term "Noble Savage" would suffice to serve as a devastating weapon against any opposition to the racist agenda.

The myth of the Noble Savage, if we examine it closely, is constructed so as to assert the existence of what it purports to critique, the existence of a belief in the absurd juxtaposition of the incompatible attributes of nobility and savagery. By projecting the absurdity of the construction itself onto a figure such as Rousseau, selected as the emblematic representation of more serious ideas (and their advocates) that are the real targets of the attack, the myth operates by oblique and obfuscatory symbolic manipulations to attain its intended purpose, the creation of a self-authenticating and self-perpetuating rhetorical program for the promotion of racial superiority and dominance. This is certainly what it "meant," in terms of how it was applied and used by the racist faction surrounding Hunt and Crawfurd in the Ethnological Society, and later by Hunt and his allies in the Anthropological Society.

We might then ask, leaving aside for the moment the seductive elements of sarcasm and polemic inherent in the construction of the "Noble Savage" myth, what did the ideologues of racial dominance consider truly noble? For Hunt (1867b: 18), anthropology itself was a "noble enterprise." But in what way? Some members of the Anthropological Society, such as John Beddoe, used the term as an epitaph for races already dead or perceived to be dying, in effect ennobling the process of racial extermination:

> Look again a little further, to New Zealand, where an anthropological problem of the intensest interest and importance has to be worked out, no less a one than this, whether that noble race of barbarians, the Maori, can be raised to the level of our civilisation, or whether they are destined utterly to perish. (Beddoe, in Hunt 1867b: 20)

We have heard the same message before, from Crawfurd himself. Hunt gives us an indication of his own conception of nobility in a note to his article on the Negro:

> Again, I would call attention to the noble words of Thomas Carlyle.[5] Speaking of labour, he well says: " . . . But yours in the West Indies, my obscure black friends, your work, and the getting of you set to it, is a simple affair. . . . You are not 'slaves' now; nor, do I wish, if it can be avoided, to see you slaves again; but decidedly you will have to be servants to those that are born wiser than you, that are born lords of you—servants to the whites, if they are (as what mortal can doubt that they are?) born wiser than you. That, you may depend on it, my obscure black friends, is and was always the law of the world, for you and

for all men: to be servants. . . . Heaven's laws are not repealable by earth, however earth may try—and it has been trying hard, in some directions, of late! I say, no well being, and in the end no being at all, will be possible for you or us, if the law of Heaven is not complied with. . . ." (1863c: 55–56)

No being at all! Nobility, in the context of the racially polarized anthropology of the era, quite obviously oscillated between the polarities of supremacy and subordination in interracial dynamics, with the latter in turn bounded by the poles of servitude and extermination. No other choices were possible, since nobility, just as much as in Lescarbot's time, was still inexorably established by "Heaven's laws," however hard Hunt may have worked to rhetorically disguise them as scientific laws. The myth of the Noble Savage was created and used to uphold this bleak construction of the universe.

Kenneth R. H. Mackenzie, whose role in the Anthropological Society seems mainly to have been the continual voicing of expressions of fawning appreciation for Hunt's every word and action, gives us an example of the usefulness of the Noble Savage myth to Hunt's faction, in remarks intended to absolve British colonists from responsibility for what was seen as the impending extinction of the Nuu-chah-nulth ("Nootka") Indians of Vancouver Island.

> We are disposed to consider it as extremely likely that the juxtaposition of the unquestionably artificial civilisation of Europe and the uncivilised native life of savagedom, may have a tendency to appal and obscure the savage mind—in fact, that the mere presentation of a foreign and novel state of existence may frighten the "noble savage," first out of his wits, and then out of existence altogether.
>
> . . . Anthropologists do not pretend to the protection of aborigines, but they at the same time have no interested motives in their extinction; to them the negro and the red man afford interest and instruction alike; but, unlike a very unfortunate, not to say malignant, set of men at the present day, they do not desire to exalt the inferior at the expense of superior races. If the tendency is that they die out, that tendency, this a natural one, cannot be fully arrested. (Mackenzie 1868: 373–74)

Thus, for the now-dominant racist faction in the Ethnological Society, the myth of the Noble Savage became yet another weapon in the ideological arsenal, ultimately useful for the scientific-racist project of helping to naturalize a genocidal stance toward the "inferior" races. But the myth was so powerful and successful that it began to capture the imagination even of anthropologists who disagreed with Crawfurd's racial theories and Hunt's political agenda. For example, John Lubbock, who traded roles with Crawfurd as president and vice president of the Ethnological Society throughout the 1860s, wrote,

> There are, indeed, many who doubt whether happiness is increased by civilization, and who talk of the free and noble savage. But the true savage is neither free nor noble; he is a slave to his own wants, his own passions; imperfectly protected from the weather, he suffers from the cold by night and the sun by day; ignorant of agriculture, living by the chase, and improvident in success, hunger always stares him in the face, and often drives him to the dreadful alternative of cannibalism or death. (1865: 595)

And E. B. Tylor, who also became active in the Ethnological Society during the time of Crawfurd's leadership, wrote a few years later, "What we now know of savage life will prevent our falling into the fancies of the philosophers of the last century, who set up the 'noble savage' as an actual model of virtue to be imitated by civilized nations" (1881: 408).

By now, the Noble Savage myth had become so well established in anthropology that it pervaded the entire discipline, influencing even those who had never known Crawfurd or shared his racist agenda, such as Franz Boas.

> I hope that . . . I have not created the impression that we are dealing with peoples living in an original state of simplicity and naturalness as Rousseau conceived of them. (Boas 1889: 68)

> The deep-seated feeling that political and social inequality was the result of a faulty development of civilization, and that originally all men were born equal, led Rousseau to the naive assumption of an ideal natural state which we ought to try to regain. (Boas 1904: 24)

Clearly, the myth of the Noble Savage had become part of the ideological foundations of anthropology in the English-speaking world—and, moreover, one that would endure for nearly a century and a half, long after most other elements of mid-Victorian anthropological ideology had fallen subject to critique or rejection. It is long overdue for critical scrutiny, and for an assessment of the racist foundations on which its original construction rests.

Part of this scrutiny must include some of the ambiguities surrounding Crawfurd's paper itself. From a scholarly perspective, these include the opaque derivation of his theoretical approach. Crawfurd seems as reticent to identify his theoretical sources as he is eager to proclaim his use of ethnographic sources, such as "my friend, Mr. Darwin," leaving the impression that all of his theoretical ideas have sprung full-grown from his own mind. Yet we can see resemblances to the inventory of environmental factors he identifies as "conditions which favour, retard, or obstruct the early civilization of man" in environmentalist-ethnological writings of the late eighteenth century: for example, in William Falconer's *Remarks on the Influence of Climate, Situation, Nature of Country, Population, Nature of Food, and Way of Life, on the Disposition and Temper, Manners and Behaviour, Intellects, Laws and Customs, Form of Government, and Religion, of Mankind* (1781), which not only resembles Crawfurd's paper in many of its themes and subjects, but which also includes a strong attack on Rousseau (459–80). It is certainly possible, and perhaps even likely, that Crawfurd encountered this work during his university days at Edinburgh, or in his later ethnological readings, and drew on it for some of his ideas. Yet, although the work includes many facets that overlap with Crawfurd's emphases, it also shows many differences—for example, in a portrayal of the state of savagery that, although generally negative, is not nearly so vehement as in Crawfurd's rendition; or, in that its critique of Rousseau is based on a different work and has little to do with his representation of savagery. Reconstructing Crawfurd's theoretical sources of inspiration is, in fact, a difficult and complex task that will have to await further study.

More immediately rewarding than a quest for its theoretical sources is a brief reflection on some of the political and strategic issues surrounding the paper's first appearance. First of all, Crawfurd was not actually present at the reading of his own paper; it was read in absentia by the secretary, Thomas Wright. Was he indisposed, or detained by unforeseen obligations? Another possibility is more suggestive. From his conclusion, it is clear that Crawfurd had expected to find "civilized white men and accomplished women" among his audience. But, in fact, neither the *ESL Minutes* nor the *Athenaeum* announcement and report of the paper mention any plans for an "Extra-ordinary Meeting" that would include a mixed audience. If this were part of the initial arrangements for the paper, abrogated by an uncooperative council or by the misogynous Hunt acting as go-between, could it be that Crawfurd resorted to the Barnumesque gesture of protesting by a boycott of his own paper?

Also, there is the curious fact that the published version of the paper in the *Transactions* identifies Crawfurd as the "President of the Ethnological Society of London." Crawfurd was indeed president in 1861, when the paper was published; but identification of authors in the ESL *Transactions* and *Journal* normally designated their status at the time their papers were presented to the society rather than at the time of publication. For example, *Transactions* 7 simply identifies Crawfurd by name and Royal Society membership for papers read before his death on May 11, 1868, but adds "the late . . . President of the Ethnological Society" to the byline of his posthumous paper read on June 9, 1868 (Crawfurd 1869d: 197). Similarly, *Transactions* 1 identifies Crawfurd simply as a fellow of the Royal Geographical Society, rather than as president of the Ethnological Society, at the time of his paper "On the Effects of Commixture, Locality, Climate, and Food on the Races of Man" given at the British Association in September 1858 and at the Ethnological Society in February 1859 (Crawfurd 1858: 76), even though he was president at the time of publication.

By contrast, Crawfurd's listing in *Transactions* 1 as "President" for his "Noble Savage" paper of April 1859, a month before the May Anniversary Meeting when elections were normally held, seems to suggest that he was already president by that time, with a change in status after February but before the next official election date in May 1859. In fact, we know that Sir James Clark continued as president until the May meeting, when he was hastily reconfirmed as president until 1860 following the disastrous nominations of FitzRoy and Tennent. We have also seen evidence of Clark's growing disaffection and the ascendancy of Crawfurd as the rising star of the society during the same period. The final authorities for publication of the *Transactions* would have included the secretaries, Wright and Hunt. We have seen enough chronological slips of Hunt's pen to not be surprised that in this case, for one reason or another, he misremembered Crawfurd's ascension to the presidency as occurring substantially before the 1860 elections. The discrepancy in the *Transactions* may simply reflect Hunt's conviction that, with its Barnumesque triumph in the creation of a compelling anthropological humbug, a triumph to which Hunt aspired but never quite managed to achieve, Crawfurd's Noble Savage paper emblematized his ascension to the rightful status of the presidency. In Hunt's eyes, Crawfurd was already president, no matter who might happen to sit in the chair.

But when Crawfurd took the president's chair officially, after the election, he took steps to impose his own order on things. His first official policy initiative, as recorded in the *ESL Minutes* (October 17, 1860, 261), was to announce that at the next meeting he would propose "that Ladies be admitted as visitors." At the next meeting, "after some discussion," the proposal was amended to, "That Ladies be admitted to the Meetings on all occasions specified by the Council" (*ESL Minutes,* November 21, 1860, 261–62). As we shall see, there is reason to believe that the discussion and amendment may have resulted from opposition by Hunt. But Crawfurd was now in control, and the policy foreshadowed by the Noble Savage paper would shape its course, and that of anthropology itself, in the years to come.

18 Crawfurd and the Breakup of the Racist Alliance

FIGURE 25. RACIAL
HIERARCHIES. Caucasian superiority, emblematically personified
by George Washington, contrasted
with anonymous representatives
of the "lower races," from John
Jeffries' *Natural History of the
Human Races* (1869: frontispiece).

Hunt had hijacked the rhetoric of political radicalism and scientific skep-
ticism to promote adherence to the most reactionary views of his era,
and, with the help of Crawfurd's more powerful political and rhetorical
strengths, had ultimately succeeded in hijacking the Ethnological Society
itself. But Hunt, as Crawfurd's creator, could not long endure remaining his
subordinate; while Crawfurd, in turn, would not passively let himself be
manipulated as Hunt's puppet. Tensions between them grew and ultimately
led to Hunt's leading a breakaway faction to found the rival Anthropological Society in 1863. From then on, the two would become irreconcilable, if
not entirely unappreciative, adversaries.

Crawfurd's political and charismatic appeal to the faltering Ethnological Society, and particularly to Hunt's racist hijacking project, rested on a combination of the diplomatic skills gained in a career of succession to progressively higher positions in the British colonial system and a polemic audacity that at times bordered on the surreal. Hunt, in a love-hate relationship that sometimes found him standing appreciatively at Crawfurd's side and sometimes leaping at his throat, gives us some vivid portraits of Crawfurd in action:

> A paper, by Lieutenant S. P. Oliver, R. A., on the "Communication between the Atlantic and the Pacific," was then read, in the course of which the following amusing cross-examination was conducted by Mr. Crawfurd in his happiest style:—
>
> Mr. CRAWFURD said that Lieutenant Oliver had, no doubt, had excellent opportunities of forming an opinion upon the comparison between the red men of America and the black men of Africa, as he had seen them in Madagascar. He would like to know which of these races Lieutenant Oliver preferred.

> Lieutenant OLIVER: I think that is a very difficult question indeed.
>
> Mr. CRAWFURD: That is just the reason why I put it.

> Lieutenant OLIVER was sorry he had given that subject very little of his attention; but he might say that the men who were with him, and who were their best men when cutting through the forests, were men from Africa . . . and there were no better men in the world. . . .

> Mr. CRAWFURD: You saw a great many monkeys and a great many savages. Did you encounter the missing link between man and the monkeys?
>
> Lieutenant OLIVER: No, certainly not.
>
> Mr. CRAWFURD: I see you have been eating lizards and iguanas. What like is iguana flesh?
>
> Lieutenant OLIVER: Iguana flesh is like what I would imagine the flesh of a young child would be.
>
> Mr. CRAWFURD: Did you like it?
>
> Lieutenant OLIVER: Well, we were generally pretty hard up when we ate it.
>
> Mr. CRAWFURD: You would not have eaten a young child, I suppose, in the same circumstances?
>
> Lieutenant OLIVER: Well, I don't know. (Hunt 1868b: 90–91)

"On the Civilization of Man" (the "Noble Savage" article's running title) was the second of a prodigious outpouring of articles Crawfurd published in the *Transactions* between 1861 and 1868, at a rate of up to nine articles per year, for a total of thirty-eight in seven years. Crawfurd's output of articles in this period was far greater than that of any other contributor to the journals of either the Ethnological or the Anthropological Society and is comparable only to the volume of writings by Luke Burke in his privately published *Journal of Ethnology*, or perhaps to James Hunt's output in his proprietary *Anthropological Review*. And, as it turns out, the similarity among the three is more than quantitative. Although some of Crawfurd's articles were rather innocuous explorations of particular ethnographic problems via his specialty, philology, most, like the works of Burke and Hunt, were polemics on racial superiority and inferiority, asserting scientific validity for the stereotypical racist hierarchies that inevitably placed whites at the top and darker races in subordinate positions on the scale of nature (fig. 25).

The core of the series was a group of articles (Crawfurd 1858, 1861a, 1862, 1865a, 1865b) presenting attacks on the ill effects of racial "commixture," in which Crawfurd denounced what he saw as the degrading effects of racial mixing and promoted white supremacy as a way of safeguarding racial purity and enabling the survival and continued advancement of civilization. In Crawfurd's (1858: 81–82) view, "The union of a superior with an inferior race deteriorates, of course. . . . When, on the contrary, the races are nearly equal, there is no degeneration," as in the mixture of European "races," particularly those of the British Isles. He views "commixture" as the predominant condition of existing races, a degradation of their original status as separate (but interfertile!) "species" and an obstacle to their scientific classification.

> That the many separate and distinct races of man, when there has been no commixture, are originally created species, and not mere varieties of a single family,—such abnormal varieties as we find to spring up occasionally among the domestic animals, and even with man himself, although more rarely, there are many facts to show. . . . The union of the highest and lowest species of the human race yields an intermediate progeny, inferior to the first, and superior to the last. . . . But the greatest difficulty in distinguishing species arises from the fact of man being, even in the lowest state of society, in the condition which, in speaking of the lower animals, we call the domestic, and consequently subject, even within each species, to the endless variety induced by domestication. . . . I think it must be obvious that to classify mankind—as

naturalists do the lower animals in the wild state—is hopeless. Such a classification with the lower animals in the domestic state is admitted to be impracticable, and with man, ever in the domestic state, the difficulty opposed to such an arrangement cannot be less. (Crawfurd 1861a: 355–56, 365, 372)

The emphasis on man as a "domesticated" animal displaying complex modifications and degradations resulting from the intermixture of originally pure and separate wild species is a characteristic element of Crawfurd's position that would be negatively commented on by Darwin (see below). But it would produce even more negative reactions from anthropologists such as Burke and Hunt, for whom its necessary advocacy of the fertility of interracial "hybrids" (Crawfurd 1865b) constituted an egregious challenge to a long-established fundamental article of racist belief. If Crawfurd's repeated evocations of the domestication metaphor can be seen as symbolic projections of his identity as a colonial diplomat and governor whose main responsibility in life was the taming and management of recalcitrant "savage" populations, so, too, at a deeper level, they might be imagined as resurgences of a Scottish pastoralist heritage, in which flocks are to be managed and bred to the advantage of the herder. At any rate, Crawfurd's continual references to the English as a "mongrel" and "bastard" race, together with occasional defenses of the humanity of Celts and Highlanders, did not do much to resolve tensions; and, at least from late 1861 onward, Crawfurd found himself enmeshed in debates not only with the antiracist faction of the society but also in increasing degree with his nominal allies such as Burke and Hunt (Crawfurd 1861b: 20 ff.).

The growing rift between Crawfurd and Hunt, no matter what intellectual and scientific principles came to the foreground of their public debates, gained impetus from important strategic divergences. They had worked quickly and effectively together to revitalize the society, holding joint meetings with other scientific societies (*Athenaeum*, February 2, 1861, 159; March 9, 1861, 329), issuing new membership appeals, easing the process for admitting new members, publicizing meetings more effectively than in the past (the 1861 Anniversary Meeting was announced in the press well over a month in advance (*Athenaeum*, April 6, 1861, 468), and stepping up the pace of meetings from monthly to biweekly (*Athenaeum*, April 6, 1861, 468). But Crawfurd offended Hunt from the outset by unilaterally taking the strategic offensive in opening the meetings to women, a move that the misogynist Hunt deeply deplored and ultimately bitterly cited as the cause of the 1863 split into opposing Ethnological and Anthropological societies (see below). Hunt, for his part, made strategic moves that could hardly have pleased Crawfurd.

In February 1861 a paper by the French explorer Paul du Chaillu, "Travels in the (Gorilla) Regions of Western Equatorial Africa," was read before the Geographical Society (*Athenaeum,* March 2, 1861, 297). The paper, and the specimens of gorilla skulls that du Chaillu brought to illustrate it, created an immediate sensation among a scientific audience longing for direct information on the legendary primate; and the excitement was intensified by the apparent implications for the developing Darwinian controversy. Du Chaillu's paper was enthusiastically commented on by Professor Richard Owen, England's foremost anatomist, who had made use of du Chaillu's specimens to prepare diagrams that he exhibited at the discussion of the paper (*Athenaeum,* March 2, 1861, 297), and further expounded on in a March lecture at the Royal Institution, presenting an "exposition of the distinctive characters between the Negro (or lowest variety of Human Race) and the Gorilla" (*Athenaeum,* March 23, 1861, 395–96). Owen saw in du Chaillu's specimens an opportunity to expand on the radical dichotomy between humans and apes that he had maintained over the past two decades (Desmond 1989: 288 ff.); but Thomas Huxley, already locked into adversarial confrontation with Owen during the Darwinian controversies at the 1860 meetings of the British Association for the Advancement of Science, struck back with a series of challenges to Owen's interpretations (*Athenaeum,* March 30, 1861, 433; April 13, 1861, 498) with criticisms, some conceded by Owen, designed to support an evolutionist perspective.

As both antagonists relied heavily on du Chaillu's specimens, the controversy seemed only to enhance the reputation of the French explorer. Du Chaillu's book, *Explorations and Adventures in Equatorial Africa* (1861a), appeared to rave reviews (*Athenaeum,* May 11, 1861, 621). Meanwhile, the Geographical Society continued to offer him enthusiastic support, even going so far, it was suggested, as to have "allowed him to make one of their rooms into a museum" (*Athenaeum,* May 18, 1861, 662). Du Chaillu's warm reception in the Geographical Society seems to have been supported by its longtime patriarch, Sir Roderick Impey Murchison (*Athenaeum,* June 1, 1861, 729); and one of Murchison's close associates was none other than John Crawfurd, who had served with him as an officer of the British Association. It may have been the Murchison-Crawfurd connection that resulted in the invitation of du Chaillu to address the Ethnological Society on "The Races of Man in Africa" on May 14, 1861, in an extraordinary meeting held only one day before the society's Anniversary Meeting on May 15.

It must have seemed to Crawfurd and Hunt that the Ethnological Society could only gain from associating themselves with the most publicized explorer of that year's society "season." But, as it turned out, the society was in for a surprise. On the very same day that du Chaillu addressed the Ethnological Society with a paper bearing the revised title "On the Physical Peculiarities, Customs and Language of the Tribes met with in Africa during a Residence of Four Years" (*Athenaeum*, May 25, 1861, 698; see also du Chaillu 1861b), John Edward Gray, an officer of the British Museum, wrote the *Athenaeum* to accuse du Chaillu of flagrant inaccuracy, misrepresentation, and plagiarism.

Over the next few months, in a series of communications that the *Athenaeum* published under the title "The New Traveller's Tales," Gray would establish that du Chaillu had copied published illustrations of known animals as claimed representations of new species, used pictures of one species to represent another, and claimed discoveries of new places and species as long as two years after publication of their discovery elsewhere (*Athenaeum*, May 18, 1861, 662–63; May 25, 1861, 695; June 1, 1861, 728). Another critic who signed himself "R.B.S." wrote to point out that du Chaillu had presented impossible chronologies that had him exploring different parts of Africa at the same time (*Athenaeum*, May 5, 25, 1861, 695). And an anonymous "Aspirant after Sporting Honours" even wrote the press to point out du Chaillu's tale of having shot two eagles in two trees with one shot, wryly asking if he could have the name of du Chaillu's gun manufacturer (*Athenaeum*, June 1, 1861, 729).

As the scandal grew, many of du Chaillu's former supporters withdrew to a skeptical neutrality (*Athenaeum*, June 1, 1861, 729). It would have been prudent for the Ethnological Society to do the same. Surely Crawfurd, the veteran diplomat who had once cited Buddhist theology in a diplomatic communication urging the British government to withdraw its support from two British subjects attacked by a mob and imprisoned in Thailand, on the grounds that they had offended Buddhist religious beliefs by killing a horse, would have seen when to disassociate himself from a losing cause (Crawfurd 1821–25: 228). But Hunt, knowing only the strategy of attack, apparently went over Crawfurd's head with a personal appeal to his friend, Richard Francis Burton, to address the society in du Chaillu's defense.

Burton, who was admitted as a member of the society on the day of du Chaillu's paper (*Athenaeum*, May 25, 1861, 698), was another ambiguous figure, an African (and Asian) explorer who, like du Chaillu, had succeeded in becoming both famous and infamous (Stocking 1987: 253). After the break between Crawfurd and Hunt became irreparable, Burton and du Chaillu would become Hunt's staunch allies in the secessionist Anthropological Society; and already in their first encounter in 1861, Burton showed his loyalty in his defense of du Chaillu.

> The Ethnological Society doubtless retains a pleasant recollection of a paper upon the tribes of Western Equatorial Africa read on the 14th of May by our latest celebrity, the enterprising M. du Chaillu. It has been suggested to me by my friend Dr. Hunt that a few remarks upon the subject of the eastern races of the same continent would be not uninteresting as tending to prove that throughout the vast breadth of the peninsula, the same language, the same manners and customs, the same religion and tone of thought—briefly the same ethnic development prevails. (Burton 1861: 316)

The strategy underlying the invitation to Burton is characteristically Hunt's. Burton, after all, could hardly act as a witness to verify any of du Chaillu's claims, since he had never visited the same part of Africa, or seen any of the places or peoples du Chaillu described. However, his affirmation on faith of du Chaillu's veracity, based on dogmatic assertions of the "sameness" of all Africans, even those unknown and unseen by him, would be a valuable testimonial in support of the racist cause.

Crawfurd must certainly have been upset by Hunt's tactics, which would link the society to targets of accusations of misrepresentation and render it an object of suspicion to the respectable audience to whom Crawfurd continually tried to appeal. He may have also been upset by the brand of racism that Hunt's strategy promoted. Actually, Crawfurd was not as stereotypical a racist as Hunt. Their backgrounds and social status were entirely different. Hunt, the "son of a gentleman" (Keith 1917: 18), had enjoyed an open door to medical studies at Cambridge, reserved at the time for members of the Church of England; whereas Crawfurd, a "highlander from Islay, who can still think and speak in the Gaelic" (Keith 1917: 17), had necessarily done his medical studies at Edinburgh. Edinburgh was a hotbed of both medical and political radicalism (Desmond 1989); and it seems natural that Crawfurd, finally made eligible to run for Parliament after the passage of the Reform Act, should have done so in 1832–37 not as a Conservative but as an Advanced Radical (*DNB* 5: 61). If the Edinburgh-Radical connection seems appropriate to Crawfurd's later avowals of an antislavery position, it can only seem inappropriate to his advocacy of racial separation and hierarchy; for many opponents of such views, including Radical politicians, medical men, and even Prichard and Hodgkin, shared the same educational heritage. But if Edinburgh had played host to Prichard and Hodgkin, it had also played host to the English racist, Knox, and the American racist anthropologist, Morton—and, ironically, the antiracist Hodgkin had been friends there with both (Kass and Kass 1988: 71). Like the intellectual environment of the university itself, Crawfurd seemed to embody a complex mixture of elements of coexisting but ultimately contradictory value systems.

In fact, Crawfurd's position, though fairly characterizable as racism, was neither simple, nor rigid, nor absolute; and we must give it closer attention. Thus Crawfurd had insisted from the very beginning that racial heredity was only one element in the achievement of civilization and that environmental factors, such as the presence or absence of plants or animals suitable for domestication and geographic isolation from or proximity to other peoples from whom inventions could be borrowed, could be equally or more significant factors than racial heredity in the advancement of a given people. Indeed, if one compares Crawfurd's arguments in the "Noble Savage" paper (1859a) with his considerable output of work on the differential effects of ecological-geographic factors on human societies (Crawfurd 1858, 1861b, 1863, 1867a, 1867b, 1867c, 1868a, 1868b, 1869a, 1869b, 1869c, 1869d), one is struck by the many resemblances of arguments and even individual examples to Jared Diamond's 1997 work, *Guns, Germs, and Steel.* Both are dealing with the same basic question, why some peoples have "advanced" to a state of technological superiority and political dominance over others, and both find their basic answer in a line of analysis that some would call geographic determinism but which seems more accurately characterizable as a kind of ecological opportunism. If Diamond's approach is conceived in antiracist terms as opposed to Crawfurd's qualified support for racism, it may be that a century and a half of accumulating more precise data in fields such as ethnography, evolutionary biology, ecology, archaeology, and epidemiology has provided Diamond with more plausible explanations than Crawfurd's admission when comparisons failed to reveal significant ecological differences: "I do not see how the difference can be accounted for, except by difference in the quality of the race" (Crawfurd 1859a: 160). But we still might ask ourselves, when was racism ever a simple result of scientific ignorance?

In any case, Crawfurd's racism was, in a sense, a "softer" racism than the hard-line racism of some of his contemporaries. We can see the contrast in his debate with Hunt at the meeting of the British Association in Dundee:

[A paper was then read on] *Skin, Hair, and Eyes as Tests of the Races of Men (previously read in London)* by Mr. JOHN CRAWFURD.

Mr. CRAWFURD then said he would be glad to hear any remarks on this paper, and first he would ask for the opinions of the founder of the Anthropological Society.

Dr. JAMES HUNT was most happy to accept the invitation to make a few remarks on this interesting paper on one of the greatest difficulties in the whole range of the science of man. . . . [H]e (Dr. Hunt) held that man's progress in the scale of civilisation, accompanied with other things, bore a relation to both skin and hair. A dark skin, accompanied with crisp hair, was invariably a mark of mental inferiority. . . .

Mr. CRAWFURD said there seemed to be no very material difference between the President of the Ethnological Society and the President or Director[1] of the Anthropological Society, and he was sure they would all be very glad that such was the case. With respect to colour, Dr. Hunt assigned inferiority to dark skin. He (Mr. Crawfurd) would deny that. Napoleon had dark hair, and a dark skin too; and he did not conceive that a better specimen, so far as the mere humanity [!] was concerned, had ever been produced. . . . Now, with respect to the inferiority of the black people, although the Hindoos were black they were incomparably superior and in a far more advanced state of civilisation than the brown-complexioned Malays. *He would advise the Dr. to give up the black inferiority altogether, for he had nothing whatever to stand upon.* With respect to the races being distinguished by hair or complexion, differences were to be found in the same family in the prosperous town of Dundee, by the same father and the same mother. Suppose a family of seven daughters. There might be cases of the kind, and he hoped there were. One had dark hair and a dark complexion; another was fair-haired; and a third was reddish, or, to be more genteel, auburn. There was not the slightest superiority in the dark-haired and dark-complexioned daughter [!] as compared with the lighter-haired and clear-skinned members of the family. There were cases of every sort of hair and every sort of complexion being found in families by the same father and the same mother. How could they make out that?

Dr. HUNT said perhaps Mr. Crawfurd would point out where a race was to be found of equal intellectual power to the fairer races when dark colour was combined with crisp hair?

Mr. CRAWFURD replied that he knew of the dark colour being combined with wool, and he had known some very pretty people have curly hair. Dr. Hunt said he would not condemn every one. That was very well put on his part, for in Dundee they could find beauty and talent in every department of colour.

Dr. HUNT, in reference to Mr. Crawfurd's remark in respect to wool, explained that he did not make use of the word wool, because wool was not hair.

Mr. CRAWFURD remarked that hair was not wool, and wool was not hair, but they were pretty nearly the same thing. There could be no distinction drawn between wool and hair, except what was obvious to the eye. They could make the same use of the one as of the other, though he would be sorry to see wool upon a pretty young lady.

Dr. HUNT replied that a dark colour of hair and eyes, combined with curly hair, was always a mark of mental inferiority, and he challenged Mr. Crawfurd or anyone else to bring forward an exception to this generalisation.

The discussion then terminated. (Hunt 1868b: 95–96; emphasis added)

Crawfurd may have partially redeemed himself by standing up before the leaders of British science—and an audience of his own Scottish countrymen—and publicly denouncing the doctrine of black inferiority by pointing out their own genetic diversity. Yet his racial views remained complex; and we should not imagine that he abjured in any way his underlying conviction of European superiority to other races, even if rejecting a simple black-white formulation of racial differences. Rather than attempt to unravel the complexly interwoven strands of Crawfurd's substantive views more than the evidence allows, let us turn again to rhetorical and political aspects of the debate.

Crawfurd's side of the Dundee debate, with its interjections of unpredictable, antilogical twists and absurdist bombshells, would amply reward a line-by-line analysis. But as always, his punch line is an appeal to the "ladies" and their Victorian gentlemen defenders, who would be properly outraged that there were opponents pernicious enough to advocate views that might be seen as undermining their virgin purity or superiority. We have already seen exactly the same strategy deployed in his conclusion to the "Noble Savage" paper of 1859. Recognizing this strategy helps to clarify a mystery that has puzzled some of the scholars who have investigated the break between the Ethnological Society and the Anthropological Society.

In 1864 Hunt wrote in a letter of dedication to Paul Broca,

My failure, however, in arousing the Ethnological Society from its torpor . . . arose entirely from the opposite views held by myself and my colleagues as to the objects of the Ethnological Society, and its duties as a scientific body.

The stand-point claimed for the science of Ethnology by the late Dr. Knox, by Captain R. F. Burton, . . . by myself, and by some others, was that of a grave, erudite, and purely scientific study, requiring the most free and serious discussion, especially on anatomical and physiological topics, for the elucidation of the many difficult problems arising out of the subjects brought forward. This, however, was far from being the opinion of a large and powerful section of the Society, headed by my venerable friend, Mr. John Crawfurd. The party under his leadership desired to place the Ethnological Society on a footing with the Royal Geographical Society, and to render its meetings fashionable and popular by the admission of ladies. You will, doubtless, smile at the strange idea of admitting females to a discussion of all Ethnological subjects. However, the supporters of the "fair sex" won the day, and females have been regularly admitted to the meetings of the Ethnological Society during the past three years.[2]

Even now the advocates of this measure do not admit their error, nor do they perceive how they are practically hindering the promotion of those scientific objects which they continue to claim for their society. On the contrary, they rejoice at their victory, and Mr. Crawfurd had publicly on more than one occasion ascribed the success which attended the Ethnological Society under his *régime* to the admission of ladies.

Apart from this fatal mistake, you will readily understand that other important, and indeed vital differences, existed as to the mode in which such a society should be conducted. Finding myself, therefore, unable to give my cordial support to a society whose apparent objects were so utterly at variance with my own views—views in which I was not without supporters—the idea occurred to me of establishing in this country a really scientific society, which, taking yours as a model, might become worthy of a great nation. (1864a: vii–ix)

Hunt reprinted the same passage word for word four years later (Hunt 1868a: 434–35), giving some indication of the importance of the issue to him. But how could it really be true that an issue such as the admission of women to meetings, so apparently peripheral to the fundamental differences between the two factions, should have actually provided the impetus for the split between the two societies? Stocking provides a reasonable explanation:

It is in this context of free-wheeling discussion of a wide range of controversial topics that one must understand the issue which by some accounts provoked the separation of the two societies: the admission of women to the meetings of the Ethnological Society. For the "anthropologicals," who sought a "liberty of thought and freedom of speech" unrivaled by any other scientific society, the presence of women made it impossible to discuss freely matters of human anatomy and physiology, or such questions as phallic worship and male and female circumcision. (1987: 252–53)

Indeed, this closely parallels Hunt's own explanation. However, if we recognize the extent to which having women in his audience was an indispensable part of Crawfurd's political strategy, we can see an alternative explanation that has little to do with intellectual issues or freedom of speech. As we have seen, Crawfurd was already using the strategy of appeal to a mixed audience of men and women in his "Noble Savage" paper of April 1859. It was Crawfurd himself who regularized the practice of mixed meetings in 1860 as his first official act after becoming president (*ESL Minutes* 1:261–62), and he put the new arrangement to strategic use in the growing tensions between himself and Hunt from 1861 onward.

In the escalating competition between Hunt and Crawfurd for audience support, it was simply to Crawfurd's advantage to have women in his audience, not so much for their own sake, but for the political advantages he could evoke by arousing the protective passions of their adult male kinsmen and companions. Hunt, by contrast, seemed to be incapable of reaching out to such an audience; his rapport and sympathies seemed to be confined to an exclusionist circle of postadolescent males, of whatever age they might happen to be, whose insecurities and hostilities were as likely to be aroused by threats from gender as from racial differences. Hunt's political survival demanded the exclusion of women and the men who were comfortable in their companionship; and in the face of Crawfurd's aggressive quasi-courtship techniques, he had no real choice but to retreat to a segregated bastion behind which he could rest, secure and impregnable from the attacks Crawfurd was able to launch with the support of a mixed audience.

If Crawfurd had in a sense originally been Hunt's creation, he quickly became a living exemplar of the Victorian specter of Frankenstein's monster, a creature who would inexorably return to haunt his maker. Again and again, his bizarre originality got the better of Hunt. We see this in the 1865 debate over whether the Ethnological Society or the Anthropological Society would prevail in the struggle for control of anthropological papers at the British Association.

> MR. CRAWFURD [said he] hoped it would not be fancied that there was any hostility between himself and Dr. Hunt, who was at one time honorary secretary of a society to which he (Mr. Crawfurd) was president. He held in his hand the Anniversary Address of the President of the Anthropological Society, which consisted of thirty-two pages of letterpress, eighteen of which were devoted to a consideration of the three titles, ethnography, ethnology, and anthropology, and the preference was given to the latter, for reasons which he could not see. Anthropology was a term of vast antiquity, first used in the first year of the sixteenth century, in the year 1501—very properly, in his opinion, at the fag-end of the dark ages—it was, to his taste, an ugly polysyllable—by

a man named Hundt, who, it was possible, might have been an ancestor of Dr. Hunt in the twelfth generation, and who was also called *Magnus Canis* — *Anglicé,* "Big Dog,"—and who wrote a work called *Anthropologia.* The word then consisted of six syllables. It was now reduced to five, or, commercially speaking, was 20 per cent less. The word was still too long, for the world called the anthropologists anthropos, with a long accent on the last syllable [i.e., "anthro-pose!"]. The whole of the word was, in his opinion, too long, and he recommended the meeting to negative resolution and amendment alike. (*AR* 3 [1865]: 357)

19　Crawfurd, Darwin, and the "Missing Link"

FIGURE 26. FIJIAN HAIRDOS. The variety and beauty of Fijian hair arrangements, from John Lubbock's *Origin of Civilisation and the Primitive Condition of Man* (1870: 48).

In arguing his program of racial superiority and dominance, Crawfurd mounted a critical attack on virtually every anthropological theory that might be imagined to support ideas of human unity or equality. His targets included, first of all, Prichard's vision of ethnology as a science of human unity (e.g., Crawfurd 1861a: 362, among many others). There followed attacks on every theory of human migration and development, such as that of paleo-Indians from Asia to North America (Crawfurd 1864b); the theory of Indo-Aryan or Indo-European languages (Crawfurd 1860); the Stone-Bronze-Iron Age hypothesis (Crawfurd 1864c); and, with growing intensity until his death in 1868, Darwin's theory of evolution.

Crawfurd had been a friend and admirer of Darwin (Darwin 1856: 89; Crawfurd 1859a: 157, 175) before the publication of the *Origin of Species*, at least in part because of Crawfurd's recognition among naturalists since his publication of *Indian Archipelago* (Crawfurd 1820) and because Darwin's *Beagle* voyage narrative (Darwin 1839a, 1839b) afforded ethnographic data and racially negative opinions that Crawfurd could effectively turn to his own uses. Indeed, Crawfurd refers repeatedly to "my friend, Mr. Darwin" in his "Noble Savage" paper; and Darwin's ethnographic polemic against the Fuegians had furnished Crawfurd with crucial props to set up the article's punch line, with its construction of the myth of Rousseau's invention of the Noble Savage (Crawfurd 1859a: 175–77).

The break between them came with Darwin's publication of the *Origin* in 1859. Crawfurd, invited to review the book for the *Examiner*, wrote to Darwin to warn him that his review would be hostile but would "not calumniate the author" (Darwin 1859b: 32). In fact, Crawfurd produced an uncharacteristically sympathetic statement of opposition, praising the "remarkable book," the ideas of which, "for the perfect integrity with which they are stated[,] are entitled to the most respectful study" (Crawfurd 1859b: 772). He quotes Darwin at length on the struggle for existence and natural selection, allowing him his own voice. When Crawfurd begins to state his own impressions and objections, he dwells, as we might expect, on the absolute separation of human races, considered as immutable distinct species.

> Hybridism, or the sterility of the offspring of parents of distinct species of the same natural family, seems to us to be a clear proclamation of nature against the confusion which the variety necessary to Mr. Darwin's theory implies. Even when two species are so closely allied that sterility in their offspring does not follow from their union, there exists a natural repugnance to intermixture. Thus, the Germanic and Lapland races who border on each other do not intermix; the Negroes and Mauritanians standing in the same relation have been distinct for some 3,000 years; and it was but a few nights ago that Captain McClintock informed us that the Red Indians of America not only did not intermix with their immediate neighbours the Esquimaux, but that no example was known of their being able even to dwell and exist among them. (Crawfurd 1859b: 772–73)

Crawfurd then begins to launch a rhetorical attack on Darwin's theory, although one that would be relatively restrained in tone until he subsequently began to confront Darwin's followers.

Mr. Darwin's theory, even if it were established, would not account for the origin of species, for it would not tell us how his some nine primordeal species, or his single progenitor of these nine, originated. The theory supposes an unlimited progress towards improvement. By it we may hope that the race to which we ourselves belong may in the course of some millions of years become angels or demigods. This is, no doubt, consolatory, and yet it is somewhat marred by the mortifying reflection that proud man may have been once an ape, a bat, or a mere monad—nay that even Isaac Newton may have had the very same progenitor as a drum-head cabbage! Millions of years hence (if the improved man then living should think it worth while to preserve a record of our present humble doings), the best of us may be looked upon as no better than clever apes. . . . The theory, indeed, is a scientific metempsychosis, not only more ingenious but far more consolatory than that of Hindus and Buddhists, for it is all hopeful progress without any counterbalance of melancholy retrogression, or still worse annihilation. (Crawfurd 1859b: 773)

Crawfurd was thus one of the first, despite Darwin's deliberate avoidance of the subject, to recognize the implications of evolutionary theory for human descent. His dislike is more than obvious. What Crawfurd finds to like in the *Origin*, despite his own antislavery rhetoric, is Darwin's exposition of the "slave-making instinct" in ants, which he quotes at great length, drawing this conclusion: "It will be observed that, as with human slave-dealing, the slave is black, and the dealer, if not white, at least red or fairer" (Crawfurd 1859b: 773).

Before publication of his review, Crawfurd had sent Darwin suggestions for the improvement of his work.

He says he has read my book, "at least such parts as he could understand." He sent me some notes and suggestions (quite unimportant), and they show me that I have unavoidably done harm to the subject, by publishing an abstract. He is a real Pallasian; nearly all our domestic races descended from a multitude of wild species now commingled. (Darwin 1859b: 32–33)

In fact, this was exactly Crawfurd's theory of human races generalized to the level of biological species.

From then until a few months before his death, Crawfurd abandoned the Noble Savage in favor of a pursuit of bigger game, Darwin's theory of evolution. The turning point came at the British Association meetings of 1863, just after the publication of Sir Charles Lyell's (1863) and Thomas Huxley's (1863) works on the "Antiquity of Man," when the press and the public were hungering for discussion of the Darwinism controversy and few scientists were willing to commit themselves. Crawfurd felt no such inhibitions; and the fortuitous combination of a cancellation of other section meetings because of excursions and the weather and Crawfurd's prime-time position before a scheduled debate between Hunt and an African-American critic of his racial theories resulted in Crawfurd's drawing the largest crowd of the entire conference and getting two columns of coverage in the *Times* (*LT*, August 31, 1863, 7).

Over the next several years, Crawfurd found himself promoted to the status of one of Darwin's leading critics in the eyes of the popular press (Ellegard 1958: 79, 81, 240) — or, at least, the better-educated part of it. Ironically, for some elements of the Christian conservative press, Crawfurd, despite his ever more vehement opposition to Darwinism, was actually identified with Darwin.

> We regret to observe that Messrs Crauford [*sic*] and Darwin's essentially antiscriptural notions with regard to the origin of Man have been again brought forward at this meeting. Professor Huxley was the champion of Mr. Darwin's mischievous theory—that Man is a development from brutes—and Mr. Crauford . . . that mankind did not spring from a single pair of human beings. (*English Churchman*, October 9, 1862, 987, cited in Ellegard 1958: 73)

For such critics, the objectionable essence of Darwin's theory was religious rather than scientific; and Crawfurd was perceived as falling in the same antiscriptural camp. From the standpoint of leading scientists, conversely, Crawfurd was hardly qualified to render scientific judgment on Darwin's theory; he was one of a variety of ideologues who stirred his own unscientific ingredients into the muddle of popular misunderstandings. Neither of these negative judgments had any significance for Crawfurd, who was in a position to celebrate his own success at yet another propaganda coup.

Having established a successful precedent of deconstructive ridicule and distortion in his Noble Savage myth, Crawfurd applied the same strategy to every other theory. He represented Darwin as promoting a theory that logically required not only that existing species of apes should transform into the existing species of men but also that "the frog ought at least to be transformed into a crocodile, the butterfly into a dove, and the bee into a falcon or eagle" (Crawfurd 1868c: 29). Darwin's theory belongs "to the realm of pure fancy" (28); the processes of change he projects are nonexistent "except in dreams" (28); his mutations of species are "more extrava-

gant than the metamorphoses of Ovid" (29); it is as "beyond human understanding" (31) as the Buddhist theory of reincarnation—or perhaps
even more so!

Darwin, it seems, is no saner than Rousseau, or at least not deserving
of any different treatment. For, as Crawfurd's (1868c: 34–38) conclusion
makes clear, the ultimate offense that Darwin has committed is to obscure
the question of racial superiority:

> But let us for a moment indulge in the belief that the Darwinian theory
> has, through the creation of a being or beings superior to apes, but in-
> ferior to man, bridged over the chasm which now separates them, and
> that the masterpiece of organic existence is at length reached; still man
> is but a generic term, for he is divided into many races, or speaking
> more correctly, into many species, greatly differing among themselves
> in bodily and mental attributes. It was incumbent, therefore, on the
> theory, to show that such differences were brought about by "natural
> selection in the struggle for life," and to indicate with which of the
> many races the mutation began; or, in other words, which of the races
> it is that stands nearest to the apes. It makes no attempt of the kind; it
> simply makes a man out of a monkey and of something else as yet un-
> known, leaving mankind an indiscriminate hodge-podge; and so, there-
> fore, the Darwinian theory, except in so far as it provokes inquiry, is of
> no value to ethnology or the natural history of man. (37–38)

By this time, Crawfurd's Noble Savage myth had achieved its purpose. We have seen its resounding success in its appropriation by Lubbock,
Tylor, Mackenzie, and others. Lubbock, at least, retained enough skepti-
cism, despite his general acceptance of the myth, to debate Crawfurd on his
scathingly negative assessments of savage life.

> [A paper was then read, on] *The Antiquity of Man* (previously read in
> London) by Mr. JOHN CRAWFURD, F.R.S. . . . Sir JOHN LUBBOCK agreed
> most entirely and cordially with Mr. Crawfurd in the main conclusions
> to which he had come, but there were one or two minor points on which
> he had a rather different opinion. . . .
> Then, he thought Mr. Crawfurd had been rather unjust to the Fee-
> jeans. When they considered the canoes these people built, the arms
> and implements they formed, and even the language to which Mr. Craw-
> furd had alluded somewhat uncomplimentarily, he thought they would
> admit that the Feejeans were more advanced than he appeared to sup-
> pose. He would say the same thing of the Esquimaux. No doubt they
> were very dirty, but one could not wash himself with ice. . . . Indeed,
> when the circumstances were considered, the Esquimaux would be found
> to have made the most of their opportunities; and he even thought that,

if Mr. Crawfurd himself, with his well-known ingenuity and great per-
severance, were to go to live in the far north among that people, he
would find it difficult to carry on a more civilised state of existence than
that in which the Esquimaux were found to be. . . .[1] The principal point,
however, on which he differed from the author of the paper was that he
(Mr. Crawfurd) was a total disbeliever in the unity of the human race,
whereas he (Sir John) was a firm believer in that unity. (Hunt 1868b:
91–92)

Lubbock, in a humorous twist of poetic justice, thus turns Crawfurd's attack on Rousseau back on him, leaving unspoken the implication that, as
Crawfurd said of Rousseau, a week's residence with the people he wrote
about "would have brought him to a saner conclusion." Unfazed by, and
perhaps unaware of, Lubbock's irony, Crawfurd returned to his attack on
his new pet rhetorical phantom, the specter of the "missing link," evoked
to haunt Darwinian evolutionary theory and its supposed support for the
unity of man.

Crawfurd did not invent the "missing link," as he apparently had the
Noble Savage. He does not refer to it in his early review of Darwin's *Origin of Species* in 1859 (Crawfurd 1859b), even though Darwin had in his
first edition of the *Origin* invoked the medieval metaphor of "one long and
branching chain of life" (Darwin 1859a: 301) and explicitly discussed the
apparent problem of the absence from the geological record of "innumerable transitional links" in the chain (e.g., Darwin 1859a: 172–79, 279–82,
301–11, 459–66). The term "missing link" was used by Huxley (1860: 25)
and another reviewer of Darwin (cited in Lyell 1863: 502) as early as 1860.

But, in fact, the term was pre-Darwinian. It had been used by Lyell
years before Darwin's publication to refer to gaps in the geological chain of
fossils implying a continuous gradation of succession of new and distinct
species.

> On passing from the lower greensand to the gault, we suddenly reach
> one of those new epochs, scarcely any of the fossil species being com-
> mon to the lower and upper cretaceous systems, a break in the chain
> implying no doubt many missing links in the series of geological monu-
> ments which we may some day be able to supply. (Lyell 1851: 220)

In this context, Lyell had used the term "link" without its later evolutionary connotations but instead as part of an argument against the transmutation of species: "The succession of living beings appears to have been continued not by the transmutation of species, but by the introduction into the
earth from time to time of new plants and animals" (1851: 501).[2]

Lyell, of course, later reversed this position when he became a supporter of Darwin's views. But, for other users of the term, what would be new in the appropriation of the "missing link" as a polemic term by the anti-Darwinists was the substitution of the notion that the linkage implied should be transmutational rather than simply successional, as well as a considerable increase in negative valorization.

Thus Crawfurd soon recognized the utility of the "missing link" as a rhetorical weapon, particularly after he successfully used it to attack Lyell and Huxley at the British Association in 1863. By the time of his 1868 debate with Lubbock, he was ready to wheel out the "missing link" as a fully developed piece of rhetorical artillery as potent as the "Noble Savage" had been a decade earlier.

> Mr. CRAWFURD . . . begged in the first place to reply to the question raised by Sir John Lubbock. . . . As to the Feejeans, he looked upon them as a race very low indeed in the scale of civilization. . . . As to the unity of the human race, of course he did not believe in that. His friend believed in the theory of special [i.e., natural] selection,[3] and he hoped to hear Sir John describe his theory of the human species, to explain how he discovered the missing link, how a monkey became a man, and how all the different races of men had undergone the change they had now done. He would like to see a single particle of evidence to show that a black man became white [Prichard's theory], or a white man became black [Blumenbach's theory], or how a black woman could be compared to the women he saw before him. (Hunt 1868b: 94)

In this 1868 debate with Lubbock, Crawfurd's rhetorical strategy is the same one he used a decade earlier in generating the Noble Savage myth. In both cases, Crawfurd deliberately misinterprets his opponents (Lubbock and the Darwinians in place of Rousseau) by attribution of beliefs they did not hold (that present species or races had been produced from other currently existing species rather than common ancestors), sarcastically emblematized by a polemic fantasy projected on his opponents ("missing links" in place of Noble Savages), all wrapped up in a concluding appeal to egocentric prejudice, complacency, and the threatened honor of Victorian womanhood.

But this time Lubbock, although willing at least partly to swallow the myth of the Noble Savage, had no appetite for another tainted concoction such as the "missing link." He expresses his distaste for the latter in the same work in which he affirms his belief in the former.

> Opponents of Mr. Darwin's theory often ask with misplaced triumph for the links connecting any two species. In fact, however, every species

is a link between other allied forms. Of course, indeed, as long as any varieties remain undescribed there will be intervals—indicating, however, gaps in our knowledge, not in nature. Moreover, it is admitted by every one that there are variable species, that is to say, species which present two or more extreme forms, with intermediate gradations. Now we may fairly ask those who assert that no two species are connected by links, how they would separate the instances of variable animals (which they admit to occur) from the case which they say does not exist. If we were to obtain to-morrow all the links between any two species which are now considered distinct, no one can deny that the two would at once be united, and would hereafter appear in our classifications as one variable species. In fact, therefore, they first unite into one species all those forms, however different, between which a complete series is known, and then argue in favour of the permanence of species because no two of them are united by intermediate links. (Lubbock 1865: 308)

Lubbock's quickness to expose the fallacy of the "missing link" obviously springs largely from having found himself the target of Crawfurd's invective. But although he retained enough of the ethnographic heritage of the dialectic of vices and virtues to find qualities to be admired even in maligned peoples such as the Fijians (fig. 26), he was generally uncritical of negative attitudes toward "savages" by Crawfurd and others. If he had had a similar motivation to take a more critical stance to the myth of the "Noble Savage," he might have been less willing to accept on faith the prejudiced descriptions of the travelers that brought him to such a negative evaluation of "savages" and their place in the racial hierarchy (Lubbock 1870: 269–70). After years spent with Crawfurd in meetings of the Ethnological Society, perhaps a week's visit with Rousseau's critique would also have brought Lubbock to a saner conclusion!

Epilogue:
The Miscegenation Hoax

In early 1864 a pamphlet called *Miscegenation* was published anonymously in the United States. P. T. Barnum gives this account of it in *Humbugs of the World:*

> Some persons say that "all is fair in politics." Without agreeing with this doctrine, I nevertheless feel that the history of Ancient and Modern Humbugs would not be complete without a record of the last and one of the most successful of known literary hoaxes. This is the pamphlet entitled "Miscegenation," which advocates the blending of the white and black races upon this continent, as a result not only inevitable from the freeing of the negro, but desirable as a means of creating a more perfect race of men than any now existing. This pamphlet is a clever political quiz; and was written by three young gentlemen of the *World* newspaper, namely, D. G. Croly, George Wakeman, and E. C. Howell.
>
> The design of "Miscegenation" was exceedingly ambitious, and the machinery employed was probably among the most ingenious and audacious ever put into operation to procure the indorsement of absurd theories and give the subject the widest notoriety. The object was to make use of the prevailing ideas of the extremists of the Anti-Slavery party, as to induce them to accept doctrines which would be obnoxious to the great mass of the community, and which would, of course, be used in the political canvass which was to ensue. It was equally important that the "Democrats" should be made to believe that the pamphlet in question emanated from a "Republican" source. . . .
>
> The scheme once conceived, it began immediately to be put into execution. The first stumbling-block was the name "amalgamation," by which this fraternizing of the races had been always known. It was evident that a book advocating amalgamation would fall still-born, and hence some new and novel word had to be discovered, with the same

meaning, but not so objectionable. Such a word was coined by the combination of the Latin *miscere*, to mix, and *genus*, race; from these, miscegenation—a mingling of the races. The word is as euphonious as "amalgamation," and much more correct in meaning. It has passed into the language, and no future dictionary will be complete without it.

Next, it was necessary to give the book an erudite appearance, and arguments from ethnology must form no unimportant part of this matter. Neither of the authors being versed in this science, they were compelled to depend entirely on encyclopaedias and books of reference. This obstacle to a New York editor or reporter was not so great as it might seem. The public are often favoured in our journals with dissertations upon various abstruse matters by men who are entirely ignorant of what they are writing about. It was said of Cuvier that he could restore the skeleton of an extinct animal if he were only given one of its teeth, and so a competent editor or reporter of a city journal can get up an article of any length upon any given subject, if he is only furnished one word or name to start with.

There was but one writer on ethnology distinctly known to the authors, which was Prichard; but that being secured, all the rest came easily enough. The authors went to the Astor Library and secured a volume of Prichard's works, the perusal of which of course gave them the names of many other authorities, which were also consulted; and thus a very respectable array of scientific arguments in favour of Miscegenation were soon compiled. The sentimental and argumentative portions were quickly suggested from the knowledge of the authors of current politics, of the vagaries of some of the more visionary reformers, and from their own native wit.

The book was at first written in a most cursory manner, the chapters got up without any order or reference to each other, and afterwards arranged. As the impression sought to be conveyed was a serious one, it would clearly not do to commence with the extravagant and absurd theories to which it was intended that the reader should gradually be led. The scientific portion of the work was therefore given first, and was made as grave, and terse, and unobjectionable as possible; and merely urged, by arguments drawn from science and history, that the blending of the different races of men resulted in a better progeny. As the work progressed, they continued to "pile on the agony," until, at the close, the very fact that the statue of the Goddess of Liberty on the Capitol [in Washington, D.C.] is of a bronze tint, is looked upon as an omen of the colour of the future American!

"When the traveller approaches the City of Magnificent Distances," it says, "the seat of what is destined to be the greatest and most beneficent power on earth, the first object that will strike his eye will be the figure of Liberty surmounting the Capitol; not white, symbolizing but one race, nor black, typifying another, but a statue representing the composite race, whose sway will extend from the Atlantic to the Pacific Ocean, from the Equator to the North Pole—the Miscegens of the Future." (1865: 204–6)

Barnum goes on to describe the adroit manipulations of politicians and the media used to make the pamphlet an international sensation and to associate it in the public mind with the Republicans—then the party of Lincoln, emancipation, and racial equality—to discredit them in that year's election campaign. Barnum's analysis has been substantially confirmed by later academic researchers (Bloch 1958; Wood 1968: 53–79).[1] Subsequent research has added details to Barnum's account but missed some of the information he provides; and later researchers seem to be unaware of the existence of his contemporary exposé of the hoax, taking an 1880 work by Joseph Sabin as the first published disclosure of the names of the pamphlet's authors (221; see also Bloch 1958: 62; Wood 1968: 58). Still, Barnum's narrative, unchallenged in the accuracy of its facts and analysis, remains unsurpassed as the vivid contemporary testimony of a "native expert" in the political and public relations world of the 1860s, who could write with the professional expertise and authoritative personal experience appropriate to one who had earned the title "Prince of Humbugs."

The hoax found many willing believers and a few skeptics on both sides of the slavery controversy; but belief was particularly fervent among the racists. John van Evrie, the American racial propagandist whose anti-Negro polemic had been a source of inspiration for Hunt, responded with a work titled *Subgenation: The Theory of the Normal Relation of the Races; An Answer to "Miscegenation"* (1864). And among the ideologues of racism whose victimization by the hoax was less innocent than willing, we find none other than James Hunt, who published a pompously indignant review.

MISCEGENATION. During the last two months there have come reports to Europe of the remarkable form of insanity which is just now affecting the people of Federal America. We should not have thought it worth while to take any notice of the publication of the pamphlet under review, if it did not give us some insight into the extraordinary mental aberration now going on in Yankeedom. It is useless, however, longer to close our eyes to the phenomenon now appearing in the New World. Before we saw this pamphlet, we expected that it was merely a hoax, which some political wag had concocted for the benefit of his party. But an examination of the works [sic] dispels that illusion, and shows that the author attempts to found his theory on scientific facts!

There is, indeed, just enough of the current scientific opinion of the day, and also enough of literary merit, to enable readers of this work to get very much confused as to the real nature of the opinions and theory therein propounded. The anonymous author starts with some general assertions, and if these be admitted, the theory is not so utterly absurd as it otherwise appears. . . . The manner in which the conclusions of science are misrepresented, and in which gratuitous assertions are made, calls for an early exposure.

In the preface we read, "Science has demonstrated that the intermarriage of divers races is indispensable to a progressive humanity." This is totally false, and such an hypothesis as the superiority of mixed races rests on no scientific data, and is contradicted by many well-known facts. The public are warned against reading the work by the author, if they desire "what is vulgarly known as amalgamation." It is because the word "amalgamation" is justly so dreaded, that the author coins another word. "Miscegenation" will not find a place in future scientific literature. . . .

Professor Huxley has recently declared that the "slave-holding interest" indulges in far greater absurdities than the abolitionists; but we confess we have never read any statement respecting the physical characters of the races of man which for absurdity equals the following. . . . A chapter, entitled, "Heart-Histories of the White Daughters of the South," is too indecent for us to quote from; we believe that only a Mulatto or a Mulatress could have strung together such licentious absurdities. (Hunt 1864b: 116–21)

Hunt concludes his review by approvingly quoting another "miscegenation" myth, an apocryphal story of sixty-four "female abolitionists" helping freed slaves in the South, who had given birth to an equal number of "little Mulattoes." The story's truth was confirmed by a Confederate military officer. Once again, as in the 1863 hoax of the "enslaved Hindoos" lampoon, Hunt had fallen victim to his own insatiable need to swallow, and to force down the throats of others, whatever garbage was offered as bait by the opponents of human equality.

Crawfurd, it seems, did not swallow the bait. Perhaps, like some of the American abolitionists, he "smelt a rat," or was one of those, like Lincoln, "who can see a joke, [and] was not to be taken in so easily" (Barnum 1865: 207, 210). Or perhaps he realized that some of his own positions—the denial of inferiority of "mongrel" races and of the sterility of hybrids, for example—were too close to those of the pamphlet to risk calling attention to himself.

But, in the final analysis, Crawfurd may have simply recognized that the triumph of the rhetorical-conceptual hoax of "miscegenation" had outshone his own earlier attempts to promote another newly invented term, "commixture," to achieve the same ideological purpose. In the five years from 1859 to 1864, three great anthropological discursive hoaxes had been successfully constructed and sold to a broad consumership: the "Noble Savage," the "missing link," and "miscegenation." The two that enjoyed the greatest immediate success would be the first to be exposed, although they would leave lasting effects on the English language. Crawfurd had been instrumental in promoting two of the three, including the Noble Savage, which would have the longest-running success of all. He had no need to risk betting his winnings on a horse of an ambiguous color.

V

THE NOBLE SAVAGE MEETS
THE TWENTY-FIRST CENTURY

20 The Noble Savage and the World Wide Web

Our story of the creation of the myth of the Noble Savage properly ends with its introduction into the anthropological disputes and political struggles over racial equality and human rights of the mid-nineteenth century. Yet we must naturally be curious about its effect on our own era, the beginning of the twenty-first century; and, in fact, we cannot adequately appreciate the significance of its introduction nearly a century and a half ago without understanding something of its continuing power and vitality in our own times. Like the ideals of equality and human rights, which it was created to undermine, the myth has undergone numerous transformations and recontextualizations, the course of which would require a separate historical investigation to reveal. However, we can at least quickly time-shift ahead to pick up the story again at the end of the twentieth century, to see how the myth of the Noble Savage continues to have an impact on our contemporary world.

If we look for the Noble Savage today, one of the more interesting places to begin is on the Internet. A recent search with one of the more discriminating search engines, one less likely than many to come up with vastly inflated lists of irrelevant sites, led to a listing of no fewer than 1,987 World Wide Web pages featuring the "Noble Savage" in some form or other—and to a recommendation from the search engine: *"Refine your search"*! The search results ranged from university course syllabi to sites identified with tribal governments (e.g., http://www.eagleswatch.com/great_sioux_nation.htm) to a discussion on the Australian Broadcasting Corporation's "Sports Factor" program (http://www.abc.net.au/rn/talks/8.30/sportsf/sstories/sf970228.htm) about Kenyan runners ("Certainly the travel writers who explored Kenya at that time really eulogised the Kenyan. I suppose it was a variation on the Noble Savage, the Rousseau-ian view of the

Noble Savage") to a listing of "Noble Savage" on the Jockey Club's web page "Number of Mares Reported Bred to Thoroughbred Stallions in 1998" ("Mares Reported Bred," http://www.jockeyclub.com/maresbred/maresall. html). Apparently Noble Savage had serviced fourteen mares that year. Noblesavage.com (http://www.noblesavage.com/) and noblesavage .net (http://www.noblesavage.net/) are domain names shared by a commercial website design service; noblesavage.org (http://www.noblesavage .org/) "is a non-profit web site [advocating] nothing but knowledge and freedom"; "The home page of the noble savage" (URL omitted for privacy) is a student website consisting of empty index links dedicated to the Inupiaq language; and "*Noble Savage*" is the home page of a Florida commercial real estate agent (http://www.users.dircon.co.uk/~bab/ch22/ns.htm).

It would be difficult to classify, or perhaps even to rationally describe, all of the constructions of the "Noble Savage" in this phantasmagoria of disparate entities, which appear, in overall perspective, to owe their existence solely to a juxtaposition of verbal absurdities capable of being warped through an infinite number of teleocognitive dimensions. When we encounter the Noble Savage in a site titled, for example, "The Secret Plot of the Muffler Men" (http://www.roadsideamerica.com/muffler/muffler .html), or in one called "Concepts exist within The Yeetle Box, assuming the shapes and forms of persons" (http://www.ameritech.net/users/bpadjen/concepts.htm)—grouped together with Love, Truth, Beauty, Worm Holes, Photosynthesis, the Great Chain of Being, and Flying Pigs— appreciation somehow seems a more appropriate reaction than analysis or critique. And yet, for a considerable number of these sites, comparisons reveal some patterns of order behind the apparent chaos. The most obvious of these patterns is the apparent tendency of such sites to fall into one or the other of two large groups, distinguished by the relatively positive or negative spin they put on the term "Noble Savage" itself.

For those sites that interpret "Noble Savage" in a positive light, we might attempt a preliminary classification of the approach as being one of romantic self-affirmation. That is, the author of such a site typically says, in more or less simple or elaborate form, "I AM a Noble Savage, and I'm proud of it!" Explanations may or may not follow the assertion; those that explain either term tend to stress elements such as integrity, intellectual curiosity and freedom, and resistance against conforming to authority.

What is the Noble Savage?

The Noble Savage is a seeker of wisdom and truth. A warrior in spirit yet still a lover of peace. Ever questing, ever questioning, ever vigilant, the Noble Savage is hope. A dream of something better than what we are forced to be. . . .

The concept of the Noble Savage is hardly new and unique. . . . I started using the concept years ago because of a cartoon found in a school calendar. . . . I was always in trouble, but usually for refusing to follow blindly where others led. . . . Since prior to my departure from the aforementioned college, I had reached the penultimate level of disciplinary punishments, the cartoon spawned my nom de guerre.

Yes, its hokey and a little stupid, but for me it is a symbol of hope. A dream of a better tomorrow. The knowledge that if I maintain my sense of humor, my honor and my courage, I can weather any storm. If you can't laugh at yourself, how can you laugh at anything else. (Noble Savage.org website: http://www.noblesavage.org/)

A prominent subset of these romantic self-affirmation sites consists of those arising from the world of popular music. One such site, for example, is devoted to a rock band called Noble Savage, which was founded in 1996 in the Washington, D.C., area, and which by 1998 was claimed to have "blown away" every competing band with whom they had appeared locally (http://www.geocities.com/SunsetStrip/2078/noblesavage.htm). Another site called "Noble Savage" (http://www.geocities.com/SunsetStrip/Club/1442/a-virginsteele-noblesav.html) is devoted to a single recording, *Noble Savage*, released in 1986 by a much better known and longer-established band, the heavy metal group Virgin Steele. The lyrics to the album's title song, "Noble Savage," can be found on-line at http://www.gti.net/korax/oldpage/virgin.htm. They link the name "Noble Savage" to qualities such as grace, power, dignity, honor, and freedom, which we might be inclined to associate with "romantic naturalism"; but also to elements seemingly less likely to fit the stereotype, such as voices of reason and kingdoms on high. A more institutional framing of the "Noble Savage" in the pop music world occurs in the name of a club in Shreveport, Louisiana, Noble Savage, which shows up in the itineraries of several bands (e.g., in the site devoted to "Melissa Reaves band tour schedule"; http://www.melissareaves.com/tour.html).

As this set of examples shows, what initially seems a relatively simple and straightforward case of romantic self-affirmation can quickly and easily shade over into a case of commercial promotion of a corporately constructed "self." In this respect, it may be that pop music is emblematic of postmodern self-identity; but beyond the problematics of self-promotion in the corporate marketplace, there are more general issues to be considered in these virtual manifestations of the Noble Savage.

One of the more obvious issues, of course, is that although the Web manifestations of the Noble Savage as positive self-affirmations may strike us at first glance as conforming to the myth as we know it, apparently stereotypical instances of "romantic naturalism" insofar as they base their claims of nobility on explicit or implied connections to "natural" behavior and attitudes (by contrast, say, with "artificial" conformity), in fact none of them evokes any personal connection with "nature" in any ecological sense or with mankind in a "state of nature." In this respect, they violate the myth rather than affirm it. But even more obviously—and in more blatant contradiction of classic "Noble Savage" mythology—as instances of *self*-affirmation, they represent claims about the self rather than about the Other. Their ascriptions of both "nobility" and "savagery" are self-ascriptions and not labels assigned to any other group of people. Out of several hundred sites examined, very few that interpreted "Noble Savage" in a positive way were not self-ascriptive, applying the term to an external subject. One of these was a review of a 1998 book by Adolf Max Vogt, *Le Corbusier, the Noble Savage: Toward an Archaeology of Modernism* (http://www.plannet.com/books/lcrbnblsvg.html); another was an article about a radio talk show host ("Jean Shepherd: Radio's Noble Savage"; http://www.advanix.net/~jsadur/shepharp.htm). Another such site, "The Noble Savage of the Americas" (www.brasilemb.org/guarani.htm), was a biography of a Brazilian opera composer, Antônio Carlos Gomes, who was initially so successful in Italy that he was considered a possible successor to Verdi. Gomes had a Guarani Indian grandmother and was actually knighted in Italy; thus the "Noble Savage" label seems to represent the kind of misguided, racistically tinged "compliment" exemplified by naming sports teams after Indian chiefs. Finally, another of the rare non-self-ascriptively positive Noble Savage sites was "the home page of the noble savage" (officially titled, like so many other sites, "The Noble Savage"), which greets visitors with this opening: "Welcome to the home page of the noble savage (in case you don't know what the savage is, it is a wolf. The wolves kill only what they eat and eat what they kill" ("home page of the noble savage"; URL omitted).

Thus positive evocations of the Noble Savage on the Web seem to be applied mostly to the self, with rare exceptions including applications to subjects such as an individual architect, a radio personality, an opera composer, or even an animal species—but not to actually existing ethnic groups or to hypothetical early humans in a "state of nature." And, finally, none of them seems to identify Rousseau as the purported source of the concept.

What about the sites that interpret "Noble Savage" in a negative way? In general, they seem to be mirror reversals of the positive sites in each of the respects we have considered here. None of them, for example, use "Noble Savage" as a self-ascription; for to do so would constitute an act of self-condemnation rather than self-affirmation. Instead, in contrast to the positive sites, virtually all of them do apply "Noble Savage" not only to others who are explicitly or implicitly assumed to be in some sort of pre- or noncivilized state of closeness to nature but also, in some cases, more specifically, to actually existing "tribal" peoples. And, characteristically, in most cases they explicitly identify Rousseau as the source of the Noble Savage idea. In other words, the negative sites overwhelmingly replicate and endorse the Crawfurdian myth.

Like the positive Noble Savage sites, the negative sites include large numbers of examples that seem to fall into characteristic groups, and individual exceptions. Among the exceptions are the Native American tribal government website and the Australian Broadcasting Corporation sports program site mentioned above and various unique sites, ranging from an essay in an alternative arts on-line magazine by a nostalgic Leninist who uses the Noble Savage as a lead-in to denouncing Rousseau for "ignoring Plato's warnings about how democracy creates demagoguery & loss of freedom" ("Alternatives to Capitalism—Part V"; http://musea.digital chainsaw.com/histor74.html) to a simple listing of "Noble Savage" without further comment on "The Internet's Best List of Oxymorons" (http://www.atlantamortgagegroup.com/oxymoronlist.htm). The characteristic groups formed by large numbers of the negative sites, more or less faithfully replicating the Crawfurdian myth, are distinguished by their authorship and/or sponsorship.

By far the largest group of authors and sponsors of negative/Crawfurdian Noble Savage websites are those associated with academic institutions. These sites take forms such as course syllabi, study guide readings, review and exam questions, answers posted by students, student term papers, faculty authors' conference papers and abstracts, postings of previously published articles and book chapters, book reviews, and various other products of academic life. One such site includes this header:

> These lecture notes are intended solely for the use of students enrolled in Anthropology [XXX]. Please do not refer to, or cite, them. While reasonable care has been taken with references, citations and attributions, I have not adhered to the normal scholarly standards applying to academic publications. (URL omitted for privacy)

Assuming that similar reservations might be held by many of the academic authors, and that the student writers are at a particular disadvantage in being forced to produce essays within severe time constraints on a subject not of their own choosing, I will not quote these sites directly or list their URL addresses. However, it might be noted that their posting on the Web has an effect similar to publication in exposing them to public scrutiny, probably more widespread in many cases than would be achieved by publication in academic journals. Thus, depending on the use made of them by an unknown potential audience, these academic Web postings that "have not adhered to the normal scholarly standards" may have greater influence in shaping opinion than those that meet the stricter standards of more traditional publications.

But quoting from the academic Noble Savage websites would, in any case, be primarily an exercise in redundancy, since they almost without exception faithfully reproduce the rhetoric of the Crawfurdian myth familiar to us from other sources. Again and again, we encounter in them the same uncited attributions of authorship to Rousseau, the same essentialist framing of nonwhite peoples in terms of the rhetoric of "savagery," the same pronouncement of summary judgments denying their purported claims to "nobility." Even if we grant that all of this is done with the best of intentions, in an attempt to problematize a kind of racial-ethnic stereotyping whose positive manifestations can produce as much distortion and damage as their negative counterparts, nevertheless the formulaic invocations of the same sarcastic catchphrases can begin to seem tiresome and overly negativistic after the first few dozen repetitions.

Perhaps the main thing to be learned from these sites is the great extent to which the myth of the Noble Savage has permeated academic discourse in the one hundred forty years of its existence. It shows up in writings on anthropology, cultural studies, philosophy, political science, literary and art criticism, American and European history, and various other disciplinary contexts. It is absorbed from the instructors' course materials and reproduced more or less faithfully by students, although some of the more reflective ones will occasionally comment on the term's absurdity or add an original interpretive twist to their responses. But it has penetrated so deeply into academic culture that it even appears in a standardized curriculum for fifth-grade arts classes (URL omitted for privacy), where students are taught to recognize the Noble Savage in apparently any early portrayal of American Indians as handsome, strong, or dignified individuals. With children in the public schools learning the phrase before they enter their teens, the persistence of Noble Savage discourse seems assured for some time to come.

Compared with academic websites, the other major group of negative-Crawfurdian Noble Savage sites is considerably smaller, and in many ways considerably more interesting: sites authored and promoted by religious fundamentalists. These seem to arise exclusively out of conservative Christian contexts, both Catholic and Protestant. However, they show considerable diversity of views and approaches among themselves and differ from the academic websites in quite striking ways.

In contrast to the common tendency of the academic sites to attack supposed belief in the Noble Savage as contrary to fact and reason, the fundamentalist sites share a tendency to attack it as contrary to faith and the word of God. Thus one such site, sponsored by an organization with the self-explanatory name Revolution Against Evolution, is titled "For the Politically Incorrect: The Anti-Biblical Noble Savage Hypothesis Refuted" (http://www.rae.org/savage.html). There may be a deeper irony in the century-spanning juxtaposition here of two of the most effective catchphrases for discrediting oppressed groups and their defenders; but the more obvious irony is certainly that while the "Noble Savage Hypothesis" may be antibiblical, "Political Incorrectness" appears to belong on the side of the angels.

The fundamentalist sites differ, of course, in beliefs and approaches, including in their identification of just what constitutes a manifestation of the Noble Savage and what part of God's word is threatened by it. Some, indeed, couch their discussions in predominantly secular terms. For example, Kerby Anderson's "National Child Care" article (http://leaderu.com/orgs/probe/docs/childcar.html) on the Probe Ministries website opens with a quote from Hillary Rodham Clinton and a discussion of proposals for national child care laws and guidelines, followed by a critique based on selectively cited studies identifying supposed risks faced by children in day care: loss of bonding, loss of a sense of "object permanence" in the child's image of the mother (citing Piaget), increased aggressiveness, physical and verbal abusiveness, increased exposure to contagions and infections, and so on. Some of these may represent legitimate concerns, while others appear to be taken out of context and sensationalized. But in any case, the determinedly secularist terminology masks the underlying motivations of the site. Only by reading between the secularist section headings and topic sentences of paragraphs do we notice the repeated hints of a dark conflict between "socialist" child care and the will of God. Not surprisingly, the conflict emerges most prominently in the article's invocation of the Noble Savage:

> Christians should not be surprised by these findings given our biblical understanding of human sinfulness. Each child is born a sinner. When day care workers put a bunch of "little sinners" together in a room without adequate supervision, sin nature will most likely manifest itself in the environment.
>
> Proponents of socialized day care begin with a flawed premise. They assume that human beings are basically good. These liberal, social experiments with day care begin with the tacit assumption that a child is a "noble savage" that needs to be nurtured and encouraged. Social thinkers ranging from Jean Jacques [sic] Rousseau to Abraham Maslow begin with the assumption about human goodness and thus have little concern with the idea of children being reared in an institutional environment.
>
> Christians on the other hand believe that the family is God's primary instrument for social instruction. Children must not only be nurtured but they must also be disciplined. (http://www.leaderu.com/orgs/probe/docs/childcar.html)

Thus the battle between good and evil, between God and socialism/liberalism, ultimately turns on the outcome of a struggle against a truly formidable enemy: the assumption of human goodness. The rhetorical similarity to Hunt's denunciation of the "assumption of human equality" is interesting. This is the only fundamentalist site that does not even bother to link the Noble Savage with nonwhite tribal peoples; instead it focuses on those whom even Rousseau himself identified as "true Savages": children. Of course, he never called them "Noble."

Other fundamentalist sites, less overtly secularist in their terminology, tactics, and targets, explicitly address themselves to theological issues of sin, punishment, and damnation. One such site with a conservative Catholic orientation, Brother Francis's "The Dogma of Faith Defended Against Right-Wing Liberals" (http://www.catholicism.org/pages/faithdog.htm), attacks opponents who believe that those outside the Catholic Church are not doomed to an eternity of punishment in Hell. At one point in his argument, discussing an encyclical issued by a nineteenth-century pope, he says,

> The Liberals of the 19th century, those disciples of Jean Jacques [sic] Rousseau, had idealized, romanticized, and all but canonized, the noble savage—the invincibly ignorant native on a desert island, entirely out of reach of Church or civil society. The Pope will try to rationalize to the Liberals of his day the fate of this poor savage as being consonant

with the justice and mercy of God. (http://www.catholicism.org/pages/
faithdog.htm)

That is, he will try to rationalize the eternal punishment of the "poor savage," a punishment inflicted simply for his "invincible ignorance" rather
than any actual offense, as a just and merciful act. As we might expect, the
primary target here is not some group of natives on a desert island.

> The Liberals are not interested, as you know, Father Stepanich, in
> the pagans and savages who have never heard the Faith preached to
> them. . . . The Liberals want to see the "invincibly ignorant" native
> in their neighbors—the Episcopalians, the Quakers, the Unitarians,
> the Christian Scientists and the Jehovah's Witnesses. (http://www.
> catholicism.org/pages/faithdog.htm)

As is so often the case in "Noble Savage" rhetoric, the "savage" once again
stands as the symbol of targets much closer to home. And, in fact, much of
the following discussion revolves around the justification for the eternal
punishment of unbaptized infants by consigning them to Limbo, a tor-
ment-free part of Hell. Those who might object that newborn children do
not deserve eternal punishment are scornfully dismissed as "addicts of sentimental theology." They are adherents of the "deadly heresy" of rationalism, and "they reflect the spirit of our times—a most un-Catholic spirit
which is the fruit of the Jewish and Masonic domination of contemporary
thought." Thus the corrupted Catholics have joined forces with their "in-
vincibly ignorant" Noble Savage counterparts and "have Communized,
Protestantized, Masonized, Judaized, and all but invalidated our supreme
act of worship, our greatest source of blessings—the Holy Sacrifice of
the Mass."

But meanwhile, on the Protestant side of the fence, the same battle is being waged along very similar lines. Gregory Koukl's "The Brighter Side of
Being Judgemental" (http://www.str.org/free/commentaries/theology/
brighter.htm) places more emphasis on angels than on infants; but it also
invokes the Noble Savage in justification of the apparently arbitrary infliction of divine punishments on the seemingly innocent.

> I don't accept this spiritual notion of Rousseau's noble savage, that
> there's this noble savage in the darkest of Africa or the jungles of Thai-
> land that is just waiting to find out about God, but he's surrounded by
> all of these false religions. He really wants to know the truth but it's
> not there. I don't believe such a man exists. Men everywhere are flee-
> ing from God, and the heathen in Africa or Thailand has no more in-
> terest in the true God than the average heathen that walks the streets

of Los Angeles. I just want to make the point that God is not under obligation to save angels or men. (http://www.str.org/free/commentaries/
theology/brighter.htm)

The pattern we see beginning to emerge from the fundamentalist websites, then, is that invocations of the myth of the Noble Savage refer not to
mistaken assumptions of the goodness of man in a state of nature but
rather to the dangers of belief in the goodness of human nature. The targets of such attacks only incidentally include non-Western peoples and
are otherwise highly variable. For a particularly richly targeted example,
we might consider an excerpt from R. J. Rushdoony's "From Ape Man to
Christian Man":

> The Tarzan stories were later versions of Rousseau's "noble savage"
> myth. Tarzan was the natural man, reared by the apes apart from civi-
> lization and possessing a natural goodness and nobility. . . . The story
> of Tarzan was the myth of the noble savage for the masses. In various
> ways, the myth was continued: the criminal, as the outsider, became in
> the films of the 1930's the new victim of civilization and often the truly
> noble hero. Then, in the 1960's blacks were given that role by the me-
> dia. . . . Before long, the new cultural heroes in the tradition of Rous-
> seau were homosexuals, one in Britain declaring that theirs was the
> truly free culture because it was totally artificial. . . . Rousseau's noble
> savage and Burrough's noble ape man were becoming destroyers. . . .
> The culture of death began to prevail.
> At the same time, however, . . . a Christian culture began to develop.
> . . . Surrounded by the evidences of a dying world, a new world is in the
> making. The old order is nearing death. Therefore rejoice! We are mov-
> ing from Rousseau's ape man to the new man in Christ. (http://www
> .chalcedon.edu/report/97may/s01.htm)

With this exposé of "Rousseau's ape man," variously manifested as a
pop fiction hero, criminals, blacks, and homosexuals claiming that "theirs
was the truly free culture because it was totally artificial," we seem to have
moved rather far beyond eighteenth-century conceptions of man in nature—although perhaps not too far beyond the nineteenth-century mind-
space of Hunt and Crawfurd that engendered the myth, especially considering the socialists, communists, and liberals linked to the Noble Savage in
the other fundamentalist websites. At any rate, the richness and variabil-
ity of their targeting lends a colorful dimension to the fundamentalist sites,
in contrast to the rather drab uniformity of the academic sites, with their
narrow, unrelentingly repetitive focus on debunking the purported "nobility" of American Indians and a few other ethnic groups.

And yet the academic and fundamentalist sites are clearly closely related in their treatment of the Noble Savage, and equally clearly differentiated from the other kinds of sites we have considered. Not only do the fundamentalist sites seem dependent on rhetorical and logical framings of the Noble Savage borrowed from academic sources, they also closely resemble the academic websites in their evocation of the myth of Rousseau's authorship, their rhetorical equation of nonwhites and "savages," and their assumption of a widespread belief in savage "nobility" that needs to be refuted. Essentially, both are promoting the same Crawfurdian myth, using at least some of the same techniques and strategies. What remains unclear in their common use of a basically defensive weapon is the question of exactly which enemy of civilization, progress, or the will of God the academic sites are defending against. Does the convergence of academic and fundamentalist representations of the Noble Savage have a deeper significance, reflecting some kind of functional identity of the two perspectives?

21 The Ecologically Noble Savage

Looking at academic publications in more traditional media in recent years, we find the Noble Savage myth and its rhetoric enjoying widespread popularity in many disciplines. As we might expect, the long-established interest of literary critics in the Noble Savage continues to be manifested in works as diverse as Gaile McGregor's *The Noble Savage in the New World Garden* (1988) and S. Sacchi's "The Noble Savage and His Civilized Counterpart in Literary Tradition" (1993), as well as in more specialized studies of individual authors and their works (e.g., Altherr 1985; Cook 1997). Likewise, the long-term presence of the Noble Savage in writings in the critical history of ideas continues in works such as Hayden White's "The Noble Savage Theme as Fetish" (1976) and Stelio Cro's "Montaigne and Pedro Martir—The Roots of the Noble-Savage" (1990a) and *The Noble Savage* (1990b). In recent writings, this tradition seems to shade over into the emergent field of cultural studies, where a more strongly critical focus gives rise to more polemicized expressions. For example, Hilaire Kallendorf (1995), a devotee of Fairchild's theories, raises a spirited defense of Columbus's vituperation of the Taino Indians by attacking positive characterizations of them as romantic Eurocentric projections of the myth of the Noble Savage. The argument in support of Columbus's negative views includes this remarkable passage:

> Let us note that in their museums, Dominicans are not accusing Columbus of hyperbole. Instead they are taking his words at face value and asking: what substantiation did Columbus have for claiming that the Tainos, identified now as the enemies of "civilisation," were full of cruelty to the point of threatening his life? One viable response would be that by this time, after several years of contact with the Tainos, he had become aware of several customs of theirs which frightened him to the

point of frenzy. . . . Today in Santo Domingo, in the Museo del Hombre Dominicano, one can view an exhibition of an authentic live burial of a Taino woman next to her husband. . . . The male skeleton appears typical, but the jaws of the female skeleton are still open from her last terrified scream. The scene creates the impression that across the centuries, through the corridors of the museum, there still resounds her final scream of submission and horror. (Kallendorf 1995: 458–59)

One wonders if the author had been watching too many antiabortion propaganda films lately. But at any rate, in addition to disciplines that have long been populated with Noble Savage representations, we also find them in a wide range of other disciplines and fields of study, including long-established disciplines such as art history (Trudel 1996), folklore (Walsh 1997), and political science (Ahmed 1991). But the fact that we also find them in more recently developed fields of study, fields with no previous history of connection to the subject—for example, film criticism (Aleiss 1991), business ethics (Green 1991), studies of tourism (Meisch 1997), and studies of death and dying ("Natural Death and the Noble Savage," Walter 1991)—is perhaps the most striking evidence for the continuing vitality and widespread appeal of Noble Savage rhetoric at the end of the twentieth century.

As for anthropology, where the myth of the Noble Savage arose in intimate connection with the institutional founding of the discipline, we might well expect that a century-and-a-half-old foundation myth has permeated so deeply into the fabric of the discipline that its influence would be almost impossible to uncover with any degree of precision. It has long since submerged into the intellectual substrata of anthropological constructions, surfacing occasionally and so casually as to almost escape notice in faculty and teaching assistant office gossip, conference bar humor, and other informal settings that remain largely off the record and off the intellectual radar scope. Sometimes a sighting occurs unexpectedly, as in this passing remark from Melvin Konner's *Why the Reckless Survive* (1990), "noted with pleasure" by an anonymous *New York Times Book Review* writer:

> I had gone to Africa to pursue not only specific scientific goals but also some personal philosophic ones, among them the confirmation of a naïve, almost Rousseauan vision of a rather noble savage. I expected to find, on the plains of Botswana, the beauty of the human spirit in "pure" form, unadulterated by the corrupting influences of civilization. The not-so-noble savages I had in fact encountered—and came to know so well, and in some instances to love—proved collectively capable of selfishness, greed, jealousy, envy, adultery, wife abuse, and frequent con-

flict ranging from petty squabbles to homicidal violence. Not that they were any worse than we are; they just weren't evidently better. . . . The noble savage does not exist and never did. ("So Much for the Noble Savage," 31)

From chance encounters like this, we sense that there must be great numbers of similar casual remarks scattered through the anthropological literature and incalculably greater numbers scattered through its oral folklore. Their occasional emergence into the light of public attention suggests not only how much anthropology but also a much wider popular audience still welcomes the continual rediscovery and reiteration of a "new" insight that few realize was originally deliberately planted in the discipline to serve the interests of mid-nineteenth-century racism, and which ironically now serves to express the intention to see others as equally human, even as it perpetuates the derogatory, essentializing terminology of those who first devised it.

And yet, despite this general tendency to recede into the background level of anthropological discourse, as in other disciplines, the Noble Savage continues to appear in prominently foregrounded places in professional writing. As we might expect, many such appearances occur in the literature of historical and critical anthropology (e.g., Guille-Escuret 1992; Linnekin 1992; Bolyanatz 1996; Duvernay-Bolens 1998), although it also appears in other anthropological contexts, ranging from cultural into physical anthropology (e.g., Dettwyler 1991). In such cases, the Noble Savage always appears as part of the introductory framing of an article or paper, and may reappear in its conclusion, but it is seldom, if ever, included in the body of the study. In other words, it occupies the normal place of a citation of authority or a theoretical construct to be established, tested, modified, complexified, problematized, verified, or falsified in the course of the study. However, unlike the "normal" (or shall we say "legitimate"?) theories and concepts that usually fill such a role, the Noble Savage is never cited or attributed to a source, except by the usual vague hints about Rousseau. And, of course, unlike other theoretical constructs, it is never subjected (nor could it be) to any kind of questioning, testing, challenge, or modification. It is simply there to be invoked and accepted on faith, as a given fact of nature, and to stimulate a visceral thrill of attraction that seems to enliven, even as it violates, the apparently scientific conventions of framing by logic and argumentation that characterize the anthropological literary genre. As a pseudological and pseudoscholarly framing device that violates the foundations of the genre that it emulates, the Noble Savage enables a unique and interesting variation on anthropological literary style, perhaps roughly characterizable as that of a scientific treatise grounded in science fiction.

Or, from another viewpoint, perhaps the continual resurrections, reincarnations, and mutations of the Noble Savage are more like those of some beloved monster in a continual series of remakes of a horror movie. The most prominent reconstruction and resuscitation of the Noble Savage in 1990s anthropology certainly reveals signs of a professional and public hunger for new stories about old bugaboos, as well as a certain taste for an imaginatively Frankensteinian bricolage of working apparitions out of disjunct components. The creature that seized such a strong hold on the anthropological imagination in the last decade of the twentieth century, as it turns out, was not actually created by an anthropologist: it was "the Ecologically Noble Savage," introduced in an article of that title by the conservation biologist Kent H. Redford (1990a).

Redford's article, first published in a popular science magazine and reprinted twice in the next three years, in *Cultural Survival Quarterly* (Redford 1990b) and a collection of undergraduate anthropology readings (Redford 1990c), began with an acknowledgment of the rich store of environmental knowledge held by indigenous peoples and an expression of misgivings about economic rationalizations for their study. He then introduced his main subject.

> The economic argument for the investigation of indigenous cultures
> has its roots in the myth of the noble savage. . . . It is the latter idea,
> that Indians lived in conformity with nature, that inspired this cen-
> tury's reincarnation of the noble savage. . . . Prominent conservationists
> have stated that in the past, indigenous people "lived in close harmony
> with their local environment." . . . The idealized figure of centuries past
> had been reborn, as the ecologically noble savage. (Redford 1990c: 11)

Without presenting further documentation that anyone other than himself had explicitly conceived of "savages" as "ecologically noble," Redford goes on to cite recent evidence that "refutes *this concept* of ecological nobility" (1990c: 12–13; emphasis added). His evidence covers a range of issues and cases, including cases of human alteration of ecosystems, sometimes extensive, in precontact America; examples that "make it clear that indigenous peoples can either be forced, seduced, or tempted into accepting new methods, new crops, and new technologies," including environmentally detrimental ones; and adaptations to market forces that trade economic advantage for threats to sustainability, such as sale of timber from Indian lands. He then briefly refers to a number of statements by others that seem to reflect unproblematic assumptions that Indians will always manage natural resources in ecologically beneficial ways, qualifies the generally negative tone of his previous remarks by reminding readers that there is also evidence of "methods used by indigenous peoples that are definitely superior to those used by nonindigenous peoples living in the same habitat," suggests that most such positive cases are likely to disappear under market and demographic pressures, and ends with an argument for the value of research on indigenous knowledge systems justified mainly in salvage-ethnography terms, with a small remaining hope that "occasionally, only occasionally," such research may yield results that are practically useful for future needs.

Many of Redford's points would seem reasonable enough to a general reader. But, in keeping with its original publication in a popular magazine, his article makes only brief, passing references to particular cases and quotes sources without any specific citations. Two years later, in a book likewise written for the popular market, another biologist, Jared Diamond (1992), would deploy a series of longer quotations and partial citations to launch an attack on "Rousseauian fantasy" (8) and European idealizations of "noble savages" (318) that he viewed as preventing realization of the extensive environmental damage wrought by indigenous peoples. But, for much of the decade, the "ecologically noble savage" debate would shift from the popular to the professional literature and take many forms, focusing on a wide range of cases and issues.

For example, around the time the "third edition" of Redford's original article was published, he and the anthropologist Allyn Stearman published an article in *Conservation Biology* warning readers that, even though indigenous groups might have conservation-oriented beliefs and goals, their use-oriented conception of conserving biodiversity was in conflict with biologists' absolute goal of preserving all species in an ecosystem in their original numbers and balance (Redford and Stearman 1993a). Although the Ecologically Noble Savage had been demoted to a passing back-page reference in this article, the ethnobiologist Janis Alcorn (1993: 424) highlighted it in a rare rhetorical counterattack, juxtaposed with the "myth of the noble state," the false belief that governments can be relied on to protect biosystems in pristine purity, in arguing that conservationists must reject idealistic absolutes in favor of real-world possibilities for actual progress in conservation—for which alliances with indigenous peoples offered some of the most promising opportunities, a point partially accepted by

Redford and Stearman (1993b), even while reiterating their more absolutist position.

A more uncompromisingly critical view of native peoples entered the Ecologically Noble Savage debate that same year, however, in Michael Alvard's "Testing the 'Ecologically Noble Savage' Hypothesis" (1993), which applied statistical models to observations and interviews regarding prey species choice by Piro hunters of Peru to argue that the hunters' behavior better suited a hypothesis of maximizing short-term return for efforts expended than one of avoiding overkill of species with vulnerable populations. The next year, Stearman reentered the debate in an article titled "'Only Slaves Climb Trees': Revisiting the Myth of the Ecologically Noble Savage in Amazonia" (1994), where she cited the case of a Bolivian people whose abandonment of nomadism and slavery had led to the abandonment of labor-intensive foraging in favor of quicker, more destructive extraction techniques as a counterexample to apparently more environmentally beneficial cases of indigenous ecological adaptations elsewhere. Stearman argued forcefully that even positive stereotypes of native peoples as conservationists can backfire politically when outsiders perceive a given group as violating the expectations they arouse—clearly a valid and important point, but also an indication of the political potency of the Ecologically Noble Savage debate and a movement away from earlier expressions of partial agreement and willingness to view issues in terms of multiple perspectives.

The escalation and expansion of the Ecologically Noble Savage debate shows even more clearly in Bobbi S. Low's article, "Behavioral Ecology of Conservation in Traditional Societies" (1996), a statistical analysis of ecological information in ethnographic source material drawn from the Human Relations Area Files, a widely used anthropological database. Here Noble Savage rhetoric is bound to issues that include the Quaternary/ Pleistocene extinction hypotheses, the collapse of the Mayan civilization, the European trade–induced depredations of beaver populations by Montagnais and Great Lakes Indians, massive cliff-jump hunting of bison by Plains Indians, Hawaiian and Polynesian extinctions of native species (Low 1996: 360–62)—and, apparently at a deeper level of significance, judging by the evidence of Low's previous work (e.g., Ridley and Low 1993), "selfish gene" theory, the "Tragedy of the Commons," and the conflict between the absolute scientific-evolutionary truth of individualistic human selfishness and romantic and Marxist illusions of common interests and altruism (Low 1996: 364–66).

A discussion of ecological and conservation issues by eleven anthropologists in *Current Anthropology* the following year (Headland et al. 1997) shows that the Ecologically Noble Savage has become enmeshed in an even more widening and varying web of contexts. Thomas N. Headland opens the discussion by juxtaposing "ecologically noble savages" with "pristine forests, isolated !Kung Bushmen, Kayapo-made forest islands, the idealization of primitivity, neofunctionalism, the belief in wild food abundance, and so on" (605), all related targets of the "revisionist" stance he favors. In the following pages he adds Marshall Sahlins's concept of hunter-gatherers as "the original affluent society," conceptions of African Pygmies as hunter-gatherers, the Maya collapse, and the viability of tropical forests as subsistence foraging ecosystems (607–8). The discussion between Headland and ten other writers, active promoters of Ecologically Noble Savage rhetoric as well as anthropologists against whose work it had been directed, shows a wide range of viewpoints pro and con and provides a useful overview of issues and sources. Objections to many of the substantive points raised by Headland and other writers on the Ecologically Noble Savage are summarized in the response by Leslie E. Sponsel (1997). The Ecologically Noble Savage continues to appear in the literature after 1997 (e.g., Meyer 1998), although at least in some cases (e.g., Dutfield 1999) perhaps with a somewhat cooler reception than the general enthusiasm that greeted its arrival in the early 1990s.

But by now, it seems that Ecologically Noble Savage has managed to attach itself to so many concepts and issues that it appears capable of assuming just about any meaning at all; and we must inevitably wonder whether something so universally meaningful can have any particular meaning. Could it have become rather like Wittgenstein's ideal floor, polished to such perfect smoothness that it has no friction left to enable anyone to walk on it? Or perhaps, as the logical positivists once said of statements about God, the kind of statement that cannot have a meaning because there is no conceivable way for it to be disproved? At any rate, the amorphous ubiquity of Ecologically Noble Savage discourse begins to resemble that of classic Noble Savage discourse nearly enough that it seems worth a closer examination of its construction and deployment strategies.

Redford's original introduction of the Ecologically Noble Savage frames it in these terms:

> The economic argument for the investigation of indigenous cultures has its roots in the myth of the noble savage. In its first incarnation, the *noble savage* was a shorthand term for the idealized European vision of

the inhabitants of the New World. Early chroniclers noted that among the Indians "the land belonged to all, just like the sun and water. Mine and thine, the seeds of all evils, do not exist for those people. . . . They live in a golden age, . . . in open gardens, without laws or books, without judges, and they naturally follow goodness." Jean-Jacques Rousseau, Thomas More, and others idealized the naked "savages" as innocent of sin. . . . The idealized figure of centuries past had been reborn, as the ecologically noble savage. (1990c: 11)

Already we sense that we are on shaky ground. The quote that follows the first mention of the "myth of" [i.e., belief in] the Noble Savage, as if to illustrate its existence—and which is then immediately followed by the name of Rousseau, as if to show his authorship—is, of course, not by Rousseau but by Peter Martyr (see chap. 2); and the "myth" it implies is obviously not the Noble Savage but rather the Golden Age. The least we can say about this foundation "myth" of the Ecologically Noble Savage is that its framing is, whether deliberately so or not, confusing and deceptive. The result is strangely reminiscent of the random outcomes of play with syntactic-conceptual algorithm devices such as "The Postmodernism Generator" (http://www.csse.monash.edu.au/cgi-bin/postmodern); for example: "'Sexual identity is impossible,' says Habermas; however, according to Parry, it is not so much sexual identity that is impossible, but rather the fatal flaw, and some would say the absurdity, of sexual identity." The automatic generation of apparently meaningful strings of keywords, buzzwords, clichés, quotes, and names seeming to fill the role of attribution of sources produces a superficial impression of semantic authenticity that may seem authoritative to those who do not know the subject, or get the joke—at least, until repeated exposures reveal the underlying mechanical repetitiveness and absurdity of such constructions.[1] But the same might be said of most of the attempts to give authoritative grounding to critiques of supposed Noble Savages, whether ecological or not.

By the time of Alvard's "Testing the 'Ecologically Noble Savage' Hypothesis," the Ecologically Noble Savage had already been promoted to a "hypothesis" suitable for scientific "testing." In fact, the hypothesis actually challenged in his study was "the conservation hypothesis," that is, "that hunting decisions are made to ensure sustainable harvests of prey. Restraint is exercised by hunters in the short term to prevent overexploitation and depletion of resources in the long term" (Alvard 1993: 359). Alvard's observations and interviews do indeed yield statistics suggesting that Piro hunters tend to concentrate on species that yield maximal caloric return for the time and effort expended; but the meaning of such statistics in relation either to "nobility" or to the tested hypothesis is not entirely clear. The interpretation that they tend to disprove either "nobility" or the conservation hypothesis rests on a key assumption.

> If indigenous people possess an intimate knowledge of their environment, it is not unreasonable to assume that native hunters are aware of the reproductive parameters and limitations of their prey species. Native hunters following a conservation strategy might be expected to use their knowledge to minimize their impact on the prey. . . . Hunters would identify those species most susceptible to uncontrolled harvesting and restrain from killing more than would be sustainable. (Alvard 1993: 363–64)

In other words, the assumption is that the "intimate knowledge of their environment" possessed by indigenous peoples is of such a kind that it would allow them to accurately assess and predict the sustainability of prey populations, measured against the possibility of significant depletion or extinction. Given that even the ability to conceptualize such possibilities, much less to develop reasonably accurate assessments of overall population figures, reproduction rates, and predictions of likely outcomes, only arose very late in Western science after considerable experience with population depletions and extinctions on a worldwide scale, this seems a high expectation for any small nonliterate population inhabiting a limited territory. Stearman's " 'Only Slaves Climb Trees' " provides information on cases that contradict Alvard's assumption:

> Even though life prior to contact and sedentarism was described as often difficult in that much of their time was devoted to the food quest, requiring almost constant movement, the Yuqui seldom went hungry. . . . [I]t is clear by their descriptions of and attitude toward the forest that nothing is perceived as truly scarce: scarcity is viewed as a temporal and spatial inconvenience that can be remedied by simply moving to another area where that scarcity does not exist. Because of a lack of functional circumscription . . . the Yuqui did not, and still do not recognize that resources are finite. . . . [T]he Machiguenga . . . are opportunistic in using resources and do not appear to recognize that heavy use of a resource will deplete it. (1994: 348, 350)

Alvard is not the only one to insist that observations of peoples actually living in a minimally destructive, apparently sustainable balance with their environment are irrelevant to the question of whether they practice conservation, since limited impact may simply result from limited population, technology, and participation in cash markets. He and others cite Hunn's concept of "epiphenomenal conservation" to distinguish such circumstantial results from "genuine conservation," which requires deliberate and self-conscious sacrifices of immediate self-interest to long-term preservation of potentially endangered species and environments. Often in such arguments the test for "genuine" conservation is expressed in terms of the presence or absence of "ethics" or "altruism." A reader not caught up in the heat of the debate might wonder whether some sort of inflation or conflation of standards has occurred—analogously, say, to efforts of early scholars to determine whether non-European peoples could practice "religion" without elaborate "rituals" or texts attributed to Divine "revelation." Could the question perhaps be, not whether their practices suit the purest Euro-American philosophical ideals of conservation, but instead, what are their conservation practices like? This would, of course, require an initial suspension of xenocynic doubt, a willingness to consider the possibility that all practices that tend to conserve species and ecosystems—whether or not "altruistic," whether "epiphenomenal" or explicitly intentional— could be described by a common label extended from one system to others with different characteristics, much as we do in comparing religions or languages. Whether or not this would be epistemologically useful, something like it seems to inform the advocacy of indigenous-Western conservation alliances by ecological pragmatists such as Alcorn (1993), for whom bottom-line successes in conserving environments and species seem more important than tests of purity of intention.

But, in fact, the interface between intentionality and efficacy forms a hotly contested ground in the Ecologically Noble Savage debate precisely because it offers a base to assert control over the all-important political implications of the available intellectual and strategic alternatives. To be sure, there are participants in the debate, such as Alvard, who frame their arguments in terms of a scientific objectivity so classical as to seem almost a throwback to Enlightenment ideals of rationalist disinterestedness and the reduction of all reality to the mathesis (Foucault 1970: 57 ff., 71ff.). But other participants in the debate from Redford (1990) onward have explicitly recognized the potentially grave political consequences for the indigenous peoples under discussion and hence the implication of scientific questions in political conflicts and their outcomes. Thus when Alvard asserts in the 1997 *Current Anthropology* discussion that the "revisions" under debate are the normal results of scientific hypothesis testing by observation, and as such ought to be considered examples of "scientific progress" (610), others express reservations about so easy an escape from political implications. Sponsel says,

> Although writers are seldom candid, science is not necessarily amoral and apolitical in implications or motivations. It is no coincidence that some of the revisionism occurs around the Columbian Quincentenary, an event which should have reminded the world that many modern states were built on genocide, ethnocide, and ecocide against indigenes. The revisionist critique of the "primitive" is often an indirect apology for Western "civilization." (1997: 621)

On a more mundane level, it could also at least be pointed out that, given the intense scrutiny of indigenous peoples' possession or lack of "altruism" and deterministically conceived analyses of their sometimes aggressively exploitative environmental responses to demographic and market forces, almost no corresponding attention has been paid to the parallel dependence (hinted at in Smith 1997: 559) of growing populations of scientists and anthropologists on a tightly circumscribed and increasingly competitive job market, where survival is dependent on increasingly aggressive exploitation of "new contributions" that must consist of either recognizably original innovations or strikingly provocative challenges to existing ideas and paradigms. The latter species of game is surely more abundant, and more likely to be immediately rewarding in terms of the caloric energy expended in its pursuit. In this view, we might expect an eventually inevitable dialectical-generational turnover as today's revisions fall victim to tomorrow's attacks, if not also—since, after all, the ideas and paradigms available as prey exist in finite numbers—a decline of predator populations in response to ideological overkill. But, in the meantime, we ought to consider what effect the introduction of Noble Savage rhetoric has had on this ecological debate.

It is striking to note that in the 1997 *Current Anthropology* discussion, after Headland's introduction of the Ecologically Noble Savage, none of the other participants invoke it to support "revisionist" stances—including not even those, such as Alvard and Stearman, who had prominently foregrounded it in their earlier writings. But this is not surprising if we recall the invention and historical use of Noble Savage discourse as a political-rhetorical weapon: as such, it is useful only in a position of initial attack. To follow with more of the same not only shows unoriginality but might perhaps expose more of its construction than could withstand scrutiny. However, two of the participants in the debate make approaches to a critique of rhetoric. Raymond Hames, although he echoes Alvard's view of revisions as scientific progress, goes on to say,

> As for ecological anthropology, [Headland] notes that "doctrines long accepted have in the past half-decade increasingly been attacked as *myths*" (my emphasis). I believe that calling an idea "mythical" or "illusory" is unproductive because it too often leads to the development of a new set of myths. . . . Frequently there is an element of truth in a so-called myth but it is overgeneralized or unqualified. When I explored the existence of game conservation by tribal peoples and found more evidence for the contrary . . . I did not declare tribal conservation a myth. Instead, I argued that a more interesting question is under what conditions we can expect to see the development of conservation or opportunism. . . . This orientation is more productive because making an empirical generalization does not help us develop a theoretical understanding of why it may be true. (1997: 614)

In contrast to this epistemological-methodological critique, John H. Bodley takes a more strongly critical stance, one that is rooted in politics as well as epistemology and that explicitly focuses on the Ecologically Noble Savage:

> In my view, the problem with ecological revisionism is its tendency to exaggerate and misattribute the myths it seeks to demolish, sometimes creating apparent anthropological conflict where none need exist, while at the same time (and perhaps more important) missing the point of the cultural ecological realities underlying the "myths" that are being trashed. The "myths" of ecologically noble savages, untouched primitives, and pristine wilderness are easy targets for revisionists and good examples of the problems this debate generates. Surely it is possible to push any anthropological observation to absurdity, and it is easy to conclude that one is the very first to discover such absurdity. To avoid such extremes . . . we also need to consider what interests our interpretations serve.
>
> . . . When anthropologists correctly argue that there are no "untouched tribals" or that the Tasaday were not "Stone Age relics," the public may mistakenly conclude that small-scale cultures are not real and indigenous peoples have no legitimate claims to cultural autonomy. . . .
>
> It is no surprise that revisionist assaults on "noble savages" and "wilderness" come at the historical moment when the global culture's unsustainable cultural imperative of perpetual capital accumulation is reducing the earth's stocks of water, soil, forests, and fisheries to dangerously low levels and disrupting ecosystems and natural cycles on an

unprecedented scale. It is of course valid to point out the limitations of homeostatic models and the misuse of ahistorical functionalism and to assail insupportable claims that small-scale cultures existed in "near-perfect equilibrium" or "perfect harmony with nature." . . . The magnitude of the difference in styles of resource management and consumption patterns between small and global-scale cultures is also very clear, and it is not a "myth." Ecological "nobility" is a false issue. Like Headland, I have seen tropical-forest peoples cut down wild fruit trees rather than climb them, but rather than concluding that they are therefore not "ecologically noble," I stress that when a group has no politically or commercially driven cultural incentive for expanding its population, production, and consumption, its members do not need to be self-conscious conservationists. (1997: 611–12)

But we must recall that, even though Sponsel and Bodley warn us of dire political consequences that could ensue from creating overly negative impressions of indigenous peoples' environmental practices, Redford and Stearman likewise warn us of grave consequences that might result from uncritically positive accounts leading to unrealistically high expectations. There seems to be no obvious reason to doubt the sincerity of either warning, or the apparent good intentions toward these peoples expressed in both positions. Perhaps more important, not only does either outcome seem logically possible, but many of us will have heard of actual instances of political repercussions arising from both positive and negative stereotyping of marginalized groups.

If we at least grant the difficulty of completely rejecting either position on ethical or political grounds, we find a similar problem in coming to a summary judgment on factual grounds: although many individual cases are disputed, most of those who attack notions of "Ecologically Noble Savages" agree that some cases seem to support conservation, while most of their opponents agree that indigenous peoples can and sometimes do cause damage to their environments. The core of the debate, then, seems to be a rather ordinary dispute over conflicting interpretations of growing information and new questions, certainly not so ethically and politically neutral as Alvard's scientific-progress model would see it but at least with apparently as much likelihood of ethical and political as of scientific legitimacy. What, then, does the Noble Savage rhetoric add to this core debate?

First of all, it seems clear that despite the key role of Noble Savage rhetoric in promoting nineteenth-century racist anthropology, its reappearance in any particular context does not necessarily imply racist motivations or agendas. Even if we doubt the possibility of the neutrality claimed by some users of Noble Savage discourse, we still have no grounds for inferring hostile intent without more evidence. In fact, for some users of Noble Savage rhetoric, the opposite appears to be true: many such usages are framed in terms of the antiracist goal of critiquing overromanticized views of native peoples that might lend themselves to racist stereotyping or counterattack and to negative political consequences. As we have seen, this is avowedly the intent of some of the participants in the Ecologically Noble Savage debate.

And yet, here as elsewhere, regardless of its users' wishes, Noble Savage rhetoric has an automatically insidious effect of undermining good intentions by using language as a lever to subtly skew representations, pushing them ever so slightly over the edge. By its inherent negativity, it forces us to frame the "other" not only in terms of an absolute distinction from "us" but also one that has acquired increasingly derogatory and detemporalizing connotations over the centuries. To be "savage" is not only to be wild but also to be ferocious, ignorant, and backward. And it has the widest potential target range of almost any racial epithet; it invites incorporation of every dark-skinned people who stand outside the favored circle of the first-person civilized, and may expand wherever necessary to include lighter-skinned peoples as well.

Noble Savage rhetoric further tends to inflate the emotional "noise" level of virtually any discussion, and so to promote logical obfuscation. One simple instance of such an obfuscation occurs in Douglas J. Buege's "The Ecologically Noble Savage Revisited":

> Professor of political science and Standing Rock Sioux writer Vine Deloria, Jr., once made the seemingly remarkable claim that prior to arrival of Europeans in North America "the land was untouched." This remark, which I take to be fairly representative of claims of ecological nobility, relies upon the assumption Deloria makes that Native Americans were so in tune with nature that they had little impact upon their natural environments. In other words, Deloria is claiming that the pre-European occupants of North America were "ecologically noble" human beings. *The phrase, "native peoples as ecologically noble," is employed by Deloria* as a metaphor. (1996: 77; emphasis added)

Thus, in deconstructing Deloria's own rhetorical inflation, the author raises the distortion level to produce a new distortion of fact. The apparently quite sincere transformation from Deloria's phrase to the author's analytic reformulation of it, and hence to the attribution of the author's own reformulation to Deloria himself, is all too typical of the cognitive delusions induced in otherwise clear-thinking scholars who succumb to the allure of Noble Savage rhetoric.

Similar kinds of obfuscation arise at the most technical level of the Ecologically Noble Savage debate, where high stakes rest on the selection of statistical models and their application to a small set of precise observations of data collected with reference to those models (e.g., Alvard 1993) and a much wider set of problematic historical inferences from observations made prior to, or without reference to, the existence of such models (e.g., Low 1996)—all of which then becomes supercharged with the rhetoric of savage nobility. The rhetorical framing produces language that appears to suggest not only that both kinds of cases lead to similarly "objective" certainty in their respective interpretations but also that "nobility" is subject to disproof by quantitative measures—although its proof by any method remains unimaginable—while savagery is a simple fact of life, something given in nature and not open to question or investigation, since it is the preexisting ground on which the investigation is constructed from the outset.

Finally, the introduction of Noble Savage rhetoric into this ecological debate has facilitated lumping together many issues that, however valid any of them may be in and of themselves, nevertheless together form a problematic conglomerate. Some of the issues raised under this broad terminological umbrella, for example, have to do with particular peoples, particular environments, or both; others, with particular types of cultures and/or particular types of environment; and still others, with more global issues. Thus parts of the Ecologically Noble Savage debate are concerned with the Piro, the Yuqui, and other Amazonian hunters and subsistence farmers, or, looking at a different continent, with the Kalahari Bushmen and the Central African rain forest Pygmies, including not only their subsistence practices and environmental impact but also their ethnogenesis, identities, and scholarly representations. Other parts are more generally concerned with the viability of equatorial rain forest ecologies as human foraging environments, or with the feasibility of sole dependence on hunter-gatherer subsistence patterns in such environments locally, or even globally, before or after the emergence of agricultural societies. Part of the debate concerns the potentially beneficial and harmful effects of foraging cultures on the environment; another part, the changes produced by agriculture; and much of it hinges on questions of demographics and environmental statistics. And yet another part focuses on the existence or nonexistence, effectiveness or lack thereof, of indigenous conservation ethics and religious beliefs.

Even to a nonspecialist, it is clear that many of these issues are quite different in nature and logically require quite different treatments. Ecologically Noble Savage rhetoric, on the other hand, tends to globalize and moralize them into an indistinguishable blur, where the generic "savage" can be interchangeably exemplified at one moment by the desert hunter and at the next by the rain forest agriculturalist, and the most isolated particular of environmental transgression by either becomes part of the global moralizing proof of the ignobility of all. Perhaps this globalizing and moralizing tendency provides a clue to understanding the similarity of academic and fundamentalist religious websites mentioned above, for the overall course of the debate strangely evokes cryptotheological echoes of Paradise, the Fall, and Original Sin. The "savage" may begin as the member of an isolated tribe who cuts down a particular tree to get its fruit; but he inevitably ends up as generic nonwhite humanity, all of whom are shown to be morally deficient by the agglomeration of the sins of the individual upon the whole. This is not to say that the "civilized" whites cannot have sins of their own; they simply exist outside the bounds of the discussion, free of the damning connotations of the terms in which they themselves have framed it. The introduction of Noble Savage discourse into this ecological debate may have gained its proponents the polemic advantage of a label more distinctive and colorful than Headland's "revisionism"; but in so doing, it has promoted logical confusion and, more regrettably, rhetorically targeted the very peoples for whose protection against counterproductive stereotyping the concept of the Ecologically Noble Savage was avowedly invented. As Max Horkheimer and Theodor W. Adorno say in *Dialectic of Enlightenment,*

> It is characteristic of the sickness that even the best-intentioned reformer who uses an impoverished and debased language to recommend renewal, by his adoption of the insidious mode of categorization and the bad philosophy it conceals, strengthens the very power of the established order he is trying to break. (1944: xiv)

If we need proof, we might briefly revisit the World Wide Web and the world of popular media. As already mentioned, we do not find instances on the Web in which indigenous ethnic groups are accorded positive representations as Noble Savages, ecological or otherwise. Thus, if we search the Web for praise of ecologically noble Others, we will have to settle for the wolves on the "Home Page of the Noble Savage" who are noble because they "kill only what they eat and eat what they kill" (URL omitted). However, we find a few sites that have drawn directly on the Ecologically Noble

Savage debate, including the site of "Scientist John Woodmorappe" (http://www.users.bigpond.com/webfx/cyber/johnw.htm). Woodmorappe, a geology M.A. who specializes in Noah's Ark and the Flood, writes frequently for "creation science" periodicals. One of his articles for *Revolution Against Evolution*, "For the Politically Incorrect: The Anti-Biblical Noble Savage Hypothesis Refuted" (http://www.rae.org/savage.html), uses citations from Alvard's 1993 article to denounce the "Ecologically Noble Savage" as "anti-Biblical and anti-Western." Besides Alvard, Woodmorappe draws in arguments from writers on primitive warfare and cannibalism to add still more contentious ingredients to the Ecologically Noble Savage stew. Despite the theological concerns underlying the article, Woodmorappe's rhetoric is generally restrained in tone and secularist in vocabulary; indeed, if a few key phrases and sentences were excised, it would be virtually indistinguishable from many academic writings on the Ecologically Noble Savage. This close resemblance to the academic and anthropological literature may produce a sense of uneasiness when contrasted with the context in which we see that the Ecologically Noble Savage has emerged from scholarly journals onto the Web—a context starkly highlighted in the article's list of topical index keywords: "radical environmentalism, rebutting anti-religious propaganda, political incorrectness, antifeminism, countering environmentalist extremism, little-known information, Judeo-Christian environmental ethic, countering politically correct propaganda, falsifications of history, environmental doublespeak, tree huggers, Rush Limbaugh's environmentalist wackos" (http://www.rae.org/savage.html).

22 The Makah Whale Hunt of 1999

For a more specifically targeted example of the political uses of Ecologically Noble Savage rhetoric, we might turn to the case of Makah whaling. On May 17, 1999, the Makah of Neah Bay, on the tip of the Olympic Peninsula in western Washington, killed a whale in a tribally sponsored hunt. It was the first whale hunt conducted by the tribe in more than seventy years. The Makah, whose primary subsistence had been based on whaling and fishing for many centuries, retained the right to continue these activities in their 1855 treaty with the U.S. government and, for the next half century, made a successful and even prosperous adaptation to participation in the worldwide marine mammal and fishing industries—successful, that is, until the collapse of the industries through the successive depletion of the gray whale, fur seal, and halibut populations on which they depended (Collins [1996] gives a good recent overview of Makah subsistence activities and changes from 1855 to 1933). Although they continued with limited hunting of gray whales for subsistence and ceremonial purposes into the twentieth century, the Makah finally abandoned even this limited hunt in the late 1920s in response to the severe population decline of the whales. When gray whale numbers rebounded to near-precontact levels and the whale was taken off the Endangered Species List in 1994, the Makah announced their intention to resume whale hunting. As they proceeded with their plans to implement the hunt, they found themselves in the midst of a rising storm of criticism (effectively described and analyzed by Dark [1999]) that reached a momentary peak with their launch of the first tentative hunting cruises during the autumn whale migration of 1998, and which rose again during the spring 1999 migration to burst out in a torrent of unprecedented intensity, violence, and overt racism when the hunt finally succeeded in May.

Such an outburst would seem at first glance to be exactly what promoters of the Ecologically Noble Savage critique such as Redford (1990b) and Stearman (1994) had predicted: the inevitable hostile backlash against romantic stereotypes of indigenous peoples living in "perfect harmony" with their environment, acting as the infinitely kindhearted guardians of all living creatures. Indeed, some of the negative reactions to the Makah hunt were couched in just such terms; and at one point, a Canadian journalist even invoked rhetoric and ideas closely related to those of the Ecologically Noble Savage literature to ironically chide the environmentalist opponents of the Makah for their unrealistic expectations.

> Everything was so much easier before the Indians slipped out of the box we'd put them in as noble and selfless keepers of the land. It turned out they wanted to feed their families and keep their home towns alive, and that meant making money from trees and fish just like everybody else in B.C. has been doing for a century or so. . . . Humans have a well-earned reputation for destroying everything they touch. And whales are noble, kind of like Indians used to be before they started wanting things. Unfortunately, nobility doesn't pay the bills. (Paterson 1998)

However, this one critical article by a detached, even if sympathetic, observer represents an exceptional viewpoint in a complex, highly polarized debate. Investigation of the deployment of Noble Savage rhetoric in the overall controversy shows a more convoluted pattern of usage, one that is less in keeping with the suppositions and predictions of Ecologically Noble Savage theory.

During the stages of preparation leading up to the successful hunt, Noble Savage rhetoric had begun to appear in the writings of whaling opponents. For example, in fall 1998, Bryan Pease wrote in the *Cornell Daily Sun*,

> Contrary to the patronizing view of many white liberals, however, not all native people can be lumped under one *noble* banner. Some Native Americans are just as conniving, barbaric, *savage* and capitalistic as their European counterparts. . . . Grey whales, and all of nature by extension, are facing threats not only from obvious corporate killers such as Mitsubishi, but also from more insidious evildoers masquerading under the guise of "cultural rights." (Pease 1998; emphasis added)

The strategy Pease employs here to situate the Makah among the even "more insidious evildoers" than Japanese megacorporations, a strategy of rhetorically splitting an uncapitalized and unmarked Noble Savage into a polar opposition between "savage" evildoers such as the Makah and their "noble" conservationist opposites, was devised by organizational opponents of the Makah hunt. It has the advantage of presenting the appearance of ordinary descriptive language, even as it automatically evokes the sarcastic force of the original term. Thus, by following this strategy, one can talk of the Noble Savage and invoke its long-established power as an offensive weapon while technically avoiding the term itself and evading charges of any direct and intentional connection with its racist connotations. For there is no question that, by the late 1990s, the racist implications of Noble Savage discourse were becoming increasingly obvious to at least some of the participants in the whaling controversy.

In fact, the use of Noble Savage rhetoric in ecological disputes had already backfired against some of the environmental activists who had deployed it in earlier confrontations with indigenous hunters. For example, at the World Conservation Congress meeting in October 1996, representatives of the Inuit Circumpolar Conference, representing Inuit seal hunters, and the International Fund for Animal Welfare (IFAW), which opposed their hunt, debated the latter organization's application to join the congress. When IFAW's request was rejected, David McLaughlin of CBC Morning News interviewed Rosemarie Kuptana, Inuit Conference president, and Ian MacPhail, a special consultant for IFAW.

> MACPHAIL: Well again, I don't want to be sarcastic but I can't help noting that the noble savages are frightfully well dressed. One of them is wearing a gold Rolex watch which I can't afford. I think they should be awfully careful about doing the Nanuk-of-the-North/starving-in-igloos story. Because I don't think that there are many really genuine noble savages living on the land on what nature provides. I would like to meet one. I'd like to shake him by the hand.
>
> MCLAUGHLIN: Can I see if I could introduce you to Rosemarie Kuptana?
>
> MACPHAIL: Well, I don't want to get involved. ("IFAW and the 'Noble Savages,'" http://www.highnorth.no/in-wi-ro.htm)

At another point in the interview, MacPhail admitted, "We use highly emotional language in order to get the public to show concern and donate money." But as the interviewer comments, "It's the very reason why the

World Conservation Union denied membership to the IFAW." Strategies are useful only until they turn counterproductive; and the IFAW was not the only conservationist organization to be caught in a backlash against its confrontation of indigenous peoples in the antisealing campaign. Alx V. Dark (1999) suggests that the criticism Greenpeace received for the adverse effects of its antisealing campaign on Inuit communities may have been responsible for its decision not to join the environmentalist–animal rights coalition opposing the Makah hunt; the same may be true of the IFAW itself, whose name is conspicuously absent from the Makah debate (e.g., the 1996 "Open Letter to the Makah Nation," http://www.highnorth.no/op-le-to.htm, signed by 341 groups opposing the hunt). For those who chose confrontation rather than retreat, it became crucial to devise more complex strategies to avoid the mistakes of the past and their political repercussions.

Thus it was that the Sea Shepherd Conservation Society, which emerged as the organizational spearhead of the opposition to the Makah hunt, developed a strategy that combined uncompromising confrontation with a passive-aggressive rhetorical stance that cast the whales, members of the Makah minority opposing the hunt, and Sea Shepherd itself in the common role of victims of the Makah whalers, whom they went out of their way to provoke into any response that could be turned against them. Moving into the territory of a tribe they outnumbered in membership by forty to one, and confronting their canoes with speedboats and oceangoing ships, it was vitally necessary to use every impression management strategy available to seize the moral high ground. Paul Watson, Sea Shepherd leader, described a 1997 confrontation:

> We found ourselves face-to-face with a traditional Makah canoe. It was not a good media image. Our large black vessel was facing off against their smaller black canoe. On the surface this did not bode well from a media perspective. I was taking the chance of being portrayed as the big bad eco-bully. (Watson 1997: 3)

Indeed, for some, perhaps including the Makah themselves, the confrontation might have brought to mind how Watson, after his expulsion from Greenpeace for his advocacy of violent tactics, had risen to fame by using his original "large black vessel" to ram a large oceangoing whaling ship. Facing off against the canoe at Neah Bay, Watson chose a rhetorical mode of attack, representing its Makah occupants in terms that suggested drunkenness, evasiveness, and deceptive claims of adherence to a "tradition" they actually knew nothing about. But the Sea Shepherd leaders needed other weapons as well to offset their public relations disadvantage. One of the strategies they chose involved a creative manipulation of Noble Savage rhetoric.

It was, in fact, the leaders of Sea Shepherd who devised the strategy of rhetorically splitting the Noble Savage into a polarized opposition of savagery to nobility. Their use of the strategy was subtler and more sophisticated than that of some of their allies, in that they avoided actually using the term "savage," leaving the savagery implied by opposing a deliberate rhetoric of nobility to an unspecified opposite. Thus, in a 1997 article titled "Confronting the Politically Correct Harpoons of the Makah," Watson highlighted the rhetoric of nobility in specific reference to the most outspoken Makah opponent of the hunt, Alberta Thompson, and to conservationist motives in general:

> Alberta Thompson is a direct descendent of a noble Makah sealing clan. . . . She eloquently stated, "The whale is to be watched, to be heard, to be admired, not to be blown away with 360 bullets and not used." . . .
>
> Some Makah argue that they have a right guaranteed by treaty to kill the whales. A right under law does not make the action ethically right. It would be a far more noble act to say yes, we have the right to kill the whale, and we choose not to exercise that right. (1997: 4, 9)

In choosing to ennoble the real opponent of the hunt (albeit in terms that could easily be dismissed as an innocent reference to high status in the traditional Makah class system) and the moral imperative of opposition to hunting in general, the nobility highlighted by the rhetoric logically calls for an implied opposite. Why not take the opposite to be simply prowhalers and pro-whaling moral choices rather than the "savage"? In part, because the Noble Savage had acquired so much discursive-conceptual momentum in English-literate circles over the last one hundred forty years that mention of the first half of the term would automatically cause nearly every reader encountering it in reference to indigenous peoples to be inexorably pushed on into recollection of the second; but if anyone doubts that this is so, there is also the way in which Watson frames his article. Having raised a red flag with his "Politically Correct Harpoons" title, which, considering its source, might put some readers on their guard, he then moved to disarm them by admitting the "political correctness" of his own cause and by citing pro-Indian credentials that include service as a medic for the

American Indian Movement at Wounded Knee in 1973. Then he proceeded to the main point of his argument.

> Many people subscribe to the myth that the objectives of the Native Americans are always in harmony with the objectives of conservation and environment. This is, of course, a racist outlook because it attributes the superior virtues of conservation ethics to Native Americans and assumes that they are of one collective mind and spirit. These mythical virtues have romantically evolved because of comparative technologies. The less technologically advanced cultures have had a lesser impact relative to the technologically advanced impact of the Europeans. Native Americans, like all other Americans, are equal to all other human beings. As a conservationist, I have come to understand that there does not exist any distinctive human culture, or race, superior to, or inferior to another. It is access to technology that defines the relative impact of a culture. (Watson 1997: 1)

Watson goes on for two more paragraphs to repeat sometimes luridly paraphrased arguments and examples from the Ecologically Noble Savage literature—for example, "the now disappearing jungle culture of the Kaiyapo of the Amazon . . . use chain saws on the magnificent hardwoods of the jungle"—but studiously avoids mentioning the term "Ecologically Noble Savage" itself. To an insider, the context and underlying metaphor of the article's stance is clear, as, in consequence, is the contextual foundation for projecting the implied opposite of the rhetorical "noble" highlighted in the following pages. To the outsider, the arguments consistently stress the moral equality of all humans, and the author certainly cannot be accused of using any such pejorative term as "savage" in reference to the Makah. Lisa Distefano, Watson's field commander of day-to-day operations during the Sea Shepherd blockade of Neah Bay, who followed Watson in highlighting the nobility of opponents of the hunt—"those noble people of the Makah tribe who always knew in their hearts what was the right thing to do"—while avoiding mention of the term "savage," remarked in her diary: "But Paul has asked me not to call anyone names. He never lets me have any fun." ("Neah Bay Diary, Dec 2 [1998]," http://www.estreet.com/orgs/sscs/wh/us/nbd/mkjnl23.html).

Nevertheless, as preparations moved toward inception of the first preliminary attempts to implement the hunt in late 1988, Watson, perhaps worried that some of the public audience might not have been getting the point, wrote, "Makah tribal officials are very good at calling us liars and propagandists, and have been doing so steadily for the last three years.

They are equally proficient at playing the race card. A sympathetic national media . . . has been saturated with the reverse racism inherent in the 'noble native' take on the hunt" (Watson 1998). Who could read the quotation mark–flagged "noble native" without making a mental correction, substituting the original term for its euphemistic stand-in? There could no longer be any doubt about what was being left unsaid in the rhetorical strategy employed by the hunt's opponents. The atmosphere of the Makah debate had become supercharged with the overtly positive rhetoric of nobility, constructed within a polarized frame that left the counterforce of its implied opposite polarity temporarily empty and unrealized. The instability of the positive overcharge could only be resolved by a strong discharge of negative energy; the rhetoric of savagery that would complete the circuit would ultimately have to be released openly into the field of polarization.

When the spark finally came with the killing of the whale on May 17, the effect was explosive. "Why is this savage brutality allowed?" one writer to CBC News Online demanded to know (http://www.newsworld. cbc.ca/viewpoint/omalley/letters.html). "Ruthless savages," exclaimed another. The *Calgary Herald* quoted Peter Hamilton, founder of the Lifeforce Foundation, as saying, "Anyone who enjoys subjecting an intelligent, sentient whale to an agonizing, slow death is a bloodthirsty savage" (http://elements.nb.ca/theme/marine/articles/article23.htm). The long-suppressed force of the negative polarity of the implied Noble Savage rhetoric had finally been released; and, in contrast to the proliferation of instances of the rhetoric of nobility before the hunt, one would have to look far and wide after May 17 to find a few isolated remnants such as the plea from a CBC listener: "I know some groups are working actively to stop such brutal killings. . . . [C]an you give me the address so that I can contact them and contribute my might [*sic*] (howsoever small it may be) to their noble efforts" (http://www.newsworld.cbc.ca/viewpoint/omalley/letters .html). And in one case, we find a different and more disturbing twist given to the rhetoric of nobility:

> To Nelson mandela [*sic*, here and throughout], oppression gave thee basis for behaving in a more noble manner than did his oppressors. There is no way the makah can be said to be responding their oppression in like manner. . . . I am willing to wake the white man's burden, and despite the history of white racism, state that . . . their relation to the whales [is] no more morally defensible than the traditional behavior of whites to Indians. (http://www.columbia-pacific.interrain.org/ compass/letter.html)

One wonders whether this might make more sense if "the traditional be-havior of whites to Indians" had been subsistence cannibalism rather than extirpation and genocide. But, generally, the rhetoric of nobility had van-ished from the scene, to be replaced by the rhetoric of savagery. The posi-tive overcharge generated before the hunt had finally been released by the posthunt explosion of negative energy.

Alx Dark's (1999: sec. 6, "Eco-Colonialism") analysis of racist and colo-nialist currents in the Makah debate up to a month before the hunt gener-ally holds true for the period after May 17 as well, with some qualifications and new elements introduced by the greatly heightened level of negative intensity after the kill. For example, although organizations opposing the hunt generally persisted in their charges that outsiders such as the Japanese and U.S. governments were the real motivating force behind the hunt— thus, as Dark says, reducing the Makah to "a passive people easily manip-ulated by non-natives"—the vast majority of individual reactions heaped condemnation on the Makah alone, with no attempt to share any putative blame with Japanese or other outsiders. Perhaps a more disturbing change was the virtual disappearance of any mention of the Makah minority op-ponents of the hunt who had previously been the object of so much of the rhetoric of nobility; from now on, it seems, the Makah were to be treated as an undifferentiated mass, equally guilty and equally savage. If these changes signaled a turn to a more racialized essentialization of the Makah as a people than had been previously apparent in the debate, they would nevertheless pale in comparison to far more glaringly blatant manifesta-tions of overt racism.

Dark (1999) identifies several colonialist-racist themes in the prehunt debate centering on issues of "tradition": stereotypes of "traditional" pu-rity versus "assimilated" corruption; non-natives' superior knowledge of what constitutes "authentic" native culture; the equation of technological change with cultural assimilation; and the inevitability of "progress" or "evolution" from "barbaric" elements associated with native culture to "civilized" elements associated with white culture. All these themes con-tinue in the posthunt debate, often mixed together with each other and with new elements of radical negativism that lead to disturbing transfor-mations. Thus, for example, one of the most prominent themes of the posthunt reactions was the repeated cry, "Take it back!"

> If the Makahs are so stuck in the past . . . perhaps we should allow
> them to stay in the past and take all modern conveniences and luxuries
> away from them and see how long they last. (Cited in Tizon 1999: A16)

> Keep the faith. Possibly we should take back non-traditional gear-
> trucks, rifles, electricity, tvs, fast food, etc. (http://www.newsworld.cbc
> .ca/viewpoint/omalley/letters.html)

To this basic colonialist assumption that "we" have absolute power over "them," which makes it possible and morally right to "take back" everything we have "given" them to raise them ("taking up the White Man's Burden") from timeless traditional savagery to modern civilization, other writers add a heavy dose of racist stereotypes and slurs. Thus a mother and daughter wrote to the *Seattle Times*, "Hey, I think we should also be able to take their land if they can take our whales. Publish this article but don't use our last names. We wouldn't want to lose our scalps" (cited in Tizon 1999: A16). While this particular letter may have set a unique standard for ignorance—after all, not only had the Makah already ceded their land to the whites in the treaty of 1855 for a guarantee of their rights to continue hunting *their* whales but also their war customs included headhunting rather than the scalping practiced by Indians and whites farther east (Swan 1868: 51)—it was hardly unique in the mindless venom of its racist stereotyping. Another writer, responding to a CBC editorial, said,

> Personnally [*sic*, here and throughout], I think it is a stupid, senseless, and needless slaughter by a bunch of jerks. They didn't go out in their canoe's as their forefathers had done, with spears, etc., no they went out with a motor driven craft, armed with high calibre rifles and took un-fair advantage of a creature that was not bothering them. . . . [W]ho do they think they are? It's time their special status ended and they were treated like any other citizen. Give them the privilege of paying taxes like the rest of us. Take them off the welfare rolls, and give them something to do besides killing wales. They still appear to be ruthless sav-ages. (http://www.newsworld.cbc.ca/viewpoint/omalley/letters.html)

The racist smearing of all Indians with the worst one knows, or has heard, about any of them should be so obvious for many readers that it would be an insult to their intelligence to dwell on it. Denunciation of the Makah in terms of a reduction of all "Indians" to the worst common denominator showed itself repeatedly in remarks such as the question of a writer to the op-ed page of the *Oregonian*: "Ancient Aztec Indian traditions included human sacrifices to their gods. Are we going to allow them to do that, too?" (http://www.oregonlive.com/oped/99/05/edo52212.html). Does the "them" refer to the descendants of the Aztecs, or the Makah? If the latter, why, other than because of their racial identity as "Indians"? Yet

it is worth noting that not only do these stereotypes display abysmal ignorance of Indians in general (they pay taxes, for example, and welfare assistance may vary as much among Indians as among whites), they also display
particular ignorance about the Makah and the historical depth and dyna-
mism of their traditions. A letter to the editor of the *Oregonian* said,

> Count me as confused, but since when does the Makah's ancient cul-
> ture—which they continue to insist is all they are observing—include
> using high-powered rifles, motorized chase boats, cellular phones and
> high-tech tracking devices to chase and kill a whale? While I would be
> against this kill under any circumstances, I could at least respect their
> culture a bit more if they were being true to their ancient cultural
> ways. (http://www.oregonlive.com/oped/99/05/ed051913.html)

The fact is that the Makah had guns and were trading skins and whale
oil for powder and musket balls by the beginning of the 1840s (Wilkes
1844: 4:487), and they were using rifles instead of spears for seal hunting
by the mid-1860s (Swan 1868: 30). Indeed, they had been persuaded to sign
the treaty partly on the basis of (unkept) promises by the U.S. negotiator
that the government would provide them with equipment to facilitate their
catch, and they had moved quickly in the following decades to incorporate
the most advanced available boats and equipment into their marine mammal hunting and fishing practices (Collins 1996). Thus, by the mid-1920s,
they were using motorized tugboats to tow the killed whales back to the
village, once as many as four in a single day (Densmore 1939: 52). If they
did not also have "motorized chase boats, cellular phones and high-tech
tracking devices," "trucks, . . . electricity, tvs, fast food, etc.," at the time of
signing the treaty, neither did the whites moving into their territory; both
were "given" these inventions by faraway, later inventors. And if, on
adopting such innovations, the Makah had not renounced their right to
whaling, neither had Italian Americans renounced their right to remain
Roman Catholics or eat pasta in order to qualify to own trucks, nor had
Jewish Americans renounced their rights to practice circumcision in order
to make themselves eligible for electricity. What, after all, did one have to
do with another? Like other Americans, the Makah had taken advantage of
innovations, incorporating them into their changing traditions over more
than a century and a half. But the basic option available to others for balancing tradition with innovation by freedom of choice must, it seems, be denied to the Makah solely on the basis of their racial identity. As one writer
to the *Seattle Times* put it, "We should tell the Makahs (and all other 'Na-

tive Americans') that, in the words of Star Trek's Borg: 'Resistance is futile! Prepare to be assimilated!'" ("Makah Whale Hunt," http://archives. seattletimes.com/cgi-bin/texis.mummy/web/vortex/display?storyID= 3747ccff44).

In the week following the hunt, it almost seemed as if there were a contest to see who could come up with the worst possible insults to hurl at the Makah. Martin O'Malley, a commentator for CBC News, thundered, "I hope the Makah 'hunters' eat their bloody whale and use the oil for their lamps. The sneak attack on the grey whale off the coast of Washington state was a revolting spectacle of phony aboriginal pride" ("A Whale for the Killing," http://www.newsworld.cbc.ca/viewpoint/omalley/martin09905 18.html). A letter to the *Seattle Times* said, "These people want to rekindle their traditional way of life by killing an animal that has probably twice the mental capacity they have. These idiots need to use what little brains they have to do something productive besides getting drunk and spending federal funds to live on" (Tizon 1999: A16). To say that some of the writers seemed to have worked themselves into a state of frenzy would be putting it mildly. One Canadian Web page opened with a quote from "William Shakespear"—"You blocks, you stones, you worse than senseless things!"—and went on to say of the hunt:

> They started [by] claiming it was essentially a religious rite to revive the old spiritual ways. Then it was then a means to improve self esteem, cure alcoholism and drug addiction. To me, this sounds as off the wall as trying to cure alcoholism by covering themselves in dog feces. . . . If they really need to hunt to feel like real men, how about hunting deer or seals with hand-made bows? They could also try Viagra. Reviving whale sacrifice sounds like a scheme hatched in a beerhall. . . . A Makah hunter is a like a cannibal who sees only long pig[1] when he meets a fellow human being. . . . To win this debate, we must persuade the Makah they are killing creatures perhaps more intelligent than themselves. Otherwise, their arguments make perfect sense. ("Makah Whale Sacrifice," http://mindprod.com/whale.html)

This particular diatribe resulted in a visit from the police and a psychiatric exam, since the writer, to protest the hunt, also announced, "I stopped taking the AIDS medications that keep me alive." It may be that suspicion of mental imbalance was one of the factors that led most newspapers and organizational websites to ignore the more overtly and violently racist communications they received. However, the *Seattle Times*, which editorially opposed the hunt, published an article by the reporter Alex Tizon that

specifically highlighted the more extreme anti-Makah and anti-Indian reactions. Tizon summarized the developments of the first week's responses:

> If words were harpoons, the Makah Tribe of the Olympic Peninsula
> might well suffer the same fate as the young gray whale killed on na-
> tional television early last week.
>
> So hostile has been the protest to the hunt that Makah tribe mem-
> bers have put their reservation, inundated with death threats, in a state
> of wartime alert. Bomb threats have evacuated Indian schools. Air-
> waves and editorial pages across Western Washington have carried
> anti-Indian vitriol not heard or seen since the Boldt Decision [uphold-
> ing native fishing rights] a quarter century ago.
>
> The Makahs have been called savages, drunkards and laggards. Pro-
> testers have entreated people to "Save a whale, harpoon a Makah."
> Calls for a return to killing Indians like in the Old Wild West have ap-
> peared in Internet chat rooms and in newsletters. (Tizon 1999: A1)

In fact, there had been a trickle of overt and implied threats at least since
the Makahs' first attempts to begin the hunt in fall 1998 — one writer, for
example, asking, "When the white people came to the west their tradition
was to kill the "savages"—native americans, should they start doing that
again in the name of tradition?" ("What Is Your Opinion?" http://www.
pacificcoast.net/~braveart/thoughts.htm; her letter appeared on the website of the West Coast Anti-Whaling Society, which describes itself as "a
group of citizens dedicated to preserving the sanctity of life"—for whales,
dolphins, and porpoises!). But after the May 17 kill, the floodgates of hate
were opened. The same themes were repeated over and over in personal
websites, talk radio, and letters to the editor, often almost verbatim. The
author of a Canadian website was one of many who asked the same question in May as the earlier writer had in October: "White people not that
long ago hunted the Makah for sport. Should that right too be revived in
the name of 'tradition,' 'self esteem' and 'unity'?" (http://mindprod.com/
whale.html). Others found new ways of expressing their violent emotions.
"The Makah whale hunters should go harpoon themselves," raged one
(http://www.nicksrant.com/nr05181999.html). Tizon's article (1999: A16)
includes some lurid examples, including these two:

> I am anxious to know where I may apply for a license to kill Indians.
> My forefathers helped settle the west and it was their tradition to kill
> every Redskin they saw. "The only good Indian is a dead Indian," they
> believed. I also want to keep faith with my ancestors.

> They are a modernized welfare race. I personally hate the Makah Tribe.
> I hope and pray for a terrible end to the Makah Tribe, very slow and
> very painful.

The reactions even included some positive affirmations of racism of a
kind rarely seen in mainstream society in the 1990s.

> Others, . . . however, said: "Yes, my comments are racist. But when the
> entire race of Indians support the killing of a whale, I guess anybody
> who opposes the hunt . . . suddenly finds themselves being a racist. I
> guess being a racist is not that bad when I consider the alternative."
> And one writer who identified himself only as Tony said: "While it
> would bother me to be termed a racist, it bothers me more that whaling
> has resumed in the Pacific Northwest. If the Makah wish to label me a
> racist then I guess most of the country is racist against them." (Tizon
> 1999: A17)

Having now seen the context to which the earlier manipulations of
Ecologically Noble Savage rhetoric led in the developing debate over the
Makah hunt, we may be in a better position to understand its significance.
Clearly, we are dealing with more than rhetorical issues, and the colonialist, racist, and genocidal feelings expressed by so many of the hunt's opponents arise from deeper and wider sources than the presence of one
catchphrase or discursive theme. But, equally clearly, the interjection and
manipulation of a polarized opposition of nobility/savagery based on the
Ecologically Noble Savage literature raised the verbal and emotional tem-
perature of the hunt's opponents, creating an unresolved tension that undoubtedly lent its energy to the strength of the violent outbursts against
the Makah and against Indians in general. With the Indians implicitly but
inexorably cast in the role of "savages" by the framing of the discourse, the
righteous violence of their nobly motivated opponents would inevitably
burst out against them.

> Natives were often referred to as "savages," and it seems little has
> changed. God Bless America and all those members of the Makah tribe
> who once again were successful in resurrecting latent feelings of racial
> hatreds. (Cited in Tizon 1999: A16)

Thus, while the predictions of the Ecologically Noble Savage literature
that romantic expectations of ecological "nobility" might lead to a backlash
against indigenous peoples perceived as violating those expectations were,
in a sense, borne out by the reactions to the Makah whale hunt, the existence of the literature itself provided an ideological and rhetorical weapon

for opponents to encourage the development of such expectations, and so intensify the violence of the reaction to them in their attacks on the Makah. It seems doubtful that any Ecologically Noble Savage theorist would have predicted such an outcome. It also may seem ironic that it was ultimately directed against the Makah, who might, after all, be thought to have something like a legitimate claim to "ecological nobility"—or, at least, to a "conservation ethic"—by virtue of their having given up whaling long before any white nation did so, when the whale populations were becoming depleted. But such a conclusion also seems unlikely, given the highly idealistic standards by which a "conservation ethic" is defined in Ecologically Noble Savage theory. Since the Makah abandonment of whaling had occurred only after they became aware that substantial population losses had already occurred, surely any Ecologically Noble Savage theorist would have characterized their actions in terms of some variant of "epiphenomenal" conservation—perhaps "expostfactorial" conservation?—to distinguish it from "genuine" conservation, which would require a combination of altruism and foresight that no culture has ever attained. But, if so, then Ecologically Noble Savage theory is as substantively empty as any other form of Noble Savage discourse, and it is hardly surprising that its role in the Makah debate was reduced to that of a weapon for rhetorical attacks and an intensifier of emotional diatribes that ultimately crossed the line into open advocacy of genocide. For this, after all, was why Noble Savage discourse was invented in the first place.

Conclusion

Sometimes, we must recognize, smoke leads us neither to a fire nor to a smoking gun but only draws us deeper into a smoke screen. The myth of the Noble Savage has succeeded in its intended purpose of obfuscation. It draws us in by its invitation to an act of disbelief in an apparent absurdity, surely an attractive prospect to any inquiring or critical mind. It invites us to consider the nature of savages, to see whether they in fact are or could ever be noble. In so doing, it diverts our attention toward particular peoples and their advocates and defenders and away from its own concealed assumptions; toward its substantive objects of reference and away from its rhetorical manipulations. By accepting the invitation, we accept the rhetorical construction of certain peoples as "savages"; and by accepting the challenge to prove or disprove their nobility, we accept the validity of an essentializing distinction of human worth drawn ultimately from the ideology of feudalist class values. To either deny or affirm the nobility of savages is to accept the terms of the myth's own construction, and so to affirm the construction of marginalized peoples in terms of their wildness, cruelty, or inhumanity and assert the superiority of values epitomized in the idealization of class differences into virtues. There *is* such a thing as nobility, there *are* such people as savages—and we imagine the absurdity to lie in the juxtaposition of the two rather than in our failure to problematize either.

Thus our commitment to an act of critical disbelief has generated a rather spectacular convergence of acts of unquestioning faith. No wonder the myth has had a run of unbroken success for nearly a century and a half. How could we even be willing to consider the possibility that we might have been such unwitting victims? And even if we were, how could we begin to expose the myth to the mundane light of historical and critical inquiry? Recently, there have been some signs of movement toward the beginnings of a more critical approach. Wilcomb Washburn and Bruce Trigger (1996: 72), for example, have referred to "the so-called myth of the Noble Savage"; and Gordon Sayre (1997: 124) points out that "critics of works containing some of what were once considered the most famous Noble Savages have declared that they are in fact not to be found there." But Washburn and Trigger (1996: 72) also refer to "the noble savage as conceptualized by Jean-Jacques Rousseau"; and Sayre (1997: 124) refers repeatedly to "the Noble Savage trope"—as if "tropes" normally exist as disembodied ideal essences in the absence of the verbal expressions on which they are grounded. All such incipient critiques, in other words, are fatally compromised by uncritical acceptance of the myth's own rhetorical polarities of nobility versus savagery, which inexorably draws discussion back into the circular entrapment of dealing with substantive issues and features of a world generated and constrained entirely by the terms in which we consent to frame it.

Historical and critical investigation remains impossible as long as we remain focused on the substance of the myth; for it defines reality in its own terms and constructs its own objects in whatever time frame we might attempt to project it into. It cannot fail to hypostatize visceral perceptions of racial contrasts into significant entities, or to absurdify tolerance and sympathy into foolish idealism, no matter where we apply it. Myths are by nature timeless; and the myth of the Noble Savage will inevitably generate more or less noble and ignoble savages, and corresponding representations of them, in every imaginable spatiotemporal context. As a substantive object of investigation, it has no history, and can never have one.

But as a rhetorical construct, the Noble Savage indeed has a history, one grounded in the dual time points of Lescarbot's invention of the Noble Savage concept in 1609 and Crawfurd's construction of the myth as we know it in 1859. Since the two crucial manifestations of what seems to be the same rhetorical construct have such apparently radically different meanings, however, the identification of dates only situates us in a matrix of interwoven historical problems. Obviously, each of the two dates presents its own problems for understanding how and why the Noble Savage was projected as a basic element in the construction of an imagined anthropological discipline, appropriate to its own temporocultural context. These problems have framed the beginning and ending of our investigation.

Next the process of transformation of meanings of the Noble Savage in the two hundred fifty years between 1609 and 1859 occupied our attention, projected in terms of a sketch of the history of the rhetoric of nobility. Neither this investigation nor selective attention to the question of representations of substantive nobility provided convincing proof of a significant presence, much less predominance, of Noble Savage imagery or beliefs in the ethnographic and derivative literatures between the writings of Lescarbot and Crawfurd. Much of what has previously been taken as expression of belief in the Noble Savage we now find to be the lingering transformations of the Golden Age discourse of comparative negation and the dialectic of vices and virtues, playing itself out in oscillating interaction with the opposing energies and increasingly negativizing forces of Enlightenment sociocultural evolutionary progressivism and nineteenth-century racism. Manifestations of the rhetoric of nobility reveal themselves to be contingent and attributive evocations of aesthetic nobility and the nobility of distinction. The many sightings of the Noble Savage since Crawfurd invented the myth in 1859 turn out to have no more enduring solidity than the myriad observations before the Copernican revolution of the movements of the sun and planets around the earth. The Noble Savage, taken either as a rhetorical or as a substantive construct, as an object of narrative representation or of belief, had no more reality than that which could be artificially and anachronistically projected onto the past by a post-Crawfurdian retrospective imagination.

Or so it would seem. One of the inevitable results of this study will be a rush of new sightings of Noble Savage manifestations, and one of its most useful results would be an enhanced critical attention to the meaning of constructing and projecting a label such as "the Noble Savage" back into its own prehistory. This would at least have the benefit of incorporating a critical examination of our own thoughts and motivations into the picture, where they properly belong. Ultimately, some of the Noble Savage sightings might even survive such a reflexively critical scrutiny and form the basis for a new conception that requires neither absolute affirmation nor denial of their existence. This would certainly lead to a more complex and sophisticated level of understanding than it is possible to achieve in this first attempt. But for a first attempt at a critical treatment, the simpler viewpoint projected here seems a satisfyingly polemic response to what was, after all, a polemic construct, and a satisfactory stimulus to further discussion.

Admittedly, this study raises more questions than it answers. Although at first glance it would appear to be a study of the history of ideas, it leaves us wondering whether there was actually any "idea" of the Noble Savage between Lescarbot's highly specific invention of the concept of savage nobility, Dryden's syntactic rearrangement of its terms into the phrase "noble Savage," with its transformed implications of feudalistic heroism, and

Crawfurd's even more radical transformation of it into a sarcastic emblem of racial inferiority. As an outline of the history of a particular rhetoric—or, more accurately, of the convergence of the two rhetorics of savagery and nobility—it is obviously only a sketch of an investigation that logically should encompass two and a half centuries of work in several literary genres and languages. In choosing an approach that favors relatively extensive discussions of examples that I take as representative of significant trends in particular genres and historical periods, I have omitted mention and discussion of some other occurrences of the rhetoric of nobility that I know of; and there are certainly many more that will have escaped my attention. I have largely avoided considering the issue of the presence of the Noble Savage in literary fiction, partly because of the extent of specialized critical literature available, partly because of the special kinds of professional priorities and techniques of representation engaged in by its authors, and largely because of my sense that scholarship in this area is especially contaminated by lengthy and extensive exposure to the assumptions of Noble Savage mythology. It may nevertheless call for special treatment of a kind I feel unable to give it.

Finally, my focus on the literature of travel-ethnography and anthropological theory may have omitted notice of predecessors of the Noble Savage constructions of Lescarbot or Crawfurd, or both. Many works referring in one way or another to the "savage" were published before Lescarbot, and Crawfurd may well have drawn on earlier sources—as he clearly did in his promotion of "missing link" mythology—to aid in his introduction of the Noble Savage into the mainstream of anthropological discourse. If such sources can be found, say, in the popular, political, or journalistic literature before Crawfurd's presentation of the Noble Savage paper to the Ethnological Society in April 1859, they would add further dimensions of interest and complexity to our discussion. In their absence, we can at least reflect on a few implications of the evidence we have considered so far.

Realizing that the myth of the Noble Savage was a political and polemical fabrication of the racist anthropology movement in nineteenth-century Britain helps to clarify the enigmatic character of its history in the English language. We have noted the term's polemic character, so distinct from the French *bon sauvage* and related terms in other languages. In French, *sauvage* does not necessarily connote either fierceness or moral degradation; it may simply mean "wild," as in *fleurs sauvages*, "wildflowers." The term once carried this kinder and gentler connotation in English as well,[1] although it does so no longer. For example, Dryden, who picked up and used Lescarbot's term "noble savage," also wrote in 1697, "Thus the salvage Cherry grows . . ." (*OED*, "Savage," A, I, 3). And Shelley, whom we have met with as the author of one of three possible other recorded uses of the term "noble savage" in pre-1860s English literature, wrote in 1820 in his *Ode to Liberty*, "The vine, the corn, the olive mild, Grew savage yet, to human use unreconciled . . ." (*OED*, "Savage," A, I, 3).

Thus we see that not only did writers previously taken as believers in the myth of the Noble Savage use the term "savage" with a simple connotation of wildness, remote from any moral or even human implication, applicable even to the cherry and the "mild" olive, but also this nonpolemic usage continued in English until well into the nineteenth century. Can we rule out the likelihood that this long-standing English usage was finally destroyed only by the transformation of the term into an ideological weapon through the fabrication of the racist anthropological myth of the "Noble Savage"?

And it may be the case that the same kind of transformation, driven by the same pernicious influence that effected the change in English usage, is slowly creeping into other languages as well. A few recent articles in French (e.g., Trudel 1996: 7 ff.; Duvernay-Bolens 1998: 143) have abandoned the long-established *bon sauvage* in favor of a new expression, *noble sauvage*; and some German scholars use *edle Wilde*, "Noble Savage," in place of *gute Wilde*, "good savage" (Bitterli 1976: 367 ff.; Sammet 1992: 932). Such cases seem rather obvious imitations of English usage, often arising in the context of explicit references to English writers such as Berkhofer (1978, cited in Trudel 1996: 8) and Lovejoy and Boas (Lovejoy et al. 1935, cited in Bitterli 1976: 371) in whose writings the "Noble Savage" plays a prominent role. Nor is it clear that the English-derived usage is moving toward general acceptance in these languages, particularly in French; for many French writers continue to use *bon sauvage* (e.g., Todorov 1989; Doiron 1991; Guille-Escuret 1992), just as some (but perhaps fewer) German writers retain the term *gute Wilde* (e.g., Kohl 1981).

But, looking beyond questions of language, it may be time for a reality check. If the issues we are dealing with are only historical and discursive, why should a reader flinch at Fairchild's condemnation of a slave longing for freedom as evidence of the "Noble Savage" as yet another example of "romantic naturalism" and European sentimental fawning over the imagined goodness of darker races? If freedom from oppressive laws is a Western romantic fantasy projected onto the Other, why should the seventeenth-century Tibetan author of the *Great Law Code of Gtsang*, who never knew of a Western audience, much less wrote for one, have denounced the laws of "barbarians" such as the Mongols and the Chinese as too strict and cruel, in the first case, and as too numerous and complex, in the second? No, clearly the urge for freedom and something like human rights, by whatever name they might be called, and a distrust for complex and oppressive laws are not simply romantic fantasies projected on exotic others by the European mind. After all, in life, just as in Western adversarial jurisprudence, there are those who suffer the verdict of winners and losers; those condemned to a lifetime of servitude and those who forfeit their lives.

Still, it may at least be possible to argue that issues of life, death, and truth are secondary. Gaile McGregor suggests,

> If it is important to note the extent of the retrospective distortion and oversimplification to which [Rousseau] has been subjected, it is, however, equally important, at least for present purposes, to realize that what he was perceived as saying has just as much relevance to the history of primitivism as what he really did say. In terms of influence exerted, in fact, such popular generalizations probably contributed more to the development of the noble savage convention than the comparatively complex ideas that may be more authentically attributed to the man himself. . . . It was quite predictable, indeed—considering these covert public pressures—that Rousseau's temperate exposition of savagery would be misinterpreted along exactly the lines we have noted. The fact is, despite his carefully iterated personal reservations about primitivism, Rousseau himself—as much as any, a product of inherited cultural predispositions—inadvertently invited such a reading. (1988: 20–21)

It would probably be going too far to point out the similarity of such an argument to that by which a rape victim, "despite [her] carefully iterated personal reservations," is judged to have "inadvertently invited" an attack. But we can certainly ask, are innocence and resistance irrelevant? Is it simply "just as relevant" to take into consideration "popular generalizations" in some times and places as, for example, the inferiority of certain races, even if as "products of inherited cultural predispositions [sic]," they exhibit characteristics that can be misinterpreted and distorted to serve as the basis for accusations and attacks? And are dead philosophers any less deserving of justice than other victims of such attacks? Justice for the dead is a major and near-universal concern in human relations and international jurisprudence; we hear appeals for it every day from Bosnia and Kosovo, from Rwanda and Burundi, from Cambodia, from families of American crime victims and the unjustly accused. Why exclude French philosophers? If Dr. Sam Sheppard, Dr. Samuel Mudd, and the Rosenbergs can be subjects of appeals to have their names cleared, why not Rousseau?

But then even some who take things such as truth, justice, intent, and the person as problematic constructs would still react with reluctance, if not repugnance, to propositions such as those advanced by McGregor. Regardless of ethics, moreover, scholars might at least worry that cavalier inaccuracy is an obvious index of incompetence. And anyone, scholar or not, who knew the function of the Noble Savage–Rousseau myth in the racist project of the 1850s and 1860s might have enough pride and intelligence not to continue lending intellectual support to such a bankrupt and questionable project that too many past generations, anthropologists, critics, and others, have already invested far too much credulity and energy in.

I find all these factors compelling enough to maintain that Rousseau's innocence is one of the most important points of this account. The issue was never the existence of something called "the Noble Savage," which neither Rousseau nor anyone else believed in; rather, it was Rousseau's generalized critique: "Man is born free, but everywhere he is in chains." This was a voice that had to be silenced, or at least discredited, especially in a discipline so closely linked to the subjects of his primary scientific and critical concerns. And thus I believe that the conclusion of a critical study of the myth is an appropriate place to offer an apology not only to those whom our predecessors wrongfully mislabeled as savages but also to Rousseau, who in trying to impart a little nobility to the future of civilized man became the sacrificial victim of our own discipline's lingering accommodation with the forces of hatred and ignorance.

To exonerate Rousseau on this one point, of course, does not absolve him from other legitimate critiques of his scholarly and ethical flaws, nor does it entail any necessity of wholesale subscription to either his ideas or those of the "Enlightenment" in general. Indeed, we have already seen how Rousseau stands in opposition to such putative Enlightenment ideals as the quest for disinterested knowledge, part of the tendency toward an ultimately dehumanizing hyperrationalism that has increasingly come under criticism in twentieth-century scholarship. Thus, for example, in *Dialectic of Enlightenment* (1944), Horkheimer and Adorno, refugees from "the self-destruction of the Enlightenment" (xiii) in the brutal chaos of fascist totalitarianism, find in the rationalism of the Enlightenment the seeds of its own destruction.

> For the Enlightenment, whatever does not conform to the rule of computation and utility is suspect. So long as it can develop undisturbed by any outward repression, there is no holding it. In the process, it treats its own ideas of human rights exactly as it does the older universals. . . . Bourgeois society is ruled by equivalence. It makes the dissimilar comparable by reducing it to abstract quantities. To the Enlightenment, that which does not reduce to numbers, and ultimately to the one, becomes illusion. (Horkheimer and Adorno 1944: 6–7)

But if their critique of the internal faults of the Enlightenment is uncompromisingly deconstructive, it is not entirely hostile or destructive. Concerning the motivations and goals of their critique, they say,

> The point is rather that the Enlightenment *must consider itself*, if men are not to be wholly betrayed. The task to be accomplished is not the conservation of the past, but the redemption of the hopes of the past. . . . The accompanying critique of enlightenment is intended to prepare the way for a positive notion of enlightenment which will release it from entanglement in blind domination. (Horkheimer and Adorno 1944: xv–xvi)

Michel Foucault (1965, 1977), whose work on the history of mental and penal institutions constitutes a profound critique of Enlightenment-derived ideas and practices, says, "The 'Enlightenment,' which discovered the liberties, also invented the disciplines" of authoritarian coercion and control over theoretically equal subjects (Foucault 1977: 222). But Foucault, in his essay "What Is Enlightenment?" also says,

> The thread that may connect us with the Enlightenment is not faithfulness to doctrinal elements, but rather the permanent reactivation of an attitude—that is, of a philosophical ethos that could be described as a permanent critique of our historical era. . . . This ethos implies, first, the refusal of what I like to call the "blackmail" of the Enlightenment. I think that the Enlightenment, as a set of political, economic, social, institutional, and cultural events on which we still depend in large part, constitutes a privileged domain for analysis. I also think that as an enterprise for linking the progress of truth and the history of liberty in a bond of direct relation, it formulated a philosophical question that remains for us to consider. . . .
>   But that does not mean that one has to be "for" or "against" the Enlightenment. It even means precisely that one has to refuse everything that might present itself in the form of a simplistic and authoritarian alternative: you either accept the Enlightenment and remain within the tradition of its rationalism (this is considered a positive term by some

and used by others, on the contrary, as a reproach); or else you criticize the Enlightenment and then try to escape from its principles of rationality (which may be seen once again as good or bad). . . .

We must try to proceed with the analysis of ourselves as beings who are historically determined, to a certain extent, by the Enlightenment. Such an analysis implies a series of historical inquiries that are as precise as possible; and these inquiries will not be oriented retrospectively toward the "essential kernel of rationality" that can be found in the Enlightenment and that would have to be preserved in any event; they will be oriented toward the "contemporary limits of the necessary," that is, toward what is not or is no longer indispensable for the constitution of ourselves as autonomous subjects. (1984: 42–43)

Considering the issue in these terms, could it still be credibly argued that a deliberate misinterpretation of the Enlightenment, by the continued misattribution of the Noble Savage fantasy to Rousseau's authorship or inspiration, is a help in, rather than a hindrance to, "the constitution of ourselves as autonomous subjects"?

But however important it may be, the reassessment of Rousseau's historical significance cannot be the endpoint of our discussion. After all, the myth of the Noble Savage was constructed a hundred years after the *Discourse on the Origins of Inequality* and played a strategically important role in manipulating the confluence of contemporary scholarly, popular, and political currents of the time, a time long after Rousseau's writing. It still continues to do so at the beginning of the twenty-first century. Not only has the myth not faded into historical obscurity with the passing of the particular circumstances that engendered it, and not only has it undergone multiple reframings and revitalizations over the decades; ultimately, it has succeeded in far outstripping the bounds of its anthropological origin and penetrated broadly and deeply into the conceptual-discursive worlds of scholarly and popular culture.

Where does the continuing negative energy of Noble Savage rhetoric come from? Fairchild (1928: 498–511), in his conclusion to *The Noble Savage*, delivers a passionate defense of his faith in rationality; denunciation of the Noble Savage is for him a denunciation of certain dark, irrational forces that he sees rising to threaten civilization. He does not identify these forces. Judging by similarities of polemic rhetoric of the time, we might suspect communism or trade unionism as likely candidates, but he does not name his target, and other intellectual or aesthetic trends of the 1920s are equally possible. The more important point is the perception of the existence of an enemy that threatens the balance of existing culture and institutions and the myth of the Noble Savage as a weapon in the ideological war against it. And this war extends beyond the 1850s and the 1920s; its continuing strength is behind the survival of the Noble Savage myth for so many years after Fairchild's partial exposure of its falsity.

Fairchild was a minor figure in a wave of critical studies of "exoticism," "primitivism," "romantic naturalism," and related topics that developed among French and American literary critics and historians of ideas in the periods preceding the outbreaks of the two world wars. Leading figures in the movement included Arthur Lovejoy (1923), Geoffroy Atkinson (1924), George Boas (Lovejoy et al. 1935), and, above all, Gilbert Chinard (1911, 1913, 1931). Chinard stands out not only because of his chronological precedence and encyclopedic scholarship but above all because of the vehemence of his rhetoric. He was, perhaps, the person most responsible for resurrecting and revitalizing the myth of the Noble Savage for the twentieth century. Even though, as a good French scholar, his focus of interest was *le bon sauvage*, Chinard nevertheless replicates the logic and intensifies the rhetoric of the Crawfurdian myth in his fervent attack on the person he sees as the most insidious enemy of Western civilization, Jean-Jacques Rousseau.

In one instance, Chinard (1913: 363) even mirrors the rhetoric of the myth: "To place 'natural man' such as Rousseau conceives him at the very root of our genealogical tree, is to give a certificate of nobility, and better still, of goodness and virtue, to all humanity." This was entirely unacceptable. Chinard's concern, he tells us, is with the literary image of the "savages" rather than with determining their true nature; but, in the heat of his attack on Rousseau and his philosophical contemporaries, he finally abandons restraint far enough to venture this opinion: "The savages remained none the less savages. With all their virtues, they belonged to a race different from ours; separated from us by thousands of miles, no visible connection existed between them and us" (1913: 361).

Although, as we have seen, Lovejoy and Fairchild quickly and definitively refuted the association of Rousseau with the Noble Savage myth, Chinard stood alone as the last scholar to devote serious attention to Rousseau's writings and still lend support to the myth. But, in fact, Chinard's opposition to Rousseau is part scholarly criticism and part political polemic, assuming the form of an indictment against Rousseau's "crimes" (Chinard 1913: 361) and "sins" (357). He compares Rousseau with Lahontan, whom he sees as a crude precursor:

Even though Lahontan spent his time abroad, one could not say that he did not exercise any influence on his contemporaries. . . . We have indicated in passing that which Diderot and Rousseau may owe to him; it is Jean-Jacques, more than any other author, that the author of the *Dialogues with a Savage* resembles. With all his faults, his fundamentally ignoble motives, he has put into his style a passion, an enthusiasm which has no equivalent except in the *Discourse on Inequality*. Like Rousseau, he is an anarchist; like him, he is bereft of moral sensibility, and to a considerably greater degree; like him, he imagines himself to be the prey of persecutions of the human race leagued against himself; like him, he is indignant about the sufferings of the miserable and, even more than him, he throws out the call to arms; and like him, above all, he attributes to property all the evils that we suffer. In this, he permits us to establish a direct connection between the Jesuit missionaries and Jean-Jacques. (1913: 186)

Wait a minute, we have to pause and ask, what is Chinard talking about here? Some kind of anarchist movement perpetrated by Lahontan, the Jesuits, and Rousseau? Is this a conspiracy theory to explain the French Revolution? Yes, as it turns out, it almost is; the Jesuits have promoted "dangerous ideas" in giving us the impression of the good qualities of "savages," and "this impression seems to have been contrary to the interests of the monarchical state and religion" (Chinard 1913: 149). He goes on to ask, "To praise the goodness of the savages and the wisdom with which they conduct the affairs of the nation in their councils, isn't this to indirectly criticize our governmental system?" (149). He proceeds further to accuse them of a number of other subversive activities, such as "reproducing the discourse of the savages" and "faithfully reporting their naïve, natural and reasonable objections," culminating in "furnishing the unbelievers with all of the [ideological] weapons which they could desire" (149–50). He concludes by warning darkly: "The *philosophes* of the 18th century would come; their ideas would find a ground well prepared" (150). In fact, Chinard's fundamental characterization of Rousseau is "un continuateur des missionaires Jésuites" (341 ff.), and the missionaries were instrumental in giving rise to "the revolutionary spirits [who] would transform our society and, inflamed by reading their relations, bring us back to the state of the American savages" (187).

I would not go so far as to say that the French Revolution had for its unique authors the excellent missionaries whom we have studied; they have nonetheless contributed in great part to that spirit of revolution that increasingly spread throughout the 18th century. (187)

It is no wonder that Chinard, in speaking of the missionaries, uses the expression *les bons pères* as often as he does *le bon sauvage*. The contempt for simple-minded advocates of "goodness" and equality who would— even if inadvertently—threaten the established order is unmistakable. Even Lescarbot, with his theory of terrorism against the "savages," characterized by Chinard as "neither . . . a pessimist nor . . . an enemy of civilization, and . . . very simply and sincerely Christian" (1913: 111) and taken as a key figure in defining *le bon sauvage*, becomes *le bon Lescarbot* (365)! Seemingly, the only ones to escape damnation by "goodness" are Lahontan and Rousseau; for their implication in the "sins" and "crimes" that led to revolutionary change are far more transgressive than mere simple-minded goodness.

But, ultimately, the force driving Chinard's attack is not the dead weight of history but rather a powerful political vector that projects from the past into the present.

> Rebelling against every constraint, against every law, against every superiority, the Baron de Lahontan or [his editor] Gueudeville, it matters little which [!], and his American savage are, speaking properly, anarchists. The *Dialogues with a Savage* is neither a political treatise nor a scholarly dissertation; it is the clarion call of a revolutionary journalist; that which Lahontan proclaims is not only Jean-Jacques Rousseau, it is Père Duchesne[2] and the modern socialist revolutionaries. (Chinard 1913: 185)

Thus it seems to be no accident that, just as the Noble Savage myth was propagated in a period of impending wars and the revolutionary "specter . . . haunting Europe," so also its twentieth-century resurrection and escalation arises in an atmosphere of buildup to world war and looming socialist revolution in which, as in the French Revolution, subordinate classes or peoples might rise up to threaten the established order.

In this, we sense the closing of a circle; or perhaps better, the recurrent swelling of a cyclic current extending all the way back to Lescarbot's generation of the Noble Savage concept. When Lescarbot departed from France on his voyage to Canada, his expedition prepared to sail in the port of La Rochelle, a Protestant community known for a certain emphasis on moral rectitude.

> But the workmen, through their good cheer (for they had every one two shillings a day's hire) did play marvellous pranks in Saint Nicholas quarter, where they were lodged, which was found strange in a town so reformed as La Rochelle is, in the which no notorious riots nor dissolu-

tions be made; and indeed one must behave himself orderly there. . . .
Some of those disordered men were put in prison, which were kept in
the town-house till the time of going. . . . I will not, for all that, put in
the number of this disordered people, all the rest, for there were some
very civil and respective. But I will say that the common people is a
dangerous beast. And this maketh me remember the Croquans' war,
amongst whom I was once in my life. . . . This confused people had
neither rhyme nor reason among them; everyone was Master there.
(Lescarbot 1609c: 64–65)

Stories and symbols are cultural attractors invested with human creative energies that may come out of, and be in one sense "about," the past;
but their origin gives them a vector of movement through the present and
on into some projection of the future that attracts a renewed investment of
constructive energy as long as humans can imagine their potential force.
Thus Renaissance humanists invested such energy in the discursive sym-
bolism of the polarity between "mine and thine," *meum et tuum*, that attracted renewed investment of energy in the generation of a critique of
property, privilege, and power over the four hundred years from Martyr to
Rousseau to Marx and beyond, but also attracted the oppositional energies
of Lescarbot and other defenders of orders of hierarchical dominance and
privilege.

In its turn, the Noble Savage myth, once constructed and adopted into
anthropological and general discourse, becomes a symbolic attractor that
draws to itself the cultural energies invested in all kinds of other symbols,
ideas, and programs of action—even some that are directly opposed to the
vector of the original impetus that set it in motion. Tylor (1871: 11), despite his declaration of relief that his evolutionist reorientation of anthropology made it possible to disregard questions of race, nevertheless accepted the hierarchy of superior and inferior races as a background or
substrate of the avowedly deracialized evolutionary theoretical foreground
he projected. Anthropology could thus continue on its Crawfurdian racist
vector, at the price of a certain fundamental dissimulation or dishonesty,
concealed by the critical smoke screen of the Noble Savage myth. Boas, on
the other hand, with his antiracist convictions shaping both foreground
constructions and background assumptions, surely has to be seen as a
source of oppositional energies, whose attraction to the Noble Savage myth
represents a compromise at once more tragic and more strategically limited, a contingent acceptance of the historical necessity of bowing to anthropology's need to observe the "paradigm of permissibility" (Flaherty
1992: 21 ff.) in order, in the long run, to continue the work of expanding

horizons that would ultimately compensate for minor strategic concessions along the way.

Anthropologists should certainly have developed an understanding of how powerful and privileged interests can manipulate symbols to reinforce and validate their own dominance over others. But if such an insight was ever gained in the field, it seems to have seldom enough been applied by anthropologists to the analysis of the relationships among power, rhetoric, and epistemology in their own culture; and it was certainly never applied to question the origin of the myth of the Noble Savage.

Rousseau himself, more astute in his understanding of the relationship of power to ideology than many subsequent practitioners of the discipline he promoted, warned,

> Destitute of solid Reasons to justify, and sufficient Forces to defend himself . . . the rich Man, thus pressed by Necessity, at last conceived the deepest Project that ever entered the Human Mind: this was to employ in his Favour the very Forces that attacked him, to make Allies of his Enemies, to inspire them with other Maxims, and make them adopt other Institutions as favourable to his Pretensions, as the Law of Nature was unfavourable to them. . . . With this View . . . he easily invented specious Arguments to bring them over to his Purpose. (1755a: 134–35)

And John Stuart Mill, the chief living target of Hunt's polemic, said,

> The tendency has always been strong to believe that whatever received a name must be an entity or being, having an independent existence of its own. And if no real entity answering to the name could be found, men did not for that reason suppose that none existed, but imagined that it was something peculiarly abstruse and mysterious. (Cited in Gould 1981: 350)

So it was with the myth of the Noble Savage, as it was with its contemporary myths of miscegenation and the missing link, the latter likewise promoted by Crawfurd as a symbolic counterforce to oppose any threat to existing balances of power and privilege. So also, in our own time, it is with rhetorical-mythological constructs such as "political correctness" and "special rights," evoked by dominant classes and their supporters to discredit and cripple any viable egalitarian opposition.[3] The ideological weapons they deployed—from appropriations of fragmentary truth derived from isolated cases of extreme rhetoric and behavior by a few of their opponents to the construction of emblematic absurdities used as polemic labels to discredit all conceivable opposition—remain the same; for the target, a group particularly susceptible to self-critique on questions of logical and ethical consistency, has repeatedly shown itself vulnerable to such attacks. Defenders of existing systems of oppression and subordination have always found it easy to evoke ideological phantoms and project them to encompass the limits of the imaginable universe; the only issue has been how to intensify the projection to more vividly impart a sense of impending threat and danger.

But anthropology may in fact have needed the Noble Savage myth, or something like it, to raise its own defensive smoke screen. As a field of study that by its nature inevitably opens doors to consideration of multiple cultural viewpoints and perspectives, it is always potentially subject to suspicions of disloyalty and subversion of its own culture and the forces that dominate it. This has been so from the first confrontations of Renaissance ethnographer-theorists with the Inquisition to the Boas censure and beyond.

In another study of problems in Renaissance theory (Ellingson n.d.), I raise the question of how the conflicts generated by the opposition between ethnology and the Inquisition were resolved after the Inquisition ended. The answer may be that the Inquisition never ended but was gradually transformed into a more secularized, less overtly violent, and less centrally institutionalized reactionary current that continued to bear down, with techniques and pressures adapted to changing times, on potentially subversive forces. Anthropology was one of these, particularly when brought into conjunction with the energizing forces of egalitarian concepts and the defense of human rights. Hunt's attempt to create an oppositional anthropology by neutralizing it into a science that excluded the ethics of "philanthropy" simply resulted in a reactionary scientistic politics of misanthropy that most serious scholars quickly turned away from.

Ultimately, a workable solution was found by anthropology's internalizing its own critique, and becoming its own Inquisition, by demonstrating a self-policing activity that would prevent it from forming loyalties to others that might endanger the entrenched wielders of power in the existing system of colonial dominance and racial subordination. Accepting the myth of the Noble Savage constituted an effective demonstration of loyalty. Affirmation of the sarcasm inherent in the term showed that anthropologists would never sell out or "go native," never cross the line that separated the "savage," as such irrevocably marked as an inferior being, from the Noble—still, in the last analysis, a status reserved not only for one side of the racial division that the myth helped to support but also, as the word implies, further restricted to a dominant elite.

Thus, once constructed, the Noble Savage myth becomes, to use John Pemberton's (1994: 11) term, a kind of "meta-spook" lurking in the background to haunt anthropological mindspace, ready to be ritually invoked to terrorize those who slip into the heresy of egalitarian "philanthropy" and defense of human rights. It has left us with a crippled language, but its effect is still more insidious. In the language of 1990s computer technology, Crawfurd succeeded in creating a discursive and conceptual virus, one that insinuates itself into our thought and words and scrambles our data and programs, ultimately corrupting our work and impairing our access to the most valuable part of the anthropological heritage: the critical awareness of our shared humanity that should have been anthropology's first and greatest gift to ourselves and the peoples we study.

Notes

INTRODUCTION

1. Indeed, Audrey Smedley (1993: 52ff.) argues, with good reason, that English conceptions of "the savage" were grounded in early expansionist conflicts with Irish pastoralists and, more broadly, in isolation from, and denigration of, neighboring European peoples. The ethnographic literature lends considerable support to such arguments. Yet emerging European views of "savagery" were the product of an international literature of exploration, widely circulated in translations, in which the experience of any single nation could play only a partial role in shaping the overall emergence of the concept. The common focus of all discussions, determined by shared new experience of a steadily growing number of nations, was the centrality of the American Indians in defining the nature of "savagery." In this process, the French played a greater role than other nations; Spanish discourse seems to have focused more on "barbarians" than on "savages" (Pagden 1982), and the English entered into the American colonial scene at a later date, after the terms of the discourse had already become established.

CHAPTER 1. COLONIALISM, SAVAGES, AND TERRORISM

1. Thus Lestringant (1997: 184) maintains that Montaigne's essay on cannibals "creates the figure of the Noble Savage," a position enabled by Lestringant's rather sweepingly substantivist view of the "real" existence of cannibals (e.g., Lestringant 1997: 7, 19) in the world at large, apart from their discursive representations, a topic that he treats with considerable sophistication.

2. Villegagnon was the military governor of the French Huguenot colony in Brazil described in Jean de Lery's (1578) ethnography, the richest ethnographic narrative of sixteenth-century America.

3. The ethnographic section of Lescarbot's work mixes together information about the Mi'kmaq and the neighboring Abenaki, in such a way that it is

not always clear which information pertains to which group. Since Lescarbot lived in much closer proximity to the Mi'kmaq, and consequently had more opportunities to observe them, this discussion assumes that he is generally referring to the Mi'kmaq if there are no indications to suggest otherwise.

CHAPTER 2. LESCARBOT'S NOBLE SAVAGE
AND ANTHROPOLOGICAL SCIENCE

1. Although Lescarbot's conclusion as to the Indians' forfeiture of rights resembles that of the Spanish theologian Sepulveda, Las Casas's opponent in the debate over Indian rights, it is based on reasoning that Spanish legalists had long rejected, that is, the priority of Christian claims over those of infidels (Pagden 1987: 90–92, 82–85). On the other hand, his argument that the Indians had wastefully disregarded and failed to exploit the resources available to them was an early evocation of a principle that would become fundamental to French and English colonial ideology, namely, the principle of *res nullius,* "empty things," which maintained that since true ownership of land depended on its use and improvement by agriculture, the Indians, stereotyped as wandering hunters, retained no right of ownership (Pagden 1995: 76 ff.).

2. There seem to be few sources that could have inspired Lescarbot to develop his Noble Savage theory. Lery (1578: 113) had written, in describing the warfare of the Tupinamba of Brazil, "They have neither kings nor princes, and consequently are all almost equally great lords"; and Montaigne (1588a: 46), primarily following Lery's ethnographic descriptions, called the warfare of the "cannibals" "noble and generous." We know that Lescarbot had at least read Lery, and both Chinard (1913: 109) and Atkinson (1924: 68) cite the general resemblance of his ideas to some of Montaigne's. It is certainly possible that some of his more relativistic statements might have been inspired by either Lery or Montaigne. However, despite their associations of nobility and warfare, neither author even comes close to enunciating a conception of savage nobility as fundamental or elaborate as Lescarbot's, which, moreover, is so inextricably rooted in Lescarbot's legal training and interests that there can be little doubt that he was its original author.

CHAPTER 5. SAVAGES AND THE PHILOSOPHICAL TRAVELERS

1. In the French edition, "mien et tien," that is, "mine and thine," the vernacular rather than the Latin form of the expression.

CHAPTER 6. ROUSSEAU'S CRITIQUE
OF ANTHROPOLOGICAL REPRESENTATIONS

1. Maurice Cranston, translator of the *Discourse on Inequality* and author of the most extensive recent biography of Rousseau (Cranston 1982, 1991),

calls the second volume of his biography *The Noble Savage;* but the title refers to Rousseau himself, and Cranston cites no instance of his use of the term.

2. Two centuries later, two other critics of civilization, Horkheimer and Adorno, would imagine a similar attack.

> You consider the existing power to be unjust—Do you want power to be replaced by chaos? You criticize the monotonous uniformity of life and progress—Shall we then light wax candles in the evening and allow our cities to be full of stinking refuse as they were in the Middle Ages? You do not like slaughter-houses—Is society to live on raw vegetables from now on? However absurd it may seem, the affirmative answer to questions such as these still falls on friendly ears. . . . A discussion between two young people: . . . A. Do you then maintain that there should be no doctors or that the old quacks should return? B. I did not say that. I am simply horrified at the prospect of becoming a doctor myself, especially a consultant with responsibility over a large hospital. Nevertheless, I consider it better for doctors and hospitals to exist than for sick people to be left to die. I also don't want to be a public prosecutor, yet I consider the existence of robbers and murderers to be a much greater evil than that of a system which sends them to prison. Justice is reasonable. I am not opposed to reason—I simply wish to define clearly the form it has taken. (Horkheimer and Adorno 1944: 237–38)

3. Precontact Makah also wore blankets of their own invention and manufacture, made from dogs' hair or cedar bark (Swan 1868: 15–16).

4. However, Smedley (1993: 230) puts this often-criticized aspect of Rousseau's life into a realistic context: "He even had to put his own five children . . . in a foundling home because he was too poor to feed them."

CHAPTER 7. THE ETHNOGRAPHIC
SAVAGE FROM ROUSSEAU TO MORGAN

1. Volney goes on to repeat a rumor that Rousseau's critique of civilized corruption had been a dishonest joke, first suggested to him by Diderot. Maurice Cranston, Rousseau's biographer, discounts this story; but in any case, if it were true, it would apply to the "First Discourse" on the arts and sciences rather than to the *Discourse on Inequality.*

2. Jacqueline Duvernay-Bolens (1998: 156), in an article published after this section was completed, states that "the thought of Volney represents an indispensable key" for understanding the shift from positive representations of "savages" exemplified by Lafitau to the raciocentric negativity of the nineteenth-century evolutionists. Her analysis stresses many of the points made here, with considerable more detail on the influence of changing theories of physiology.

3. Carl Resek's (1960) is the major scholarly biography of Morgan. A concise overview of Morgan's ethnographic work in relation to his theoretical stance is given by Robert E. Bieder (1986: 194–246).

CHAPTER 8. SCIENTISTS, THE ULTIMATE
SAVAGE, AND THE BEAST WITHIN

1. In this regard, Linnaeus's narrative might be seen as reflecting something like the sense of wonder that Greenblatt (1991) sees in explorers' narratives of America. As we have seen, Linnaeus's excitement was energized by a feeling that he, too, was exploring a New World.

2. Compare Rousseau's (1755b: 90) description of the savage: "His imagination paints no pictures; his heart yearns for nothing; his modest needs are readily supplied at hand; and he is so far from having enough knowledge for him to desire to acquire more knowledge, that he can have neither foresight nor curiosity."

CHAPTER 10. PARTICIPANT OBSERVATION
AND THE PICTURESQUE SAVAGE

1. Darwin had concluded that similar behavior by the Indians of Tierra del Fuego was evidence of inferior intellectual development, rather than "acting a part"; see above, chapter 8.

2. Since "appetizing" is obviously English in form, Murray's claim must be understood as having imported a French word—most likely *appettisant*—and adapting it into an Anglicized form. However, the *OED* cites uses of "appetizing" dating back to 1653. Thus the most Murray might conceivably have done is to reintroduce a term that had formerly been used in English but had fallen into neglect by Murray's time.

3. Catlin's commitment to the defense of Indian rights certainly had a strong component of self-interest, since he supported himself and his family through lectures and traveling exhibitions of his "Indian Museum" of paintings and artifacts and thus benefited from promoting public interest in them. Still, his defense of their rights was far stronger and more consistent than most writers of the period. His efforts at freelance promotion of his work eventually failed; but he still maintained his commitment to personal financial support of specific groups of Indians, even in the face of disastrous circumstances that led to his bankruptcy and perhaps to the ill health of his family and the deaths of his wife and son (McCracken 1959: 192–98).

4. He does, however, associate them with a related rhetoric of feudal knighthood, which nevertheless remains distinct in context and implication from his usage of "noble" and its derivatives.

CHAPTER 11. POPULAR VIEWS OF THE SAVAGE

1. Actually, the passage cited is already secondhand opinion in Moffat (1842: 57–58), who is quoting an earlier missionary's impressions of the Bush-

men. Moffat himself balances this negative assessment with a discussion of what he sees as the Bushmen's good qualities.

CHAPTER 13. RACE, MYTHMAKING, AND THE CRISIS IN ETHNOLOGY

1. On the other hand, cases such as the late-twentieth-century use of antidiscrimination rhetoric by proponents of anti–affirmative action laws, using the discourse of equality to perpetuate the effects of past racial discrimination, show the pitfalls of taking avowals of egalitarian intent at face value.

2. Kass and Kass (1988: 591) maintain that the theory, advanced by Keith (1917) and repeated by Stocking (1971), that a conflict in the Aborigines Protection Society between the "student party" and the "missionary party" led to the "forced" withdrawal of those who formed the Ethnological Society is a "misunderstanding" unsupported by the historical evidence.

3. Still later, they were reported as actually being African Americans, living in an Ohio insane asylum, from which it was claimed they had been procured in the first place and finally returned there when their popularity had worn out (Kunhardt, Kunhardt, and Kunhardt 1995: 150).

CHAPTER 14. HUNT'S RACIST ANTHROPOLOGY

1. The Jamaica massacre investigation committee was formed under the inspiration of Hunt's nemesis, John Stuart Mill, to pursue the investigation of Edward John Eyre, governor of Jamaica, for his role in the Morant Bay incident of October 1865 in which a protest by black former slaves against injustices led to mutual hostilities that resulted in the deaths of 18 whites and retaliatory killings of 439 blacks by Eyre's martial-law forces (Curtin 1955: 195–96). Huxley joined Darwin, Lyell, and eventually a total membership in the hundreds on the committee. The comparison with the African explorer du Chaillu's shooting gorillas is an obvious and typical example of Hunt's racial rhetoric.

CHAPTER 17. THE MYTH OF THE NOBLE SAVAGE

1. Advertisements earlier in the year had referred to the lecture as "The Art of Money Making." Barnum's autobiography, and his later biographers, give it the title, "The Art of Money-Getting."

2. Despite Barnum's image as a cynical exponent of the promotion of "humbugs," and despite the extent to which his "ethnological" exhibits may have profited from contemporary racist attitudes, it is at least questionable that he would have been entirely pleased with racist appropriation of his techniques. Later elected to the Connecticut State Legislature, his speech in support of voting rights for African Americans of May 26, 1865, with its passionate evoca-

tions of common humanity and racial equality and critique of "ethnological" rationalizations of racism, must stand as one of the nineteenth century's more eloquent acts of opposition to the triumph of racist ideology and practice (Barnum 1855–89: 575–88).

3. Bloxam (1893: 90) gives the date as April 18; but *Athenaeum* (April 4, 1859, 521; April 30, 1859, 585) records the date, in both the announcement and report of the meeting, as April 20. This would accord with the scheduling of meetings on the third Wednesday of the month, as agreed by the ESL Council in 1858.

4. Compare Dryden:

> I am as free as Nature first made man
> 'Ere the base Laws of Servitude began,
> When wild in woods the noble Savage ran.
>   (1672: 34)

5. Carlyle's diatribe is from his essay, "Occasional Discourse on the Nigger Question" (1849). The essay, containing some of the most egregiously offensive racist invective of the period, advocates a return to forced labor for the freed slaves of Jamaica as the starting point for a generalized attack on democracy and workers' freedoms in Europe. A rebuttal to Carlyle was published the following month by John Stuart Mill (1850).

CHAPTER 18. CRAWFURD AND THE BREAKUP OF THE RACIST ALLIANCE

1. Crawfurd is taking a dig here at Hunt's manipulation of titles within the Anthropological Society in order to allow others, such as Captain Richard Burton, to formally hold the office of president for the sake of publicity and name recognition while he remained in control under a different title.

2. This would place the admission of women to the society's meetings in 1861, but women had been occasionally admitted at least as early as 1857 at "Extra-Ordinary Meetings"(*ESL Minutes*, May 6, 1857, 234) where the normal male-only rules were temporarily relaxed. Their regular admission to "Ordinary" meetings was established under Crawfurd's presidency in 1860 (*ESL Minutes*, October 17–November 21, 1860, 261–62).

CHAPTER 19. CRAWFURD, DARWIN, AND THE "MISSING LINK"

1. Perhaps Lyell had read Greenwood's *Curiosities of Savage Life*: "It is somewhat more than doubtful whether the Esquimaux should be classed with the savage. True they have no religion, no political organization, are filthy in their habits and persons, and have a natural appetite for raw flesh and fish: still it may be easily enough shown that so far as the exigencies of locality and climate will permit they have adopted civilization; the best proof of this being that

Europeans cast among them for but a single generation become thoroughly Esquimaux in their habits, not by preference, but by sheer compulsion. Indeed to live with the Esquimaux the very first essential is to do as the Esquimaux do" (1863–64: 1:416–17).

2. The debate over transmutation was the result of Robert Chambers's anonymous publication a few years earlier of the *Vestiges of the Natural History of Creation* (1844), which argued for the transmutation of species.

3. "Special selection" here overtly refers to species; but in its opposition to the term "natural selection" used by Darwin and his followers, do we see a foreshadowing of the twentieth-century opposition of the polemic term "special rights" to terms such as "civil rights" and "human rights" by enemies of the latter?

EPILOGUE: THE MISCEGENATION HOAX

1. Barnum's only point challenged by later researchers is his attribution of coauthorship to "E. C. [actually S. C.] Howell." Bloch (1958: 62–65) and Wood (1968: 58) question Howell's contribution, mainly on the basis of a lack of contemporary corroborating evidence. But the doubt arises in the context of their taking the Howell attribution as an 1880 suggestion of Sabin, rather than a contemporary statement by Barnum. Given Barnum's intricate connections with the New York press and his apparent inside knowledge of the details of construction of the miscegenation hoax, his assertion of Howell's contribution is less easily dismissed than one made sixteen years after the event.

CHAPTER 21. THE ECOLOGICALLY NOBLE SAVAGE

1. Compare the following statements from *The Postmodernism Generator:*

"Art is dead," says Baudrillard; however, according to Bailey, it is not so much art that is dead, but rather the economy of art.

"Sexual identity is unattainable," says Lyotard; however, according to Ashwander, it is not so much sexual identity that is unattainable, but rather the praxis, and thus the futility, of sexual identity.

"Class is intrinsically used in the service of the hegemony of hierarchy over class," says Foucault; however, according to Bassett, it is not so much class that is intrinsically used in the service of the hegemony of hierarchy over class, but rather the collapse, and subsequent dialectic, of class.

"Narrativity is part of the stasis of art," says Baudrillard; however, according to Ardois-Bonnot, it is not so much narrativity that is part of the stasis of art, but rather the futility, and eventually the rubicon, of narrativity. (http://www.csse .monash.edu.au/cgi-bin/postmodern)

See also "The Surrealist Compliment Generator" (http://pharmdec.wustl.edu/ cgi-bin/jardin_scripts/SCG): for example, "Oh how my pathological scar desires to read poems through the ruddied girth of your soul!"

CHAPTER 22. THE MAKAH WHALE HUNT OF 1999

1. An expression reported by mid-nineteenth-century travelers to have been used by Maoris or other Polynesian islanders as a euphemism for human flesh as cannibal food.

CONCLUSION

1. Until the late fifteenth century, "savage" was also used in English in the positive sense of indomitable, intrepid, or valiant; the *OED* cites such usages as "an hardy knyght, stout and savage" and "a worthy clerk, bath wys and rycht sawage"(*OED*, "Savage," A, I, 7).

2. Duchesne, far from being a revolutionary socialist, was a Roman Catholic church historian who became embroiled in the early-twentieth-century controversy over "Modernism" in Catholic theology.

3. The myth of "political correctness," for example, makes creatively polemic use of decontextualized half-truths and extreme viewpoints and episodes to insinuate the operation of a totalitarian thought police established by a sinister, invisible authority to stifle free and natural self-expression—and in so doing, is characteristically invoked to divert attention from the victimization of the targets of racist and sexist attacks and to evoke sympathy for their attackers. The language itself reveals the hoax: are we to assume that the antidote for the purported problem is something like "political perversity"? But, of course, the absurdity of the expression provides a seductive catchphrase that lends itself to putdowns of real blunders, overreactions, and extremist postures; and so, like "the Noble Savage," the term is validated by appeal to a wider range of users than those whose political agenda it was created to serve. I will even use it myself in moments of barroom humor, but always with reflexive awareness of the leer lurking behind the smile. Most of the voluminous "PC" debate focuses, for quite understandable reasons, on substantive issues, and ultimately on the question of whether "it" does or does not "really" exist. But it also deserves a thoroughgoing historical-political examination as a rhetorical construct, a kind of study that, as far as I know, has yet to be done. Richard Feldstein takes the first steps toward such a rhetorical study in the first chapters of his *Political Correctness* (1997); but his "Brief History of the Term" (4–7) is just that, and the focus quickly shifts from PC-bashers' rhetoric to psychoanalytic reflections on their ego-projection conflicts.

References

[Aboriginal Committee] Great Britain. Parliament. House of Commons. Select
Committee on Aboriginal Tribes
1837   *Report of the Parliamentary Select Committee on Aboriginal
Tribes (British settlements).* Reprinted, with comments, by the
"Aborigines Protection Society." London: Published for the So-
ciety by W. Ball, A. Chambers, and Hatchard & Son.

Acerbi, Joseph [Giuseppe]
1802   *Travels through Sweden, Finland, and Lapland, to the North
Cape, in the Years 1798 and 1799.* London: Joseph Mawman.

Agassiz, Louis
1854   "Of the Natural Provinces of the Animal World and Their Relation to the Different Types of Man." In Nott and Gliddon
1854: lviii–lxxvi.

Ahmed, A.
1991   "Death of the Noble Savage." *New Statesman & Society* 4
(146): 16–17.

Alcorn, Janis
1993   "Indigenous Peoples and Conservation." *Conservation Biology*
7: 424–26.

Aleiss, Angela
1991   "Bon Sauvage: *Dances with Wolves* and the Romantic Tradition." *American Indian Culture and Research Journal* 15 (4):
91–95.

Altherr, Thomas L.
1985   "Tombo-Chiqui: Or, the American Savage: John Cleland's Noble
Savage Satire." *American Indian Quarterly* 9 (4): 411–20.

Alvard, Michael S.
1993   "Testing the 'Ecologically Noble Savage' Hypothesis: Inter-
specific Prey Choice by Piro Hunters of Amazonian Peru." *Human Ecology* 21 (4): 355–87.

1997   [Response to Headland 1997.] *Current Anthropology* 38 (4):
            609–11.
Astley, Thomas *See* Green, John
Athenaeum
    1830–1921 London: J. Lection.
Atkinson, Geoffroy
    1924   *Les Relations de Voyages du XVIIe Siècle et l'Evolution des
                Idees.* Paris: E. Champion.
[AR] Hunt, James, ed.; Anthropological Society of London
    1863–70   *Anthropological Review.* London: Trubner and Co.
Axtell, James
    1985   *The Invasion Within: The Contest of Cultures in Colonial
                North America.* New York: Oxford University Press.
[BAAS] British Association for the Advancement of Science
    1858   *Report of the Twenty-seventh Meeting of the British Associa-
                tion for the Advancement of Science; Held at Dublin in August
                and September 1857.* London: John Murray.
    1859   *Report of the Twenty-eighth Meeting of the British Associa-
                tion for the Advancement of Science; Held at Leeds in Septem-
                ber 1858.* London: John Murray.
Bannon, John F.
    1962   "Pierre-François-Xavier de Charlevoix, S.J." In Charlevoix
                1744b: 1, n.p.
Barnett, Louise K.
    1975   *The Ignoble Savage: American Literary Racism, 1790–1890.*
                Westport, Conn.: Greenwood Press.
Barnum, P. T. (Phineas Taylor)
    1855–89   *Struggles and Triumphs: Or, The Life of P. T. Barnum, Writ-
                ten by Himself.* Ed. George S. Bryan. New York: Knopf,
                1927.
    1865   *Humbugs of the World.* New York: Carleton. Facsimile reprint.
                Detroit: Singing Tree Press, 1970.
Barrow, John
    1804   *Travels in China.* London: T. Cadell and W. Davies.
Beddoe, John
    1859   "On the Physical Characteristics of the Jews." *Transactions of
                the Ethnological Society of London* 1 (1861): 222–37.
    1870   "President's Address." *Journal of the Anthropological Society
                of London* 8: lxxviii–lxxxiii.
    1910   *Memories of Eighty Years.* Bristol: Arrowsmith.
Belon, Pierre
    1553   *Les observations de plusieurs singularitez et choses memo-
                rables: Trouuees en Grece, Asie, Judee, Egypte, Arabie et autres
                pays estranges.* Paris: Guillaume Cauellat.

Berkhofer, Robert F., Jr.

1978   *The White Man's Indian: Images of the American Indian from Columbus to the Present.* New York: Knopf.

Biard, Pierre

1611   "Letter from Father Biard, to Reverend Father Christopher Baltazar, Provincial of France, at Paris." *Jesuit Relations* 1: 139–83.

Bieder, Robert E.

1986   *Science Encounters the Indian, 1820–1880.* Norman: University of Oklahoma Press.

Biggar, H. P.

1907   "Introduction: Marc Lescarbot." In Lescarbot 1609d: 1:ix–xv.

Bitterli, Urs

1976   *Die "Wilden" und die "Zivilisierten": Grundzüge einer Geistes- und Kulturgeschichte der europäish-überseeischen Begegnung.* Munich: Beck.

Bitton, Davis

1969   *The French Nobility in Crisis, 1560–1640.* Stanford: Stanford University Press.

Bloch, Julius M.

1958   *Miscegenation, Melaleukation, and Mr. Lincoln's Dog.* New York: Schaum.

Bloxam, George W.

1893   *Index to the Publications of the Anthropological Institute of Great Britain and Ireland, 1843–1891.* London: Anthropological Institute.

Boas, Franz

1889   *The Aims of Ethnology [Die Ziele der Ethnologie].* New York: Hermann Bartsch. English translation in George Stocking, ed., *A Franz Boas Reader: The Shaping of American Anthropology, 1883–1911.* Chicago: University of Chicago Press, 1989, pp. 67–71.

1904   "The History of Anthropology." Address at the International Congress of Arts and Science, St. Louis, September 1904, in *Science* 20: 513–24. Reprinted in H. J. Rogers, ed., *Congress of Arts and Science,* 5:468–82. Boston: Houghton Mifflin, 1906. Reprinted in George Stocking, ed., *A Franz Boas Reader: The Shaping of American Anthropology, 1883–1911,* 23–36. Chicago: University of Chicago Press, 1989.

Bodley, John H.

1997   [Response to Headland 1997.] *Current Anthropology* 38 (4): 611–13.

Bolyanatz, Alexander H.

1996   "The Sexual 'Noble Savage': Tahitians as Tilillators or Tacticians?" Paper presented at the annual meeting of the American Anthropological Association, San Francisco, November.

Brasser, T. J.
1978   "Early Indian-European Contacts." In Trigger, ed., 1978: 78–88.

Brodie, B. C.
1856   "Address to the Ethnological Society of London." *Journal of the Ethnological Society of London* 4: 294–97.

Buege, Douglas J.
1996   "The Ecologically Noble Savage Revisited." *Environmental Ethics* 18 (1): 71–88.

Burke, Luke
1848   "Outlines of the Fundamental Doctrines of Ethnology; or, the Science of the Human Races." *Ethnological Journal* 1 (1): 1–8; 1 (3): 129–41; 1 (5): 235–39.

Burton, Richard F.
1861   "Ethnological Notes on M. du Chaillu's 'Explorations and Adventures in Equatorial Africa.'" *Transactions of the Ethnological Society of London* N.S. 1: 316–26.

Callender, Charles
1978   "Miami." In Trigger, ed., 1978: 681–89.

Carlyle, Thomas
1849   "Occasional Discourse on the Nigger Question." *Fraser's Magazine* 40 (December): 670–79. Reprinted in H. D. Traill, ed., *The Works of Thomas Carlyle 29: Critical and Miscellaneous Essays 4*, 348–83. New York: AMS Press, 1969.

Carnap, Rudolf
1955   "Meaning and Synonymy in Natural Languages." *Philosophical Studies* 6 (3): 33–47.

Cartier, Jacques
1580   *A Shorte and Briefe Narration of the two Nauigations and Discoueries to the Northweast Partes called Newe Fraunce.* Trans. John Florio. London: H. Bynneman. Facsimile ed. Ann Arbor: University Microfilms, 1966.

Catlin, George
1841   *Letters and Notes on the Manners, Customs, and Condition of the North American Indians.* 8th ed. London: H. G. Bohn, 1851.

Chambers, Robert
1844   *Vestiges of the Natural History of Creation.* London: John Churchill. Reprint. Chicago: University of Chicago Press, 1994.

Champlain, Samuel de
1603   *Des savvages, ov, Voyage de Samvel Champlain.* Paris: Clavde de Monstr'œil. Reprinted with English translation in

H. P. Biggar, ed., *The Works of Samuel de Champlain*, 1:81–189. Toronto: Champlain Society, 1922–36.

1613a   *Les Voyages dv Sievr de Champlain*. Paris: Iean Berjon. Reprint. N.p.: Readex Microprint, 1966.

1613b   *Les Voyages dv Sievr de Champlain*. Paris: Iean Berjon. Reprinted with English translation in H. P. Biggar, ed., *The Works of Samuel de Champlain*, 1:189–469. Toronto: Champlain Society, 1922–36.

Chardin, John [Jean], Sir

1686   *Travels of Sr. Iohn Chardin into Persia and ye East Indies*. London: Moses Pitt.

Charlevoix, Pierre-François-Xavier de

1720–22a   *Journal d'un voyage fait par Ordre du Roi dans l'Amerique Septentrionnale*. In Charlevoix 1744a: vols. 5–6.

1720–22b   *Journal of a Voyage to North-America, Undertaken by Order of the French King*. London: R. and J. Dodsley, 1761. Facsimile reprint. Ann Arbor: University Microfilms, 1966.

1744a   *Histoire et description generale de la Nouvelle France*. Paris: Chez la veuve Ganeau. Microfiche. Ottawa: Canadian Institute for Historical Microreproductions, 1984.

1744b   *History and General Description of New France*. Ed. and trans. John Gilmary Shea. New York: J. G. Shea, 1868. Reprint. Chicago: Loyola University Press, 1962.

Chastellux, François-Jean, marquis de

1780–82   *Travels in North-America, in the Years 1780, 1781, and 1782*. Trans. George Grieve. London: G. G. J. and J. Robinson, 1787. [French ed. 1786.] Rev. ed. Howard C. Rice. Chapel Hill: University of North Carolina Press, 1963.

Chateaubriand, François-Auguste-René, vicomte de

1801a   *Atala; René; Les aventures du dernier Abencérage*. Introduction, notes, appendices et choix de variantes par Fernand Letessier. Paris: Garnier, 1958.

1801b   *Atala*. Trans. Irving Putter. Berkeley: University of California Press, 1980.

1802   *Génie du Christianisme*. Paris: Migneret.

1826   *Les Natchez*. Publies avec une introduction et des notes par Gilbert Chinard. Paris: E. Droz, 1932.

1827   *Travels in America*. Trans. Richard Switzer. Lexington: University of Kentucky Press, 1969.

1848–50   *Memoires d'outre-tombe*. Ed. du centenaire integrale et critique en partie inedite etablie par Maurice Levaillant. Paris: Flammarion, 1948.

Chinard, Gilbert

1911   *L'Exotisme Americain dans la litterature française au XVIe siècle*. Paris: Hachette.

1913	*L'Amerique et le reve exotique dans la litterature française au XVIIe et XVIIIe siècle.* Paris: E. Droz, 1934.
1931	Introduction to Lahontan 1703–5.
1932	Introduction and notes to Chateaubriand 1826.

Church, Alonzo

1950   "On Carnap's Analysis of Statements of Assertion and Belief." *Analysis* 10 (5): 97–99.

Collins, Cary C.

1996   "Subsistence and Survival: The Makah Indian Reservation, 1855–1933." *Pacific Northwest Quarterly* 87 (4): 181. http:// www.washington.edu/uwired/outreach/cspn/html/98winter/ article1.html.

Cook, M.

1997   "Bougainville and One Noble Savage: Two Manuscript Texts of Bernardin-de-Saint-Pierre." *Modern Language Review* 89: 842–55.

Cranston, Maurice

1982   *Jean-Jacques: The Early Life and Work of Jean-Jacques Rousseau, 1712–1754.* Chicago: University of Chicago Press, 1991.

1991   *The Noble Savage: Jean-Jacques Rousseau, 1754–1762.* Chicago: University of Chicago Press.

Crawfurd, John

1820   *History of the Indian Archipelago. Containing an Account of the Manners, Arts, Languages, Religions, Institutions, and Commerce of Its Inhabitants.* Edinburgh: Constable.

1821–25 *The Crawfurd Papers: A Collection of Official Records relating to the Mission of Dr. John Crawfurd sent to Siam by the Government of India in 1821.* Bangkok: Vajirañana National Library, 1915. Reprint. Westmead: Gregg International Publishers, 1971.

1834   *To the Inhabitants of the Borough of Marylebone.* London: John Crawfurd, 27, Wilton Crescent, Belgrave Square, 8th January 1834. Snell, Printer, Paddington. Two copies in *Broughton Papers*, vol. 5, ff. 208, 213. British Library Additional Manuscript 47,226.

1858   "On the Effects of Commixture, Locality, Climate, and Food on the Races of Man." *Transactions of the Ethnological Society of London* N.S. 1 (1861): 76–92. [Given at BAAS, September 1858; ESL, February 16, 1859]

1859a   "On the Conditions Which Favour, Retard, or Obstruct the Early Civilization of Man." *Transactions of the Ethnological Society of London* N.S. 1 (1861): 154–77. [Given at ESL, April 20, 1859]

1859b   Review of Darwin, *Origin of Species. Examiner*, December 3, 1859, 772–73.

1860　"On the Aryan or Indo-Germanic Theory." *Transactions of the Ethnological Society of London* N.S. 1 (1861): 268–85. [BAAS, July 1860; ESL, December 19?, 1860]

1861a　"On the Classification of the Races of Man." *Transactions of the Ethnological Society of London* N.S. 1: 354–78.

1861b　"On the Connexion between Ethnology and Physical Geography." *Transactions of the Ethnological Society of London* N.S. 2 (1863): 4–23. [ESL, November 1861]

1861c　*Ethnological Society of London: Special Statement.* In *Ethnological Society: Council Minute Book, Vol. 1.* RAI Library, Museum of Mankind. Call no. A 1.

1862　"On the Commixture of the Races of Man as Affecting the Progress of Civilization (Europe)." *Transactions of the Ethnological Society of London* N.S. 2 (1863): 201–13. [ESL, June 1862]

1863　"On the Relation of the Domesticated Animals to Civilization." *Transactions of the Ethnological Society of London* N.S. 2: 387–468.

1864a　Comments on Alfred Russell Wallace, "On the Progress of Civilisation in Northern Celebes," in "Anthropology at the British Association, A.D. 1864." *Anthropological Review* 2: 334.

1864b　"On the Early Migrations of Man." *Transactions of the Ethnological Society of London* N.S. 3 (1865): 335–50. [ESL, April 1864]

1864c　"On the Supposed Stone, Bronze, and Iron Ages of Society." *Transactions of the Ethnological Society of London* N.S. 4 (1866): 1–12.

1865a　"On the Commixture of the Races of Man as Affecting the Progress of Civilization." *Transactions of the Ethnological Society of London* N.S. 3: 98–122.

1865b　"On the Supposed Infecundity of Human Hybrids or Crosses." *Transactions of the Ethnological Society of London* N.S. 3: 356–62.

1866a　"On Cannibalism in Relation to Ethnology." *Transactions of the Ethnological Society of London* N.S. 4: 105–24.

1866b　"On the Physical and Mental Characteristics of the Negro." *Transactions of the Ethnological Society of London* N.S. 4: 212–39.

1867a　"On the Migration of Cultivated Plants in Reference to Ethnology—Articles of Food." *Transactions of the Ethnological Society of London* N.S. 5: 178–91.

1867b　"On the History and Migration of Cultivated Plants in Reference to Ethnology—Fruits." *Transactions of the Ethnological Society of London* N.S. 5: 255–76.

1867c　"On the Migration of Cultivated Plants in Reference to Ethnology—Saccariferous Plants." *Transactions of the Ethnological Society of London* N.S. 5: 318–24.

1868a "On the Vegetable and Animal Food of the Natives of Australia in Reference to Social Position, with a Comparison between the Australians and Some Other Races of Man." *Transactions of the Ethnological Society of London* N.S. 6: 112–22.

1868b "On the History and Migration of Cultivated Plants Used as Condiments." *Transactions of the Ethnological Society of London* N.S. 6: 188–206.

1868c "On the Theory of the Origin of Species by Natural Selection in the Struggle for Life." *Transactions of the Ethnological Society of London* N.S. 7 (1869): 27–38. [ESL, January 1868]

1869a "On the History and Migration of Textile and Tinctorial Plants in Reference to Ethnology." *Transactions of the Ethnological Society of London* N.S. 7: 1–15.

1869b "On the History and Migration of Cultivated Narcotic Plants in Reference to Ethnology." *Transactions of the Ethnological Society of London* N.S. 7: 78–91.

1869c "On the History and Migration of Cultivated Plants Yielding Intoxicating Potables and Oils." *Transactions of the Ethnological Society of London* N.S. 7: 92–106.

1869d "On the History and Migration of Cultivated Plants Producing Coffee, Tea, Cocoa, etc." *Transactions of the Ethnological Society of London* N.S. 7: 197–206.

Cro, Stelio

1990a "Montaigne and Pedro Martir—The Roots of the Noble-Savage." *Revista de Indias* 50 (190): 665–85.

1990b *The Noble Savage: Allegory of Freedom.* Waterloo, Ont.: Wilfrid Laurier University Press.

Croly, David G., George Wakeman, and E. C. Howell

1864 *Miscegenation: The Theory of the Blending of the Races, Applied to the American White Man and Negro.* London: Trubner.

Cull, Richard

1854 "On the Recent Progress of Ethnology." *Journal of the Ethnological Society of London* 4: 297–316.

Cull, Richard, and Richard Owen

1853 "A Brief Notice of the Aztec Race, Compiled by Richard Cull, Hon. Secretary; Followed by a Description of the So-Called Aztec Children Exhibited on the Occasion, by Professor Owen, F.R.S., Read at a Special meeting, 6th July 1853." *Journal of the Ethnological Society of London* 4 (1856): 120–37.

Curtin, Philip D.

1955 *Two Jamaicas: The Role of Ideas in a Tropical Colony 1830–1865.* Cambridge, Mass.: Harvard University Press.

Dark, Alx V.
1999   "The Makah Whale Hunt." *Native Americans and the Environment,* April 1999. http://conbio.rice.edu/nae/cases/makah/index.html.

Darwin, Charles
1839a   *Journal of Researches into the Geology and Natural History of the Various Countries Visited by H.M.S. Beagle under the Command of Captain Fitzroy, R.N., from 1832 to 1836.* London: Henry Colburn. Facsimile reprint. New York: Hafner, 1952.
1839b   *Journal of Researches into the Natural History and Geology of the Countries Visited during the Voyage of H.M.S. Beagle Round the World: Under the Command of Capt. Fitz Roy, R.N.* 2d ed. London: John Murray, 1845. Reprint. New York: Heritage Press, 1957.
1856   Letter to J. D. Hooker, May 9, 1856. In Darwin 1903: 89.
1859a   *The Origin of Species.* Facsimile reprint of 1st ed. Cambridge, Mass.: Harvard University Press, 1964.
1859b   Letter to Charles Lyell, December 2, 1859. In Darwin 1896: 2:32–33.
1871   *The Descent of Man, and Selection in Relation to Sex.* London: John Murray. Facsimile reprint. Princeton: Princeton University Press, 1981.
1896   *Life and Letters of Charles Darwin.* Ed. Francis Darwin. New York: Appleton.
1903   *More Letters of Charles Darwin.* Ed. Francis Darwin and A. C. Seward. New York: Appleton.

da Vinci, Leonardo
1489–1518?   *The Notebooks of Leonardo da Vinci.* Ed. Jean Paul Richter. New York: Dover, 1970.

Degerando [de Gerando], Joseph-Marie
1800   *The Observation of Savage Peoples.* Trans. F. C. T. Moore. Berkeley: University of California Press, 1969.

della Valle, Pietro
1665   *The Travels of Sig. Pietro della Valle, a Noble Roman.* London: Printed by J. Macock, for John Place.

Densmore, Frances
1939   *Nootka and Quileute Music.* BAE Bulletin 124. Washington, D.C.: Smithsonian Institution.

de Pauw, Cornelius
1776   "Amerique (Hist. & Géographie.)" In Diderot, ed., 1751–80. *Supplément* 1: 343–54.

Desmond, Adrian
1989   *The Politics of Evolution.* Chicago: University of Chicago Press.

Dettwyler, Katherine A.

1991   "Can Paleopathology Provide Evidence for Compassion?" *American Journal of Physical Anthropology* 84 (4): 375–84.

Diamond, Jared

1992   *The Third Chimpanzee.* New York: Harper.

1997   *Guns, Germs, and Steel.* New York: Norton.

Diamond, Stanley

1974   *In Search of the Primitive.* New Brunswick: Transaction Books.

Dickason, Olive P.

1984   *The Myth of the Savage: And the Beginnings of French Colonialism in the Americas.* Edmonton: University of Alberta Press.

Diderot, Denis

1772a   *Supplément au voyage de Bougainville.* Gilbert Chinard, ed. Paris: Droz, 1935.

1772b   *The Supplément au voyage de Bougainville.* In Diderot, *Political Writings,* trans. and ed. John Hope Mason and Robert Wokler, 31–75. Cambridge: Cambridge University Press, 1992.

Diderot, Denis, ed.

1751–80   *Encyclopédie: Ou Dictionnaire Raisonné des Sciences, des Arts et des Métiers.* Neufchastel: Samuel Faulche. Facsimile reprint. Stuttgart: Frommann, 1967.

DNB

1908   *Dictionary of National Biography.* Ed. Leslie Stephen and Sidney Lee. New York: Macmillan.

Doiron, Normand

1991   "Rhétorique Jésuite de l'éloquence sauvage au XVIIe siècle: Les *Relations* de Paul Lejeune (1632–1642)." *Dix-Septieme Siècle* 43 (4), no. 173: 375–402.

Donovan, C.

1853   "The Aztec Children." *Illustrated London News* 23, no. 634 (July 23, 1853): 43–44.

Dryden, John

1665   *The Indian Emperour, or, The Conquest of Mexico by the Spaniards: Being the Sequel of The Indian Queen.* London: Printed by J. M. for H. Herringman, 1667. In Edward Niles Hooker and H. T. Swedenberg, Jr., eds., *The Works of John Dryden,* 9:1–112. Berkeley: University of California Press, 1966.

1668   "A Defence of an Essay of Dramatique Poesie, being an Answer to the Preface of *The Great Favourite, or the Duke of Lerma.*" In Edward Niles Hooker and H. T. Swedenberg, Jr., eds., *The Works of John Dryden,* 9:3–22. Berkeley: University of California Press, 1966.

1672   *The Conquest of Granada by the Spaniards.* London: Henry

Herringman, 1672. In Montague Summers, ed., *Dryden: The Dramatic Works*, 3:1–176. London: Nonesuch Press, 1931–32. Reprint. New York: Gordian Press, 1968.

1675   *Aureng-Zebe: A Tragedy*. London: Henry Herringman. In George Saintsbury, ed., *John Dryden: Three Plays*, 265–355. New York: Hill and Wang, 1957.

Dryden, John, and Robert Howard

1664   *The Indian Queen, a Tragedy*. London: Printed for H. Herringman, 1665. In Edward Niles Hooker and H. T. Swedenberg, Jr., eds., *The Works of John Dryden*, 8:181–231. Berkeley: University of California Press, 1962

du Chaillu, Paul

1861a   *Explorations and Adventures in Equatorial Africa; with Accounts of the Manners and Customs of the People, and of the Chace of the Gorilla, Crocodile, Leopard, Elephant, Hippopotamus, and other Animals*. London: Murray.

1861b   "Observations on the People of Western Equatorial Africa." *Transactions of the Ethnological Society of London* N.S. 1: 305–15.

Duchet, Michele

1971   *Anthropologie et histoire au siècle des lumières: Buffon, Voltaire, Rousseau, Helvetius, Diderot*. Paris: F. Maspero.

Du Halde, Jean-Baptiste

1735   *Description geographique, historique, chronologique, politique, et physique de l'Empire de la Chine et de la Tartarie Chinoise*. Paris: P. G. Lemercier.

Dutfield, Graham

1999   "The Public and Private Domains: Intellectual Property Rights in Traditional Ecological Knowledge." *Oxford Electronic Journal of Intellectual Property Rights* WP 03/99. http://users.ox.ac.uk/~mast0140/EJWP0399.html.

Duvernay-Bolens, Jacqueline

1998   "De la sensibilité des sauvages à l'époque romantique." *Homme* 37 (145): 143–68.

Ellegard, Alvar

1958   *Darwin and the General Reader: The Reception of Darwin's Theory of Evolution in the British Periodical Press, 1859–1872*. Chicago: University of Chicago Press.

Ellingson, Ter

N.d.   "A Great Universal City: Nicolay's Humanist Ethnographic Theory." In preparation.

Engel, Samuel

1776   "Recherches géographiques et critiques sur la position des lieux septentrionaux de l'Amerique." In Diderot, ed., 1751–80. *Supplément* 1: 354–62.

ESL Minutes

1844–69   *Ethnological Society [of London]: Council Minute Book, Volume I.* Royal Anthropological Institute Library, Museum of Mankind, MS no. A1.

ESL Regulations

1855   *Regulations of the Ethnological Society of London.* London: W. M. Watts.

Fabian, Johannes

1983   *Time and the Other: How Anthropology Makes Its Object.* New York: Columbia University Press.

Fairchild, Hoxie Neale

1928   *The Noble Savage: A Study in Romantic Naturalism.* New York: Columbia University Press.

Falconer, William

1781   *Remarks on the Influence of Climate, Situation, Nature of Country, Population, Nature of Food, and Way of Life, on the Disposition and Temper, Manners and Behaviour, Intellects, Laws and Customs, Form of Government, and Religion, of Mankind.* London : Printed for C. Dilly.

Feldstein, Richard

1997   *Political Correctness: A Response from the Cultural Left.* Minneapolis: University of Minnesota Press.

Fenton, William N., and Elizabeth L. Moore

1974   "Introduction." In Lafitau 1724: 1:i–cxix.

FitzRoy, Robert

1858   "Outline Sketch of the Principal Varieties and Early Migrations of the Human Race." *Transactions of the Ethnological Society of London* 1 (1861): 1–11.

Fitzsimmons, Raymund

1970   *Barnum in London.* New York: St. Martin's Press.

Flaherty, Gloria

1992   *Shamanism and the Eighteenth Century.* Princeton: Princeton University Press.

Flammarion, Camille

1886   *Le Monde avant la Création de l'Homme.* Paris: Marpon et Flammarion.

Foucault, Michel

1965   *Madness and Civilization.* New York: Random House.

1970   *The Order of Things: An Archaeology of the Human Sciences.* New York: Vintage Books.

1977   *Discipline and Punish: The Birth of the Prison.* New York: Pantheon.

1984   "What Is Enlightenment?" In Paul Rabinow, ed., *The Foucault Reader,* 32–50. New York: Pantheon.

Fowler, Loretta
    1996   "The Great Plains from the Arrival of the Horse to 1885." In Trigger and Washburn, eds., 1996: I/2: 1–55.

Fredrickson, George M.
    1971   *The Black Image in the White Mind: The Debate on Afro-American Character and Destiny, 1817–1914.* New York: Harper and Row.

[Galileo] Galilei, Galileo
    1632   *Dialogues Concerning the Two Chief World Systems.* 2d rev. ed. Trans. Stillman Drake. Berkeley: University of California Press, 1967.

Gobineau, Arthur de
    1854   *The Inequality of Human Races.* Trans. Adrian Collins. London: William Heinemann, 1915.

Gould, Stephen Jay
    1981   *The Mismeasure of Man.* Rev. and expanded ed. New York: Norton, 1996.

Green, John
    1745–47   *A New General Collection of Voyages and Travels.* London: Printed for Thomas Astley. [This collection, actually compiled and edited by Green, is usually mistakenly attributed to Astley, the publisher, in bibliographies.]

Green, M. K.
    1991   "Images of Native-Americans in Advertising—Some Moral Issues." *Journal of Business Ethics* 12 (4): 323–30.

Greenblatt, Stephen
    1991   *Marvelous Possessions: The Wonder of the New World.* Chicago: University of Chicago Press.

Greenwood, James
    1863–64   *Curiosities of Savage Life.* London: S. O. Beeton.

Guille-Escuret, Georges
    1992   "Cannibales isolés et monarques sans histoire." *Homme* 32 (122–24): 327–45.

Guyot, Arnold
    1849   *The Earth and Man: Lectures on Comparative Physical Geography, in Its Relation to the History of Mankind.* Trans. C. C. Felton. 7th ed. Boston: Gould and Lincoln.

Hakluyt, Richard
    1589   *The Principal Navigations, Voyages, Traffiques & Discoveries of the English Nation.* Glasgow: J. MacLehose and Sons, 1903–5.

Hames, Raymond
    1997   [Response to Headland et al. 1997] *Current Anthropology* 38 (4): 614–15.

Harris, Marvin
    1968   *The Rise of Anthropological Theory.* New York: Crowell.
Headland, Thomas N., Michael S. Alvard, Stephen Beckerman, John H. Bodley, Peter M. Gardner, Raymond Hames, Alice E. Ingerson, Dominique Legros, Eric Alden Smith, Leslie E. Sponsel, and Allyn Mac Lean Stearman
    1997   "Revisionism in Ecological Anthropology." *Current Anthropology 38* (4): 605–30.
Healy, George R.
    1958   "The French Jesuits and the Idea of the Noble Savage." *William and Mary Quarterly,* 3d Ser., 15 (2): 143–67.
Hennepin, Louis
    1683   *A Description of Louisiana.* Trans. John Gilmary Shea. New York: John G. Shea, 1880. Reprint. Ann Arbor: University Microfilms, 1966.
    1698   *A New Discovery of a Vast Country in America.* London: Printed for M. Bentley, J. Tonson, H. Bonwick, T. Goodwin, and S. Manship. Reprint, Reuben Gold Thwaites, ed., Chicago: McClurg, 1903.
Herzog, Don
    1998   *Poisoning the Minds of the Lower Orders.* Princeton: Princeton University Press.
Heylyn, Peter
    1629   *Mikrokosmos: A Little Description of the Great World.* 4th ed. Oxford: William Turner and Thomas Huggins.
Hodgen, Margaret T.
    1964   *Early Anthropology in the Sixteenth and Seventeenth Centuries.* Philadelphia: University of Pennsylvania Press.
Honigman, John J.
    1976   *The Development of Anthropological Ideas.* Homewood, Ill.: Dorsey Press.
Horkheimer, Max, and Theodor W. Adorno
    1944   *Dialectic of Enlightenment.* New York: Continuum.
Howitt, William
    1838   *Colonization and Christianity: A Popular History of the Treatment of the Natives by Europeans in All Their Colonies.* London: Longman, Orme, Brown, Green, & Longmans.
Hunt, James; see also *AR*
    1863a   "Introductory Address on the Study of Anthropology." *Anthropological Review* 1: 1–20.
    1863b   "On the Physical and Mental Characters of the Negro." *Anthropological Review* 1 (3): 386–91.
    1863c   "On the Negro's Place in Nature." *Memoirs Read before the Anthropological Society of London, 1863–64:* 1:1–60.
    1864a   "To Dr. Paul Broca." In Carl Vogt, *Lectures on Man: His Place in Creation, and in the History of the Earth,* ed. James Hunt,

v–x. London: Anthropological Society of London/Longman, Green, Longman and Roberts.

1864b   "Miscegenation." *Anthropological Review* 2: 116–21.

1866   "Race in Legislation and Political Economy." *Anthropological Review* 4 (13): 113–35.

1867a   "The President's Address [Annual Meeting. January 1, 1867]." *Journal of the Anthropological Society of London* 5: xliv–lxx.

1867b   "The Manchester Anthropological Society." *Anthropological Review* 5: 1–27.

1867c   "On the Doctrine of Continuity Applied to Anthropology." *Anthropological Review* 5: 110–20.

1868a   "On the Origin of the Anthropological Review and Its Connection with the Anthropological Society." *Anthropological Review* 6: 431–42.

1868b   "Anthropology at the British Association." *Anthropological Review* 6: 88–103.

1868c   [Crawfurd memorial resolution] "Proceedings of the Society: May 19th, 1868." *Journal of the Anthropological Society of London* 6: clxxi.

Huxley, Thomas H.

1860   "The Origin of Species." Reprinted in Huxley, *Darwiniana: Essays*, 22–79. New York: D. Appleton, 1896.

1863   *Evidence as to Man's Place in Nature*. New York: D. Appleton.

ILN (*Illustrated London News*)

1843a   "The Ojibbeway Indians." 3, no. 86 (December 23, 1843): 401–2.

1843b   "Jockosot." 3, no. 86 (December 23, 1843): 404.

1853a   "Zulu Kafirs." Advertisement, 23, no. 632 (July 9, 1853): 6.

1853b   "The Aztec Lilliputians." Advertisement, 23, no. 632 (July 9, 1853): 6.

1853c   "The Court." 23, no. 632 (July 9, 1853): 7.

1853d   "The Aztec Children." 23, no. 632 (July 9, 1853): 11–12.

1853e   "Aztec Lilliputians." Advertisement, 23, no. 633 (July 16, 1853): 22.

1853f   "Can the Aztecs Speak?" 23, no. 635 (July 30, 1853): 66.

1853g   "The Aztec Children." 23, no. 639 (August 20, 1853): 144.

1853h   "Meeting of the British Association at Hull." 23, no. 644 (September 17, 1853): 225–27.

1853i   "The Aztec Children." 23, no. 648 (October 8, 1853): 307.

Jaucourt, Louis de

1765   "Sauvages." In Diderot, ed., 1751–80: 7:29.

Jeffries, John

1869   *The Natural History of the Human Races*. New York: Edward O. Jenkins.

[*Jesuit Relations*]
> *The Jesuit Relations and Allied Documents.* Ed. Reuben Gold Thwaites. 73 vols. Cleveland: Burrows Brothers, 1896–1901.

Kallendorf, Hilaire
> 1995 "A Myth Rejected: The Noble Savage in Dominican Dystopia." *Journal of Latin American Studies* 27: 449–70.

Kass, Amalie M., and Edward H. Kass
> 1988 *Perfecting the World: The Life and Times of Dr. Thomas Hodgkin, 1798–1866.* Boston: Harcourt Brace Jovanovich.

Keith, Arthur
> 1917 "How Can the Institute Best Serve the Needs of Anthropology?" *Journal of the Royal Anthropological Institute* 47: 12–30.

Knox, Robert
> 1859 "Abstract of Observations on the Assyrian Marbles, and on their place in History and in Art." *ESLT* 1 (1861): 146–154.

Kohl, K. H.
> 1981 *Entzauberter Blick: das Bild vom Guten Wilden und die Erfahrung der Zivilisation.* Berlin: Medusa.

Konner, Melvin
> 1990 *Why the Reckless Survive — And Other Secrets of Human Nature.* New York: Viking.

Kunhardt, Philip B., Jr., Philip B. Kunhardt III, and Peter W. Kunhardt
> 1995 *P. T. Barnum: America's Greatest Showman.* New York: Knopf.

Labat, Jean Baptiste
> 1728 *Nouvelle Relation del Afrique Occidentale.* Paris. Excerpts reprinted in Green 1745–47: 2:1 ff.

Lafitau, Joseph-François
> 1724 *Customs of the American Indians Compared with the Customs of Primitive Times.* Ed. and trans. William N. Fenton and Elizabeth L. Moore. Toronto: Champlain Society, 1974–77.

Lahontan, Louis Armand de Lom d'Arce, baron de
> 1703a *New Voyages to North-America.* London: H. Bonwicke et al. Reprint. Chicago: A. C. McClurg, 1905.

> 1703b *Suite du voyage, de l'Amerique, ou, Dialogues de Monsieur le Baron de Lahontan et d'un sauvage dans l'Amerique.* Amsterdam : Chez la veuve de Boeteman, 1704.

> 1703–5 *Dialogues curieux entre l'auteur et un sauvage de Bons Sens qui a voyage, et memoires de l'Amerique Septentrionale.* Ed. Gilbert Chinard. Baltimore: Johns Hopkins University Press, 1931.

Las Casas, Bartolomé de
> 1542/1552 *A Short Account of the Destruction of the Indies.* Trans. Nigel Griffin. London: Penguin, 1992.

Latham, R. G.
    1853   "Ethnological Remarks upon Some of the More Remarkable Varieties of the Human Species, Represented by Individuals now in London." Paper presented at the British Association for the Advancement of Science, Hull, September 9; summary in *Journal of the Ethnological Society of London* 4 (1856): 148–50.

Lawrence, William
    1817   *Lectures on Comparative Anatomy, Physiology, Zoology, and the Natural History of Man.* 7th ed. London: John Taylor, 1838.

Leems, Knut
    1767   *General and Miscellaneous Remarks Concerning Lapland.* Abridged translation in Acerbi 1802: 2:135–321.

Lery, Jean de
    1578   *History of a Voyage to the Land of Brazil, Otherwise Called America.* Trans. Janet Whatley. Berkeley: University of California Press, 1990.

Lescarbot, Marc
    1609a   *Nova Francia, or, The Description of that Part of New France which is One Continent with Virginia. . . .* Translated out of French into English by P. E[rondelle]. Londini: Impensis Georgii Bishop.
    1609b   *Histoire de la Novvelle France.* Paris: Iean Milot.
    1609c   *Nova Francia: A Description of Arcadia.* Trans. P. Erondelle. London. Reprint. London: Routledge, 1928.
    1609d   *The History of New France.* 3d ed. Paris: Adrian Perier, 1618. Trans. W. L. Grant. Toronto: Champlain Society, 1907–14. Reprint. New York: Greenwood Press, 1968.

Lestringant, Frank
    1997   *Cannibals: The Discovery and Representation of the Cannibal from Columbus to Jules Verne.* Berkeley: University of California Press.

Levaillant, Maurice
    1948   Introduction and notes to Chateaubriand 1848–50.

Levin, Harry
    1969   *The Myth of the Golden Age in the Renaissance.* Bloomington: Indiana University Press.

Linnaeus [Linne], Carl von
    1732   *Lachesis Lapponica, or a Tour in Lapland.* Trans. James E. Smith. London: White and Cochrane, 1811.

Linnekin, Jocelyn S.
    1992   "Ignoble Savages and Other European Visions: The La Perouse Affair in Samoan History." *Journal of Pacific History* 26: 3–26.

Loftis, John
   1966   "Commentary: The Indian Emperour." In Edward Niles Hooker
               and H. T. Swedenberg, Jr., eds., *The Works of John Dryden*,
               9:293–330. Berkeley: University of California Press, 1966.
Lovejoy, Arthur O.
   1923   "The Supposed Primitivism of Rousseau's 'Discourse on In-
               equality.'" *Modern Philology* 21: 165–86.
Lovejoy, Arthur O., Gilbert Chinard, George Boas, and Ronald S. Crane, eds.
   1935   *Primitivism and Related Ideas in Antiquity: A Documentary
               History of Primitivism and Related Ideas I.* Baltimore: Johns
               Hopkins University Press.
Low, Bobbi S.
   1996   "Behavioral Ecology of Conservation in Traditional Societies."
               Human Nature — An Interdisciplinary Biosocial Perspective 7
               (4): 353–79.
LT (*London Times*)
   1863   [John Crawfurd]. August 31, 1863, 7.
   1868   [Obituary of John Crawfurd]. May 13, 1868, 5.
Lubbock, John
   1865   *Prehistoric Times, as Illustrated by Ancient Remains and the
               Manners and Customs of Modern Savages.* 2d ed. New York:
               Appleton, 1872.
   1870   *The Origin of Civilisation and the Primitive Condition of Man.*
               New York: Appleton, 1873.
Lyell, Charles, Sir
   1851   *A Manual of Elementary Geology: or, The Ancient Changes of
               the Earth and Its Inhabitants, as Illustrated by Geological
               Monuments.* 3d ed. London: John Murray.
   1863   *The Geological Evidences of the Antiquity of Man: With Re-
               marks on Theories of the Origin of Species by Variation.* Lon-
               don: John Murray.
McCracken, Harold
   1959   *George Catlin and the Old Frontier.* New York: Bonanza.
McGregor, Gaile
   1988   *The Noble Savage in the New World Garden: Notes toward a
               Syntactics of Place.* Toronto: University of Toronto Press.
Mackenzie, Henry
   1787   *Man of the World.* London. Citations in Fairchild 1928.
Mackenzie, Kenneth R. H.
   1868   "Sproat's Studies of Savage Life." *Anthropological Review* 6:
               366–78.
Mariner, William
   1827   *An Account of the Natives of the Tonga Islands in the South
               Pacific Ocean.* 3d ed. Edinburgh: Constable.

Martyr, Peter (Martire, Pietro)

1511–21   *The Decades of the Newe Worlde or West India.* Trans. Richard
            Eden. London: William Powell, 1555. Reprinted in Edward
            Arber, ed., *The First Three English Books on America,* 43–200.
            New York: Kraus Reprint Corp., 1971.

Mason, John Hope, and Robert Wokler

1992   Introduction to Denis Diderot, *Political Writings,* ix–xxxv.
            Cambridge: Cambridge University Press.

Mead, Margaret

1932   *The Changing Culture of an Indian Tribe.* New York: Columbia
            University Press.

1975   "Visual Anthropology in a Discipline of Words." In Paul Hock-
            ings, ed., *Principles of Visual Anthropology,* 3–10. The Hague:
            Mouton.

Meek, Ronald

1976   *Social Science and the Ignoble Savage.* Cambridge: Cambridge
            University Press.

Meisch, L. A.

1997   "Gringas and Otavalenos—Changing Tourist Relations." *An-
            nals of Tourism Research* 22 (2): 441–62.

Mersenne, Marin

1636   *Harmonie Universelle.* Reprint. Paris: CNRS, 1963.

Meyer, Landon

1998   "Biodiversity Conservation and Indigenous Knowledge: Re-
            thinking the Role of Anthropology." *Indigenous Knowledge
            and Development Monitor* 6 (1): http://www.nuffic.nl/ciran/
            ikdm/6.1/myer.html.

Mill, John Stuart

1850   "The Negro Question." *Fraser's Magazine* 41 (January): 25–
            31. Reprinted in John M. Robson, ed., *Collected Works of John
            Stuart Mill 21: Essays on Equality, Law, and Education,* 87–95.
            Toronto: University of Toronto Press.

Moffat, Robert

1842   *Missionary Labours and Scenes in Southern Africa.* London:
            John Snow. Facsimile reprint. New York: Johnson Reprint
            Corp., 1969.

Montagu, Mary Wortley

1716–18   *Turkish Embassy Letters.* London: Virago, 1994.

Montaigne, Michel de

1588a   "Of the Caniballes." In *The Essays of Michael, Lord of Mon-
            taigne,* 2:32–54. Trans. John Florio. London: J. M. Dent,
            1897.

1588b   "Of Coaches." In *The Essays of Michael, Lord of Montaigne,*
            5:186–221. Trans. John Florio. London: J. M. Dent, 1897.

Montesquieu, Charles-Louis de Secondat, baron de La Brède et de
    1748   *The Spirit of Laws.* Ed. David Wallace Carrithers. Berkeley: University of California Press, 1977.

Mooney, Michael Macdonald
    1975   "Introduction." In George Catlin, *Letters and Notes on the North American Indians,* ed. Michael Macdonald Mooney, 1–83. New York: Clarkson N. Potter.

Morgan, Lewis Henry
    1851   *League of the Ho-dé-no-sau-nee, or Iroquois.* Rochester: Sage.
    1877   *Ancient Society: Or Researches in the Lines of Human Progress from Savagery, through Barbarism to Civilization.* New York: Henry Holt. Facsimile reprint. New York: New York Labor News, 1971.

Morton, Samuel G.
    1839   *Crania Americana: Or, a Comparative View of the Skulls of Various Aboriginal Nations of North and South America, to which is Prefixed an Essay on The Varieties of the Human Species.* Philadelphia: J. Dobson.

Murray, Charles Augustus
    1839   *Travels in North America during the Years 1834, 1835 & 1836, Including a Summer Residence with the Pawnee Tribe of Indians in the Remote Prairies of the Missouri and a Visit to Cuba and the Azore Islands.* London: R. Bentley.

Nicolay, Nicolas de
    1567–68   *Les quatre premiers livres des navigations et peregrinations orientales.* Lyon: Gvillavme Roville.

Nott, Josiah C., and George R. Gliddon, eds.
    1854   *Types of Mankind or, Ethnological Researches.* Philadelphia: J. B. Lippincott, Grambo.
    1857   *Indigenous Races of the Earth; or, New Chapters of Ethnological Inquiry.* Philadelphia: J. B. Lippincott.

Ogilby, John
    1670   *Africa.* London: Printed by Tho. Johnson for the author.
    1671   *America: Being the Latest, and Most Accurate Description of the New World.* London: Printed by the author.

Pagden, Anthony
    1982   *The Fall of Natural Man: The American Indian and the Origins of Comparative Ethnology.* Cambridge: Cambridge University Press.
    1987   "Dispossessing the Barbarian: The Language of Spanish Thomism and the Debate over the Property Rights of the Indians." In Anthony Pagden, ed., *The Languages of Political Theory in Early-Modern Europe,* 79–98. Cambridge: Cambridge University Press.

1993   *European Encounters with the New World: From Renaissance to Romanticism.* New Haven: Yale University Press.

1995   *Lords of All the World: Ideologies of Empire in Spain, Britain and France c. 1500 – c. 1800.* New Haven: Yale University Press.

Paterson, Jody

1998   "Indians Can't Live on Nobility." *Victoria Times Colonist,* September 4, 1998. http://website.lineone.net/~s.ward/MIN/98Nov/Makah.html.

Pearce, Roy Harvey

1953   *The Savages of America: A Study of the Indian and the Idea of Civilization.* Baltimore: Johns Hopkins University Press, 1965.

1988   *Savagism and Civilization: A Study of the Indian and the American Mind.* Berkeley: University of California Press.

Pease, Bryan

1998   "Cultural Wrongs." *Cornell Daily Sun.* http://people2.clarityconnect.com/webpages5/dcc14/cultural.html.

Pemberton, John

1994   *On the Subject of "Java."* Ithaca: Cornell University Press.

Picart, Bernard

1712–31   *Ceremonies et coutumes religieuses de tous les peuples du monde.* Amsterdam: J. F. Bernard.

Plano Carpini, John of [Giovanni di], Archbishop of Antivari

1248   *History of the Mongols.* In Christopher Dawson, ed., *The Mongol Mission: Narratives and Letters of the Franciscan Missionuries in Mongolia and China in the Thirteenth and Fourteenth Centuries,* 3 –72. New York: Sheed and Ward, 1955.

PM (Penny Magazine)

1832   "Civilized and Savage Life." 8 (May 19, 1832): 69.

1834   "The Physical Powers of Savages." 125 (March 15, 1834): 99–100.

Prévost, Abbé

1746–92   *Histoire générale des voyages.* Paris: Didot.

Prichard, James Cowles

1813   *Researches into the Physical History of Man.* London: J. and A. Arch. Annotated facsimile reprint, ed. George Stocking. Chicago: University of Chicago Press, 1973.

1843   *The Natural History of Man.* London: H. Bailliere.

1848   "On the Various Methods of Research Which Contribute to the Advancement of Ethnology, and of the Relations of That Science to Other Branches of Knowledge." *BAAS Report* 17: 230–53.

1851   *Researches into the Physical History of Mankind.* [4th ed. of 1813] London: Houlston and Stoneman.

Purchas, Samuel
  1625   *Hakluytus Posthumus, or Purchas His Pilgrimes: Contayning a History of the World in Sea Voyages and Lande Travells by Englishmen and Others.* Glasgow: J. MacLehose and Sons, 1905–7.

Putter, Irving
  1980   Introduction to Chateaubriand 1801b.

Rameau, Jean Philippe
  1760   *Code de musique pratique.* Paris: Imprimerie Royale. Reprint. New York: Broude Brothers, 1965.

Redford, Kent H.
  1990a   "The Ecologically Noble Savage." *Orion Nature Quarterly* 9 (3): 24–29.
  1990b   "The Ecologically Noble Savage." *Cultural Survival Quarterly* 15, no. 1 (1991): 46–48.
  1990c   "The Ecologically Noble Savage." In William Haviland and Robert Gordon, eds., *Talking about People: Readings in Contemporary Cultural Anthropology,* 11–13. Mountain View, Calif.: Mayfield, 1993.

Redford, Kent, and Allyn Stearman
  1993a   "Forest-dwelling Native Amazonians and the Conservation of Biodiversity: Interests in Common or Collision?" *Conservation Biology* 7 (2): 248–55.
  1993b   "On Common Ground? Response to Alcorn." *Conservation Biology* 7 (2): 427–28.

Resek, Carl
  1960   *Lewis Henry Morgan: American Scholar.* Chicago: University of Chicago Press.

Richards, Evelleen
  1989   "The 'Moral Anatomy' of Robert Knox: A Case Study of the Interplay between Biological and Social Thought in the Context of Victorian Scientific Naturalism." *Journal of the History of Biology* 22 (3): 373–436.

Richardson, Ruth
  1987   *Death, Dissection and the Destitute.* London: Routledge and Kegan Paul.

Ridley, Matt, and Bobbi S. Low
  1993   "Can Selfishness Save the Environment?" *Atlantic Monthly* 272 (3): 76–86.

Riffenburgh, Beau
  1994   *The Myth of the Explorer: The Press, Sensationalism, and Geographical Discovery.* Oxford: Oxford University Press.

Rousseau, Jean-Jacques
  1749–61?a *Essai sur l'origine des langues, ou il est parlé de la mélodie et le*

l'imitation musicale. In Rousseau, *Oeuvres 13: Écrits sur la Musique*, 141–222. Paris: Lequien, 1821.

1749–61?b   *Essay on the Origin of Languages, Which Treats of Melody and Musical Imitation*. In Rousseau and Johann Gottfried Herder, *On the Origin of Language*, trans. and ed. John H. Moran and Alexander Gode, 1–74. New York: Ungar, 1966.

1753b   *Lettre sur la musique françoise*. In Rousseau, *Oeuvres 13: Écrits sur la musique*, 229–85. Paris: Lequien, 1821.

1755a   *A Discourse upon the Origin and Foundation of the Inequality among Mankind*. By John James [i.e., "Jack"] Rousseau, Citizen of Geneva. London: R. and J. Dodsley, 1761.

1755b   *A Discourse on Inequality*. Trans. Maurice Cranston. London: Penguin, 1984.

1768   *Dictionnaire de musique*. Paris: Duchesne.

1782–89   *Confessions*. Ed. P. N. Furbank. New York: Knopf, 1992.

Rubruck [Ruysbroek], William of [Willem van]

1255   *The Journey of William of Rubruck*. In Christopher Dawson, ed., *The Mongol Mission: Narratives and Letters of the Franciscan Missionaries in Mongolia and China in the Thirteenth and Fourteenth Centuries*, 89–220. New York: Sheed and Ward, 1955.

Ruffières, Charles Robert des

1868   "Report on the Failure of the Amalgamation Scheme." *Journal of the Anthropological Society of London* 6: cxcvii.

Sabin, Joseph

1880   *A Dictionary of Books Relating to America, Vol. 12*. New York: J. Sabin's Sons.

Sacchi, S.

1993   "The Noble Savage and His Civilized Counterpart in Literary Tradition." *Rivista di Letteratura Moderne e Comparate* 45 (1): 5–34.

Sagard, Gabriel

1632a   *Le grand voyage dv pays des Hvrons*. Paris: Chez Denys Moreav, rue S. Iacques, a la salamandre d'argent. Reprinted in Sagard 1632b: 273–406.

1632b   *The Long Journey to the Country of the Hurons*. Ed. George M. Wrong; trans. H. H. Langton. Toronto: Champlain Society, 1939.

Sahlins, Marshall

1972   *Stone Age Economics*. Chicago: Aldine-Atherton.

Sammet, Gerald

1992   "Erbschleicher der moralischen Integrität: Christoph Kolumbus, der edle Wilde und ein Geist, der uns brüderlich grüsst." *Merkur: Deutsche Zeitschrift für europäisches Denken* 46 (9–10): 932–37.

Saxon, A. H.
    1989   *P. T. Barnum: The Legend and the Man.* New York: Columbia University Press.

Sayre, Gordon
    1997   *Les Sauvages Américains: Representations of Native Americans in French and English Colonial Literature.* Chapel Hill: University of North Carolina Press.

Schalk, Ellery
    1986   *From Valor to Pedigree: Ideas of Nobility in France in the Sixteenth and Seventeenth Centuries.* Princeton: Princeton University Press.

Schiller, Francis
    1979   *Paul Broca: Founder of French Anthropology, Explorer of the Brain.* Berkeley: University of California Press.

Schoolcraft, Henry R.
    1857   *History of the Indian Tribes of the United States: Their Present Condition and Prospects, and a Sketch of Their Ancient Status. Information Respecting the History, Condition, and Prospects of the Indian Tribes of the United States,* vol. 6. Published by order of Congress, under the direction of the Department of the Interior—Indian Bureau. Philadelphia: J. B. Lippincott. Facsimile reprint. N.p.: Historical American Indian Press, [1976?].

Scot, Edmund
    1602–5   *A Discourse of Java, and the First English Factory There, with Divers Indian, English, and Dutch Occurrences.* In Purchas 1625: 164 ff. Abridged reprint in Green 1745–47: 1:284–305.

Semmel, Bernard
    1962   *The Governor Eyre Controversy.* London: MacGibbon and Kee.

Sinclair, Andrew
    1977   *The Savage: A History of Misunderstanding.* London: Weidenfeld and Nicolson.

Skinner, Quentin
    1987   "Sir Thomas More's *Utopia* and the Language of Renaissance Humanism." In Anthony Pagden, ed., *The Languages of Political Theory in Early-Modern Europe,* 123–57. Cambridge: Cambridge University Press.

Smedley, Audrey
    1993   *Race in North America: Origin and Evolution of a Worldview.* Boulder: Westview.

Smith, Eric A.
    1997   [Response to Headland et al. 1997] *Current Anthropology* 38 (4): 618–19.

"So Much for the Noble Savage"
    1990   *New York Times Book Review,* August 19, 31.

Sorber, Edna C.
1972   "The Noble Eloquent Savage." *Ethnohistory* 19 (3): 227–36.

Sponsel, Leslie E.
1997   [Response to Headland et al. 1997] *Current Anthropology* 38 (4): 619–22.

Stanton, William Ragan
1960   *The Leopard's Spots: Scientific Attitudes toward Race in America, 1815–59.* Chicago: University of Chicago Press.

Stearman, Allyn M.
1994   "'Only Slaves Climb Trees': Revisiting the Myth of the Ecologically Noble Savage in Amazonia." *Human Nature—An Interdisciplinary Biosocial Perspective* 5 (4): 339–57.

Stocking, George W., Jr.
1968   *Race, Culture, and Evolution.* New York: Free Press.
1971   "What's in a Name? The Origins of the Royal Anthropological Institute, 1837–1871." *Man* 6: 369–90.
1973   "From Chronology to Ethnology: James Cowles Prichard and British Anthropology, 1800–1850." In Prichard, *Researches into the Physical History of Man.* London: John and Arthur Arch, 1913. Reprint. Chicago: University of Chicago Press. Pp. ix–cx.
1987   *Victorian Anthropology.* New York: Free Press.

Swan, James G.
1868   *The Indians of Cape Flattery, at the Entrance to the Strait of Fuca, Washington Territory. Smithsonian Contributions to Knowledge* 220. Washington, D.C.: Smithsonian Institution, 1870.

Switzer, Richard
1969   Introduction and notes to Chateaubriand 1827.

Tennent, Sir James Emerson
1859   *Ceylon: An Account of the Island Physical, Historical, and Topographical.* London: Longman, Green, Longman, and Roberts.

Thwaites, Reuben Gold
1903   Introduction and notes to Hennepin 1698.

Tizon, Alex
1999   "E-mails, Phone Calls Full of Threats, Invective." *Seattle Times,* May 23, A1, 16–17.

Todorov, Tzvetan
1989   *Nous et les autres: La réflexion française sur la diversité humaine.* Paris: Seuil.
1993   *On Human Diversity: Nationalism, Racism, and Exoticism in French Thought.* Trans. Catherine Porter. Cambridge, Mass.: Harvard University Press.

Trigger, Bruce G.

1985   *Natives and Newcomers: Canada's "Heroic Age" Reconsidered.* Kingston: McGill-Queen's University Press.

Trigger, Bruce G., ed.

1978   *Handbook of North American Indians 15: Northeast.* Washington, D.C.: Smithsonian Institution Press.

Trigger, Bruce G., and Wilcomb E. Washburn, eds.

1996   *The Cambridge History of the Native Peoples of the Americas.* Cambridge: Cambridge University Press.

Trouillot, Michel-Rolph

1991   "Anthropology and the Savage Slot: The Poetics and Politics of Otherness." In Richard G. Fox, ed., *Recapturing Anthropology: Working in the Present,* 17–44. Santa Fe, New Mex.: School of American Research Press.

Trudel, François

1996   "Le 'Noble Sauvage' est inuit: La construction d'une figure de l'Ungava au XIXᵉ siècle." *Etudes Inuit* 20 (2): 7–38.

Tylor, Edward Burnett

1863   "Wild Men and Beast-Children." *Anthropological Review* 1: 21–32.

1871   *Primitive Culture: Researches into the Development of Mythology, Philosophy, Religion, Art, and Custom.* London: J. Murray.

1881   *Anthropology: An Introduction to the Study of Man and Civilization.* London: Macmillan. Reprint. New York: Appleton, 1934.

van Evrie, John H.

1861a   *Negroes and Negro "Slavery": The First an Inferior Race; the Latter Its Normal Condition.* New York: Van Evrie, Horton & Co.

1861b   *White Supremacy and Negro Subordination; Or, Negroes a Subordinate Race, and (So-Called) Slavery Its Normal Condition.* 2d ed. New York: Van Evrie, Horton & Co., 1870.

1864   *Subgenation: The Theory of the Normal Relation of the Races; An Answer to "Miscegenation."* New York: J. Bradburn.

1869   "Death of the Best Man in England." *New York Weekly Day-Book,* November 6, 1869. Reprinted in *AR* 8 (1870): 97.

Vico, Giambattista

1725   *The New Science.* 3d ed. Naples, 1744. Trans. Thomas G. Bergin and Max H. Fisch. Ithaca: Cornell University Press.

Voget, Fred W.

1975   *A History of Ethnology.* New York: Holt, Rinehart, Winston.

Vogt, Adolf Max

1998   *Le Corbusier, the Noble Savage: Toward an Archaeology of Modernism.* Trans. Radka Donnell. Cambridge, Mass.: MIT Press.

Volney, C. F. [Constantin François]
    1787   *Travels through Syria and Egypt, in the Years 1783, 1784, and 1785.* London: G. G. J. and J. Robinson.
    1791   *Volney's Ruins: Or, Meditation on the Revolutions of Empires.* Boston: Josiah P. Mendum, 1877.
    1803   *A View of the Soil and Climate of the United States of America.* Trans. C. B. Brown. New York: Hafner, 1968.

Walsh, Martin W.
    1997   "May Games and Noble Savages: The Native American in Early Celebrations of the Tammany Society." *Folklore* 108: 83–91.

Walter, T.
    1991   "Natural Death and the Noble Savage." *Omega — Journal of Death and Dying* 30 (4): 237–248.

Washburn, Wilcomb E., and Bruce G. Trigger
    1996   "Native Peoples in Euro-American Historiography." In Trigger and Washburn, eds., 1996: I/1: 61–124.

Watson, Paul
    1997   "Confronting the Politically Correct Harpoons of the Makah." *Ocean Realm,* Spring 1997. http://www.estreet.com/orgs/sscs/essays/orealm/ormakah.html.
    1998   "Where Is the Whales' Manifesto? Sea Shepherd's Response to the Makah Manifesto." http://www.estreet.com/orgs/sscs/wh/us/mkmanif.html.

White, Hayden
    1976   "The Noble Savage Theme as Fetish." In *First Images of America,* 121–35. Berkeley: University of California Press.

Wilkes, Charles
    1844   *Narrative of the United States Exploring Expedition, During the Years 1838, 1839, 1840, 1841, 1842.* New York: G. P. Putnam, 1856.

Winterbotham, William
    1795   *An Historical, Geographical, and Philosophical View of the Chinese Empire.* London: J. Ridgway and W. Button.

Wood, Forrest G.
    1968   *Black Scare: The Racist Response to Emancipation and Reconstruction.* Berkeley: University of California Press.

Wood, J. G.
    1871   *The Uncivilized Races of Men in All Countries of the World.* Hartford: J. B. Burr.

Index

Abenaki, 389

Abernethy, John: debate with Lawrence, 250

Aboriginal Committee (British Parliament Select Committee on Aboriginal Tribes): bleeding hearts, 227; critique of term "savage," 226; investigation of colonial abuses, 230; rhetoric of nobility, 227

Aborigines, Australian. *See* Australian Aborigines

Aborigines Protection Society, 227, 273; and Anti-Slavery Society, 222; and Ethnological Society of London, 237, 240, 264, 288

Acerbi, Giuseppe: colonialist exploitation of Saami, implication in, 139; Golden Age litany of comparative negations, negative treatment of, 137–38; Saami, 134–39; —, reindeer herding camp, 129; —, sauna, discovery of, 135–36; —, smell of, sensual shock at, 136–37

Adam, Antoine, 165

Adario. *See* Kondiaronk

Adorno, Theodor W., and Max Horkheimer: on corrupt language, 357; on Enlightenment, 379–80

Agassiz, Louis, 151–52, 215, 269

Ahmed, A., 343

Alcorn, Janis, 351; on myth of noble state, 346

Aleiss, Angela, 343; on Noble Savage, 1

alienation: as colonialist representational strategy, 12

Altherr, Thomas L., 342

altruism and conservation ethic: in Ecologically Noble Savage debate, 351, 372

Alvard, Michael S.: on Ecologically Noble Savage, 2, 347, 349–50, 352, 358; on hunting by Indians, 349; on Noble Savage, 2; and scientific objectivity, 351–52, 354, 356

amalgamation: earlier equivalent of "miscegenation," 324

American Indian Movement, 364

American Indians (*see also under names of individual tribes*): antipathy of Anglo-Americans, 107; —, Volney on, 111; assertions of equality with Europeans, 51, 54; bestial representations, Champlain, 49; —, of Europeans, in Indian woman's reversal of metaphor, 288–89; —, Greenwood, 216; —, Hennepin, 55, 58; —, sensationalized image of "dog-eaters" in Nuu-chahnulth Wolf Ritual, 193; —, Volney, 116–17; —, of women by Hennepin, 58; childishness of, claimed by de Pauw, 164; —, claimed by Volney, 111; children's

425

American Indians (*continued*)
and animals' response to strangers,
Catlin on, 181; —, Murray on,
172–73; critique of Europeans, 50,
51, 59–60, 72; —, Dryden's fictionalized Montezuma, 38; —, Kondiaronk, Charlevoix's account of,
73–75; —, Kondiaronk, as Lahontan's fictionalized Adario, 68–76; —,
Mishikinakwa, "Little Turtle,"
Miami chief, as Volney's philosophical counterpart to Lahontan's Adario, 112–13, 116; —, Rousseau's
wet blanket, 80, 91–92; eloquence
of, Grangula, Iroquois chief, and
Lahontan's attempt to literally
translate metaphors, 73; —, Iroquois, Hennepin on, 56; —, Kondiaronk, Charlevoix's account of,
73–75; —, Kondiaronk, as Lahontan's fictionalized Adario, 68–76; —,
Lady Diplomatist, 288–89; evolutionary infancy of, according to de
Pauw, 163–64; French funeral
psalms reframed as war song duel,
20; hospitality, 26–27, 50, 53, 110,
172, 183; humor, Catlin on, 182;
humor, Murray on, 172; hunting,
22–23, 113, 169; —, Alvard on,
349; —, Catlin on, 181; —, Charlevoix on, 105; —, Lafitau on, 77–78;
—, Lescarbot on, 22–24; —, Makah
seal hunting, 368; —, Makah whaling, 80, 359, 368; —, Morgan on,
119–20; —, Murray on, 174–75; —,
as paradigm case for the savage,
xiii, 47, 295; —, Plains, 179; —, as
suggested cause of Quaternary/
Pleistocene extinctions, Low on,
347; perception as vanishing race,
107; prostitutes, fictional, by
Chateaubriand, 205; pursuit of
trade alliances with Europeans,
14–15, 16, 49; racial essercializa-
tion in reaction to Makah whale
hunt, 367; squah, derogatory term

for Indian women, used by Chastellux, 107–8; traveling shows in London, 244–45; —, and P. T. Barnum,
244; warfare, and Jesuit military
imagery, 79; warfare, Lafitau on, 77,
78–79; women, erotic appeal of to
Europeans, 48, 49, 205; —, as
hideous, asserted by Chastellux,
107–8; —, Lady Diplomatist,
288–89
Anderson, Kerby, 337
Anglo-Americans, antipathy to American Indians, 107; Volney on, 111
Anthropological Review, 246, 256,
261, 287, 305
Anthropological Society of London.
See ASL
anthropology: adherence to Noble
Savage myth, 3, 4, 299, 387; American racist school, 127, 151–53, 215,
217, 269; internalized self-critique,
387; Lescarbot's projection of future
discipline, 27–28, 80; Noble Savage
myth in late twentieth century,
343–45; Rousseau's projection of
future discipline, 1, 84–90
Anti-Slavery Society: and Aborigines
Protection Society, 222
Arthur, George, 228
ASL (Anthropological Society of
London): John Beddoe, presidency
of, 281; conflict with ESL, 263, 281,
303, 314–15; James Hunt, presidency of, 248; studies by Stocking,
240
assimilation: as colonialist representational strategy, 9, 11, 12, 45
Astley, Thomas, 94
Atahuallpa, Inca emperor, 35
Atkinson, Geoffroy, 382; on *bon
sauvage*, 8; on Lescarbot, 33, 34
Australian Aborigines, 244, 252; bes-
tial representations, by Greenwood,
213–14
Aztec Lilliputians, 244, 245–46; and
P. T. Barnum, 246; illustrations of,

Text: 10/13 Aldus
Display: Aldus
Composition: G&S Typesetters, Inc.
Printing and binding: Edwards Brothers